The Many Faces of Judge Lynch

The Many Faces of Judge Lynch

EXTRALEGAL VIOLENCE AND PUNISHMENT IN AMERICA

CHRISTOPHER WALDREP

palgrave
macmillan

THE MANY FACES OF JUDGE LYNCH
Copyright © Christopher Waldrep, 2002.
All rights reserved. No part of this book may be used or reproduced in any manner
whatsoever without written permission except in the case of brief quotations
embodied in critical articles or reviews.

First published 2002 by
PALGRAVE MACMILLAN™
175 Fifth Avenue, New York, N.Y. 10010 and
Houndmills, Basingstoke, Hampshire, England RG21 6XS.
Companies and representatives throughout the world.

PALGRAVE MACMILLAN is the global academic imprint of the Palgrave
Macmillan division of St. Martin's Press, LLC and of Palgrave Macmillan Ltd.
Macmillan® is a registered trademark in the United States, United Kingdom and other
countries. Palgrave is a registered trademark in the European Union and other
countries.

ISBN 0–312–29399–2 hardback

Library of Congress Cataloging-in-Publication Data can be found at the Library of
Congress

A catalogue record for this book is available from the British Library.

Design by Letra Libre, Inc.

First edition: November 2002
10 9 8 7 6 5 4 3 2 1

Printed in the United States of America.

For Pamela

Contents

Acknowledgments		*ix*
Introduction		1
Chapter One	Prologue: The Origins of the Word	13
Chapter Two	The Word and the Nation	27
Chapter Three	"California Law": The West and the Nation	49
Chapter Four	"What We Call Murder": Lynching and the Meaning of Legitimacy in Reconstruction	67
Chapter Five	"The Indignation of the People Knew No Bounds": The Lynching Narrative in the 1870s and 1880s	85
Chapter Six	"Threadbare Lies": Making Lynching Racial	103
Chapter Seven	Tuskegee, the NAACP, and the Definition of Lynching, 1899–1940	127
Chapter Eight	"High-Tech Lynchings": Making the Rhetoric National	151
Epilogue	Hate Crimes	185
Notes		193
Bibliography		233
Index		257

Acknowledgments

S teve Whitfield generously gave this manuscript a careful reading, as did Tom Appleton. Michael Les Benedict, Roberta Senechal de la Roche, Dan McMillan, and Michael Fitzgerald read portions of the text. I benefited greatly from all their insights and comments and claim all the remaining errors for myself. I presented portions of this manuscript at the Citadel, at a Southern Historical Association meeting, the Southern Intellectual History Conference, and Vernon Burton's southern history reading group at the University of Illinois. The discussion generated by these presentations stimulated my thinking enormously. Michael Bellesiles encouraged me to first write about this topic in his anthology *Lethal Imagination: Violence and Brutality in American History* (New York: New York University Press, 2000). I am still benefiting from my participation in Michael Johnson's 1991 National Endowment for the Humanities seminar, "Slavery and Freedom." Deborah Gershenowitz's support has been essential.

Gordon Cotton and Martha Huie provided indispensable help as I grappled with elements of this story. Jack Davis alerted me to the importance of Jesse James Payne and shared his materials on that case. Judy Schafer, Cory Andrews, and Joe Tregle, Jr., helped me locate New Orleans newspapers. Christian Fritz shared his work on popular sovereignty. William Carrigan deserves mention for his excellent work on the lynching of ethnic Mexicans. Beyond that, I must thank him especially for loaning me the transcript of Jesse Washington's trial. Michael Hussey at the National Archives has been enormously helpful. Susan Sherwood at the San Francisco State University Labor Archives found materials without being asked. I am most grateful.

Chapter seven originally appeared as "War of Words: The Controversy Over the Definition of Lynching, 1899–1940," *Journal of Southern History* LXVI, No. 1, February 2000, 75–100. I thank that journal for permission to republish here.

My colleagues at Eastern Illinois University heard more about lynching than anyone should have to endure, primarily in our monthly history colloquia. David K. Smith kept me supplied with books on the French Terror and Anita Shelton guided me through the meanings of Russian terrorism. Newton Key and Lynne Curry generously shared their insights and knowledge. My colleagues at San Francisco State University are proving just as supportive. Bill Issel, Chris Jackson, and Barbara Loomis have directed me to useful sources. The San Francisco State University Foundation supported this project. Librarians and archivists at both these institutions and many more provided the most important support of all. I thank them all.

As always my family played an important role in this project. Pamela makes it all worthwhile. In my first book I said that Janelle and Andrea learned to read books as I learned to write one. I am still learning to write, but now they are catching up, beginning their own writing.

Introduction

Ernest Withers's photography studio is at the end of a darkened hall-way off Memphis's famous Beale Street. Pictures of Martin Luther King and Elvis Presley decorate the walls, as does a framed full-page newspaper article detailing Withers's experiences as one of Memphis's first black police officers. The day I came to visit, Withers roamed the room talk-ing into a cell phone. Why do you want to talk about Emmett Till? he asked his caller. He is dead; two men were acquitted. When the caller theorized that more than the two acquitted men had committed the crime, Withers snapped: What difference does that make?[1]

Putting his phone away, Ernest Withers greeted me. Like the person on the phone, I also was interested in Emmett Till, the black youth murdered in Mississippi by J. W. Milam and Roy Bryant in 1955. I knew that Withers had been part of the team of black journalists deployed by the *Chicago Defender* to investigate the crime. Withers sat at his desk, telling me that thousands of young black men have died at the hands of Memphis police. Whites lynched Withers's great-great-grandfather during the Civil War. This was an injus-tice just as surely as the Till killing. Emmett Till became famous only because a Chicago union leader named Rayfield Mooty, a cousin of the Till family, in-fluenced Till's mother to open the casket, shocking the world with her son's mutilated face, Withers said. So many others had died in incidents some-times not even called lynchings, to be forgotten or overlooked in the first place. Why is it that no one cares about them?

It was, I thought, a good question. A few years ago I would never have imagined that one day I would be so anxious to talk to an eyewitness to the most famous lynching trial in American history. I have studied vigilantes and mobs for all of my professional life as a historian, but I had always pushed lynching aside. Without thinking about it very much, I realize now that I thought lynching seemed more a subject for sociologists than historians. Even the books written by historians seemed sociological, either case studies or quantitative analyses limited to lynchings between 1880 and 1930 or 1940. History is often said to be the study of change over time; few students of lynching have identified much change in the nature of lynching.

My thinking changed after 1991 when I began researching a book on the South's criminal justice system.[2] I discovered that the place I had chosen as the focus of my studies, Warren County, Mississippi, had been the scene of many killings called lynchings, more than most Southern counties. Since I was trying to learn all I could about Warren County, I decided to start studying more closely what scholars had to say about lynching.

What I found surprised me. Since newspapers were virtually the only source available for lynchings, modern scholars had a hard time defining "lynching."[3] Some scholars claim to rely on something called the "NAACP definition" of lynching. This definition emerged from a 1940 summit conference between the National Association for the Advancement of Colored People (NAACP) and rival organizations. As commonly presented, it contained four elements:

1. there must be evidence that a person was killed;
2. the person must have met his death illegally;
3. a group of three of more persons must have participated in the killing;
4. the group must have acted under the pretext of service to justice or tradition.[4]

In fact, there was no "NAACP definition" of lynching. The papers of the NAACP in the Library of Congress document staff debates, confusions, and disagreements—but no consensus—over the meaning of lynching. Thurgood Marshall apparently had so little regard for the 1940 definition that he refused to count as lynchings killings by posses.[5] A 1947 request by President Harry Truman's Committee on Civil Rights for a definition of lynching threw the NAACP into confusion. An NAACP staffer asked the legal department to review various and contradictory definitions advanced over the years by the NAACP, pleading with the lawyers to "please supply me with an official definition for specific use by our department." The legal department responded that its staff never believed the 1940 definition to be adequate since it required evidence that a person was killed, eliminating maimings and attempted lynchings.[6] The issue remained unresolved. A year later, the same staffer complained to Walter White that the NAACP had never settled whether killings by peace officers should be counted as lynchings. "We have never clarified for our own purposes these particular distinctions," the staffer wrote. She went on to say that "I have never learned of our decision to clarify our definition." The NAACP, in short, had no definition of lynching. And yet, scholars deploy the "NAACP definition," which the NAACP itself found unworkable, as a mantra to fend off critics.[7]

The reality is that most of what we know about lynching comes from newspaper reports. The decisions of small-town newspaper editors close to the scene of the killing, who were usually a part of the community that sanctioned the killing, determined whether the nation regarded particular killings as "lynchings" or "murders" or heard about them at all. From this evidence, lynching scholars tried to recapture lynchers' thinking through quantitative analysis, their debates asking whether economics or patriarchy drove lynching.[8] They looked for links between lynching and such variables as cotton production, the price of cotton, or the number of legal executions.[9]

Such questions cannot be answered quantitatively without very precisely defining the thing being studied, lynching. The more I thought about lynching the more difficulties I found in trying to narrowly and scientifically define some particular behavior as lynching. Writers at the end of the twentieth century exaggerated the supposed ritual character of racial violence.[10] Earlier writers fully understood that people called lynchers often killed casually, with no ceremony at all. The questions debated at the beginning of the century reveal the often nonritual character of extralegal violence called lynching. Can the police lynch anyone? If so, can we go back and recover police killings not contemporaneously counted as lynchings? Can a dead person be lynched? Mobs sometimes went to funeral homes and extracted bodies of dead persons to be burned. What about the almost-dead or dying persons? A mob killed Cleo Wright as he was about to die anyway. Can one person lynch another person? Are three killers required before murder becomes lynching? What do we do with cases, like that of Emmett Till, where the number of killers is in dispute or unknown?

At one point I even wondered if Harry Thaw's notorious killing of Stanford White could not be defined as a lynching. In 1906, Thaw shot and killed Stanford White before a crowd of witnesses. Thaw's memoir of the affair reveals a remarkably cold-blooded killer: "I felt sure he was dead. But [as] I wanted to take no chances, I walked toward him, and fired two more shots." Thaw acted alone and no one has ever accused him of lynching White. Yet Thaw killed White "under the pretext of service to justice." White was a debaucher of women, a libertine, and many agreed that Thaw's revolver had made New York safer for virginal women. The nation rallied around Thaw and even ministers defended the killing. Three trials failed to convict Thaw of murder. If community approval is the essence of lynching, then Harry Thaw lynched Stanford White. If a white man today killed a black man for the purpose of defending womanhood, and did so with the widespread approval of white America, should he not fairly be called a lyncher? Yet, race alone can not define lynching: In some years mob law killed more whites than blacks.[11]

I became impatient with such technical questions. Lynching was a word with the power to justify or challenge the nation's tolerance for extralegal violence. Some of the most exciting research into lynching deals not only with lynching itself but with the words used by its opponents to describe and characterize the horror. In 1984, Trudier Harris recognized that the words black writers used to record whites' ritualized killings of African Americans have helped configure the black experience. "The black writer," Harris wrote, "becomes a kind of ritual priest in ever keeping before his black audience the essence of one of the forces that have shaped their lives."[12] Ida B. Wells was just such a "ritual priest." Her chief claim to historical fame comes more from the enduring rhetoric she fashioned than anything else. Wells consciously constructed arguments based on sources whites could not refute, presenting them with language in a manner that commanded authority. Proponents of lynching relied on language as well. Jacquelyn Dowd Hall has argued that rape talk formed "a kind of acceptable folk pornography," conversation that legitimized and incited violence.[13] James H. Madison writes that after a 1930 Indiana lynching, competing "storytellers" fought to establish a dominant narrative of the event.[14] From this scholarship I learned that use of the word lynching could be defined as a "speech act" or as "discourse," but I finally realized that the act of labeling certain behaviors as lynching should be called rhetoric. Rhetoric implies a consciousness of audience, an attempt to influence a public. Throughout American history both apologists and opponents of lynching have used the word to influence public opinion.

This book is not a history of lynching as a behavior. Rather, my intent here is to trace the history of the word lynching, as a variable in determining Americans' acceptance of extralegal violence. Rather than a history of lynchers, this is a history of how the people who championed their cause, or fought against it, manipulated the meaning of lynching. This does not mean that I think words matter more than behavior. Words shape behavior. Perhaps this book will lay the foundation for some future study of the behavior called lynching. But students of the act of lynching have underestimated the importance of language. We have tried to pull neutral data from politically charged descriptions of violence without first looking carefully at how particular words came to describe particular acts. Ironically, few in the heyday of lynching missed the politics of language. All sides understood the importance of language as they fought to make extralegal violence seem legitimate or illegitimate. From its beginnings, lynching talk prompted tensions between those impatient to control what they defined as crime and those determined to protect the rights of accused persons. Abolitionists engaged the slave South in debate about violence. The antislavery press scored points when it plausibly accused white Southerners of lynching.

I got a clear demonstration of how this process works as I finished this book. On September 11, 2001, television and radio news broadcasters reported the attacks on the World Trade Center and the Pentagon. Caught off guard, these journalists composed their copy as they spoke. Their unrehearsed reporting, and interviews with various scholars and experts, showed working journalists searching for the proper word, the best analogy, to describe what many admitted they found almost beyond description. When Senator John McCain, and others, said the attacks clearly constituted "an act of war," they used terminology designed to foreclose any but an immediate military response by the United States. Historian Alan Brinkley shrank from such language ("this is not an act of war in any conventional sense"), seeking to reassure Americans that no "large-scale military activity will at least immediately follow this." Throughout the day, I watched and listened as the phrase "act of war" took hold, along with a concomitant Pearl Harbor analogy. I would not say the words caused American bombers to attack Afghanistan, but calling the attacks "an act of war" clearly made an argument for military action. Language crafted by news broadcasters and politicians guided the thinking of citizens as they absorbed the horrors on their television screens.[15] Long before television, writers and politicians fashioned the labels Americans relied on to comprehend the smaller-scale horrors lynchings represented, labels that were also calls to action.

Within particular topics scholars know full well the power of language. This understanding is particularly striking in Holocaust studies. Recently, in an examination of American "Holocaust consciousness," Peter Novick found that Americans only began to seriously engage the Holocaust as an entity in its own right, rather than as an element in the larger universe of Nazi barbarisms, after 1961. American journalists did not popularize the word "Holocaust" until they encountered it in Israel, while covering the Eichmann trial. Before Eichmann, there had been no widely accepted popular term to describe what had happened. Thus, in 1946, David P. Boder could not secure funding or recognition for his project to interview the Jewish victims of Nazi murder. Boder acted before a common language had been achieved. Without the necessary rhetorical support, Boder foundered and his work slid into obscurity. Building that rhetorical support meant creating a name and popularizing it, persuading people to recognize "Holocaust" as the word describing Nazi racist violence.[16] In America, Ida B. Wells, T. Thomas Fortune, and other African American leaders made lynching into the label we use to describe the episode of racial violence that gripped the country after the Civil War.

Focusing on the processes of such language creation has had interesting consequences for my understanding of American regionalism. After a colleague read a draft of this book, he complained that after a while, all the violence began to look the same. He insisted that the South has always been, and remains today, the most violent part of the nation. I know this is the standard view, and it is not wrong. Yet, I confess that as I began to examine lynching talk in California, Ohio, and New Jersey, I noticed more similarities than dissimilarities between descriptions of brutalities in those regions and those in the South. Moreover, as I read what Northerners and Southerners said about violence, I realized that the evidence now available does not allow us to say absolutely and conclusively that Southern culture nurtured some peculiar instinct to violence that white Southerners could not control. I was struck more by white Southern newspaper writers' participation in the national culture than by their distinctiveness. Southerners had no trouble finding language in the national lexicon to describe and explain their actions. They could easily excuse their violence with metaphors and analogies copied from other regions. Language describing white Southerners' violent habits generated a national toleration for extralegal violence that, in turn, encouraged white Southerners' most violent tendencies. White Southerners seemed to draw strength from arguments on behalf of their violence.

White Southerners, and the nation as a whole, created an intellectual environment that sometimes tolerated, and on occasion actively encouraged, mobbing. The creation of that tolerating environment took place in the imaginations of men and women, in oral conversation, and on the pages of newspapers and magazines. It was a political act, or rather, series of acts, just as surely as voting or making a campaign speech. It may be that this toleration had as much to do with high levels of Southern violence as did culture.

This creation of a rhetorical environment tolerant of extralegal violence has made all of America violent, not just the South. The United States is the most violent industrialized country in the world. The National Center for Health Statistics reports that the homicide rate in the United States is four times higher than in comparable industrialized countries. In the 1990s, the American homicide rate was seventeen times higher than in Japan and ten times higher than in Germany. In 1999 15,533 persons died in the United States by murder and "nonnegligent manslaughter." This figure represented a significant improvement over 1998, when 16,974 died by murder and nonnegligent manslaughter. The Uniform Crime Reports carefully caution readers that these numbers do not include justifiable homicides, attempts to murder, or assaults to murder.[17] In 1968, when 14,589 American soldiers died in Vietnam combat, protesters filled the streets, yet no one protests the murder rate.[18] Americans accept high murder rates as unavoidable, the product of a culture that has, somehow, made violence instinctive. We are murderous because we cannot help ourselves.

Understanding America as a peculiarly violent place and conceiving of lynching as racial, early-twentieth-century lynching opponents charged that only Americans lynch. But while the antilynchers hoped to change the American character, turning the nation away from that form of racial violence, scholars have often argued that Americans cannot help themselves. Richard Maxwell Brown writes that our revolutionary origins established a tradition of violence. David Hackett Fischer says that people from rougher cultures settled the brutal precincts in America, bringing European tendencies to violence with them. Others, like David Courtwright, insist that our frontier experience inclined us to violence. Still others have claimed our constitutionalism promotes violence by placing sovereignty in the hands of the people, leading ordinary citizens to think they have the right to decide when the killing of criminals is legitimate.[19]

Obviously most murders cannot be called "lynchings," by any definition. Harry Thaw consciously calculated his act as a service to justice; many more murders stem from moments of passion or emotional miscalculation. Yet, it is also true that the idea that a person can be justified, in some circumstances, in killing another person is more prevalent among Americans than among Canadians or the residents of other industrialized countries. The belief that Americans have "no duty to retreat" from violent confrontations and the notion that it is manly to fight are tied up with the parallel idea that public opinion determines the legitimacy of murderous violence.[20] Lynching means many things, but one meaning is murder endorsed by community. This can be racial, and when it is, the lynchers' community does the endorsing. But it does not have to be; it is a mistake to conceive of lynching as only racial. Westerners have lynched whites (and Mexicans, and Native Americans, and Chinese) more often than blacks, as have Northerners and Easterners. The original impulse to lynch was not racial. Racial violence is a subset of a larger problem.

The current state of air travel makes what the general reader of history takes from this study especially important. The arrest of Richard C. Reid for attempting to explode a bomb on a transatlantic flight reminds us that airline passengers can confront violence and when that happens, they will likely do so with no police officer or judge available. In a sense, airliners represent an environment not so different from the frontier, where migrants made their own law. What flashes through the mind of a passenger as he or she closes his or her fingers around the throat of a would-be hijacker is set by what the society believes is an acceptable level of extralegal violence. In the case of Richard C. Reid, passengers held him until proper authorities were available, but they could have imagined themselves as part of a society where killing such a miscreant would be acceptable or even expected.[21]

This book is a history of how our society has reached a point where such violent expectations no longer prevail. The story of lynching should first tell us that our history never "caused" us to be violent. The fact that we have for so long debated the meaning of lynching shows that violence is not automatic for Americans, but rather the product of a complex and subtle mechanism that legitimates violence through language, description, and popular opinion. Americans have used words and rhetorical "truths" to convince themselves that their violence is right or, if not right, then instinctive and uncontrollable, a force of nature or history. Plausibly calling something a lynching compellingly argues that the violence had popular support. The contested language used to describe our violence documents just how controversial popularly sanctioned violence has been. Language itself is political and represents past political decisions to sanction or not sanction violence. This debate continues even today and remains important for us all.

This book documents how Americans have used language to work out a framework for judging the legitimacy or illegitimacy of mob law. First, two competing notions about lynching emerged in the American Revolution. One version saw lynching as the work of officers exceeding their authority while the other saw lynching as the work of ordinary people acting entirely outside the law. The second idea soon predominated, rendering lynching as the work of a community or neighborhood united against outrageous crimes. As Americans migrated West, those who could convincingly claim to act on behalf of "Judge Lynch" had taken an important step toward legitimacy and power by making themselves seem the representatives of their "whole" community. By the end of the nineteenth century, though, African American civil rights activists had defined lynching on a black-white nexus. In the twentieth century, the nation stripped power and autonomy from the neighborhoods, subjecting local acts of violence to national debate. Acts of violence openly endorsed by neighborhoods or communities that were called lynching began to decline. This forced reformers to redefine the word or lose the use of it. In the scramble for new meaning, the old definition of lynching as community sanctioned did not disappear—the essence of lynching rhetoric has been to attack the larger society for supporting or tolerating extralegal violence. Nonetheless, reformers dismissed the old checklist of descriptors that had once determined whether a killing should be called a lynching or not. Lynching no longer had to have the overt support of the community. No big crowd was needed. In short, almost any racial killing, especially in the South, could be called a lynching as a way of reproaching the whole region. By the end of the century, though, a new term had evolved to challenge lynching as the premier descriptor of racial violence. The new rhetoric, *hate crime*, understood racial violence as the act of a depraved individual, not a corrupt community.

The first chapter looks at the "invention" of lynching. Obviously no scholar will ever identify the first extralegal execution. It may not even be possible to know decisively who first uttered the term "lynching." We can look at the earliest rhetoric about the origins of lynching, comparing that rhetoric to the reality on the Virginia Southside oral culture. Making that comparison shows that stories about the first lynching advanced arguments for or against extralegal violence in the Revolutionary period. Virginians used the word lynching in a self-conscious attempt to legitimate their violence.

The second chapter follows the word from neighborhood jargon, largely confined to the oral culture, into national rhetoric that implicitly criticized the larger community or neighborhood for sponsoring violence. The word lynching entered the national lexicon after an 1835 Vicksburg, Mississippi, riot because at that moment it served Americans' competing rhetorical needs. Opponents of Andrew Jackson saw rioting as evidence of popular sovereignty run amok. Abolitionists could use the riot in their propaganda to show how slavery brutalized white Southerners. Debate over the Vicksburg lynchings touched the most controversial issues of the day.

Abolitionists capitalized on this new weapon in their rhetorical arsenal only to find it compromised by migration westward. The third chapter shows how Westerners justified their extralegal violence on the same basis for which it had been criticized earlier. Abolitionists and Whigs said that communal violence exposed the neighborhood as depraved. But now, rather than signaling social defect, Western community support for an act of violence made the violence legitimate. Even the abolitionist press found it difficult to refute Westerners' logic: American citizens have a right to monitor their courts and act in place of constituted authorities when those authorities prove inept or corrupt in the face of terrifying crime.

The fourth and fifth chapters each cover roughly the same post–Civil War time period. The fourth chapter shows that racial violence not openly endorsed by the entire community, or most of it, did not qualify as lynching. To call Ku Klux Klan racial violence lynching would have implied that the Klan had the universal support of their Southern white communities. The fifth chapter looks at violence that did meet the 1870s definition of lynching, the nonracial punishment of criminals outside the law. In this decade the nation came closest to achieving a national lynching consensus across regional lines. Journalists invented no new excuses or justifications for lynching, but they did harden and regularize the old explanations, making a formula or metanarrative for describing mob violence. Horrific crime,

crime so brutal that it scandalized whole neighborhoods, sparked lynchings. In places where courts operated poorly or not at all, the press thought, a community should punish the criminal itself, outside the law. The will of the community had to be respected, especially when it was unanimous and impulsive.

In the 1880s and 1890s black journalists persuaded Americans to think of lynching as racial. Since lynching implied community support, calling acts of racial violence lynchings enabled civil rights proponents to use each lynching as evidence of the need for societal reforms. Some journalists understood full well in the 1870s that Judge Lynch had racist tendencies, sometimes killing blacks more readily than whites, but only in the 1890s did black opponents of lynching succeed in making the practice seem almost exclusively racial. The sixth chapter looks at Ida B. Wells, the great lynching crusader, showing how her own thought evolved from acceptance to rejection of community-sanctioned punishment of criminals outside the law.

The seventh chapter examines the fight between early-twentieth-century antilynching organizations over the meaning of lynching. The National Association for the Advancement of Colored People (NAACP), the Tuskegee Institute, and other organizations fought bitterly over the meaning of lynching, though that quarrel is largely forgotten today. The disagreement over the definition of lynching was not a distraction from the primary issue. The NAACP needed a loose definition of lynching as part of its long-term fight against a racially corrupt society. The Tuskegee Institute urged a strict, scientific definition, expecting that one day lynching could be brought to an end. In a sense, the fight was between pessimism and optimism. The NAACP saw white racism as deeply rooted in American culture and never expected to declare victory and disband. Tuskegee actually hoped to end racial violence one day.

In the twentieth century, neighborhood lynchings became the subject of national debate. Chapter eight tracks lynching talk through the last half of the twentieth century, as it became increasingly "high-tech," meaning that improved technology allowed national news outlets to make lynching a matter for national debate. At the same time, the meaning of lynching became further confused. Authorities complicated the meaning of lynching by their efforts to speed up criminal justice, to execute criminals so quickly that no lynching would be necessary. "Legal lynching" became a twentieth-century reality.

Finally, the last chapter looks at the development of hate crimes. By 1985, Americans saw community-sanctioned lynching as largely a thing of the past. Hate crime became the new term for individual acts of violence driven by prejudice. Hate crime rhetoric implied violence in defiance of community norms, not acts sanctioned by the neighborhood. The term lynching implicated a whole community or neighborhood, suggesting that everyone in town supported the lynching whether they participated directly or not. A "hate crime" insulted or outraged the community, challenging rather than enforcing societal values. Proponents of hate crime laws hoped this new rhetoric would change the course of America, moving the nation away from its racially violent past.

From the first moment when an American mouth opened and the word lynch came out, lynching has carried enormous political power to indict a whole community or mobilize that community to violence. Used effectively, it can persuade people that violence is legitimate for having popular sanction or illegitimate for expressing a corrupt popular will. This was true on the American frontier where regulators sought language that would justify their extralegal violence as just, fair, and necessary. Abolitionists came the closest to winning large numbers of Northerners to their banner when they charged that slavery made Southerners violent, turned them into lynchers. Westerners manipulated the word, too, insisting that American citizens, the people, have a right to judge their courts and take to the streets when they find their criminal justice system inadequate or inept or corrupt or just too slow. In the 1870s, the biggest and most powerful newspapers "opposed" lynching but recognized that some truly terrible crimes drove communities almost to madness, especially when the courts could not effectively control crime. In such cases, Judge Lynch had to be acquitted by reason of temporary insanity. White Southern conservatives exploited this national understanding of outraged popular passion. They racialized extralegal violence in the sense that they insisted that any killing of a black person must be legitimate under contemporary standards for judging such things. African Americans fought back, turning the word lynching into a synonym for a racially motivated killing.

Debate over racial lynching occurred within a larger argument among Americans. This dispute involves the appropriate role of violence in American society and the government's monopoly of violence. The arguments for lynching, that some crimes explain or justify mob action, that the public has a right to punish criminals in some circumstances, are all bigger than questions about race. They continue today in the debate over capital punishment. White Southerners invented nothing when they "began" lynching. Southern whites turned to their most brutal acts of violence after many Americans claimed for themselves a right to violence. Understanding the political uses rhetoriticians have made of lynching unveils realities behind Americans' so-called instinctive violent urges. Americans have sometimes consciously decided to turn to violence, but the decision was not instinctive. It came only after debate and argument.

One final note. Throughout this book I will be referring to "lynchings" and "lynchers" even though such terms cannot be defined and function as rhetoric. I will not define lynching, though I use the nineteenth-century definition as a reference point. Nineteenth-century folk understood lynching to mean an act of violence sanctioned, endorsed, or carried out by the neighborhood or community outside the law. (They did not often define community in this context—a group of people geographically proximate to one another sharing a common ethic approximates their thinking.) Across time, critics have sometimes called acts of violence lynchings as a way of accusing some social network of sponsoring the violence—even when an individual or small group acted without the explicit knowledge or support of any larger society. Corrupt violence, some charged, could be a lynching if it had a community's tacit or unspoken support. Thus, as Jamil Adbullah Al-Amin, formerly known as H. Rap Brown, goes to trial charged with murder as I write these words, his supporters say he may be lynched. They do not worry that a mob will break open the jail and hang Al-Amin from a tree. Rather, they fear he will not get a fair trial. They see as perverted not only the criminal justice system that tries Al-Amin, but also the larger society sponsoring such a legal structure. If a racially corrupt system sentences a black man to death, they say, he has been lynched. (Actually, he was ultimately sentenced to life in prison.) Such an accusation does not really fit the nineteenth-century idea of what a lynching would be, but it does reflect the old idea that a lynching is a killing outside truly legitimate law sanctioned by the citizenry generally.

I will reflect local contemporaneous usage: if people at the time called an event a "lynching," so will I. Constant use of phrases like "extralegal crowd violence" seems awkward and unrealistic, since people at the time did call some events "lynchings." I will also bring up cases not called lynchings to suggest the arbitrary nature of labeling and to discuss the concept of "legal lynching."

CHAPTER ONE

Prologue
THE ORIGINS OF THE WORD

There is no beginning and there can be no end to lynching. Today newspapers report lynchings in Mexico, Germany, South Africa, the Middle East, and Kenya.[1] Romanians who cheered the death of dictator Nicolae Ceauscescu in 1989 proclaimed "Lynching is not a crime," a claim that seems jarring to many Americans.[2] One scholar described a 1644 French mob attack on three minor government officials as a "lynching."[3] In 1769 Ireland, a mob dismembered a police informer's body and nailed the pieces to a prison door.[4] Eighteenth-century Chinese mobs hunted down and killed sorcerers, and in the nineteenth century, they burned thieves alive.[5] Lynchings, or crowd actions that looked like those events Americans have chosen to call lynchings, have never been unique to the United States. They have occurred for centuries in Europe, Africa, and Asia.

Imagining the beginnings of lynching is a political act. Nineteenth-century writers searched for the origins of lynch law to justify it. In 1837, when Francis J. Grund, the Austrian-born supporter of Andrew Jackson and author of *The Americans in their Moral, Social and Political Relations*, found that "Lynch law" sprang from the Bible, he strove to promote the practice. Lynching had been "begot in those happy times, in which religious customs took the place of the law." Rather than attributing lynching to the American frontier, Grund claimed New England pilgrims, governing little communities through mutual agreement and consent, did not "spare the rod" when disciplining miscreants. Grund credited the American Revolution not with inventing lynching but with transforming its meaning. Revolutionaries substituted tarring and feathering for the Puritans' flogging and thereby nationalized the practice, "being at first employed in a patriotic cause, [which] created an universal prejudice in its favor."[6]

In 1887, the California historian Hubert Howe Bancroft found the origins of *Popular Tribunals* ("the illegal administration of justice by the people") in the Enlightenment. Bancroft began building his argument by pointing out that feudal regimes once determined the guilt or innocence of accused persons in clandestine proceedings. "Almost every state," Bancroft wrote, "had its system of secret tribunals, where judgments, most unexpectedly to the victims, were passed in darkness and executed in the light." The guilty and innocent alike feared such arbitrary power.[7] According to Bancroft, the Enlightenment emancipated citizens' minds, forcing governments to allow popular sovereignty. When the government failed to execute the popular will properly, the public had the duty to rise up and enforce law outside state institutions. Enlightenment thinkers may not have coined the term lynching, but Bancroft found it in Galway, Ireland, in 1493, or, perhaps, in 1687 when a Judge Lynch suppressed piracy in American waters by "execut[ing] justice summarily, regardless of the forms of law."[8] Grund and Bancroft both hoped their readers would conclude that such deep origins in human history legitimated the collective violent expression of popular sovereignty.[9]

Americans have also traced the origins of lynching to criticize it. The most serious challenge to Grund and Bancroft's logic came eighteen years later from a scholar named James Cutler. Cutler's work on lynching remains the standard even today; he was the only scholar to study lynching throughout the course of American history in depth. Cutler published his lynching research after receiving his Ph.D. from Yale (1903) and while teaching political economy at Wellesley College. Cutler later joined Case Western Reserve University as a sociology professor. He remained at Case Western for nearly forty years, establishing the School of Applied Social Sciences and writing monographs on training for social work and education, never again returning to the subject of lynching.[10]

In 1905 Cutler began his look at lynching by asking "Why is lynching a peculiarly American institution?" Cutler reviewed Bancroft's evidence for the universality of lynching and rejected it. The Galway story, Cutler said, "may be dismissed with but little consideration." The pirate story rated no better ("equally fanciful and fictitious"). Instead, Cutler found exclusively American origins for the term, if not the practice.[11] The United States differs from other countries because Americans have a peculiarly dangerous attitude toward law, Cutler explained. He felt that without the long traditions found in Europe, Americans naturally have less respect for law. And American citizens also respect law less for having made it themselves. In such a place, "it is inevitable that the legal machinery will prove powerless to control popular excitements."[12]

By finding the first lyncher in Virginia, he sought to justify a particular idea about ordinary Americans' rights to violence outside the law. The first lyncher certainly did not live in Virginia. The first man to call himself a lyncher probably did, a fact that proves nothing about the origins of any behavior that might be called lynching but may tell us something about the beginnings of lynching rhetoric.

CHARLES LYNCH

According to the mythology, the first Judge Lynch lived in either Bedford or Pittsylvania County, Virginia. Those favoring Bedford County as the site of the first lynching have advanced Charles Lynch as the original Judge Lynch while the competing Pittsylvania story features William Lynch. Bedford County narratives normally present Charles Lynch as a leading citizen and stalwart patriot, who responded to a Tory plot to seize Virginia's lead mines in the summer of 1780. Since the mines provided the bullets necessary to save Virginia from the British, the emergency preempted defendants' rights.[13] When the Tories mounted their insurgency, moreover, the General Court in Williamsburg had practically ceased to exist because of the war. According to another version of the story, the court did function, but the Tories defeated their prosecutions by providing false alibi witnesses.[14]

Parts of the legend are correct. Charles Lynch really was a member of the Bedford County elite, a colonel in the militia, a magistrate, and a legislator. Lynch and other Virginia militia officers brutally put down sporadic outbreaks of Tory sentiment in Virginia's southwestern counties. Colonel William Campbell of Washington County, hearing that Tories conspired to seize the lead mines in Montgomery County and murder county leaders, marched his soldiers to the rescue. His laconic report after a hunt for disaffected Virginians survives today: "Shot one, Hanged one, and whipt several."[15]

Men engaged in such shooting, hanging, and whipping had no choice but to think about how others saw their actions. They saw themselves as punishing treason, but from the English point of view, they committed treason themselves. And they violated their own Virginia law. In March 1780 another Virginia militia colonel, William Preston, wrote Governor Thomas Jefferson that a magistrate had reported that seventy-five men had taken an oath to King George III, vowing "to perpetuate the most horrid murders [on all] Individuals in Authority in this Quarter." Among the persons targeted for murder was Preston himself, along with his family.[16] Jefferson's response provides a clue to how the governor saw such behavior. Jefferson warned Preston, "We must avoid any irregularity which might give" those accused of treason "legal means of withdrawing themselves from punishment."

Jefferson worried that Preston, angry at the threats to his family, might disregard the nuances of due process. The governor wrote that he approved "much"—but pointedly not all—"of your most active endeavors" to apprehend the guilty. Jefferson also instructed Preston to protect the lead mines immediately. To the extent that Preston read urgency into Jefferson's words, the admonition to protect the lead mines may have weakened the governor's plea for due process.[17]

In June word circulated among Virginia militia officers that Tories had organized around New River and had already committed murders and various other outrages.[18] In August new reports of murders and horse thefts perpetuated by Tories spread through Virginia.[19] In response to news of this "horrid Conspiracy," Colonel Lynch marched his soldiers from Bedford County into Montgomery County to protect the lead mines.[20]

According to the most detailed account of Lynch's work, he and his fellow justices of the peace tried accused Tory conspirators, carefully following proper due process, even as they violated the letter of the law denying them jurisdiction over felonies. According to legend, convicted defendants received thirty-nine lashes administered at the base of a tree in Lynch's yard.[21] As he began arresting alleged traitors, Lynch received a letter from Preston expressing the worry that Lynch did not give his prisoners proper trials. Lynch wrote back, "What sort of tryals you have been inform'd I have given them I know not, but I can assure you I only Examine them strictly & such as I believe not Very Criminal I set at Liberty." The others, Lynch assured Preston, received "a proper tryal."[22] Lynch was a law-abiding citizen, or so he presented himself to Preston.

Lynch may have held militia trials or he may have been talking about county court examinations in the only county where he would have had authority to hold such proceedings, Bedford County. Lynch only rarely attended county court, although he was the senior justice, but he could well have played a role behind-the-scenes in the numerous treason prosecutions Bedford County's court processed that summer. In July the court ordered five men fined and jailed for "Breach of a certain act of assembly entitled 'an Act for the punishment of certain offences.'" Originally passed in October 1776, this statute had been beefed up in May 1780, and gave county courts the power to punish certain treasons without going to the General Court. But in August of 1780 Preston described himself as "a stranger" to the new law, "as we have not been able to procure a Copy of the Act & have only heard of it."[23] Perhaps Preston was really scrambling to locate a copy of the latest enactment from Williamsburg. It seems more likely that Preston saw himself as a stalwart backwoods patriot, more interested in justice than legal technicalities.

On August 29 the court ordered seven more men jailed for high treason. Officially, these defendants were to go to the General Court for trial, as specified in the original statute. But so many languished in the Bedford County jail that in October the justices expressed sympathy for their gaoler, or jailer. He had to feed and house such "a number of Disaffected persons" for an indeterminate time that it worked a financial hardship on him. The court appealed to the legislature for financial relief.²⁴

Bedford County records do not show that any of these treason defendants were whipped. But something irregular was going on. A suspiciously high number of defendants pleaded guilty to high treason, a crime punishable by death, suggesting they had been—at the very least—energetically interrogated before reaching County Court. Nancy Devereaux, the wife of one prisoner, alleged an ethnic dimension even in these earliest proceedings, writing that there "is a missunderstanding [sic] between Colo Lynch and the Welsh in General." Devereaux described herself as "very uneasy at present lest my Husband should not have the Strictest Justice."²⁵ There are documents surviving today that purport to be the confessions of men Lynch seized and interrogated.²⁶

By August doubts about Lynch's methods had reached Jefferson. The governor did not refer to "Lynch's Law" by name, but his meaning seems clear when he wrote to Lynch, conceding that treason should be met with "the most vigorous, decisive measures." Jefferson applauded Lynch's "activity," saying it deserved great commendation: "The method of seizing them at once which you have adopted is much the best." Lynch had positioned himself as a man of action, more concerned with patriotic justice than legal details in an emergency. This was such a powerful argument that it could not be dismissed out of hand. Jefferson conceded the point.²⁷

But he carefully mixed cautions in with his approval, so much so that one wonders if he did not design the praise to make the criticisms more palatable. Jefferson warned Lynch to "take care" that Tory defendants "be regularly tried afterwards." Jefferson urged Lynch not to worry about the expense of hiring men to guard prisoners to be transported to the capital. Signaling his doubts about the country magistrate's legal abilities, Jefferson urged Lynch to consult a lawyer regarding procedure. The Commonwealth's Attorney in your county, Jefferson advised, can suggest the proper course of action.²⁸

Jefferson came close to insulting Lynch's intelligence when he explained that those thought guilty of treason at the county level must be sent to the capital for further trial. Even a militia officer professing himself "a stranger" to the latest laws knew that. It is not possible to know just how Lynch reacted to Jefferson's letter. There is evidence that Jefferson's plea could not overcome Lynch's view of extralegal violence as effective. After August still more defendants pleaded guilty to high treason.[29]

By 1782, Lynch himself used the term "lynch law" to describe informal justice, executed outside the courts. He did so in correspondence with a Captain Sanders, who was hired to manage Welsh lead miners. Lynch relied on Sanders though he realized Sanders fed the miners nothing but bread and water and, according to Lynch, drove them hard, using "irregular and violent" methods to extract their labor. When the Welsh miners refused to work, Lynch and Sanders broke the strike. Afterward, Lynch worried that "a party" conducted a whispering campaign against Sanders. Given Lynch's own account of Sanders' rough methods, it seems odd that Lynch expressed surprise that those speaking against Sanders "gained the ear of some I did not expect." Lynch explained that the feeling against his manager resulted from the "Lynch Law" Sanders administered. He denigrated the critics of "Lynch Law" as "torys & such," "lynched" for illegally trading with slaves.[30]

Charles Lynch's decision to turn his own name into a verb suggests a preference for political will, force of personality, and knowledge of good over institutional solutions, due process, and other attributes of constitutionalism. It certainly suggests the frontier hero seeking justice outside of law so much a part of American mythology. Charles Lynch, in other words, lived the fundamental tension in American life between politics and the Constitution, between seeking good over procedural values and institutional constraints.[31]

No matter how legitimate Lynch and his fellows saw their extralegal violence, they did break the law. Lynch's fears that the victims of lynch law might sue led him to seek protection from the Virginia legislature. A member of the General Assembly, he persuaded fellow lawmakers to pass a special law indemnifying himself and his friends. In 1782 the assembly declared that William Preston, Robert Adams, Jr., James Callaway, and Charles Lynch suppressed a plot by "evil disposed persons" to levy war against the Commonwealth of Virginia. The General Assembly articulated what would become the standard apology for lynching when it defined what Lynch and his fellows did as not strictly warranted by law, "although justified from the imminence of the danger."[32]

Charles Lynch did not invent the idea of using extralegal violence against "evil disposed persons." Charles Lynch can be documented not only doing things that might be called lynchings, but also using the word himself. Lynch's ally Preston presented himself as a rugged frontiersman with little time or patience for statutory technicalities. Jefferson described Lynch's work as "the most vigorous, decisive measures." And Lynch himself insisted that even if he acted outside the strict letter of the law, his prisoners all received "a proper tryal," suggesting that Lynch believed he could act fairly even while not strictly following established procedures. He never made a class argument himself, but Charles Lynch as the first lyncher positions lynching as "establishment violence" performed outside the technical letter of the law, but done by a member of the governing elite.

WILLIAM LYNCH

William Lynch's claim to be the original Judge Lynch is even more sketchy than that of Charles. An ordinary farmer, William Lynch left a smaller footprint in Virginia archival records than did Charles. There is evidence that in 1780 Tories hatched a conspiracy in Pittsylvania County and that locals used some sort of irregular legal procedure to suppress it. In 1780 Thomas Jefferson wrote that Pittsylvania County Tories plotted "a very dangerous Insurrection" and reported to Virginia's Congressional delegation that "[t]he Ring-leaders were seized in their beds."[33]

The "Ring-leaders . . . seized in their beds" included Benjamin Lawless, who was repeatedly hauled into Pittsylvania County Court from 1779 to 1781. In November 1779, the County Court examined evidence that Lawless had stolen two gunlocks, but decided the evidence did not warrant a trial. In March 1780 the County Court held another hearing to examine new charges against him. This time he stood accused of stealing three slaves, but the court again released him, finding the evidence insufficient. Finally, in July 1781, the County Court examined Lawless on charges of high treason. This time the magistrates decided the evidence justified sending Lawless to General Court. Since the General Court records are missing, what happened next is not known. Given that William Lynch has been described as the first lyncher and Benjamin Lawless as his original victim, it may be significant that William Lynch testified against Lawless in 1779 and 1781. He probably did in 1780 as well, but the records for that year only note that "divers witnesses" attended the proceedings against Lawless.[34] William Lynch had taken part in a long effort to convict Lawless, an effort that remained frustratingly unsuccessful at least until 1781.

As the civil courts faltered, the militia assumed control. At the end of 1780 a politically active merchant named David Jameson wrote that a court martial in Pittsylvania County had crushed an insurrection plotted by "the lower rank of people." The court martial convicted three insurrectionary leaders, but errors in the proceedings meant that the trio would get a new trial. Jameson wrote that he very much disliked trying people in court martials and "wish[ed] to see that only in use w[hi]ch. the Constitution points out."[35] Unlike Charles Lynch, William Lynch occupied no position of leadership in his county. There is no evidence he played any significant role in the militia. Furthermore, there are no contemporary documents showing William's impatience with the technical letter of the law.

In 1811, diarist Andrew Ellicott chanced to interview William Lynch, recording their meeting in his diary. Ellicott listened as the old man described the first "Lynch-men" of the Revolutionary War, claiming his lynchers organized in 1776. Lynch described in detail how he and his gang tortured prisoners until they confessed. In some instances he placed men his "court" had condemned on horses with their hands bound and a rope around their necks. Apparently this allowed Lynch to say he did not actually execute his victims, although the result was that he did, as the horse inevitably wandered off in pursuit of food.[36]

In his interview with Ellicott, William Lynch presented himself as a patriotic man of action with little time for legal technicalities. He comes across, as described by Ellicott, as very much like the Charles Lynch documented in Jefferson's correspondence. More to the point, he presented himself as a stock type: as the rugged, independent-minded frontiersman. Such yeomen had ordered the Carolina backcountry well before the Revolution, so the idea had been in circulation for a long time before William Lynch ever met Ellicott, a quintessential American in the New Republic with a scientific and entrepreneurial mind.[37]

In this era, many questioned just how far popular sovereignty should extend. Federalists thought the new constitutional order allowed only a very limited role for the people. The people should vote but then remain passive for fear of upsetting political stability and threatening law and order. Alexander Hamilton and George Washington saw little difference between peaceful protest and riot, "the vengeance of armed men." Proponents of popular sovereignty, such as the jurist James Wilson, emphasized the right of the people to control or supervise their government. At the end of the eighteenth century, some Americans organized "Democratic Societies" to promote the democratic impulses they understood to be inherent in the American Revolution. Federalists feared the democratic societies as heretical, illegitimate for being informally "self-created" rather than the product of constitutional processes. They merely pretended to represent the people; only duly elected representatives could do that. The Federalist orator and intellectual Fisher Ames condemned the societies for promoting "club sovereignty," a term that resembles "club law," which some later writers used to describe vigilante groups.[38]

Against this intellectual backdrop, Lynch's cruelty appalled Ellicott and he wrote sarcastically, "this was called aiding the civil authority." He added that "it seems almost incredible that such proceedings should be had in a civilized country governed by known laws." Ellicott concluded that Lynch had a "strong but uncultivated mind" and expressed surprise that he was "a great stickler for equality and the rights of man as established by law!"[39] Ellicott never published his interview. For him, meeting the first lyncher was a matter of historical curiosity.

In 1836 Edgar Allan Poe found lynch law more appealing. In his magazine, the *Southern Literary Messenger,* Poe proposed William Lynch as the first lyncher, publishing a constitution he said Lynch had written for his band of vigilantes. In this charter Lynch complained of "a set of lawless men" stealing horses, counterfeiting, and many other crimes that Poe thought justified vigilantism. Lynch's charter did not claim that the war had shut down the General Court or that the Court met too infrequently or at too great a distance: He insisted, instead, that criminals rendered the law ineffective by suborning a false alibi. Poe excused Lynch, writing that the Virginian faced "a trained band of villains."[40]

In Poe's portrait, William Lynch swept aside legal formalism to fight crime. Poe pictured William Lynch as fighting ordinary crime rather than Tory traitors and acting out of general frustration with the law rather than because the courts failed to function.[41] Poe's William Lynch sounds a lot like David Crockett's popular 1834 self-portrait of himself as frontier hero. Like William and Charles Lynch, Crockett described his work as a justice of the peace as not always strictly legal. Nonetheless, "my judgments were never appealed from" because they "stuck like wax." Crockett explained that "I gave my decisions on the principles of common justice and honesty between man and man, and relied on natural born sense, and not on law, learning [*sic*] to guide me; for I had never read a page in a law book in all my life."[42] Since Poe had a reputation for good-natured hoaxes, it might be well not to take his lyncher's charter too uncritically. After all, Poe published the charter in the heyday of journalistic pranking.[43]

LYNCHING ON THE FRONTIER

At the end of the Revolution, based on cases like those of Charles and William Lynch, Virginians described extralegal violence as lynching. Nonetheless, Charles and William Lynch are significant only if they permanently established the term in the language. This is not a trivial point. If we see lynching as rhetoric used to legitimize a pervasive practice through description, then it matters how Americans picked up the term and used it to justify extralegal violence after Charles and William Lynch pass from the scene.

Since published early national writers rarely used the word lynching, it is not easy to connect Charles and William Lynch to later use of their name. For forty years after the Revolution, lynching remained largely locked in the oral culture. There are facts beyond dispute that suggest, if not prove, just how the term spread across America. For example, Virginia veterans of the Revolutionary War familiar with Colonel Lynch's methods began fanning out across the continent even before the war came to an end. Between 1810 and 1830 the population of the West swelled from 665,980 to nearly two million.[44] In 1830 the Irish-born writer Tyrone Power could still see crowds of American migrants, moving West with all their worldly goods.[45] Two-thirds of Virginia's Revolutionary veterans who lived long enough to apply for a pension left their home state. In their pension applications, some of the veterans remembered serving under Colonel Lynch, guarding the lead mines and fighting Tories. They went to Maine and Canada and to Texas and to every state between, but the largest groups went to Kentucky and Tennessee, with Indiana and Georgia coming in third and fourth.[46]

These migrants regularly indulged in vigilante violence. As ethnologist and explorer Henry Rowe Schoolcraft toured the Ozarks in 1818 and 1819 he noted that outraged frontiersmen "hot for revenge" often "obtained" justice "in a summary way."[47] Traveling about America between 1818 and 1820, James Flint found a Cincinnati magistrate who had dismissed a man accused of burglary only to see a gang seize the man, tie him to a tree and whip him until "blood sprung in every direction." This, Flint told his readers, was called "a court of uncommon pleas."[48] John James Audubon wrote "delineations" on various aspects of American culture, based on his observations from 1808 through 1834. Audubon devoted one such "delineation" to the regulators endemic to the Ohio and Mississippi River valleys.[49] In 1824 another English travel writer, Adam Hodgson, reported hearing of a young slave burnt to death in Charleston, South Carolina, as a punishment for murder. Still another English writer, publishing his account the same year Hodgson issued his, described extensive vigilante activity in Illinois and Indiana.[50]

Travelers encountering these migrating people often commented on their predilection for argot. In 1824 the writer Arthur Singleton called the migrants' "Phraseology" "novel." They referred to his luggage as "plunder," "as if you were a bandit," he grumbled. Singleton noticed that Virginians in Kentucky still talked like Virginians, calling a river "a run" and "tucking" a *t* at the end of words like onct, twict, and skifft.[51] Travel writer Godfrey T.

Vigne explained to his English readers that Americans can instantly identify a speaker's residence through the words, accents, and expressions peculiar to each state.[52] Tyrone Power exclaimed that he liked Western men in part because they used "a phraseology peculiar to themselves."[53]

Descriptions of this peculiar phraseology do survive. From these fragments, it is clear that these migrating Virginians talked about lynching and even invoked "Judge Lynch" as an icon for extralegal justice fairly meted out. In the first decades of the nineteenth century a number of English travelers visited America, publishing accounts of their visits, often to encourage or discourage would-be English migrants. These writers spoke with ordinary Americans as they traveled about the country and their published travel accounts are a source for the speech patterns of frontier folk. Some "travelers" simply repeated stories published elsewhere and all relied on gossip and second-hand information to enliven their prose. In some places, at some times, while these travelers did not personally meet Judge Lynch, they did hear conversation defending Lynch law. In 1819 Indiana, travel writer William Faux heard talk of "Lynch's law, that is, a whipping in the woods."[54] Nine years later the observer and recorder of pioneer life James Hall described "*Linch's Law*" as the "*lex loci* of the frontiers."[55] In March 1830, another writer, James Stuart, journeyed through Alabama and then Arkansas, encountering more Lynch's law stories. The people Stuart met defined Lynch's law as a community-administered summary punishment of some miscreant. In Arkansas, Stuart learned of a murderer "lynched" on the Mississippi River by steamboaters.[56] In 1832 Washington Irving found "Lynch's law" on the Indiana frontier when whites tied an Indian horse thief to a tree and whipped him.[57]

Irving was not the only nineteenth-century novelist to encounter lynching on the frontier. The South Carolina writer William Gilmore Simms discovered lynching and understood that frontier folk used the word to justify their crowd violence. Simms loved language, understood the power of rhetoric, studied the complexities of vernacular dialect, and laced his frontier novels with jargon he picked up in his travels. For him, the frontier was a linguistic space, filled with strange words with meanings unfamiliar to his readers. In his 1834 novel *Guy Rivers,* Simms explained that "regulators are just, simply, you see, our own people." When "the whole country's roused, then Judge Lynch" holds court. The people give "the rascal" "Lynch's Law, after old Nick Lynch, who invented it in Virginny, long before your time or mine."[58] Though fictional, *Guy Rivers* parallels the observations made by the travel writers. White frontiersmen thought their extralegal violence legitimate when it represented the will of "the whole country." They also traced its origins to Virginia, implying that its ancient origins proved its legitimacy.

Simms' explanation not only defined a particular behavior, but also justified lynching. The legitimacy of crime fighting could be contested. Even duly
appointed officers could not assume that the public would regard their actions as legitimate. James Flint's account of the Cincinnati magistrate illustrates the problems faced by one contender for authority. When the
Cincinnati squire could not position his court congruently with the practices
of a large proportion of his constituents, he had to resign his commission.[59]

Vigilantes acting outside the law also had to win public support to be considered legitimate. The notorious frontier criminals Micajah and Wiley
Harpe illustrate the point. The Harpe brothers came from North Carolina
where, according to one historian, they grew up Tory in "an environment of
hatred for and by neighbors." Whatever made the Harpes into violent preda-
tors, contemporaries thought them remarkably bloodthirsty. When the two
launched a three-state murder spree at the end of the eighteenth century,
local law enforcement could hardly handle the problem, and in southern Illinois, Kentucky, and Tennessee, ordinary citizens banded together to pursue
the outlaws. The governor of Kentucky authorized this vigilantism when he
issued a proclamation confessing that "the ordinary methods of pursuit have
been found ineffectual" and offering a reward to "any person" apprehending
the Harpes. A group of seven finally tracked down Micajah Harpe and be-
headed him. Many celebrated the death of such a vicious murderer, but the
posse could not count on legitimacy. Vengeance more than justice motivated
Moses Stegall, the group's organizer: The Harpes had murdered his wife and
baby. Stegall cut Harpe's head off with the same knife used on his family.[60]
In a world where legally constituted authorities could exert only slight influence, and law enforcement depended on the will of the people, the line between mob and posse was uncertain. Some observers saw lynching as evil,
using the word to denounce it. In 1828, the editor of the *Pensacola Gazette* cen-
sured his mayor with an editorial headlined "Lynch's Law."[61] The mayor had
not bothered with proper legal process before ordering an accused thief
whipped. Like Charles Lynch, the mayor acted because he had no faith in
regularly constituted courts and confronted a string of unsolved crimes.
Hunt understood lynching to mean a minor government official illegitimately exceeding his authority. In 1832 Washington Irving had little good to
say about lynchers. "When I compared the open, noble countenance and
frank demeanor of the young Osage, with the sinister visage and high-
handed conduct of the frontiersman, I felt little doubt on whose back a lash
would be most meritoriously bestowed." Joseph Holt Ingraham expressed
similar doubts in his 1835 book.[62]

More often, Judge Lynch played a useful rhetorical role in an unsettled environment where rival forces contended for legitimacy. Whether a vigilante or-

ganization seemed a legitimate expression of public opinion or an outlaw gang depended heavily on the words used to describe their activities. Writers less brilliant than Washington Irving or even Joseph Holt Ingraham more faithfully reproduced the arguments of the lynchers themselves. James Hall explained that in a lynching, the citizens formed themselves into a "'regulating company,' a kind of holy brotherhood, whose duty it was to purge the community of its unruly members."[63] James Stuart provided the most complete justification for Lynch law on Alabama's cotton frontier, gaining his information from conversation with Alabama whites. Since he recorded mythology heard many times removed from its original source, it is not surprising that it varies considerably from the Charles and William Lynch story. "I have heard," he wrote, "and I believe correctly," that the practice of lynching came just after the Revolution. Stuart thought lynching originated in the mountainous parts of "Carolina," when the inhabitants gave extralegal judicial authority to a person named Lynch, who exercised it with such patriotic impartiality "that his decisions were almost looked upon as having the force of law."[64] It may be that William Lynch's postwar residence in South Carolina accounts for the Alabamians' belief that lynching originated in the Palmetto State.

In Alabama, Indiana, Kentucky, and other places where locals called their extralegal punishments lynchings, the connection with the Revolution gave them a respectability they might not have had otherwise. The main point was that Judge Lynch symbolized extralegal justice handed down impartially. Stuart's story suggests that in some places proponents of summary justice invoked Judge Lynch to justify themselves. They accepted William Lynch's presentation of himself as a man of action in troubled times, an expression of popular will, and the essence of fair and impartial justice administered outside the law. Frontier figures, who could plausibly position themselves as the new Judge Lynch, won an important rhetorical victory, one that legitimized extralegal violence, in the world of small politics they inhabited.[65]

Even into the 1830s, Judge Lynch still remained an unknown personage to most Americans. In certain localities, his name circulated widely, but in an oral culture it went unrecorded in print. In the 1830s, cheap newspapers began putting newsprint in the hands of new readers. Papers copied each other, passing the same stories from one locality to the next. In the 1830s, America was becoming a national market for news. It could be said that cheap newspapers invented the American "public," a national community of readers sharing the same language and forming common narratives and journalistic conventions. Judge Lynch now stood ready to rise above neighborhood political disagreements and escape the oral culture to become a national figure.

CHAPTER TWO

The Word and the Nation

I n 1859 a writer in *Harper's Monthly* remembered that he had first heard of Lynch law when residents of Vicksburg, Mississippi, executed five gamblers in 1835. The incident became a "sensation," this anonymous writer recollected, and "soon the terms 'Lynch law' and 'lynching' became familiar as household words."[1] The spread of lynching in the American vocabulary constitutes another "invention" of lynching. Before the Vicksburg incident, lynching was not widely seen in print; thereafter it became common, a "sensation." Lynching meant violence endorsed by society; those who accused the Vicksburgers of lynching the gamblers implicitly charged that the whole South, or Jackson's political party, was corrupt. Alternatively, they saw lynching as a healthy reaction by an outraged public against gambling. The Vicksburg hangings seized the nation's attention, providing fodder for debate over the role of popular sovereignty, the people's right to take to the streets.

VICKSBURG

The Vicksburg riot, occurring in 1835, cannot be said to have inaugurated a season of disorder. So much more rioting occurred in the mid-1830s than in previous years that scholars disagree as to whether 1834 or 1835 should be called "the riot year."[2] And this wave of violence coincided with the rise of a print culture that added many fresh readers to the rank of newspaper readers. The rise of Andrew Jackson symbolized for many an innovation in the meaning of popular sovereignty that placed real power in the hands of ordinary people. Jacksonian democracy seemed to politicize mob violence and the reading about mob violence in cheap newspapers. Newspapers began widely to report violence that might not have received coverage in earlier years. A full year before the Vicksburg troubles, the *New York Sun* commented that "It is not a difficult matter to get up in our city one of those elegant assemblages called a mob."[3] Religion, race, moral outrage, abolitionism, and politics all sent rioters into the streets.[4] Well before anything happened in Vicksburg, some in New York accused the "reckless prints" in their city of encouraging mob violence.[5]

Some of the proceedings in the months before the Vicksburg hangings seem very like lynchings, though the word lynching did not often appear in the press. In 1834 miners in the Dubuque, Iowa, mines set up an ad hoc court and tried Patrick O'Conner for murder. A nearby newspaper reported the proceedings very sympathetically, making the informal court seem as regular as constitutionally constituted courts operated by the government. "If there exists no means of application of the laws over that region, it then follows that their own safety and preservation depend on regulations of their own adoption." This journalist did not know the word lynching or Lynch Law, but continued with a classic rationale for lynching nonetheless: "The unanimous agreement of the people to put a man to death for the crime of murder, rendered the act legal to all intents and purposes."[6]

When a St. Louis crowd administered fifty lashes to a cheating gambler in 1833, the *St. Louis Republican* called it a lynching.[7] In 1834, one thousand people turned out in Natchez, Mississippi, to whip and then tar and feather an acquitted wife killer. One modern historian calls this a lynching; *Niles' Register* did not. A traveler named Colonel James R. Creecy witnessed the episode and called it a lynching. His book, though, did not appear until 1860.[8] In 1835, a Louisville newspaper described the tarring and feathering of a brute named Coleman as a lynching. Coleman had enticed a little girl, just eight or nine, into an empty office "for the purpose of attempting to gratify his base and hellish appetite." Coleman's attempted rape enraged local citizens. "This," the *Louisville Advertiser* said, "is the first case of the kind that has been tried in this city for a long time before *Judge Lynch*." The *Advertiser* story appeared July 11, before news of the Vicksburg lynchings had reached Louisville.[9] Neither the St. Louis nor the Louisville incident attracted much attention outside their respective cities.

The Vicksburg story begins when the good citizens of that town gathered to celebrate the Fourth of July. The local militia company called the Vicksburg Volunteers were on prominent display for the celebrations and represented the core of legitimate authority in Vicksburg and surrounding Warren County. A local gambler named Cabler from a rough part of town called the Kangaroo showed up uninvited. Cabler seemed positively determined to expose Vicksburg's militia company as weak and ineffective, insulting its commanding officer and striking a citizen in front of the militia soldiers. With his teasing and insulting behavior, Cabler succeeded in convincing the crowd that legitimate authority could not handle the threat he posed. When Cabler armed himself and again confronted the militia, the Vicksburgers arrested him. According to the *Vicksburg Register,* the Vicksburgers took him to the woods to lynch him because they knew the law could not effectively punish him. Turning him over to the law "would have been a mockery." Lynching did not mean a hanging or any other fatal punishment. Rather than hanging Cabler, Vicksburgers lynched him, which meant a whipping followed by tar and feathers.[10]

Two days later, on Monday, July 6, Vicksburg's militia company marched into the Kangaroo, searching for any gambling apparatus it could seize and destroy. The *Vicksburg Register* said the citizens had held a meeting and decided on this course of action. No doubt the Vicksburg Volunteers intended to reestablish their authority after their humiliation on the fourth. A crowd of civilians trailed after the soldiers, watching to see what would happen when the militia confronted the gamblers. When the company kicked open the back door of a gambling house operated by a man named North, the gamblers inside fired four or five shots into the crowd, killing Dr. Hugh S. Bodley instantly. According to the *Register,* at this point indignation overcame all other feelings and the crowd stormed the house. Vicksburgers hanged five gamblers for killing Bodley.

The *Register*'s editor, William Mills, published his paper each Thursday, so he reported the hangings on July 9, the first Thursday after the Monday when they occurred. Mills himself may have been present at the event, or perhaps Marmaduke Shannon, his printer. He credited his account to "a witness of the acts detailed," endorsing the story as correct and reliable. Mills and Shannon also approved of the violence, complaining that legal authority had been unable to control the "Professional Gamblers" that plagued the city. The gamblers supported tippling houses where they decoyed the youthfully credulous, "stripping them of their possessions" and sending "them forth into the world the ready and desperate instruments of vice."[11]

In nearby Madison County, at roughly the same time as the gamblers were hanged in Vicksburg, citizens killed whites and slaves who were allegedly plotting a servile insurrection. For abolitionists, the extralegal executions in Madison County would better serve to illustrate the evils of Southern slavery than the Vicksburg killings. The Madison County affair, however, never attracted the attention accorded to the Vicksburg hangings. Vicksburg became a lynching icon; Madison County did not. Yet, because the two sets of killings occurred at the same time, the racially inspired executions in Madison County influenced how Americans viewed Vicksburg. Vicksburg seemed more racial for being chronologically associated with Madison County.[12]

Mills did not try to defend what happened in Madison County, but he thought the Vicksburg hangings entirely justified and offered as proof the assertion that every resident in Vicksburg and Warren County supported the killings. "We have never known the public so unanimous on any subject," Mills declared.[13] Mills probably hoped to make them truly unanimous by claiming they already were. The legitimacy Mills claimed on behalf of his fellow Vicksburgers would inevitably be tested before a larger audience: "it is not expected that this act will pass without censure." Though Mills lamented that outsiders would have a hard time understanding the gamblers' threat, and understanding why Vicksburgers had no choice save to act outside the law, he still worried that other cities might condemn the hangings. While Mills argued that Vicksburg public opinion made the hangings legitimate, some Americans had already begun to question the idea that isolated neighborhoods could be so autonomous as to escape outside judgment when they practiced extralegal violence. The *Vicksburg Register* regularly carried news of the outside world and, Mills knew, bigger papers with larger circulations many miles from Vicksburg would read and reprint his article. Nonetheless, Mills still thought some judgments should be kept in the neighborhood. He expected people living outside Vicksburg to respect his community's unanimous verdict. Had America agreed with Mills and seen discrete neighborhoods as morally autonomous, as "island communities," then the Vicksburg editor might have succeeded in making the hangings legitimate.

The process by which the news spread reflected, first, the state of transportation in 1835. The Mississippi River connected Vicksburg to the larger society and steamboats carried the news of the extraordinary events in Vicksburg to the outside world. On July 6, the day Vicksburgers hanged the gamblers, two boats passed through town. If those boats picked up the news, there is no evidence they passed it along. On Tuesday, as the five bodies still swung from the gallows, the eighty-six-ton sidewheeler *Scotland* stopped at Vicksburg, en route from Louisville to New Orleans. On Thursday, the day the *Register* published its account, two more boats docked at Vicksburg, one going North and one, the *Freedom,* passing through Natchez, Mississippi, on its way to New Orleans. The day after the Vicksburg press ran the story, the Natchez paper had picked up a copy of the *Register* and printed its version of the episode.[14]

New Orleans newspapers disagreed over whether the Vicksburgers had any right to kill the gamblers. Based on oral information garnered from the passengers and crew on the *Scotland,* the New Orleans press first broke the story on Saturday, July 11. Details were thin, affording Crescent City journalists the freedom to invent details. The *Louisiana Advertiser* said the affair started in a gambling house, where prostitutes, their pimps, and decoys inveigled innocent young men into their den and fleeced them.[15] The New Orleans papers went on to explain that Vicksburgers held meetings to abate the menace, issuing warnings and deadlines. The *Advertiser* said that "a committee" went to "wait on" the gamblers, only to be rebuffed. As the members of the committee retreated to consider what to do next, the gamblers fired shots from the windows of their house, killing Bodley. The *New Orleans True American* claimed Bodley had been shot eleven times. The townspeople quickly rallied and rushed the house, seizing and then hanging its five occupants "INSTANTER!!" As the *Advertiser* set its story in type, an additional report came down the river and the editor appended a paragraph reporting that "Dr. Bodley was murdered in the gaming house, after having won a considerable sum of money at the table, which was the original cause of this execution of summary justice, or Lynch law as it is called." While the *Advertiser* thought the hangings outrageous, the *True American* speculated that "perhaps" justice had been done. After all, the *True American* said, the gamblers had several times escaped legal justice.[16]

Over the weekend Mississippi steamboats brought additional dispatches into New Orleans. By Monday, July 13, the *Advertiser* had a new rendering of events, one that redeemed Bodley by reporting that he never frequented gambling houses. This fresh account jettisoned rhetoric about prostitutes and inexperienced young men, substituting specific details instead. In the new version, the trouble started when a "Mr. Fisher" got into a fight with a "Mr. Francis Cobler." When Cobler drew a knife, the crowd seized him, tied him to a tree, and whipped him and then poured tar over his body. The next day, Vicksburgers armed themselves and marched, "in military array," to the gamblers' house, determined to destroy the place. According to this account, Bodley led the assault, crashing through a door into a fusillade of gunfire. Neither of the *Advertiser* accounts showed any sympathy for the Vicksburgers. The *Advertiser*'s first story called the killings dreadful and horrible. In its second story, the paper went to greater lengths, reporting that "the unfortunate men" had "claimed to the law for the privilege of AMERICAN CITIZENS," a trial by jury.[17]

The *Advertiser* went on to report a scene in which the "unhappy sufferers" begged for a drink of water, the crowd denying them even that. The *Advertiser* indignantly demanded that the governor of Mississippi investigate, warning that "our venerable republic will crumble into dust" if nothing was done. This was the essence of sentimental writing at the dawn of the generation that would produce *Uncle Tom's Cabin,* empathizing with the unfortunate, warning that apathy could lead to catastrophe. Before lynching could fully flourish, a later generation would have to eschew such sentimentality.[18]

The *Advertiser* affixed the label lynching on the Vicksburg killings. Based on the oral information carried by the *Scotland,* the *Advertiser* described the killings as "summary justice, or Lynch law as it is called." In 1830, James

Stuart heard talk of a lynching from the steamboat *Constitution*'s master while traveling up the Mississippi River.[19] So the word had already circulated in the Mississippi Valley riverboat culture before anything happened in Vicksburg. Perhaps a passenger, a crew member, or the *Constitution*'s master himself, someone as familiar with the term as the master of James Stuart's boat had been, first labeled the Vicksburg killings as lynchings.

The New Orleans papers could be the final arbiter no more than Mills. The *Louisiana Advertiser* and the *New Orleans True American* had exchange agreements with other newspapers. The *Weekly Advertiser,* edited by staunch Whig John Gibson, exchanged papers with the *New York Courier and Enquirer,* the *New York Gazette,* the *New York Atlas,* and other big-city papers. These papers gave many thousands of readers outside Louisiana access to stories first published in New Orleans.[20] Before news of the Vicksburg hangings reached New York, though, the story ran in St. Louis, Memphis, and Charleston, South Carolina. The Southern press often presented the Vicksburg story sympathetically. On July 22, Charleston papers tendered the gamblers as "obnoxious" and "insolent," continuing their trouble even after being warned. The *Charleston Courier* echoed the *True American:* Justice was done as the gamblers had escaped legal justice "several times" before.[21]

The story took three more days to reach the North. When Northern newspapers confirmed that Vicksburgers had lynched the gamblers, they viewed the affair less sympathetically than Southern papers. The Springfield, Illinois, *Sangamo Journal,* which counted Abraham Lincoln among its readers, thought the "transaction" "disgraceful."[22] The *Chicago Democrat* ignored the news while the *Chicago American,* a Whig paper, provided extensive coverage, convinced it proved the evils of Jacksonian democracy. The *American* copied its story from the *St. Louis Herald,* which took its article from Mills's *Vicksburg Register.*[23] In two more days the story reached the Northeast. At first, the *Boston Daily Advertiser and Patriot* could scarcely credit what it read in the New Orleans papers. "We trust," the editors wrote, that accounts are exaggerated.[24] In Maine, the *Portland Daily Advertiser* confused the Madison County killings with those in Vicksburg, reporting that Vicksburgers "straightaway hanged" a white man for encouraging blacks to revolt.[25] On July 27 newspapers in New York, Boston, and Philadelphia carried the *Louisiana Advertiser* story.[26] The *New York Sun* published a story not attributed to any source but based on reporting in the *Advertiser* and the *True American,* including the report that Bodley died after winning money in the same gambling house he assaulted. The *Sun* also repeated the *Advertiser*'s use of the term Lynch law, though reversing it to "Law Lynch."[27] When the *Advertiser* published its corrected story, the *Sun* followed suit, printing its revised version on July 31, but dropping the final paragraph in which the *Advertiser* beseeched the governor to investigate on fear of losing the republic.[28]

Several papers followed up their accounts of lynchings in Vicksburg with stories explaining the derivation of the word lynching, clearly a new and unfamiliar term. In a story picked up by many papers, the *Wheeling (Virginia [now West Virginia]) Gazette* claimed that lynching began in Washington County, Pennsylvania, when frustrated farmers punished a poacher outside the law.[29] The *Boston Daily Advertiser and Patriot* printed the *Wheeling Gazette* story but also told its readers that a history of Devonshire included doggerel suggesting European origins for a similar, if not quite identical, term:

> I oft have hear of Lydford Law.
> How in the morning they hange and draw,
> And sit in judgment after.[30]

Some newspapers traced lynching to the American Revolution, with journalists remembering having heard old men speak of applying "Lynch's Law" to Tories.[31]

Back in Mississippi, Mills had begun to read outsiders' reports on the affair and complained of "the gross mis-statements made by some newspapers." The Vicksburgers did not think "the occurrences which took place in this city on the 6th inst[ant]." qualified as lynchings.[32] The most complete account of the affair, published in the *Vicksburg Register* and reprinted in *Niles' Register,* described the initial whipping as a lynching but the subsequent killings as "executions."[33] A local diarist called the killings "rash & bloody transactions." A letter written from Vicksburg termed the executions an "outrage" carried out by a "mob," but, again, not lynchings. Published travel accounts described the incident as a "massacre" or an "execution."[34]

Why, then, did journalists use lynching so freely in reporting the Vicksburg story? An 1833 St. Louis "lynching" hardly made a ripple outside St. Louis. Part of the answer to this question may be that the Vicksburgers killed five men at once, a spectacular thing to do in any context, though other massacres of even larger numbers of people went largely unnoticed. The Madison County vigilantes killed many more people than the Vicksburgers and attracted less attention. The Vicksburg hangings occurred just as technology changed the journalistic environment. A new kind of popular journalism with an appetite for sensational stories got its start at nearly the same time as the Vicksburgers hanged the gamblers. Journalist Benjamin H. Day published a thousand copies of the first issue of the *Sun* in 1833, just two years before Vicksburg. Day's rival, James Gordon Bennett, launched his penny paper, the *Herald,* on May 6, 1835. By the time the Vicksburgers hanged the gamblers, Day and Bennett had learned to use crime reporting to sell newspapers. Within six months of its first issue, the New York Sun printed 8,000 newspapers a day. Four years after that it printed 30,000 a day. The Herald published 77,000 copies a day by 1860, more than any other paper in the world. Railroads allowed a wider distribution and provided new opportunities for reading as bored passengers bought reading material from onboard newsboys. Better corrective eyewear and improved lighting also promoted reading. Trains carrying the printed word broke the isolation of neighborhoods. Widely distributed print meant that communities could no longer act without outside evaluation.[35]

Language contributed to the penny papers' success. The penny press purported to give its readers sensational insights into the world of crime. Emphasizing thieves' slang and cant allowed the National Police Gazette to situate its readers in the world of police and crime. The Gazette used argot so much it experimented with running a column dedicated to translating criminal slang, a sort of rogues' lexicon. Even without the column, the paper always laced its stories with criminal cant, supplying translations in footnotes or parenthetically.[36] Lynching was just one more crime word—one not seen in print much before the Vicksburg story and thus somewhat exotic. By the end of August, the penny press had begun to report lynchings regularly. On August 22, the New York Sun headlined a story it had clipped from the Pennsylvania Gazette, "Lynch Law." The Sun did not try to define the new word, and some of its lynchings seem far afield. A missed attempt to assassinate a lawyer in the midst of a trial, killing two bystanders instead, was deemed a lynching according to the Sun.[37] In September, the Sun reported lynchings in Louisiana, Maine, Virginia, and Tennessee, and even claimed that "western Indians" lynched. Lynching could happen almost anywhere, but both the Herald and the Sun agreed that Southerners were especially prone to the practice. The Herald reported that white Southerners thought anyone critical of slavery should meet "Judge Lynch."[38] This worried the Herald if for no other reason than such ideas might spread to New York and incite the lower orders to riot.[39] Finding so many lynchings after Vicksburg helped establish the Vicksburg executions as a landmark in the public consciousness.[40]

The penny press succeeded in selling Vicksburg because there was a market, in fact, three markets, for the story. The violence in Vicksburg happened at a time, and in a way, that seemed to prove at least three "truths" in current contention. The first of these "truths" was an effort to connect gambling with crime. Opponents of gambling constituted a market for the Vicksburg story because it seemed to validate what they already believed about the evils of gambling. Second, Vicksburg sold to those eager to condemn Andrew Jackson as a promoter of mobs. Finally, abolitionists bought papers to read about Vicksburg as well. From their perspective, Vicksburg (along with the Madison County killings) proved that slavery spawned anarchic violence. Of course, all these contentions could be true and, in a sense, all were true. The value of the Vicksburg lynchings lay in their wide usefulness; they had a multitude of meanings.

GAMBLERS

The Vicksburg killings came at a time of increasing public distaste for gambling. Americans had long accepted gambling as a legitimate fund-raising device, but just a few months before Vicksburg the *Louisville Advertiser* detected a "new-born zeal" against gambling in that city. Though the *Advertiser* suspected a rival paper of political chicanery, promoting antigambling to distract the voters, its columns document a new interest in the suppression of gambling. "There is something in the wind," the *Advertiser* reported, a new "hubbub."[41] The first reported lynching to appear in *Niles' Register* came in 1833 when St. Louis residents had lynched gamblers. The local paper applauded the lynching.[42] Victorians had a generalized fear of the urban trickster. The figure of the sophisticated urbanite, often a gambler or a prostitute, taking advantage of young country folk, was powerful in antebellum America. In a time when many Americans were on the move, it reflected a reality. Years after the Vicksburg killings, a travel writer named Frederick Hawkins Piercy took "one incident full of pathos" out of Vicksburg. It seems the Vicksburg gamblers had fleeced the son of a widow visiting Vicksburg on his mother's business. The gamblers stole not only the widow's money, but her son as well, turning the innocent country youth into a hardened criminal. The poor mother wrote pleading letters, finally sending another son. In July 1835, this young man arrived in Vicksburg to see his brother hanged alongside his fellow criminals.[43] In Victorian America, such stories resonated. Within days of the Vicksburg killings, residents in Cincinnati, Louisville, Baltimore, and Natchez expressly welcomed "Judge Lynch" to rid their cities of gamblers.[44] Because Vicksburg seemed to fit into the big picture of gambling criminals and outraged citizens, it seemed more significant than it would if seen as an isolated incident.

JACKSONIAN DEMOCRACY

The Vicksburg killings also occurred in the midst of heated political debate between the Jacksonians and their opponents. Andrew Jackson's supporters celebrated his election as a triumphant democratic revolution. The very best newspapers supported the Whigs with learned editorials and erudite treatises. Jackson fought back with chanting crowds in the street, marching behind flaming torches and live eagles. These crowds besieged the homes of leading Whigs, chanting, groaning, heckling. Whigs thought such behavior riotous and insisted Jackson had unleashed the mob in the street. In 1832, they did not use the word lynching, but there is a sense that they saw Jackson as a kind of Judge Lynch, the inventor, in his way, of lynching. By making these charges, Whigs politicized riots and mobs. Whigs believed Jackson's decision to withdraw the public's money from the Bank of the United States (an act of lawlessness in itself, according to the Whigs) had excited the laboring classes and threatened the public tranquility. From September 1832 through the end of 1833, *Niles' Register* published just three articles on riots or lynchings. By the end of this period, financial panic gripped New York. In February mass meetings protested Jackson's policies. Between March and September 1834, Niles printed nineteen articles on riots. More than half of these articles attributed the disorder to Irish laborers or other unruly Jacksonians.[45]

While its Democratic rival remained mum, the *Chicago American* had decided by August 29 that "riots and mob-law are the order of the day in the Eastern and Southern states." Riotous discontent was a "hydra-headed monster," no sooner put down in one place than present in another.[46] In September, the *American* ran a story headlined "JUDGE LYNCH IN NEW HAMPSHIRE." The "notorious gentlemen" came to the Granite State in the form of a mob that used ninety yoke of oxen to drag a black schoolhouse into a swamp and ordered the teacher to leave town.[47] "MORE LYNCH LAW" came on October 17, when the *American* reported that a mob had whipped a Kentucky abolitionist.[48] A few days later, the *American* thought it a lynching when a single black man flogged a white man who had mistreated a lady. "His gallant conduct," the article impishly noted, "almost entitles him to a white wife."[49]

The Vicksburg killings, and other rioting that followed, gave the Whigs an answer to the Jacksonian Democrats' popular sovereignty. The most effective response came from the pen of a young Springfield, Illinois, lawyer on January 27, 1838. Abraham Lincoln, just twenty-seven years old, delivered his speech, "The Perpetuation of Our Political Institutions," to the Young Men's Lyceum of Springfield. Lyceums educated the public through lectures and debates on important issues. More practically, they allowed young professional men to establish their intellectual prowess before a local audience. In Springfield, prominent Democrats as well as Whigs argued on behalf of their parties.[50] In his speech, Lincoln worried that "outrages committed by mobs . . . have pervaded the country." He called on every American to pledge never to violate the law of the country or to tolerate its violation by others.

Law, Lincoln urged, "should become the *political religion* of the nation."[51] Lincoln couched his speech in bipartisan patriotism, but nonetheless made a political appeal. He understood that the only way Whigs could combat Jackson's man-of-the-people appeal was with a law-and-order message. The Whigs needed something to trump popular sovereignty; Lincoln found it in law and constitutionalism.

Lincoln seemed more persuasive because he articulated the thoughts of many ordinary Americans, especially Whigs. On August 2, the Whig diarist Philip Hone, an opponent of emancipation, complained that "a terrific system" called "*Lynch Law* . . . prevails in some of the southern and western states." By the end of September, leading newspapers in South Carolina, Virginia, and Pennsylvania all agreed that the entire nation seemed "ready to take fire." On September 5, Hezekiah Niles worried that the country seemed "unhinged." Judges in Florida criticized "Vicksburg Justice."[52]

Even some white Southerners found anarchic violence troubling. William Gilmore Simms supported westward expansion and worried about class conflict, hardly Whig positions. Nonetheless, the Vicksburg hangings shook his confidence that lynch law promoted good order. Simms understood that Vicksburg greatly enlarged the numbers of his readers familiar with the word lynching. He had used the word "Lynch law" in 1834, translating its meaning for the uninitiated. In his subsequent work, published after 1835, he never again provided his readers with a definition of lynching. In fact, he excised his 1834 explanation in later editions of the same work. For Simms, and many Americans, the real invention of lynching as a widely used word came on July 6, 1835.

More importantly, after Vicksburg, Simms changed his thinking about "Lynch law." One Simms biographer holds that the writer supported extralegal justice until the end of his life, citing a letter Simms wrote in 1868. An ardent supporter of slavery, Simms urged "trusty whites" to arm themselves and organize every precinct in response to the black criminality emancipation unleashed. Such evidence of how Simms reacted to the shock of emancipation does not change the fact that in his novel *Mellichampe,* published just after Vicksburg, Simms criticized lynching in a chapter entitled "Picture of Lynch Law." While his 1834 work quoted a character defending lynching, the 1836 book has a character named Barsfield saying that he became a Tory after being tarred and feathered for speaking against the Whigs. His crime, Barsfield says bitterly, was "free thinking in a free country." In his 1840 novel, *Border Beagles,* Simms wrote that a lynching was only partially justified by the victims' criminality. In his *History of South Carolina,* Simms rehearsed the argument for Revolutionary vigilantism, and then warned that when men take the law into their own hands, they usually find it "very difficult to keep themselves within the bounds of justice." Wrongs were done, Simms wrote of the Revolution.[53] Simms's fiction documents changes in the meaning of lynching after Vicksburg. For the proponents of extralegal violence, an important battle had been lost, a fact Simms's fiction illustrated.

ABOLITIONISM

Abolitionists found the Vicksburg story useful as well. Some have traced the slave panic boiling in the background of the Vicksburg riot to publication of *The Life and Adventures of John A. Murrell, the Great Western Land Pirate,* which purported to reveal a great slave conspiracy to rebel against whites. Up and down the Mississippi Valley whites organized vigilante patrols and redoubled their watchfulness.[54] The killings in Madison County encouraged Northerners to see the Vicksburgers' violence as part of a larger pattern of lawlessness. The Vicksburg killings also came in the midst of the American Anti-Slavery Society's pamphlet campaign. More than 175,000 items went through the New York post office in July 1835. Abolitionists targeted this propaganda onslaught at white Southerners they hoped to convert, especially ministers, politicians, and newspaper editors. Instead of winning converts, the postal campaign inspired hysteria. On July 29, two days after newspapers broke news of the Vicksburg killings in the largest Northern cities, whites mobbed the Charleston, South Carolina, post office, burning abolitionist literature. Whites across the South organized vigilance committees and worried about how to deal with the abolitionists' pamphlet campaign.[55]

The Vicksburg violence provided abolitionists with a new word, a tool in their war against slavery, one they were not slow to apply in new and creative ways. On October 21, a mob in Utica, New York, attacked the New York state antislavery convention. Abolitionists promptly published a booklet denouncing the "Lynch Law system." Entitled *The Enemies of the Constitution Discovered,* the pamphlet's author, "Defensor," presented popular violence as a shocking new development. Defensor claimed that if someone just a year before had foretold lynching, such a wild prediction would not have been believed. Defensor reminded his readers that in Vicksburg five citizens of the United States had been "seized and executed without even the pretence of legal authority, contrary to the express letter of the constitution of the United States." Thereafter the Charleston, South Carolina, post office had been invaded and the mail burned, another violation of law. Defensor also printed a lengthy narrative by Amos Dresser, an abolitionist distributing literature in Kentucky and Tennessee. White Southerners seized this abolitionist and "convicted" him before a mob for, in his words, "being a member of an Anti-Slavery Society in Ohio; 2d, of having in my possession periodicals published by the American Anti-slavery Society; and 3d, 'they BELIEVED I had circulated these periodicals.'" Dresser received a whipping, administered by a city officer with a heavy cowskin.[56]

The main focus of Defensor's pamphlet, though, was the proslavery mob that attacked the Utica convention. The Utica mob, Defensor said, acted contrary to the law and the Constitution, while insisting it was *patriotism to disregard the laws.* By October the term lynching had become so commonplace in the press that "even the boys in the street talked of Lynching and bloodshed." In Utica, after an antislavery convention assembled at a church, a mob crashed inside, filling the aisles, screaming and chanting, breaking up the meeting. Led by Jacksonian congressman Samuel Beardsley, the mob continued to harass the abolitionists even after they adjourned their ill-fated meeting. The mob then ransacked the offices of the *Utica Standard and Democrat.* Defensor said, "They assailed every individual who passed in the street, whom they suspected of having acted a prominent part in endeavoring to preserve the peace of the city."[57]

The violent suppression of abolitionism, Defensor declared, was "a new system of measures, unknown to the framers of our constitution," threatening the national peace. Defensor refuted the notion that "the *people* can do every thing" with "the immutable principles of justice." The power of the people is "not unbounded."[58]

Defensor attacked lynching as a threat to American constitutionalism. The Vicksburg hangings allowed abolitionists to position themselves as American patriots, stalwart defenders of order. This was a useful antidote to their opponents' complaints that they threatened the Union and good order. One abolitionist paper thought lynching threatened not only law and order generally, but civilization itself. "Lynch law is a *crime* of the darkest dye in organized society, and in no case justifiable," the *True American* declared. It would be better to surrender all pretense to civilization than to tolerate even a single lynching. To those who ask if a murderer should go "unwhipt of justice" if the law is unable to respond, the *True American* did not hesitate: "We say yes," adding that lynchers themselves commit murder.[59]

Abolitionist rhetoric proved especially effective when the violence endangered Northerners. In the 1840s and 1850s abolitionists regularly charged that white Southerners were so prone to violence that no opponent of slavery dared set foot in the South for fear of being lynched. One abolitionist made the charge poetically:

> And if [abolitionists] step a single inch on
> Our Southern soil, we'll catch and lynch 'em,

Pour out upon them all our fury,
And hang them without judge or jury. . . . [60]

Abolitionists understood the reality this verse parodied; Southerners really did threaten Northerners with violence. On the floor of the U. S. Senate, Senator Henry S. Foote of Mississippi warned Senator John P. Hale of New Hampshire that, were he ever to dare take his abolitionist heresy to Mississippi, "he would grace one of the tallest trees of the forest, with a rope around his neck."[61] Hale had incensed Foote and other Southerners by proposing an antiriot bill for the District of Columbia. Southerners insisted that abolitionists advocated theft and that the public had a right to punish such slave-stealing thieves extralegally. "When the arm of the law is too short to reach such a criminal," Foote exclaimed, "he may be justly punished by a sovereignty not known to the law." Another senator asserted that the Revolutionary War established the legitimacy of mob law.[62] Preston Brooks's caning of Charles Sumner continued this debate, allowing abolitionists to extend their indictment of Southerners to include not just lynchings of individuals but of "the sovereign states of the Union in the persons of their representatives."[63]

When Southerners defended their rioting by presenting themselves as coolly carrying out the people's business, abolitionists fought back by charging that Southern rioters were barbaric and cruel. The abolitionists built their argument on the notion that Southern rioting really differed from that in the North. At least one modern student of rioting now concludes that Northern rioters were less violent than those in the South and Northern authorities, unlike their Southern counterparts, did not easily tolerate rioting.[64] In fact, Southerners could accurately say that Northerners did lynch people and did so with considerable brutality. Even William Lloyd Garrison did not at first associate lynching with the South. In 1834, he ran a story about a tarring and feathering in Pennsylvania, carried out "in the true Yankee style."[65] In New York, the *Rochester Union* reported that a Negro only narrowly escaped lynch law after he attempted to rape a German girl.[66] An Illinois mob seized an escaped slave charged with rape, lashed him to a tree, and then allowed his female victim to "slash, cut, and jab" his body before encouraging her brothers and husband to shoot him.[67] "Club law" prevailed in Nebraska as settlers organized against outlaw depredations.[68] The *Milwaukee Sentinel* reported the lynching of a murderer after a crowd overwhelmed the military guard. The soldiers' performance disgusted the *Sentinel*. The soldiers fell back without a blow struck or a gun fired after being rushed by only twenty-five men. Apparently, the militia sympathized with the rioters, the *Sentinel* fumed.[69] Iowa lynchers executed one murderer after another, with one newspaper counting six hangings in eight weeks.[70] A St. Louis mob destroyed a brothel. Women mobbed a man charged with child abuse in Livingston County, Illinois.[71]

Abolitionists responded to reports of Northern lynching, first by claiming that it served as evidence that Southern thinking had invaded the North and, second, by asserting that Southern violence had an element of barbaric cruelty missing—so far—in the North. Through the antebellum period Northern newspapers periodically printed reports of Southern slaves burned alive. In 1853, the *Booneville (Missouri) Observer* reported the burning of an unidentified slave for murdering Elizabeth Rains. According to the *Observer,* the slave murdered Rains as part of his effort to rape her. The *Observer* excused the burning as made necessary by "the frequent attempts of late years" of slaves to rape white women. The newspaper conceded that the punishment would be regarded as "cruel, if not barbarous." The paper answered such complaints by asserting that a white rapist would have been treated the same way. In 1853, the *Columbia (Missouri) Statesman* reported the near burning of Hiram, a slave charged with "attempting the crime of rape upon a daughter of one of our most respectable citizens." Authorities put Hiram on trial, but a crowd broke into the court room, seized the defendant, and hustled him into the street. He was not hanged only because the editor of the *Statesman* and other community leaders importuned the crowd to desist. And because the rope broke. Returned to jail, Hiram again awaited trial only to be seized a second time. This time the mob intended to burn Hiram, hanging him instead only after the victim's father announced that he wanted the slave hanged rather than burned.[72]

Abolitionists incorporated such stories into their attacks on slavery. Lynching supported Garrison's thesis that slavery made the oppressor violent. He regularly ran reports clipped from Southern papers in columns headed "THE SOUTH . . . VIOLENCE AND BLOOD ITS INHERITANCE" or "THE BLOOD-REEKING SOUTH" or, more simply, "SOUTHERN ATROCITIES." These columns contained short accounts of "Terrible Tragedies," "Horrid Murders," "School Teachers Cut to Pieces," "Whole Sale Poisonings," and "Singular Deliberate Murders." "Great Outrages" appeared alongside "Domestic Tragedies."[73] Garrison criticized "Vicksburg Lynch law" as though white Mississippians had invented the practice.[74] On September 26, 1835, Garrison ran a column headlined "MORE LYNCH LAW" and "YET ANOTHER DISGRACEFUL OUTRAGE" with stories of mob violence in Kentucky and Virginia. In Kentucky a mob set upon "Mr. Thom," actually James A. Thome, whipped him, and would have killed him had not some moderate gentlemen intervened on his behalf. In Virginia, four white men were arrested for attempting to spread revolution among the slaves. Judge Lynch's "jury" decided two of the four should be whipped—lynched. Garrison quoted a Virginia paper as saying the lynchers were "gentlemen of the first respectability, who are not only willing but anxious to be governed by the law, when it is adequate to the protection of their firesides and property."[75] The South was "A REFUGE OF OPPRESSION," Garrison alleged in a headline covering a story about a New Jersey abolitionist tarred and feathered in Georgia.[76] The South, Garrison charged, "*thirsts for the blood of abolitionists*" because "human life is held at a cheaper rate" there than in the North.[77]

Southern journalists sometimes counterattacked. In 1854 the *Mississippi Free Trader* researched an 1841 incident where abolitionists had charged that whites had burned two slaves because one of the slaves had "merely raised his hand against a white man." The *Free Trader* tried to destroy this "foul abolition calumny" by tracking down and interviewing citizens from the neighborhood where the burnings had occurred. The *Free Trader* discovered that the two slaves had kidnapped one white man's daughter and another's wife. Both women had been raped repeatedly before they could be rescued, the *Free Trader* said. The *Free Trader,* like the Missouri papers, claimed that white men would have suffered the same fate, had they committed the same crime. Further, if white men had met the same fate for a similar crime, the *Free Trader* said, the "*philanthropists* of the North" would have ignored the incident. The *Free Trader* concluded by asserting that if ever a crime justified a terrible punishment, the crimes of the two burned slaves qualified. The slaves perished terribly, the paper acknowledged, but justly, "and they who read the story will acknowledge in their hearts a perfect harmony between the crimes they perpetrated and the fate they met."[78]

These attacks on the legitimacy of lynching proved effective. Most papers carrying the Vicksburg story despised abolitionists as troublemakers, but they found lynching to be lawless and upsetting, a threat to the status quo—everything they hated in the abolitionists. The *Boston Daily Advertiser and Patriot* railed against abolitionists' "indiscreet zeal" and advised Northerners not to discuss slavery questions.[79] The *Morning Courier and New-York Enquirer* blasted the "mad wickedness of the immediate Abolitionists." The *Courier and New-York Enquirer* lectured its readers that "Unwarranted interference between master and slave" could not be tolerated as it disrupted the law and the Constitution.[80] But the Boston paper saw Vicksburgers' passion as raging out of control, condemning the Mississippi mob as "infuriated" and "exasperated."[81] The *Lexington Kentucky Intelligencer* printed a letter from a correspondent describing the Vicksburg crowd as "blind with excitement," and claimed that "the populace, breathing fury and vengeance, are up for blood."[82] Even the *Morning Courier and New-York Enquirer* warned Southerners not to interfere with abolitionists' constitutional rights.[83] The *New York Her-*

ald announced itself ready to defend Arthur Tappan, "fool and blockhead as he is" if pro-Southern mobs threatened him with violence.[84]

Violence that followed Vicksburg made it seem as though white Southerners, and their Northern sympathizers, had launched a riotous war against abolitionism. By the time President Abraham Lincoln rallied Northerners against the South with his stirring declaration that secession represented anarchy,[85] abolitionists had for years alleged that slavery encouraged a violent tendency toward lynch law across the South. This argument played well because so many Americans feared anarchy.[86] Newspapers and warring politicians regularly charged rivals with promoting disorder. Congressmen for and against slavery accused each other of stirring up tumult so often some observers might be forgiven for thinking popular excitement represented a more serious problem than slavery.[87] Journalists scrutinized reports of lynch mobs with an eye toward the crowd's demeanor. Cool lynchers, in control of their wits, seemed more legitimate than an excited crowd. When Northerners characterized Southern lynchers as excited, they leveled a serious charge, one that challenged the legitimacy of Southern rioting. In 1835, for example, many Northerners thought Vicksburgers threatened order because they had been "blind with excitement" when they hanged the gamblers.[88]

Though there had been mob violence before, newspapers made it appear as though the Vicksburg hangings seemed to open a floodgate of lynchings. In August, crowds gathered in Baltimore to vent frustration and anger at the Bank of Maryland. Handbills circulated calling on citizens to "arouse and rally around the free and unbiass'd judge Lynch who will be placed upon the seat of justice and the people enmasse [*sic*] will be the members of the Bar." The flyer went on to denounce regular lawyers and judges connected with bank corruption. When these crowds became riotous, the U.S. Army turned out to restore order, though the troops did not stay long. They quickly marched to Washington, D.C., to control an antiabolition riot in that city.[89]

Judge Lynch reached St. Louis in April 1836. After a mob burned a free black man from Pittsburg alive, one journalist wrote that he had "just returned from witnessing the most horrid sight that ever fell to the lot of man, the execution of 'Lynch Law' upon a yellow fellow." The "yellow fellow" was Francis McIntosh, who had injured a constable and killed a deputy sheriff while trying to rescue a fellow sailor from custody. The mob broke McIntosh out of jail and chained him to a tree. Two thousand gathered to watch the spectacle, yelling for the fire to be slow.[90]

In late summer of 1835 Cincinnati newspapers urged their readers to "lynch" abolitionists' publications after James Birney moved his abolitionist newspaper to the Queen City. "What is gambling in its most disgusting form," the *Cincinnati Evening Post* demanded, "compared to the circulating of these fire-brands?" Birney fired back, criticizing antiabolitionists as "mobocrats" and reporting that antiabolitionist rioting actually swelled abolitionists' ranks by making the cause seem attractive to decent people.[91] He copied without comment a story saying that the governor of Mississippi had endorsed "Lynch Law."[92] When the *Cincinnati Republican* ran a story headlined "LYNCH LAW IN CINCINNATI" denouncing the arson of some buildings occupied by "blacks of the lowest and most abandoned character," Birney was glad to see the editor "improv[e] in his love of law and order." Birney hoped that the editors at the *Cincinnati Whig* and *Republican* were both "getting over their passion for lynch law."[93]

Residents of Cincinnati were, in fact, not over that passion. On July 12, 1836, a mob broke into the offices where Birney published his newspaper, the *Philanthropist*.[94] This mob failed to put Birney out of business, but it sparked a city-wide debate in which the opponents of abolitionism articulated a rationale for lynch law. The founding fathers, one writer asserted, placed "many a Tory *dangling* from a *bough,* or garnished in his *right loyal and courtly dress of tar and feathers.*" The founders "respected the laws so long as they were productive of the public good." Such men were hardly "slaves of the law."[95] This rationale for violence, for lynching, may have encouraged a second mob attack on the *Philanthropist*. On July 30 a fresh mob, estimated at between 1500 and 5000, dismantled the *Philanthropist* office, scattered Birney's type in the street, and tore his presses apart. The debate over the legitimacy of mob violence continued after this second attack, when law and order forces gained the rhetorical upper hand and defined mob law as a threat to good order and financial security.[96] The *Philanthropist* began referring to the antiabolition newspapers as "THE MOB PRESS."[97]

A year later another mob attacked the press of Elijah Lovejoy in Alton, Illinois. Lovejoy had published his abolitionist newspaper, the *Observer,* in St. Louis. Like other abolitionist journalists, Lovejoy reprinted articles about Southern "Lynch Law" after Vicksburg.[98] After the St. Louis mob burned McIntosh, a local judge named Luke Lawless supplied a grand jury with the classic justification for lynch law, saying that the killing "was the act . . . of the multitude . . . of congregated thousands, seized upon and impelled by that mysterious, metaphysical and almost electric frenzy." Such an act, the judge said, was "beyond the reach of human law." The judge blamed the killing on abolitionists and singled out Lovejoy for censure. The acerbic Lovejoy promptly printed the judge's comments in his newspaper.[99]

Criticizing the McIntosh lynching and scolding the judge generated such a storm of protest that Lovejoy decided to leave town. Before he could pack up and move his newspaper to Alton, Illinois, a mob attacked his press. Free soil offered no sanctuary; mobs armed with tar and feathers stalked him. Failing at that, they invaded his home and wrecked his newspaper office. A mob besieged the building where Lovejoy and his press retreated, hurling stones and then setting the roof ablaze. In the midst of the tumult, one of the proslavery men shot and killed Lovejoy. The mob then entered the building and demolished the press.[100]

Reports of such violence sometimes led Northerners to rethink their tolerance of slavery. The Ohio superintendent of schools announced that he had once believed he had no choice but to tolerate slavery since it was protected by the Constitution. Proslavery violence led him to change his mind, he explained. Illinois Senator Stephen A. Douglas once proclaimed himself ready to defend the constitutional rights of slaveowners "to the last"—but not when they turned to mob violence. In 1855 the *New York Times* published a letter from a Southern correspondent denouncing the burning of "a negro man" charged with rape in Sumpter County, Alabama. "The crime was great," the *Times* correspondent acknowledged, "but good heaven, what shall we say of the punishment." The slave had been roasted for twelve hours. "The Feejees are no longer savages. Sumpter County, Ala., has achieved the *proud* position, the *high* honor of deed without parallel in the annals of brutality in any land." Such brutality was worse than lynch law, the *Times* correspondent continued, "it was demoniac revenge."[101]

White Southerners defended themselves from abolitionist attacks. The governor of Mississippi, ironically named Charles Lynch, would not be the last Mississippi governor to feel the need to justify his state after an outbreak of mob violence. Lynch told the legislature that Northern abolitionists had been instigating "occurrences of a highly exciting and offensive nature." Lynch wanted to stamp "upon these incendiary movements our indignant and decided disapprobation." In such matters, Lynch insisted, "there can be but one opinion." Lynch reported that Southerners could appeal to Northerners' justice and propriety to outlaw abolitionism. Governor Lynch must have had Madison County in mind rather than Vicksburg when he declared that "Mississippi has given a practical demonstration of feeling on this exciting subject." Hanging the white men charged with inciting the slaves to revolt "may serve as an impressive admonition to offenders." Necessity, he explained, "will sometimes prompt a summary mode of trial and punishment unknown to the law."[102]

Ordinary Southerners could not resist openly endorsing lynch law. The *American Beacon,* published in Norfolk, Virginia, took note of an abolitionist who had ventured into Lynchburg, Virginia. "Let him be watched," the paper warned, "and it is not to be doubted that the citizens of the town that bears the name of Judge Lynch, still remember the nature of the remedy of the great law giver."[103] The Lynchburgers printed handbills giving a description of the abolitionist and raised a hue and cry throughout the county. "Abolition pamphlets have been traced to him," the *Beacon* reported ominously, "and the vengeance of the people is at his heels."[104] The "vengeance of the people" meant neighborhood popular sovereignty.

Another endorsement came from someone giving his name as "Mississippian." He or she told readers of a Nashville newspaper that white southerners did not dare ignore "the merciless storms of blind fanaticism." Mississippian made a law-and-order argument. First, Mississippian sought to make Northerners understand the gravity of the threat white Southerners faced from abolition lawlessness. "Suppose societies were openly organized in the South with the avowed object of burning and destroying the manufactories of the seaports and cities of the North," Mississippian asked. That, in essence, Mississippian thought, was precisely the threat abolitionists posed to the South. In the face of such a threat, something must be done. Mississippian hoped whites could respond lawfully, but that would require some new legal recourse. Mississippian's answer, his only way to avoid lynch law, hardly seemed realistic. All free blacks must be expelled from the country, Mississippian first demanded. Then, a law must be made making it "highly penal" to circulate any book or pamphlet calculated to excite insubordination among the slaves. Mississippian conceded there might be constitutional objections to his plan, "But the principle is unquestionable, that the criminal jurisdiction of a State, in matters of domestic police is exclusive." Maintaining order, in other words, was the job of the states and nothing should be allowed to take priority over that.[105]

No one can ever say when or who invented extralegal punishment of an individual by a crowd. That practice must be as old as time. The use of the word lynching for such activity may have begun in Virginia during the Revolution. While the term "Lynch law" seldom appeared in print for decades after the Revolution, extralegal violence occurred and the word circulated in oral conversation. Many Americans first heard of lynching in 1835, when newspapers picked up the term "Lynch law" and applied it to Vicksburg and, later, many other incidents. For researchers tabulating lynchings based on newspaper reporting, 1835 marks the beginning—the "invention"—of lynching as illegitimate mob violence. The mass killing of five people by a mob might have attracted a lot of attention at any time, especially when accompanied by an even larger mass killing in a nearby county. The political currents of the day made this evidence of deranged popular sovereignty seem especially meaningful, emblematic of troublesome forces abroad in the land. Northern journalists used lynching as the icon of Southern violence as a threat to good order.

In the antebellum era, abolitionists and journalists challenged the legitimacy of popularly sanctioned extralegal violence. At the end of the nineteenth century, some still saw racial violence as legitimate. Others made some headway in establishing lynching as a peculiarly Southern tradition, illegitimate and cruelly violent. As they did so America prepared to move West, toward its "Manifest Destiny." In the territories, Westerners would make their own law. Judge Lynch was about to be rehabilitated.

CHAPTER THREE

"California Law"

THE WEST AND THE NATION

I n the nineteenth century, abolitionism represented the most serious, concerted effort to deter Americans from collective popular violence. By characterizing lynching as the product of slavery, a system allowing whites to freely torture, brutalize, and even murder black Americans with impunity, abolitionists' attacks on slavery challenged the entire Southern culture. Lynching, they thought, implied societal support of or sponsorship for illegitimate killings. This critique most effectively battled white Northern indifference because it charged that slavery planted in white people's minds a tendency toward agitated violence and lawlessness. White Northerners who cared little about the plight of slaves did fear anarchy and disorder.[1]

Westerners tripped up the abolitionists on this front. Migration westward unleashed extralegal violence that led Westerners to craft arguments justifying their actions. Western communities sponsored extralegal punishment of evildoers, they said, because they had no courts or at least no effective courts. They also insisted that the persons they lynched could never be reformed. Only the hopelessly evil died in the hands of Western lynchers, or so Westerners claimed. Many Northerners embraced such arguments, making it more difficult to criticize white Southerners' judgments that the inadequacy of their courts made racial vigilantism necessary. By seeming to legitimize vigilantism, westward migration called into question abolitionists' most powerful and important rhetorical weapon against slavery and, later, the Republicans' best argument against Southern whites' localized racial violence.

CALIFORNIA

It is a great irony that while the Southern states vigorously protested California's admission to the Union as a free state in 1850, California newspapers constructed a narrative in support of vigilantism that would serve white Southerners well. The California justification for lynching became so widely accepted that Northerners opposed to mob violence found their position undermined and scorned. Even opponents of extralegal violence found it hard to dispute the "lessons" established in San Francisco and elsewhere in California. When California joined the Union as a free state in 1850, the South lost a political battle, but in the long run, Southern white racist supporters of vigilantism and lynching gained immeasurably more from California's support of extralegal violence.[2]

The arguments Californians used to justify their lynching began before California entered the Union. Well before the Forty-niners reached California, Americans had learned that frontiersmen had to be violent because they had inadequate courts or none at all.[3] In Abraham Lincoln's own state of Illinois, twenty years before his election as president, settlers had "regulated" thieves and murderers, enforcing community justice in a manner not unlike later Southern lynchers.[4] If surviving letters and diaries truly reflect what emigrants moving West thought, they almost never doubted their right to punish outside the law behavior they called deviant. As wagon trains formed for their westward trek, the sojourners wrote constitutions, spelling out what behavior would be considered criminal. According to these documents, the emigrants had not just the right, but also the duty, to punish misbehavior. People choosing to travel outside the jurisdictions of established courts voluntarily subjected themselves to "California law." The emigrants talked openly of resorting to Judge Lynch, a term they almost never used critically. Without proper courts, men on the plains had no alternative, or so they said. In the mining camps, claim-jumpers often settled their disputes with fists and guns, resorting to no law, not even to their homemade constitutions.[5]

Such thinking became so common that by the time of the sectional crisis in the 1850s, the Western vigilante had become a stock character in frontier travel accounts. In *Western Characters or Types of Border Life in the Western States,* J. L. McConnell explained that because bands of villains infested the territories, settlers had no choice but to use "the code of Judge Lynch" as "their statute book." One journalist claimed that "Judge Lynch's officers" occupied every tent, ready to draw pistols in a second.[6] In this view of lynching, the protagonists were not "idle, turbulent, hot-headed, and insolent" Southerners, but stalwart Westerners.[7] James Fenimore Cooper and other writers promoted the idea that violence toughened frontiersmen into true American heroes.[8]

Before the time the first California vigilantes rode, the reading public had been primed to accept such violence as legitimate. A scholar named David A.

Johnson has counted over two hundred "lynchings" in California between 1849 and 1853. That particular number may or may not be valid, but it is evidence that there were a lot. Newspapers reported these mob actions as articulations of popular sovereignty. Crimes "enraged" or "excited" or "incensed" "the people," leading them to hang individuals the newspapers described as irredeemably evil.[9] Even so, California newspapers worried about criticism from the East. Opponents of Westerners' violence announced "an intense desire" to get their views before Eastern readers.[10] No wonder the Californians vigorously defended their lynching, fearing that the rest of the country might judge them harshly. In 1851 the *Alta California* cautioned "our friends at the east" against criticizing Western lynchers.[11] Five years later, another correspondent pronounced himself "well aware" that Easterners might regard such proceedings as riotous and criminal. But, he hastened to add, that would be wrong.[12]

Spontaneous punishment of criminals by various ad hoc groups had become a habit in California by the time of statehood. At least by January 1849 members of Congress worried that "Colt's pistols" had become the common law in California.[13] Whites used violence sometimes called "lynching" to oust Mexicans from California. In a book entitled *Gringo Justice*, Alfredo Mirande writes that whites drove Mexicans off their California gold rush claims, lynching dozens of Mexicans for gold.[14] When Mexican entrepreneurs underpriced their Anglo competitors, the whites resorted to violence. One source claims Anglo lynchers executed seventy-five Mexicans because the Mexicans offered to haul goods between Indianola and San Antonio more cheaply than white freighters.[15] In 1851, Downieville citizens hanged a woman named Juanita (or Josefa) after charging her with murder.[16] Hastily organized lynch courts and more-or-less officially sanctioned posses called Rangers regularly ran down and hanged Mexicans charged with a variety of crimes.[17] One old Californian reminisced that he had seen many lynchings ("distressing affairs") while in Los Angeles, which he deplored, "[y]et the safety of the better classes in those troublous times often demanded quick and determined action. . . ."[18]

California's best-organized vigilante organization began in San Francisco sometime after February 1851 when Thomas Burdue, thought to be an alias for James Stuart, supposedly robbed and beat a storekeeper named Charles J. Jansen. Jansen identified Burdue and authorities arrested Burdue/Stuart amidst mob tumult and cries of "Lynch 'em!" Happening upon an angry crowd pressing to hang Burdue as Stuart, a passerby named William T. Coleman worked his way to the front where he found civic leaders pleading with the mob to go home. Acting out of "a holy fear of mobs," Coleman leaped to the front of the crowd and proposed an extralegal drumhead trial on the

spot. Witnesses would be heard and a "prosecutor"—Coleman himself—
would present the case, but the whole proceedings would take only three
hours and would be promptly followed by a hanging. Coleman described
himself as taken aback by the response to his proposal. The crowd shouted
its tumultuous approval. Nonetheless, when Coleman held his "trial," the
jury could not agree, so the prisoner was returned to the authorities. Later,
the district court did convict Burdue, sentencing him to fourteen years. Still
later, the court learned that their prisoner really was Thomas Burdue and
not James Stuart at all.[19]

In the midst of the trials and investigation of Thomas Burdue, San Francisco merchants organized a night watch to control crime more effectively. In
some cities, such night watch organizations led to formally constituted police departments. In San Francisco, the night watch turned to vigilantism.
On June 9, San Francisco citizens met and decided to organize themselves as
a Vigilance Committee. In July the committee reached its peak, examining
hundreds of suspected thieves and other criminals as well as witnesses. The
committee hanged four men: John Jenkins, James Stuart (presumably the
real James Stuart), Samuel Whittaker, and Robert McKenzie. Whittaker and
McKenzie died after California's governor personally led a small force to rescue the two from the committee, only to have the vigilantes recapture and
hang the pair in August. As late as May 1852, the executive committee still
held meetings, but the Vigilance Committee really ceased to be a force in the
city after September.[20]

But the spirit of vigilance in San Francisco was only dormant, not dead.
In November 1855 the San Francisco Evening Bulletin endorsed a letter complaining that "one of the most cold-blooded assassinations that we have
ever known" would go unavenged if the alleged murderer was left to be
tried by the courts. "Our laws have entirely failed," the paper declared. The
anonymous author sneered at those who urged that the accused murderer,
a man named Charles Cora, be given a fair and impartial trial. The course
open to the community, this author wrote, is the reorganization of the
Vigilance Committee.[21] In January another anonymous letter writer predicted that Judge Lynch would soon "resume his authority" as no jury
could be seated to do justice in the Cora case.[22] Other writers complained
that gamblers infested the city, "a more dangerous class of persons to the
welfare of any State or community cannot exist."[23]

In May 1856, James P. Casey shot James King of William, editor of the
Evening Bulletin. The disagreement between Casey and King resembled that
between many newspaper editors and the aggrieved subjects of their writing.
Newspaper editing was extremely hazardous in the nineteenth century, not
just in the West, but everywhere. King had published an article accusing

Casey, a member of the Board of Supervisors, of being an ex-convict, a former inmate of New York's Sing Sing prison. According to the *Bulletin,* a mob assembled almost immediately after the shooting; Casey's friends hustled him to a police station for his own protection. The *Bulletin* described the crowd that assembled in front of the jail as large and agitated. The mayor appeared, urging the crowd to disperse quietly, only to be shouted down with cries of "There's too much law and too little justice in California."[24]

As King lay dying, James Nisbet took over his editing chores, continuing King's efforts to revive the Vigilance Committee. On May 18, the *Bulletin's* campaign for vigilantism finally bore fruit. The people had been oppressed for two years by corrupt government and elections controlled by vagabonds and thieves, Nisbet declared, but at long last, they could take it no more. The paper predicted that the Vigilance Committee would "rid our community of all the pests of society." With military-like precision, the Vigilance Committee formed on different streets, converging at the jail. Joseph B. Crockett estimated the size of the crowd in the street at 20,000, jamming the streets in all directions with people on housetops and hanging out of windows. Crockett did not think the authorities put up any real resistance to the crowd. "After some parleying," he wrote, they threw open the jail doors, allowing the crowd to take Cora and Casey. The *Evening Bulletin* reassured its readers that the committee included the best citizens, "men of firmness and judgment."[25]

In a letter to his wife written May 19, immediately after the Vigilance Committee organized, Crockett made the classic lynchers' argument. Thieves, murderers, and desperadoes had preyed on the city unchecked, he wrote, until the crime aroused public indignation "to a degree which never has been witnessed in any other country." The community, "the whole community," had united behind the idea of hanging Cora and Casey. Although he said little about Cora, Crockett dismissed Casey as "a man of very bad character."[26]

Despite Crockett's confidence that "the whole community" supported the vigilantes, Nisbet worked diligently to solidify local support for the lynchers. On May 20, the *Bulletin* published letters supporting the Vigilance Committee, most seemingly aimed at local readers. One letter, signed ANGLO-SAXON, reminded citizens that they had been "ground down by taxation, to support a phalanx of convicts, bank robbers, burglars, ruffians, shoulder-strikers, and pimps." Anglo-Saxon asked, "Have you forgotten what a mockery the law has been?" "Caxton," a vigilante himself, wrote, "I gloried in the power *of the people,*" the thousands gathered. Caxton just knew that such a large crowd meant that a spirit of law, not lawlessness, prevailed.[27]

The letters published by the *Bulletin* included writers attempting to position the Vigilance Committeemen as defenders of California womanhood.

The *Evening Bulletin* published a letter from "B.J.L," describing herself as "proud to behold in this city so many flocking to the standard of reformation." "B.J.L." declared, "My voice is the voice of many of my sex. We bid you God-Speed in the right." Anglo-Saxon closed his letter by asking his readers to act on behalf of the women of San Francisco, whose "tears . . . appeal to you."[28] White Southerners would make the same argument later, of course. Men so often positioned themselves as defenders of women because such arguments were persuasive—violent men seemed more legitimate when they selflessly defended women. The letter from "B.J.L." suggests that women willingly played this game, expecting and demanding protection from their men.

In June, the Vigilance Committee directly confronted the law in California. By the end of May some residents of San Francisco petitioned California's governor, J. Neely Johnson, to put down the Vigilance Committee with state troops. On June 3, Johnson issued a proclamation declaring San Francisco to be in a state of insurrection. Johnson selected William Tecumseh Sherman to take charge of California troops and put down the insurrection. Some in California hailed Johnson's strong stand, complaining only that it took him so long to act. By June 9, the situation in San Francisco became more confused and tense than when the vigilantes hanged Cora and Casey.[29]

The tension escalated even more when Vigilance Committee leaders dispatched "an efficient member of the Committee" named Sterling A. Hopkins to arrest James Reuben Maloney. Maloney had chartered a schooner to transport arms into San Francisco. Maloney intended his mission as a trap for the vigilants. He had hoped they would try to board his craft and seize the arms—a violation of a federal law against piracy. The vigilants took not only the arms, 150 muskets, but Maloney and two other men as well, later releasing the three. The Committee decided to arrest Maloney when it learned he was wandering from saloon to saloon, boasting of how he would shoot members of the Committee on sight. Hopkins found Maloney, but discovered several men, including a justice of the California Supreme Court, guarding him. Hopkins scuffled with the justice, David S. Terry. As they struggled, Terry produced a knife and plunged it into Hopkins's neck. Terry and Maloney escaped to an armory, but ultimately surrendered to the Vigilance Committee.[30]

Some in San Francisco apparently feared that support for the Vigilance Committee might dwindle in the face of such a direct confrontation with truly legitimate authority. Governor Johnson's allies in San Francisco told him that the Vigilance Committee "caught the elephant" when they arrested Terry. "We are constantly gaining ground in public sentiment," William Kibbe told Johnson in July.[31] Vigilante partisans must have seen the same shifts in public opinion as they worried in the newspapers that the confrontation with the California Supreme Court threatened the committee's very existence. To prevent that calamity, the *Evening Bulletin* published a letter hailing the Vigilance Committee as "an extraordinary tribunal, erected by the people." One vigilante accused Terry of leaving Sacramento "with an unnatural blood-thirsty desire . . . to precipitate matters to bloodshed and open warfare."[32] At the end of July, the *Bulletin* went to the crux of the committee's problem with Terry. "Terry has shown himself capable of acting in a manner directly opposed to the will of the people." In other words, Terry, representing law, threatened popular sovereignty, as manifested by the Vigilance Committee.[33] The vigilants debated what to do with Terry; they seemed hesitant to put him before one of their own courts, although they finally did so. In the end, the committee "convicted" Terry but released him anyway, unconditionally, and he resumed his seat on the California Supreme Court, much to the disgust of many San Franciscans.[34]

The earliest reporting of the Vigilance Committee in the *Evening Bulletin* suggests that the vigilantes understood that their most important battles would occur in print. From the start, it seemed clear that the campaign waged by the *Bulletin* and other papers on behalf of the vigilantes paid off. Initial estimates put the number of vigilantes at three thousand, a number that quickly swelled to ten thousand.[35] When Governor Johnson appointed Sherman to assert state power in San Francisco, the general found that the vigilantes' control of the press thwarted his best efforts to unseat them. Public opinion sided too strongly with the vigilantes to permit effective militia action. Sherman soon resigned, frustrated by the opposition he faced and his inability to secure arms for his men. Several militia companies subsequently joined the vigilantes.[36] Any lingering doubts about the vigilantes' power disappeared entirely in November, when city elections placed members of the Vigilance Committee in office. The vigilantes took formal control of the city they had controlled outside the law for five months.[37]

The vigilantes understood that success at home did not guarantee success across the nation, and they also realized that the rest of the country would judge them by how well they could build a case justifying their violence. The *San Francisco Herald* resented the "senseless calumnies industriously circulated at the East and in Europe to the prejudice of our city and State."[38] The vigilantes had concrete reason to worry about Eastern public opinion. Johnson petitioned President Franklin Pierce for federal aid in putting down the insurrection, pointing out that the Constitution gave the federal government power to suppress "insurrections." In San Francisco, fear of federal intervention went beyond the theoretical. The vigilantes nervously monitored movement of U.S. Navy vessels; rumors spread of imminent military intervention by the federal government.[39] If Eastern public opinion turned decisively against them, many feared Pierce would dispatch the Army to San Francisco.

The Argument for Vigilantism

To keep Eastern public opinion on their side, and to forestall federal intervention, Californians built an argument in four parts. The character of the people migrating westward formed the first element in what became the California justification for lynching. Westerners pointed out that many of the first immigrants to California came only to make a fortune, "by plunder, rapine, and stratagem." According to one account, a father told his California-bound son to "make money—honestly if you can—*anyhow, make money.*"[40] California journalists denounced most of the population as "unprincipled and vile." Vicious, these people made one of their own a county supervisor and another U.S. marshal, deranging society.[41]

Such vicious persons made a mockery of the law, the Californians said. According to an anonymous correspondent the *San Francisco Evening Bulletin* identified as a leading merchant, gambling dens and houses of prostitution operated openly. Vagabonds and thieves controlled the elections. Gamblers, in fact, had taken over the government and intended to convert the whole community into "a gaming fraternity." Once in office, they ground persons of property down with heavy taxation. Fires set by arsonists ravaged the city, and the law allowed the desperadoes to roam at will.[42]

Even Governor Johnson probably accepted the first element in the argument. Johnson's brother was in San Francisco in June and reported that the persons the Vigilance Committee singled out for punishment were "very bad men." In fact, William Johnson wrote, San Francisco would be better off without such characters. William Johnson's assessment probably explains why he urged caution when writing his brother. William Johnson thought his brother had taken the right stand in asserting the Constitution, but, even so, he should "let the villains look out for themselves."[43]

Amid raging criminality, the people had no choice but to rise up and wrest control of the law and government from the lawless, the vigilantes claimed. Just as Southern congressmen rationalized violence against abolitionists on the basis of popular sovereignty, Californians claimed that "the voice of the whole people" demanded vigilance in their state.[44] Frank Soule, John H. Gihon, and James Nisbet, three early historians of the 1851 movement, declared that "This was not a mob, but the *people,* in the highest sense of the term."[45] In 1856, Governor Johnson's brother, William Johnson, estimated that eight-tenths of San Francisco residents supported the Vigilance Committee, though he thought that in their hearts they knew they violated the Constitution.[46] Others, more friendly to the vigilantes, put the portion supporting the committee at nine-tenths with no indication of secret doubt in anyone's heart.[47] In its earliest reports, the *New York Times* described the rise of vigilantism as "A REVOLUTION IN SAN FRANCISCO." The *Times* correspondent said that the revolution affected the whole social and political character of the state. "I am not now at liberty," he wrote, "to say more now than that the action of the citizens of San Francisco will not be confined to the execution of Cora and Casey." The people will no longer be controlled by criminals, the *Times* said, and will make their property secure.[48] Johnson's advisors agreed with this assessment of the enormity of the situation. One wrong move on the governor's part, they worried, could set the whole state ablaze.[49]

On June 19, 1856, an orator named William Durr told a cheering crowd of San Franciscans that while Americans owe their Constitution reverence and obedience, "the right to revolutionize is reserved to us." Durr asserted popular sovereignty at the local level, insisting on "the privilege of so regulating our local affairs that our lives and property will be made safe through the correct administration of the law under the Constitution." This merger of constitutional principles with local sovereignty prompted cheers and applause.[50] When San Franciscans did organize the 1856 Vigilance Committee, the *San Francisco Evening Bulletin* reported that "execution of the law has reverted back to the whole people."[51] Other writers agreed that "the entire public sentiment of the state" favored the lynchings, with only the governor, the judges, and most lawyers in opposition. San Francisco newspapers denounced as "stale catchwords" such concepts as constitutionalism and trial by jury.[52]

The final element in the argument came in the form of reports that peace and quiet followed the lynchings. The vigilantism worked. Soule, Gihon, and Nisbet calculated that the Vigilance Committee had freed the city from "reckless villains" at a cost of four guilty men hanged without ordinary legal form. These writers thought it made no more sense to criticize the vigilantes than to "blame a drowning wretch for clinging to a sinking brother, or to a straw. . . ."[53] At the end of 1857 the San Francisco Vigilance Committee dared any honest man to deny that vigilance had achieved a great reform of public morals and politics. The people had won control of the electoral process and elections were now unstained by corruption, the committee claimed.[54]

California journalists and their Eastern allies had established a four-part metanarrative, a "truth" larger than the particular events described. In essence, the truth was that when dissolute folk flock to a place and corrupt its institutions, the sovereign people can demand vigilance; and when they do, they will succeed. There were those who found the argument unpersuasive. Many Whigs doubted the whole enterprise of going West in the first place. When Whig papers published letters describing California as a lawless and anarchic place, they did so to warn Easterners not to go there.[55] In the Whig camp, Southerners no less than Northerners often had no patience for lawlessness. In North Carolina, the *Greensborough Patriot* quoted a California mob's denunciations of law with disapproval. The *Richmond Whig* warned that if Californians did not stop their violence "we ought to hand them back to Mexico."[56] The *Wilmington (Delaware) Herald* reviewed arguments for vigilantism and concluded, "Mob law must be put down; there *can* be no security for life or liberty outside the barriers of justice."[57] For Whigs, mob rule represented public opinion out of control. The *Baltimore Sun* captured the essence of the Whig critique when it attacked the vigilantes as irresponsibly dependent on public opinion.[58]

California opponents of vigilantism fed material to their Eastern allies. In 1856, many Eastern papers printed a letter from James R. Maloney insisting that the vigilantes organized at a time when judges above suspicion presided over well-organized and effective courts. A year later Edward McGowan published an angry account of his mistreatment at the hands of San Francisco lynchers. Maloney related that he had opposed the 1856 Vigilance Committee from its inception and had immediately joined the militia when called by the governor. McGowan served in a sheriff's posse guarding the jail. When the sheriff admitted the mob into his jail, McGowan threw down his gun and went to a saloon. The vigilantes captured Maloney on June 21, holding him until the fourth of July, when they expelled him from the state. Moloney reported that alleged ballot box frauds had been much exaggerated. Such reports led the *Missouri Republican* to conclude that party hacks and loafers hungry for a free lunch filled the ranks of the vigilantes. Lynchers recruited men into their ranks by appealing to their masculinity. Two could play that game. "Genuine manhood," the *Southern Press* told its readers, means "breasting the surges of popular prejudices." In other words, real men did not succumb to the siren call of vigilantism.[59]

The law-and-order view, though, did not generally prevail. More often, newspapers in the South and the rest of the United States repeated and accepted the narrative presented by the San Francisco newspapers. Californians recognized this and expressed gratitude that their movement met with approval in the East.[60] The *Savannah (Georgia) Daily Morning News* published the *Baltimore Sun* article attacking the vigilantes but observed that only those who were there should judge whether the vigilantes' actions could be excused or not. Though the *Mobile Daily Register* thought the 1851 vigilantes excited, savage, and barbaric, by 1856 the paper praised Californians whose "heart[s] swelled with indignation" as they solemnly determined to clean out crime and corruption.[61] Even some Whig papers found the Californians' arguments appealing. Like many papers, the *Vicksburg Weekly Whig* copied its California news from the *Alta California,* a newspaper strongly supportive of the vigilantes. Relaying stories from the *Alta California,* the *Weekly Whig* kept its readers supplied with a steady stream of articles explaining the San Francisco crisis as made necessary by official corruption that stifled the people's sovereignty. No wonder the Vicksburg paper thought accounts of San Francisco lynchings sounded "marvelously" like France's 1848 revolution, which saw a mob overturn the government and establish universal male suffrage. It could not be denied, the *Whig* claimed, that vigilante leaders had shown "a great deal of tact, as well as military and administrative talent."[62]

Outside the South, California vigilantism also found approval, a fact that strengthened the hand of Deep-South advocates of extralegal violence. The *San Francisco Evening Bulletin* told its readers that even the *London Times,* "always safe to quote as being the authority least in favor of America generally," spoke approvingly of the vigilantes' "grace and dignity."[63] The *New York Herald* compared the San Francisco Vigilance Committee with the Revolutionary Committees of Safety, "the mainsprings of our Revolutionary success." The *Herald* hoped that the lesson of California would not be lost on New York. New York, the *Herald* pointed out, was every bit as immoral as California and the government just as corrupt.[64] When the California Vigilance Committee published a document explaining that majority rule was a republican principle and one that warranted vigilantism when corrupt officials seized power, the proslavery *Kansas City Enterprise* printed the text verbatim. Some California correspondents wrote to their Eastern hometown papers, explaining and justifying what was going on. In South Carolina, the *Charleston Courier* printed a letter from San Francisco explaining that "thinking and disinterested men" truly favored law and order through vigilantism. No law was administered until the vigilantes organized themselves, these writers insisted.[65]

In the short run, the most important success scored by the vigilantes in the propaganda wars came when President Pierce decided to do nothing. Answering Johnson through his secretary of state, Pierce declined to put down the "insurrection." The federal government did prosecute two vigilantes for piracy after the Vigilance Committee ordered state arms seized from a schooner in San Francisco Bay. A South Carolinian named William Blanding, newly appointed as United States Attorney, pursued this case without enthusiasm. He knew that opponents of the vigilantes had instigated the case before his appointment. His only goal, he said later, was to secure a fair trial for the defendants. He pronounced himself happy at losing the case and reported to Washington that the verdict met with wide public approval.[66]

Such was the extent of federal willingness to restore order in California. Pierce couched his decision in legalisms and constitutional principles, but his judgment also reflected public opinion.[67] William T. Sherman bitterly noted that "as [the vigilantes] controlled the press, they wrote their own history." Governor Johnson was even more direct, blaming the success of the pro-lynching narrative on "the contemptible scribblers of the dirty sheets."[68]

Pierce's decision kept the vigilantes' message alive through 1856 and 1857; white Southerners immortalized it. In the South, whites began using the California lynchings to excuse their own violence, explicitly referring to San Francisco when challenged.[69] Southerners endorsed extralegal violence in California as based on a core American belief in violent popular sovereignty. When a neighborhood or a community endorsed violence, then that violence became legitimate, Westerners and Southerners agreed. And Westerners impressed Easterners with the efficiency of mob violence. As late as 1870 one New York newspaper, while praising an Illinois governor for seeking the conviction of lynchers in his state, felt it had to concede that, "undoubtedly," there are times when lynching is necessary. "The Vigilance Committee of San Francisco, for example, attained what in any other way, years would have been required to secure."[70]

It is a measure of how deeply ingrained the justification for extralegal violence had become that even opponents of slavery accepted it. The *Washington National Era* pointed out that the California vigilante episodes were nothing less than a revolution against the existing code of laws, the Constitution, and citizens' personal rights. But the paper felt compelled to concede that the Californians acted wisely and patriotically. Even the *National Era,* with all its doubts, thought it had no choice but to recognize "the People" and their "noble" right to popular sovereignty. To their credit, the *National Era* editors saw the basic problem with the San Francisco model. Recognizing the right of revolution meant that ordinary people were entitled to rise up if they disapproved of their courts. In practice this might mean, in the words of the *National Era,* that "any formidable mob" assailing established institutions could claim legitimacy. And while the newspaper accepted arguments that San Francisco had been corruptly governed to the extent that violence became necessary, it pointedly attached some of the blame for this state of affairs to the vigilantes themselves. Californians faced an extraordinary evil, the *Era* conceded, but it was an evil of their own making. California citizens had not been energetic enough in their civic responsibilities. Distracted by a search for wealth, they neglected the primary meetings, the conventions, and the nominations that make up the machinery of elections, allowing unprincipled men to come to power.[71]

The *National Era*'s criticism of California voters amounted to an effort to limit the influence of San Francisco. Only when voters failed to do their duty was lynching warranted. Voters should pay attention, preventing the unscrupulous from gaining power. This effort to blunt San Francisco as a precedent for future mobbing failed. The San Francisco lynchers dominated the newspapers for so long, and their actions seemed so profound, that their influence proved pervasive and long lasting. The national debate over San Francisco set in the minds of many the notion that when the people judged their courts inadequate, they had a right, in the face of horrible crime, to act outside the law—an element in a developing definition of lynching.

Lynchings in other states seemed good evidence that California's lynchings influenced the nation. On August 7, 1855, a Washington County, Wisconsin, grand jury charged a farm hand named George De Bar with murder. Wisconsin newspapers fanned the flames of popular passion much as had the San Francisco press, describing the murder of John Muehr by De Bar as "One of the most diabolical murders in the history of this State."[72] The community judged their courts inadequate; when De Bar pleaded not guilty, the crowd exploded in outrage, fearing, newspapers reported, that the courts would fail to convict him, as they had failed to do in similar cases before.[73] As officers and the Wisconsin militia escorted De Bar from court, a crowd overwhelmed the guard and bludgeoned, dragged, and hanged De Bar. The press explained that De Bar perished because officers could not resist "the wild rage, or excited fury of a mob."[74]

William T. Sherman strongly believed such instances proved that San Francisco had unhinged popular respect for the law. In 1884, he wrote a friend that the influence of the San Francisco Vigilance Committee continued even to that year. "It is quoted here, and every where as an example to justify mob violence," the old general grumbled.[75]

KANSAS

Between the two incarnations of the San Francisco Vigilance Committee, Congress enacted the Kansas-Nebraska Act. After Congress passed the law (in May 1854), pro- and antislavery forces rushed to Kansas, unleashing a wave of violence called "Bleeding Kansas." Violence was not all that linked the Kansas troubles with the San Francisco lynchings. In both San Francisco and in Kansas, violent people claimed that living in an unsettled Western frontier community excused vigilantism. In both places, people dissatisfied with existing government and courts turned to crowd violence. And, also in both places, they vindicated themselves on the basis of popular sovereignty. Western migration had created a rhetoric justifying extralegal violence that both sides relied on in Kansas as well as in California.

Historians often describe the violence in Kansas in almost military terms, a regional civil war before the main event, a "shooting war" between free-soil Kansans and Missouri border ruffians. Much of the rhetoric at the time, however, followed the conventions of lynching and vigilantism. One Southern newspaper described proslavery "border ruffians" in a fashion that resembled the stereotypical Western regulator: "Imagine a fine looking man, with a heavy beard and moustache, felt hat, red shirt, (no coat), blue pants, heavy boots drawn over the pants, immense Spanish spurs, a pair of waterproof scabbards, each containing a large 'navy repeater.'" Such fine men might be "Rough in their manners, but [were] generous as sailors." Like all Western crime fighters, they took a dim view of outlawry, opposing the "whole negro stealing pack" of abolitionists.[76]

The proslavery side tried to depict the free soilers as fit subjects for lynch law. Proslavery folk thought "negro stealing" a serious crime, one that warranted mob action. The intemperate *Squatter Sovereign* of Atchison, Kansas, declared itself order loving and law abiding, "but until we make laws, we are HIGHER-law men. We go in for hanging thieves of *all* kinds."[77] This threat hardly masked a none-too-subtle jab at abolitionists as lawless stealers of slaves. The threat to good order came from "treacherous hordes" of abolitionists.[78] The free soilers' crimes went beyond even "negro stealing," according to the proslavery side. In 1856, one Missouri newspaper reported that murders "without number" and "innumerable" arsons occurred in Kansas.[79] The *Kansas City Enterprise* accused abolitionists of robbing travelers, attacking and destroying towns, and massacring settlers. "Shall these things continue?" the *Enterprise* demanded, adding: "Those who think so are mistaken, and do not know the kind of men who reside on the western frontiers."[80] Such criminality required formation of a vigilance committee, "after the fashion of San Francisco," according to the *Enterprise*. The newspaper promised that "the *people* will redress their own wrongs in their own way—and terrible will be the remedy."[81] In characteristic fashion, the *Squatter Sovereign* urged that the Northern criminals be turned back "though our rivers should be colored with the blood of the victims and the carcasses of dead abolitionists."[82]

In some cases, proslavery newspapers nearly threatened to lynch their enemies. When Governor Andrew H. Reeder arrived in Kansas on October 7, 1854, proslavery forces feared he secretly planned to make Kansas a free state, thinking he could succeed in spite of public opposition "for he knew not . . . the passions of an impulsive people." One proslavery writer expected Reeder to learn to fear "Judge Lynch . . . sitting at the foot of his bed," ready to eject him from Kansas. Proslavery Missourians began organizing committees of vigilance.[83]

Abolitionists most credibly charged proslavery men with lynching in 1855, when a proslavery mob abused an abolitionist lawyer named William Phillips. According to the *Liberator,* the crowd shaved half of Phillips's head, tarred and feathered his body, and rode him about the town of Weston on a rail. In 1855, the proslavery side hardly denied the charge of lynching, confirming that "we will continue to lynch and hang, to tar and feather and drown every white-livered abolitionist who dares to pollute our soil."[84]

Once they won control of the territorial legislature and courts, proslavery Kansans abruptly shifted gears, presenting themselves as law and order men, keeping peaceable and quiet in the face of abolitionist depredations through law, not Judge Lynch. Now only abolitionists pushed the San Francisco argument, championing higher law, including vigilantism and extralegal popular sovereignty in the face of "pretended laws" not truly emanating from the people.[85] When a Leavenworth mob hanged two murderers apparently unconnected with political agitations, the *Kansas Free State* excused the killings. Mob law, the paper concluded, "is to be deprecated, but that which renders it necessary—such as incompetent government, unjust judges, and corrupt officials, are [as] much to be deprecated."[86]

The *National Era* and other free-soil newspapers not only accepted the premises advanced by California vigilantes, but also applied them to Kansas. Just as unscrupulous villains had been allowed to steal power in California, they had in Kansas as well, in the form of proslavery ruffians.[87] In Kansas, the antislavery *Freedom's Champion* advocated bringing "rabid pro-slavery partizan[s]" before "Judge Lynch."[88] At rock bottom, the argument in Kansas was over which side really represented a majority of the settlers. Such questions get at the essence of lynching rhetoric. Lynchers always claimed to represent the People and crafted rhetoric to advance their claims. Both sides in Kansas had precisely the same goal; no wonder both sounded like lynchers.

MONTANA

The Kansas troubles illustrate the pervasiveness of lynching rhetoric and the power of popular sovereignty to excuse mob action. Yet, while Kansans used existing lynching rhetoric, they added little to it. Within a few years, few people equated Bleeding Kansas with Judge Lynch or lynch law. Kansas seemed more a fiasco, a tragedy, than a vindication for anything. Lynchings

in Montana, by contrast, really did solidify the argument in favor of lynching. The Montana vigilantes generated one of the most important works in
lynching literature, a bold argument for extralegal violence that even today
stands virtually unchallenged on its central points. As in California, the new
wave of violence attracted national attention and generated fresh efforts to
justify extralegal punishment of criminals. And, also as in California, the
lynchers insisted they had the right to act based on their assessment of the
state of local courts.

Between 1848 and 1858, migrants moving west to mine gold went to California. The mining frontier did not reach Colorado and Nevada until 1858.
As late as 1860, few settlers went to what is now Montana. When John
White discovered gold in Grasshopper Creek, the Montana gold rush began,
bringing the usual mix of miners and the people who preyed on miners. On
March 3, 1863, Congress created the Idaho Territory (which included what is
now Montana), but the territorial legislature did not meet until very late in
1863 and the legislators were slow in organizing the eastern Idaho area (now
Montana). President Lincoln appointed territorial supreme court justices to
organize territorial courts.

Lincoln picked a passionate Ohio abolitionist named Sidney Edgerton as
chief justice for the Idaho Territory. In September, Edgerton made his way
into the territory. Like many abolitionists, Edgerton had attacked white
Southerners for instigating mob law. In Congress, Edgerton had complained
that Northerners did not dare travel in the South, not because of Southern
laws but because of "a power above law and above Constitution. That power
is the power of the mob, controlled by the priveleged class."[89]

Edgerton was to run the courts in the Third District, which included the
mining camps of Bannack and Virginia City, an area heavily populated with
Democrats friendly to slavery. Edgerton migrated west with his nephew, a
lawyer named Wilbur Sanders. When Edgerton and Sanders arrived at the
mining camps, they claimed to find crime, including murder, raging out of
control. Nonetheless, Edgerton delayed setting up a court system, explaining
that he had no marshal to carry out his orders or even to administer his oath
of office. But even without Edgerton's court, there were courts functioning
in the Idaho mining camps. The miners set up their own courts and elected
judges, coroners, and sheriffs. On May 24, 1863, Bannack miners elected
Henry Plummer as sheriff.

Political considerations colored the relationship between Edgerton and
the miners. Sanders and Edgerton were Radical Republicans and were vastly
outnumbered; Plummer was a popular Democrat. Sanders, aided and advised by Edgerton, organized a vigilance committee to control crime. The
committee alleged that Plummer led a double life, pretending to enforce the

law, but secretly leading a bandit gang. Sanders and Edgerton, in fact, blamed Plummer for all the crime around the mines. The committee hanged Plummer and his deputies.

The local press built a powerful and influential justification for the hangings. Thomas J. Dimsdale, also a Republican, edited the *Montana Post* from 1864 until his death in 1866. Defending Edgerton and Sanders, Dimsdale claimed that over one hundred persons had been murdered by the "road agent" gang that Plummer masterminded. In 1866, Dimsdale published a book entitled *The Vigilantes of Montana* declaring the hangings necessary. Anyone reading Dimsdale's book, and believing it, would have to agree that Western settlers had no choice but to lynch criminals like Plummer. Dimsdale created a powerful justification for lynching and his book proved amazingly influential.[90] Historians of the Montana lynchings have accepted nearly every element of the lynchers' defense of their violence. Few doubt, for example, that crime raged through the mining camps, forcing the vigilantes to act.[91]

Dimsdale built his justification for lynching on a weak foundation. Travelers with no connections to the vigilantes (or to Plummer) reported little crime in the months leading up to the hangings, certainly no intolerable or out-of-control crime wave.[92] Moreover, the evidence the vigilantes relied on to hang Plummer was shockingly weak. Writing in 1973, Dan Cushman doubted the vigilantes' view of the so-called Plummer gang, questioning whether any such group really existed. Cushman concluded that though Plummer deserved what he got, "the charges set forth would never have stood up in court." The evidence was hearsay and "no actual proof exists that Plummer profited by a dollar from road agentry."[93] A man named Red Yeager claimed Plummer led the road agent gang shortly before Plummer was hanged.[94] The most detailed research into Plummer's life finds that he worked effectively as sheriff, collecting money from his constituents to build a jail.[95] Plummer worked in tandem with the miners' courts. The miners' courts were not manifestations of mob law and differed considerably from the vigilantes in that they did not work behind closed doors. They kept good order, publishing their laws in local newspapers, keeping records, and acting in public. Later the Supreme Court sanctioned miners' court decisions and Congress incorporated the miners' codes into federal law.[96]

Historians' repeated and continued characterization of Plummer as a "bandit" echoes lynching rhetoric. Lynchers always seek to cast their victim in the worst possible light. They did this with Plummer, and historians still, for the most part, accept this part of the argument. This view of Western lynchings has promoted the notion that American citizens have the right to size up their courts and, when they find them wanting, take over the functions of the criminal justice system. Western lynchers also argued that the persons they killed could never be reformed, an idea that persists to this day. Death penalty advocates implicitly or explicitly make the same argument.

After the Civil War Americans found that the violence in California made it difficult to doubt the logic of vigilantism. Such thinking handicapped abolitionists. It certainly undermined Reconstruction efforts. California established the basic model that justified vigilante action when outsiders corrupted the legal processes. Many Northerners found it tough to both accept the California logic and automatically repudiate Ku Klux Klan violence. One historian now seeks to rehabilitate "carpetbaggers" by comparing them to Easterners who traveled West, ambitious for personal advancement. California's argument for lynching reveals that Americans did not automatically view adventurers traveling West in a favorable light.[97] An essential ingredient in the California argument was that avarice motivated people traveling West.

Some white Northerners may have found white Southerners' claims that the Ku Klux Klan truly represented the entire South just as plausible as the San Francisco Vigilance Committee's insistence that it acted for all San Franciscans. After 1868, some white Southerners insisted that the Ku Klux Klan was, "in fact, *the* government of the Southern States, fully as much as the California 'Vigilance Committee' once governed California."[98] White Southerners could say that the Ku Klux Klan faced reprobate hordes just as did the good people of California. In the South, as in California, stalwart citizens had to act outside the law to restore order, according to this view. California vigilantism had rhetorical implications long after the courts restored order on the West Coast. California legitimized the crowd in the street shortly before the Civil War began. This undermined the work of abolitionists and made it difficult for Republicans to deny the legitimacy of Reconstruction-era Ku Klux Klansmen.

CHAPTER FOUR

"What We Call Murder"

LYNCHING AND THE MEANING
OF LEGITIMACY IN RECONSTRUCTION

A fter the Civil War, crowds of white men broke open jails, seized black prisoners, and hanged them in ways that closely resembled what Americans chose to call lynchings at the end of the nineteenth century. Brutal racial violence characterized the period from the 1860s through the 1890s.[1] Yet contemporaries did not call these acts of violence "lynchings," because white societal support for the killings was not yet solid or beyond dispute.[2]

In fact, while the underlying violence may not have changed all that much, post–Civil War "lynchings" did differ from those in the so-called lynching era. Historians call the period after the Civil War "Reconstruction," a time when the national government tried to "reconstruct" race relations in the American South. The period at the end of the nineteenth century is often called the "Gilded Age." Changes in language mark the difference between the Reconstruction era's revolutionary violence and that found in the Gilded Age, when white conservatives held power more securely.

In a truly revolutionary environment, competitors for power make bids for popular support. With old power structures in disarray, the insurgents have a genuine opportunity to seize power. This happened in Reconstruction, when Republicans and Conservatives articulated, negotiated, and enforced competing claims for public support and popular sovereignty. Across the South, both Republicans and Conservatives presented themselves as the truly legitimate expression of popular will. They shared an ambition to represent *the people,* though they disagreed over what people they represented. The Republicans had fought the Civil War to make the United States function as a unified whole. According to the most determined Republicans, a crime against a citizen's civil rights in the most obscure Southern hamlet outraged the entire republic. Republicans defined community in new, more national, ways. Conservatives were more reluctant to surrender the old Anti-federalist understanding of America as a collection of mostly independent communities. They had an older conception of community, believing that violence condoned by the white people in an autonomous neighborhood, community, or state could be legitimate even when condemned by white "outsiders" from other states or black "outsiders" from within their own states.[3]

Since competitors for power try to fix labels on events, actions, and movements that paint themselves as legitimate and their enemies as less so, language becomes critically important in revolutionary situations. While modern historians have denounced Klansmen as terrorists and lynchers, the implications of the powerful language used to label the Klan have yet to be explored.[4] Conservatives defended the perimeter around their constituents' popular sovereignty by blasting their enemies in the newspapers and in political speeches as outsiders, "scalawags" and "carpetbaggers." Their goal was to plant this language in ordinary conversation, in the public consciousness. How Klan violence should be described became a particularly hard-fought battle, one that in some ways continues even today. The words terror, lynching, and outrage have become important weapons in this subtle, even subconscious fight over appropriate language to describe the Klan. In Reconstruction, Republicans fought to persuade the public to conceptualize each Klan act as an outrage, repugnant to the entire public, an attack on the public good, defined nationally. If most Americans found such violence outrageous rather than legitimate, white conservatives had lost an important battle. Republicans battled conservatives for legitimacy in language.

Lynching implied a killing carried out by a coherent community, an expression of localized popular sovereignty of the sort Southern white conservatives advocated. Western lynching influenced their thinking. When Western writers talked of resorting to Judge Lynch, they meant a town meeting and communal trial followed by consensus and, often, an orderly execution. Lynchers were no mob, "but emphatically the people," their defenders insisted.[5] The Reconstruction Klan aspired to be seen as lynchers because they wanted to "emphatically [be] the *people*." But they never achieved that status. The Klan's failure to establish itself as a lynching organization does not mean that organization did not do exactly what later lynchers did, but it does call into question claims that white Southerners universally favored extralegal racial violence. In this environment, in some places, at some times, the insurgents did have a chance at success.

THE KU KLUX KLAN

First organized as a social club in Pulaski, Tennessee, probably in May or June 1866, the Ku Klux Klan shifted to violence with the advent of Congressional Reconstruction. In 1867 Congress passed the Reconstruction Act, dividing the South into military districts. The authors of this legislation meant to make state governments established by presidents Lincoln and Johnson provisional and replace them with new governments elected under new state constitutions. Congress extended the franchise to blacks, requiring that the states allow former slaves to vote for the new state governments. This plan to unseat white conservative governments and enfranchise blacks enraged many Southern whites and transmuted the Ku Klux Klan into a vigilante organization. As such, it proved wildly popular among defeated whites. By January 1868, Nashville newspapers had taken notice of Klan activity. "For something like six months," the *Nashville Press and Times* reported, "perhaps longer," a secret society called the Ku Klux Klan had been recruiting "young men of rebel proclivities" in southern Tennessee. The Klan probably did not even appear in Mississippi until after that state's biracial constitutional convention met in January 1868. By February the Klan had become active in Alabama and in Georgia by March. In South Carolina, the Klan organized in the spring of 1868 after whites failed at an effort to defeat ratification of the Republicans' new state constitution.[6]

Although Republicans characterized the Invisible Empire as a grand conspiracy headed by former Confederate general Nathan Bedford Forrest, Klan vigilantes only briefly acted under any kind of central direction. Local Klansmen decided for themselves who to attack, taking votes at regular meetings. Some observers claimed that, as time passed, the "better class" dropped out of the Klan, to be replaced by a "younger and more lawless set." Such claims may be hard to substantiate, but planters did complain that Klansmen frightened off their laborers and even destroyed their cotton during raids. At least one Mississippi planter understood that Klan violence gave "our enemies an opportunity" to undermine conservative white Southern political leadership.[7]

The success the Klan had at winning over white Southerners mattered a great deal. A major part of the Klan's appeal came from its claims to white unity. It vigorously denied that politics had anything to do with its violence because politics implied division, a splintered and uncertain white community. In 1868 the Pulaski Klan angrily denied that "we are *politicians*."[8] Georgia newspaper editor Ambrose Wright insisted "there was no politics in it, so far as I know." When the Klan claimed to target people who were "a curse to the community," they did not mean a community rent by division. Wright said that every "outrage" he had described in his county was "spoken of commonly as Ku-Klux." His questioner asked him to define "Ku-Klux." Wright answered "that it is synonymous with lynch law," meaning apolitical violence carried out on behalf of the community, not as an outrage to the community.[9]

The Klan's success in achieving the solidarity associated with lynching depended on the locality. The chief of the Leon County, Florida, club boasted that half the white voters belonged, "and I suppose all would have belonged to it, if it had been convenient." The Klan's claim to represent all the people, the vox populi, may have been most credible in the South Carolina backcountry.[10] In York County, South Carolina, one Klansman estimated that four or five hundred men belonged to the order. Another said that "all" white persons in western York County belonged to the Klan, adding that there were "very few exceptions." The army officer charged with tracking down the Klan in York County reported that ten small Klans had been organized in Yorkville, while another ten to eighteen had formed in the countryside. This officer said that the Klan so thoroughly dominated white public opinion in York County that the state courts did not dare act against it.[11]

In places where not all whites actually joined the Klan, observers sometimes claimed that all were implicated nonetheless. The Republican postmaster in Tuskegee, Alabama, explained that he did not charge the better people of his county with direct participation in Klan violence, "but I think they are to blame indirectly, because they permitted these things to be done by young men and reckless men, without ever censuring or manifesting any displeasure."[12] In Tallapoosa, Alabama, one white planter estimated that all the "good" citizens in his county opposed Klan violence. He thought that if all the white people had met together and passed resolutions denouncing the Klan, they could have stopped the violence. These good people did not do so, because they feared making themselves "obnoxious." Though a minority in this neighborhood, Klansmen had very effectively established a feeling of dominance, so much so that their opponents dared not challenge them.

On a more practical level, foes of the Klan worried that the Klan would burn them out of their homes.[13] An Alabama Republican declared, "A man might as well go and dig his grave as to go to Blountsville and apply against a Ku-Klux or try to warrant him." Another said "A great many" voters wanted to vote Republican but did not only because of their fears.[14] One Georgia Unionist estimated that most people were not in the Klan, but were afraid to speak against it. According to this Unionist, only the lower classes carried out Klan "depredations."[15] Republicans believed many opponents of the Klan failed to speak out only because they feared its violence.

One explanation for the alleged universality of Klan violence came from the South's culture of violence. Abolitionists had long argued that slavery had led Southerners to violence. Some observers continued this argument after the fall of slavery. In 1865 the *Louisville Journal* reported that lynch law remained as active in Kentucky as it had been before the war. A "large and excited crowd" hanged James Miller after he stabbed Tilford Gregory, the paper said. Race had nothing to do with the killing, as both Miller and Gregory were white. At least one black newspaper quickly picked up the story and reprinted it as evidence of a continued white Southern tendency to lynch law.[16]

When the Klan became active, how blacks reacted depended on how they saw themselves politically, which could be measured by the language they chose to use. After the Civil War, some blacks feared a white "reign of terror." At this time, terror meant violence perpetrated by established but illegitimate authorities, as it did in the French Revolution, not violence directed against authority.[17] In 1868, a black California newspaper called the *Elevator* worried that "rebel leaders" plotted "a war of extermination against all Union men, white as well as black." If white "rebels" were as united and powerful as the *Elevator* feared, then their hangings of blacks and whites could be called lynchings. Black and white Republicans had no claim to authority or legitimate place in the community. The *Elevator* did call whites' violence lynchings, reporting in one instance that "a force of armed Democrats" had attacked a Republican newspaper in Louisiana and lynched its editor. The *Elevator* implied that whites had so totally united behind violence-prone leaders that Republicans had been squeezed into outsider status. In essence, the *Elevator* conceded blacks' marginal status, admitting that they had not yet established themselves as a significant part of the polity.[18]

White conservatives credibly were able to apply the term lynching to their acts when they actually attracted the kind of following among whites the *Elevator* feared. In 1868 a crowd of Tennessee men gathered outside their white Republican sheriff's door at midnight. They taunted the man by groaning loudly in his yard and called for him to come to his door. J. S. Webb appeared only after they promised not to hurt him. But when he came to his door, they grabbed him and took him to the center of his yard. They cut switches "and told me they were going to lynch me if I did not resign the office of sheriff."[19]

Republicans fought such overt lynching claims by warning that innocent people could be hurt by lynchers acting outside the rules of evidence required in courts. When unauthorized men take the law into their hands, they said, mistakes could easily happen. "Do you think," Indiana Senator Daniel D. Pratt demanded of one white conservative, "Judge Lynch is less liable to make mistakes than the ordinary courts of the land?" The conservative responded that too often criminals act secretly and cannot be convicted in regular courts for want of evidence. "I have more than once seen where, in my opinion, the want of evidence let off the guilty persons." Pratt pointed out that this answer meant that lynchers punished people for whom no evidence of guilt existed.[20]

More often Republicans did not have to debate Judge Lynch's efficacy, because the Klan could not position itself plausibly as representative of the entire white population. Racism pervaded the white South, but while most whites supported white supremacy, a significant number preferred to maintain white control without vigilante violence. One Georgia native declared himself a Democrat, but not "one of these fighting democrats." He added, "If we cannot beat them at voting[,] we cannot beat them at shooting."[21] North Carolina lawyer David Schenck never wavered from his commitment to white supremacy. "I utterly loathe the negro," he candidly wrote, adding that "all my sympathies and hopes are with the white race." Shortly later he thanked God "I have been true to my race and color."[22] But Schenck did not feel he had to toe the white line on every issue. When North Carolina Republicans proffered a new state constitution, Schenck favored accepting it as "the best we can do." This stance cost him friends, but Schenck felt he could risk the criticism. Even after he went on record favoring the Republicans' proposed constitution, Klan organizers still wanted Schenck to join their "Invisible Empire." Schenck enlisted only after being assured that no violence would follow. The Klan, Schenck was told, "was purely a secret political society using lawful measures." When the Klan turned violent, Schenck abandoned it, leaving the order entirely in 1870.[23] Schenck's insistence that he never participated in Klan violence might be dismissed as self-serving—except that his claims are found on the pages of his private journal and hardly seem prepared for public consumption.[24]

Such sentiments forced the Klan to attack not only blacks, but also whites opposed to their violence. Some members of the Klan had been forced into the order. South Carolinian John S. Millar may have had "kindly feelings" for the Republicans, but he joined the Klan when vigilantes raided his house. In some cases Klansmen forced reluctant recruits to implicate themselves in serious crimes so they could not easily oppose the Klan. After Klansmen killed Charley Good, they drafted local whites to place his body in the river. Once these men had aided and abetted a murder, they could hardly refuse other assignments, for fear of being turned over to authorities themselves.[25]

Klansmen designed their killings to resemble lynchings, hoping to win community support by making it look like they already had it. Often Klan apologists denied the Invisible Empire carried out acts of violence. When these apologists admitted it had, they insisted it made life and property safe and glorified the Ku Klux Klan as upholding the law.[26] Western lynchers claimed to uphold the law as well, and Klansmen must have used a Western model, turning out crowds to hang their victims from a tree or makeshift gallows, pinning a notice announcing the reasons for the hanging to the dangling corpse.[27]

Like Western lynchers, the Klan professed to strike only at immoral, dissipated deviants, positioning itself as the arm of all decent white people. Crowds of Klansmen seized blacks and hanged them from trees, often riddling their dangling bodies with gunfire, consciously replicating the look of a lynching and thereby making an implied claim to community support.[28] Testimony by the victims of Klan violence confirm its lynch-like character. Klan vigilantes sometimes attached placards to the corpses they had hanged, following Western practice. One sign described a dead man as an arsonist. Another insisted that the victim had been hanged for "threatening to ravish."[29] Western communities used such placards to set boundaries between acceptable and unacceptable behavior, marking the executed person as a deviant. By putting their own placards on the bodies of their victims, Klansmen similarly claimed—falsely—to represent the entire white community.

The Klan also sought to position itself as the defender of all white people by insisting that it acted to protect white women. Klan initiates took an oath to protect "female friends, widows and their households" from black attackers and rapists.[30] Hardly an original thought, this was a nearly universal strategy for nineteenth-century vigilantes. In this case, Klan vigilantes hoped to use it to rally rank-and-file whites under an all-white banner. Conservative newspapers certainly understood this strategy's political usefulness, reporting black sexual crimes so enthusiastically they seemed bent on whipping their readers into a frenzy. These newspapers saw politics behind black male sexuality, blaming Republican Union Leagues for black outrages, as well as "League judges" who were unduly sympathetic to black Republicans charged with crimes.[31] Democrats sometimes alleged that the people they killed had raped white women. When J. W. King testified before Congress, he claimed that the black victim of Ku Klux Klan violence had been "a very quiet, inoffensive man." Democrats on the committee counterattacked by demanding to know if the man had not been guilty of raping a white woman. "I heard," King responded, "there was a charge by the Ku-Klux, that some negro, during the war, attempted to commit a rape on a white woman in the neighborhood, and in the scuffle he had lost a finger and that this man was minus a finger."[32] In North Carolina Pride Jones insisted that at least by the late 1860s, "women were afraid to go about the country for fear of being ravished by negroes."[33]

Whites saw politically active black men as sexually threatening and sometimes attacked that part of their bodies most closely associated with their sex. Henry Lowther of Wilkinson County, Georgia, was in the county jail, charged with organizing a company of armed blacks. Lowther's son told him that he had heard that it was up to Captain Eli Cummins whether he got out of jail or not. Lowther asked Cummins to visit him in the jail. When Cummins came, he asked, "Harry, are you willing to give up your stones to save your life?" Such a question gave one pause. Lowther remembered sitting for a moment before answering that he would. "If they come for you, will you make [a] fight?" Cummins asked. That night 180 men tied Lowther and removed him from the jail. Lowther begged for his life. "They asked," Lowther remembered later, "whether I preferred to be altered or to be killed." The mob castrated Lowther, leaving him bleeding with instructions to get medical attention. He went from house to house before finally finding a doctor willing to treat him.[34]

The Klan effort to build white community support included efforts to enforce racial loyalty by punishing women they considered immoral. Lawyer H. C. Jones of Decatur, Georgia, admitted to acting as a vigilante himself, joining a mob that went to the house of a Miss Harrill, suspected of arson, and telling the woman she must leave the area. Describing Harrill as "a vile wretch, a disgrace to the neighborhood in every way," Jones said later that he felt he had violated the law, but believed himself justified "under the circumstances." People had to act outside the law, Jones explained, when they could not rely on the state government. As evidence of this, Jones explained that too many criminals had been pardoned.[35]

Mobs attacked whites and blacks for consensual sex across racial lines. Doctor William T. Blackford served as probate judge in Hale County, Alabama, until sixty to seventy vigilantes raided his house in 1871. Blackford escaped out a back window, but the night riders claimed later they had caught him "splitting a nigger," having sex with a black woman. The vigilantes testified later that "the community" condemned Blackford, adding, "the whole community said that was so." According to white conservatives sympathetic to the raiders, if not actually vigilantes themselves, Blackford's departure from the county restored order. "We have very good order there," one said, "we have had fine order since Dr. Blackford left there."[36] According to this view, Blackford was an isolated deviant who ran afoul of his neighborhood. The Ku Klux Klan carried out the will of outraged white society, restoring order. In Monroe County, Mississippi, whites assailed Santee Butler after they alleged he had been intimate with a white woman. In another case Andy Burns had two white women living in his yard. Vigilantes shot Burns, but did not kill him. After the shooting, the women left Burns to live in a house belonging to Santee Butler. "I presume," a county resident explained later, "that Santee was playing the same game that Andy was." When the vigilantes whipped Butler, they made a bid to present themselves as the arm of outraged morality.[37]

A DIVIDED LANDSCAPE

In some places, Republicans resisted the Klan. In Limestone County, Alabama, a mob tried to break into the jail only to be repelled by an organized opposition.[38] In Floyd County, Georgia, the Klan was so weak it could kill a nineteen-year-old boy only by masquerading as Union soldiers. They told the boy they needed him to go after the Klan. The ruse worked. He went with the "soldiers" and died, trapped and alone with his enemies.[39] Allen M. Gunn of Gravella, Alabama, courageously confronted a crowd that first denounced him as a Republican and then beat him senseless. Despite such pressure, Gunn would not surrender. "My father's *blood* purchased the american constitution, as a faithful and dutiful son, My blood Shall Seal IT before I yield one inch." Despite such powerful rhetoric, Gunn felt frustrated that pen and ink failed to communicate the depth of his angry determination to resist Klan violence.[40]

Such views may have been most common in northern Alabama's stoutly Republican hill country. One former Illinois soldier living in Alabama claimed that "a vendetta" existed in Morgan County between the Ku Klux Klan and the "anti-Ku Klux Klan." Sheriff Francis Marion Treadaway tied one Klansman by his feet, dangling him over a well. As his deputies flourished their knives about the rope, Treadaway asked the Klansman to identify his fellow vigilantes. He did.[41] Another Alabama judge, John A. Lewis of Opelika, disapproved of Republicans and disliked whites teaching in "colored schools" operated by the Freedmen's Bureau. But when local whites attacked the school and its teacher, Lewis offered to station his wife and daughter in the teacher's house to forestall further violence. Using his wife and daughter, of course, trumped the vigilantes' claim to defend white womanhood. In effect, Lewis offered to demonstrate that a Republican could be trusted with respectable women and that the Klan did not truly protect Southern womanhood. In Conway County, Arkansas, Governor Powell Clayton's militia turned the tables on the Klan and the white knights found themselves on the run. One writer called Conway County "a battleground" between the ex-Confederate Klansmen and Unionists, the scene of "a second civil war."[42]

Political affiliation helps explain some of the resistance to Klan violence. Even in those parts of the South where no second civil war broke out, old

Whigs stomached unity with the Democrats only with great difficulty—even when the Democrats invoked race to rally white voters to their side. Treadaway acted out of a commitment to the Republican party and its principles. Lewis' politics also help explain his stance. He acted "in concert" with the Democrats by 1870, but he had been an old-line Whig and determined opponent of the antebellum Democrats. One Republican candidate for Congress dismissed the Klan as "entirely political."[43] By "political" he meant that the Klan resorted to violence as part of a plan to advance one white faction over another. For proof, Republicans pointed to the politics of the people attacked. Klan victims were almost always Republicans. The Klan answered this charge by insisting that their victims were all deviants—who also happened to be Republicans.[44]

The political nature of Klan violence mitigated against its confusion with lynch law, usually presented as the apolitical punishment of crime. Klansmen disarmed blacks and assassinated politically effective black leaders, thus carrying out their advertised mission of protecting white society from rampaging blacks. Sometimes, though, they advanced the fortunes of the Democratic party at a time when not all whites had yet signed onto the Democrats' standard. The hearty hatred of Democrats nursed by some old Whigs led some whites into the Republican party, at least for a time. Even in the York County, South Carolina, Klan stronghold, some whites objected to vigilante violence as political when carried out on behalf of only a segment of white society rather than for the good of all whites. In some cases, Klansmen forced reluctant whites into their organization. Charles Foster joined the Klan only to avoid a beating. As a grocer, he had sold liquor, and Klansmen warned him he would be whipped for this if he did not join their order.[45] Many more joined the Klan thinking the vigilantes intended to protect whites from black violence, only to leave the order disenchanted. Osmond Gunthorpe grumbled that when he joined the Klan he did not think of it as a political organization. "I understood it was an organization for the protection of each other against . . . the negroes rising."[46] Once Gunthorpe decided the Klan had a political agenda, representing one segment of the white community against another, he quit.

By 1869 Klan violence had attracted national attention. North Carolina Klansmen committed fifteen murders and hundreds of cuttings, shootings, beatings, and other crimes. Republicans armed themselves and feared for their lives. The failure of local law enforcement to control Klan violence contributed to the spectacle. By disguising themselves and arranging for dens to strike far from home, the Klansmen thwarted efforts to identify them in court. In South Carolina, after Republican candidates won the 1870 election, Klansmen carried out raids almost nightly for months. This violence prompted President Ulysses S. Grant to suspend the writ of habeas corpus in nine South Carolina backcountry counties. Federal marshals and the Seventh Cavalry arrested large numbers of Klansmen.[47]

Republicans sought to de-legitimize the Klan and its efforts to thwart American nationalism. They had long insisted that "our friends at the South" should be protected from old rebels.[48] Now they circulated reports of Klan violence to mobilize the nation against parochially sanctioned violence. In the mid-1870s, Republican newspapers like the *Chicago Tribune* filled their columns with horror stories of white violence against blacks. The "Mississippi Plan" meant violent efforts designed to prevent black voting, an affront to what the nation's soldiers fought for in the Civil War. "Bulldozing" meant the same thing: local efforts to thwart Republican nation building.[49] Klan violence gave Congressional Republicans ammunition to use in urging more vigorous Reconstruction policies. In the Senate, Henry Wilson called for protection of American citizens. It must be done, he orated, for the good name of the United States of America; the South had compiled a record "such as no Christian and civilized land . . . can present." Shocking and appalling acts of violence required federal protection of citizens' rights.[50] In 1873, whites in Grant Parish, Louisiana, stormed the little town of Colfax, occupied by black Republicans who were claiming political control of the parish. In the resulting massacre, perhaps a hundred black men perished. Three years later, a gang of Tennessee whites, with the assistance of a Crockett County deputy sheriff, opened the jail and killed a black inmate named P. M. Wells confined inside.[51]

In both the Colfax and the Crockett County cases, the local U. S. Attorney investigated the violence and persuaded grand juries to indict the killers. In Louisiana, James R. Beckwith drew up an indictment that charged 98 white persons with violating the civil rights of black citizens. His superiors in Washington refused to furnish him with the resources necessary to arrest so many suspects, so Beckwith only brought nine defendants to trial. In Tennessee, William W. Murray, a Southern Unionist through the war and Union Army veteran, ordered twenty men arrested. Both Beckwith and Murray relied on an 1870 federal law based on the Fourteenth Amendment of the Constitution, forbidding the states from discriminating against their citizens.[52]

When the Republicans like Beckwith and Murray attempted to use the federal courts to protect black citizens from white violence, they ran into trouble not only with local juries, but also when their cases reached the U.S. Supreme Court on appeal. In Louisiana, Beckwith succeeded in convicting only three men, and the Supreme Court overturned those convictions. In Murray's case, two judges asked the Supreme Court if the federal government could prosecute such a case along the lines Murray proposed. The

Supreme Court ruled that it could not, that the actions of the Crockett County mob amounted to a private action by individual citizens, not the kind of state action forbidden by the Fourteenth Amendment.[53]

NOT LYNCHING BUT OUTRAGE

Republicans needed strong language to denounce Klan violence, but their denial that all Southerners, or even all white Southerners, supported the Klan made lynching the wrong word. Republican Arthur A. Smith described how members of a white mob had been indicted for lynching after they seized a black man, but he quickly added, "Do not understand me to say that these persons were lynched." Authorities had relied on an act passed to suppress lynching. The law had labeled them as lynchers, but that, Smith explained, was a mere legal technicality. They were not true lynchers.[54] In his great Reconstruction novel *A Fool's Errand,* Albion Tourgee quoted Klansmen as plotting to "execute" a victim.[55] But when they did, a "loud-voiced young man" objected: "we'll all be running our necks into hemp," he warned, adding, "It's what we call murder, gentlemen, in civilized and Christian countries!"[56] Tourgee describes the killing of "old Jerry," a black man found hanged from an oak not forty steps from the courthouse, as a *hanging* rather than a lynching.[57] In another passage, Tourgee's hero looks keenly at a Klansman and charges, *"you are a murderer!"* The Klansman acknowledged the appropriateness of the term: "It is a hard word . . . ; yet I do not know but I must submit."[58] Tourgee's central character worries about being "assassinated," fearing his "individual destruction."[59] The voices echoing from the pages of Tourgee's prose do not cry lynching; instead they shriek "murder," "assassination," and "outrage."

The word lynching appears only rarely in the extensive record of Reconstruction violence. At times Southern whites seemed uncertain whether they could credibly advance the word or not. William Shapard remembered hearing a Klansman say that his organization had been "gotten up" to "straighten out matters and hang people and lynch them." Shapard's mention of lynching surprised the congressman questioning him. "He told you he was connected with an order to lynch people?" Hearing his own word repeated back to him seemed to shock Shapard himself, and he backed away from his earlier testimony, saying: "He didn't use the language you use."[60] Shapard's testimony is confusing and hard to parse, but reveals a sensitivity to the language used to describe Klan violence.

Leonard L. Weir's testimony deserves special consideration. Few people, once hanged, live to describe the experience. Weir did. Weir was a white man living in Limestone County, Alabama, where he worked as a carpenter and served as justice of the peace. Whites in Weir's neighborhood circulated a rumor that Weir had urged a black man to steal a mule. Weir suspected that his real crime was his Civil War Unionism and postwar Republicanism. Disguised Klansmen grabbed Weir, mounted him on a horse, and carried him to a likely tree. Saying that "here's about as good a limb as we will find," the Klansmen prepared him for his execution. Blindfolded, Weir could feel himself being hoisted from the ground by his neck. The noose did not snap Weir's neck, but choked him instead. He lost consciousness for a time, and then awoke on the ground, realizing that the rope must have broken. After a debate, the Klansmen released him. In some ways, Weir's story resembled an attempted lynching. Had Weir's neck instead of the rope snapped, his body would have been left dangling from a tree. He would have appeared to have been lynched, especially if decorated with a placard announcing his "crimes." In fact, though, Weir's story really reveals just how Klan violence diverged from lynching. Because they realized they might release him, Weir's would-be killers blindfolded him, followed a circuitous route, and argued over whether to execute him or not. Such secrecy combined with uncertainty hardly seems characteristic of a "genuine" Western lynching, one where an outraged community acts in concert. Finally, the small size of the gang that seized Weir—six or eight men—makes the incident look more like a clumsy kidnapping than a lynching. Perhaps most importantly, throughout his lengthy testimony before a Congressional committee, Weir never claimed to have been lynched.[61]

Although white Republicans like Weir seem never to have considered Klan violence akin to lynching, blacks, as we have seen, did for a time accuse white conservatives of lynching. As time passed black Republicans became less and less likely to do so. In 1868, African American journalists at the *San Francisco Elevator* associated the Klan's "reign of terror" with "lynching." As late as September 1874, the *Elevator* still complained that whites subjected blacks to "indiscriminate lynching."[62] Thereafter the *Elevator* accused Southern white conservatives of carrying out "murders," "outrages," "atrocities," and "massacres." The paper headlined, "Shooting, Hanging and Whipping," adding that "the Bullet, Knife, Halter and Torch [are] the Weapons." But there were no more lynchings. As the *Elevator* explained, things had changed, "the case is different." From the *Elevator*'s perspective, the key difference was that "The negro is a political power." If African Americans were a political power, and a legitimate part of the community, then the term lynching no longer fit.[63]

The word black and white Republicans preferred when describing Klan violence was outrage. While lynching suggested a killing carried out by the community, outrage implied a crime against the community. To call a Klan act of violence an outrage denounced it as the work of a minority. Republican rhetoric followed a long search conducted by the abolitionists to find the right word to describe white Southern violence. Abolitionists had accused Southerners of committing "crimes," "horrors," "atrocities," and "outrages." The word outrage worked well because it implied a crime against the nation's conscience. As Philip Hone wrote in 1835, an outrage was violence calculated "to make humanity shudder." Riots, tarrings and featherings, and murders all constituted outrages according to the abolitionist press.[64] "ANOTHER FIENDISH OUTRAGE" the Boston Liberator headlined in 1831 after "a mob of slavites" had attacked a Petersburg, Virginia, resident for favoring emancipation.[65] Northerners abused by Southerners proved the need for national citizenship rights. Like postbellum Republicans, the abolitionists understood outrage to mean an affront to the national morality. Exciting a riot or a mob, the Liberator charged, was treason.[66]

Republicans denied that the entire community, even the entire white community, endorsed Klan violence. To have admitted such would have signaled a major defeat for Reconstruction. Frederick Douglass identified three distinct classes in the South. The "Ku-Klux stripe" was only one segment in the white population. Other whites more or less accepted the new order.[67] The black Mississippi politician John Roy Lynch explained that between 1868 and 1872, most whites did not really hamper Reconstruction, and they accepted it between 1872 and 1874. Though a black man, Lynch reported success in recruiting white voters into the Republican ranks.[68]

In Reconstruction, opponents of the Klan complained of hundreds, even thousands, of outrages in Southern states.[69] This rhetoric can be found in Republicans' private correspondence, not just in the newspapers. Governors hoped outrage rhetoric would make federal authorities more amenable to protecting the rights of citizens everywhere in America.[70] Judges ordered Klansmen arrested for outrages.[71] Ordinary citizens had no trouble knowing what constituted an outrage. As one man wrote, when Klansmen robbed loyal men of everything they could take away, even taking the food out of their cooking pots, taking them out of bed "to be hung for voating for Mr Lincolen," that was an outrage.[72]

Republican propagandists hammered the word into the minds of its readers. For months in 1871 few issues of the New York Tribune rolled off the presses without a column devoted to "SOUTHERN OUTRAGES." The paper headlined "KU-KLUX OUTRAGE," "ANOTHER TERRIBLE KU-KLUX OUTRAGE," "RECENT OUTRAGES," and offered "PARTICULARS OF OUTRAGES."[73] In New Orleans the Republican-controlled state legislature investigated whites' "outrages," "massacres," "slaughters," and "murders."[74] Republicans distinguished "outrages" carried out by private citizens, even when "systemic," from the "terrorism" sponsored by local governments.

The word outrage also implied a challenge to white conservative definitions of community as a small autonomous neighborhood. Republicans wrote laws to define national citizenship and establish rights enjoyed by all citizens. Even the most ordinary of Americans understood this fact. One Ohioan listed a series of "outrages," reminding President Grant that he had "promised protection to all citizens of the united states."[75] Albion Tourgee also eschewed "lynching" in favor of "outrage" as the correct word to describe Klan violence. A Union Army veteran who came to North Carolina after the war to become a judge, Tourgee's opinion is especially important. In addition to serving as a politician, Tourgee was a writer and novelist and paid particular attention to language. Tourgee found the experience impossibly frustrating. He explained that whites commonly classed the racial violence he confronted as "outrages." Tourgee wrote that all sorts of violence qualified as "outrages." He clearly intended his catalog of horrors to shock Northern readers:

> The entry of the premises, and surrounding the dwelling with threats against the inmates; the seizure and destruction, or appropriation of arms; the dragging of men, women, and children from their homes, or compelling their flight; the binding, gagging, and beating of men and women; shooting at specific individuals, or indiscriminately at inhabited houses; the mutilation of men and women in methods too shocking and barbarous to be recounted here; burning houses; destroying stock; and making the night a terror to peaceful citizens by the ghastly horror of many and deliberate murders,—all these come within the fearful category of "outrages."[76]

In 1871 Congress organized a joint committee to investigate Klan violence. Moderates, like Congressman James A. Garfield, explained that they wanted to ascertain whether conditions in the Southern states warranted further legislation. Other Republicans, however, chafed impatiently, insisting Congress already had all the information it needed about Southern outrages. John Coburn of Indiana wanted to put "the strong arm of the law . . . in motion" and not merely a committee of inquiry into the field. Despite such objections, in April Congress created a joint committee of seven senators and fourteen representatives to investigate the safety of American citizens' lives and property. The committee organized on April 20 and began taking testimony one month later. Witnesses came to Washington, while subcommittees fanned out across the South to hear from the victims of Reconstruction violence as well as from conservative white Southerners sympathetic to the vigilantes.[77] The testimony collected by the committee is a rich source for the study of Reconstruction rhetoric. Witness followed witness from June to December 1871, their words carefully transcribed by patient government stenographers. The resulting thirteen-volume record documents Klan outrages, while preserving black and white Southerners' logic, discourse, dissembling, ordinary conversation, taunts, and argument.

Conservatives tried to dismiss the Congressional investigation as an "outrage committee," but the term outrage both stung and stuck. Southern conservatives insisted the Republicans acted from purely partisan motives, but they clearly understood that every new report of a Southern outrage weakened their argument.[78] The *Atlanta Constitution* fought back with a satirical advertisement headlined, "WANTED, A LIBERAL SUPPLY OF KU KLUX OUTRAGES IN GEORGIA . . . ," suggesting that the Republicans falsified outrage stories.[79] Asked about "outrages" by Congressional Republicans, Alabaman Edward Clement Sanders objected to such language. Killings carried out on behalf of an indignant community could hardly be classed as "outrages," he insisted. When asked what term he would use, Sanders answered, "I call it justice." Sanders's candor surprised his interrogator. "Murders do you mean to say; several murders?" Yes, that was what Sanders meant. Killings of disreputable blacks, carried out by mobs, amounted to "justice" and were legitimate, Sanders answered.[80]

Republicans had considerable success inserting the word outrage into language as a description of Klan violence. They did not permanently manage to label acts of Klan violence as outrages, but the word remained in use for at least 75 years. The earliest historians, the ones most hostile to Republican Reconstruction, found it hard to resist describing Klan attacks as "outrages."[81] In 1939 Stanley Horn defended the Klan but could not avoid the term outrage, even when he encased it in quotes and dismissed the violence it described as "harmless hazing."[82] But while the Republicans changed the language, their effort to use outrage rhetoric to discredit the Klan ultimately failed. Most whites decided in the 1870s and 1880s that on moral questions the United States was still a collection of localities, not a fully unified nation. Republicans could not persuade enough Northerners that assaults on citizens in Southern villages should outrage the entire nation.

In the 1870s the white South began to consolidate itself in a way that would replace surreptitious Ku Klux Klan violence with public violence, carried out in daylight by an apparently unified white society. In 1871 many white Southern opponents of the Klan found a home in a wing of the Democratic party called the New Departure. Proponents of a New Departure pledged themselves to easing racial tensions, promising moderation, and opposing racial divisions. After 1873, to the horror of the New Departurists, white conservatives' arguments for racial polarization caught hold. In some places this happened when blacks realized whites' worst fears by scoring electoral victories. When blacks armed themselves in self-defense, this too frightened whites and emboldened those calling for a "white line."[83] In state after state white conservatives defeated the New Departure as white voters became more conservative. With unity achieved at last, whites could operate without fear of their fellows.[84]

Perhaps in the 1880s the same number of white Southerners objected to racial violence as in the 1860s and 1870s. Yet the difference seems as clear as night and day. Gilded Age lynchers acted with community approval, rarely donning the masks and robes favored by the Klan. Rather than skulking in the dark, they killed their victims in broad daylight and posed for photographers, freely distributing postcard pictures of themselves and their victims. The Klan's goal of uniting Southern whites behind racial violence had not necessarily been entirely achieved, but the Invisible Empire's campaign had achieved considerable success nonetheless. More than the Reconstruction Klan, lynchers credibly claimed to act on behalf of all whites. A kind of consensus had been won. Opponents of lawless violence felt constrained to concede that white superiority required violence. Opposition existed, but it had been effectively silenced.

White conservatives' success at turning Klan attacks into lynchings signals the importance of language in Reconstruction. Albion Tourgee, himself a victim of this discourse, ruefully recognized conservatives' skill. "Scalawag," "carpetbagger," and "redeemer" were all conservative inventions, of course; and white Southern newspapers reinvigorated the old slander, "nigger," as well. White conservatives called themselves "redeemers," slyly invoking evangelical Christianity. White conservatives deployed these words with great skill, winning a permanent place for them in the language. These words became so much a part of the language that it became difficult even to talk about Reconstruction without implicitly passing judgment against the Republicans. As one Alabama newspaper explained, white rhetoric had served as an "engine of moral power."[85]

Recognizing the importance of language in Reconstruction allows the restoration of contingency and the recovery of the essential tendentiousness of the period. It requires that we not close the book on white Southerners as hopelessly mired in a racism that did not change from the colonial era until 1964— if then. In the American South at the end of the Civil War, white conservatives and Republicans fought a war. An important part of this struggle involved language. Republicans fought to label Klan violence as outrageous. White conservatives denied they outraged their communities; they wanted to be seen as acting on behalf of their neighbors and for the local rather than the national. Republicans both challenged Klan claims to represent all white communities, defined as small neighborhoods, and proposed a new, nationalized definition of community. To describe the Klan as guilty of lynching not only ignores an important part of Reconstruction history, but it also assumes that all white Southerners opposed Reconstruction or that they all accepted the Klan's definition of community.

Understanding why racial violence in the Reconstruction era was not called lynching helps explain the difference between Reconstruction and the lynching era. Reconstruction was a revolutionary time, a time when power as expressed in language was genuinely up for grabs. Once the white population seized power and rallied itself into a racial bloc, then, and only then, could they kill confident that they had the support of what they defined as the community. And they understood a community-sanctioned killing to be a lynching.

CHAPTER FIVE

"The Indignation of the People Knew No Bounds"

THE LYNCHING NARRATIVE IN THE 1870S AND 1880S

It is no surprise to find nineteenth-century America laced with mob violence. It may be a bit surprising to learn that in the 1870s few of the killings contemporaneously called lynchings involved black people. In the midst of westward expansion, most people understood lynching to mean punishment carried out by a community outside the law when the court system was too weak to protect the lives and property of good citizens. As Republicans and Conservatives fought over the legitimacy of white racial violence, the nation reached a consensus regarding nonpolitical extralegal violence designed to control crime.

In the 1870s, Americans continued to move to the West, and the East industrialized. The law seemed ill equipped to deal with either phenomenon: People migrating west stepped outside any court's jurisdiction, and industrialists consolidated economic power that would challenge the state. Economic depression sharpened the picture of government as weak and irrelevant to the lives of ordinary workers. In this environment, violent extralegal crime control took many forms, a kind of chaotic anarchy boiling close to the surface of American society.

But journalists made order out of the chaos, crafting a kind of template, a standard story of the violence. The articles they wrote generally condemned lynching, but they also saw the acts as sometimes necessary or at least understandable. The best evidence of the power of such thinking comes from Ida B. Wells, who later became famous as a great crusader against lynching. Before 1892, Wells wrote later, she "accepted the idea meant to be conveyed—that although lynching was irregular and contrary to law and order, unreasoning anger over the terrible crime of rape led to the lynching." Perhaps, Wells added, "the brute deserved death anyhow."[1] Wells captured American thinking about lynching. In the 1870s, the best white newspapers saw popular violence—not racial or political violence, but folk violence against truly evil criminals—as unfortunate, perhaps, but a sensible popular response to monstrous crime.

Even as Wells "accepted the idea meant to be conveyed," other black journalists mounted an attack on white racist violence. Through the 1870s, as leading white newspapers temporized on lynching, courageous black writers attacked white racial violence. They would have liked to persuade everyone that racial lynching was evil, of course, but they focused their efforts on rallying the black community. This proved a tough sell. Not until the 1890s did these black writers convince large numbers of African Americans to reject the white justification for racial lynching. Wells did not begin working to lead African Americans against the rhetorical citadel that journalists had constructed in defense of popular violence until 1892. And even these early black opponents of lynching did not reject all extralegal violence. They urged blacks to respond with violence to white brutalities.

LYNCHING IN THE 1870S

In the 1870s journalists used the terms "lynching," "vigilantism," and "mob law" almost interchangeably. Vigilantism implied a continuing organization, but the press sometimes reported that community-sanctioned vigilantes lynched their victims in episodes of mob law. When the press called a killing by a crowd "murder" rather than "lynching," though, it intended to condemn the killers. The newspapers deemed lynchings no better than murder when a crowd acted without community approval. The New York Times just barely called the killing of sixteen blacks by a Tennessee mob a lynching in 1874. The article labeled the killers "lynchers," but only once, in the twelfth and final paragraph. The headline called the affair "WHOLESALE MURDER." In some ways these Tennessee killings looked like lynchings. One hundred masked men rode to the jail, overpowered the sheriff, and seized his prisoners. What made the affair murder was that the masked men, or "maskers" as the Times called them, acted because of a vendetta, not on behalf of their community. Reporters found the origins of the trouble in a dispute between one white man and one black man over a fifty-cent debt. Such feuds did not represent the will of the people, even if a crowd did the killing.[2]

Whether they qualified as murder or not, lynchings in this era did not look so different from other times. Mobs most often hanged their victims after breaking into jail. In the 1870s, 85 percent of the incidents reported as lynchings in the *New York Times* involved death by hanging.[3] This does not mean that lynchers chose to hang their victims 85 percent of the time. It means that in 85 percent of the incidents journalists chose to call lynchings, the killers hanged their victims. Journalists associated hanging with lynching. In 88 percent of these lynching episodes, mobs broke open jails to extract prisoners. In the 1870s, the *New York Times* only described as lynchings eighteen incidents in which posses ran down fugitives without ever allowing them to be arrested. Again, this may not reveal much about the actual behavior of mobs. Journalists may have printed jail break stories more often than posse stories because there really were more jail breaks. But it is just as likely that jail breaks attracted journalists' attention more easily than posse killings because they occurred in a town large enough to serve as county seat—and to have a newspaper. Posses acted in more remote villages or rural areas.

While the typical lynching involved a jail break followed by a hanging, journalists classified shootings and stabbings as lynchings as well. In one incident, an Oregon crowd placed an accused rapist in a small boat with his executioner. The boat passed out of sight, the waiting crowd heard a gunshot, and then the boat returned with one less passenger. The *New York Times* headlined its story an "EXTRAORDINARY CASE OF LYNCHING."[4] In one 1878 killing, the lynchers cut the throat of their victim and threw his body in a bayou. The *Times* called that the "LYNCHING OF A BRUTAL NEGRO."[5]

Newspapers took note when lynchers seemed well organized or "quiet" or "determined." Many today assume that 1890s lynchings necessarily followed some ritualized format. Perhaps this follows William Blackstone's insistence that a legally recognized custom had to be "peaceful."[6] While many events called lynchings involved no particular ritual at all, even in the 1870s, journalists were on the lookout for hints of a set protocol. In some cases, lynchers arranged extralegal "trials," complete with juries and witnesses. In the case of the Oregon rapist shot in a boat, the crowd held a "trial" with the father of the victim acting as judge.[7] At least by 1880, the *Nashville Banner* thought there was a "usual custom" for the extralegal execution of accused persons, which involved hanging the person and then shooting the dangling body. Westerners, though, sometimes boasted that they killed culprits with "no fuss and no ceremony."[8] Newspaper reports of lynchings suggest a wide variety of procedures, with no particular ritual or custom, regardless of what the *Banner* thought.

When lynchers hanged their victims, they often did so in hopes of extracting a confession while jerking the person up and down repeatedly. Other times, lynchers resorted to the rope in a conscious effort to copy state executions. When a Maryland mob prepared to kill John Diggs, someone proposed that Diggs be tied to the legs of a wild horse so that he might be kicked to death. Saying that "we are carrying out the law," the "captain" of the mob rejected this creative recommendation. Instead, the mob formed a circle around Diggs, prayed for him, and then hanged him. A Tennessee mob prepared to burn a black man charged with rape, "but it being recollected that the law provided hanging as the penalty . . . , it was finally determined to follow that course."[9] At times, prisoners made any attempt at ritual impossible. One Tennessee prisoner forced a mob to shoot him by refusing to leave his cell, hiding behind the door, and fending off his attackers with a chair leg. Members of the mob tried to burn him out by throwing flaming bits of paper into the cell. When that did not work, someone finally got a shot at him, hitting him in the leg, severing an artery. That brought him down, allowing the mob to drag him from his cell and finish him off with additional shots.[10]

Out of this welter of not-so-ritualized violence, patterns emerged, more in the published description of lynching than in the behavior itself. Reporters wrote articles that essentially retold the same story, a standard narrative for lynchings, a formula that could be repeated, and would be repeated, for decades. This standard narrative archived in print a process for calculating the legitimacy of crowd violence. The calculation began when newspapers discovered that a terrible crime, shocking to the community, had been committed. Next, the crime aroused the neighborhood to a frenzy of infuriated, uncontrollable hunger for vengeance. If this happened where the courts did not function effectively, and where the public unanimously supported mob action, then popular sovereignty justified lynching.

SHOCKING CRIMES

Journalists' hyperbole when reporting crimes seemed almost designed to inspire public hysteria.[11] The *New York Times* pronounced the person lynched guilty of his or her crime in 45 percent of the incidents reported through the 1870s. Often these articles focused more on the guilt of the person lynched than on the lynching itself. The *Times,* like other newspapers, often presented the victims of the original crime sentimentally, making the lynched person less sympathetic. Children made up a disproportionate percentage of the crime victims that inspired lynch mobs. Rapists had a peculiarly perverse preference, or so the newspapers claimed, for four-year-old girls.[12] The press tended to describe the victim as a young female, sometimes very young, or, if not so young, accomplished, popular, and beautiful. One 1881 report described a victim as "a decided blonde . . . delicately formed, with soft brown curls and deep blue eyes." The papers thought a crime against such a beauty was "the most horrible ever known" in South Carolina.[13]

The universal desire of nineteenth-century men to be seen as defenders of their women manifested itself in the 1870s as it had before and would later. Although historians have sometimes argued that hard economic times led men into lynch mobs as a way of maintaining gender hegemony, men needed no particular economic motive or catastrophe to drive them into this stance. In the 1870s, lynchers claimed to act on behalf of women well before white male Southerners made a fetish of their duty to protect the flower of white womanhood in the 1890s. The context for this male claim of gender hegemony was the so-called unwritten law that allowed an outraged husband, brother, or some other male protector to kill the male seducer of the husband's wife or the brother's sister. No written law conferred such a license to kill, but juries sometimes freed the defendants in such cases as temporarily insane. Observers generally believed that the jurors did not really consider the defendant insane but rather justified under the unwritten law. Nineteenth-century Americans generally believed that this popular "law" trumped the statutory variety.[14]

There was clearly a gendered dimension to this widely recognized right of vengeance. Men had the right to protect women, and the right to protect implies the right to subordinate. But, in some cases, juries also acquitted or forgave women who killed their assailants. While the overwhelming majority of the beneficiaries of the unwritten law were men, a few women also avenged their sexual dishonor with society's approbation. Nineteenth-century feminists demanded the right of revenge for all women. The unwritten law championed male privilege but favored a more general right of vengeance for both genders. The unwritten law can be documented at least as far back as 1843; thus, it can be said that at least from 1843 on, many Americans, perhaps most, recognized a right of sexual vengeance.[15]

In the context of this tolerance for vengeance, newspapers tended to forgive or at least understand lynchers acting to protect women's honor. Some newspapers seemed less tolerant of male libertines or "the free love set" (a reference to radical utopian socialists like John Humphrey Noyes) than of lynchers. Through the 1870s, the press described lynchers as "friends" of the raped women they avenged. In 1873, when Matt Tarpey murdered a woman in Monterey County, California, Western newspapers called him "THE WOMAN MURDERER," and reported "Intense Indignation" and preparations for lynching. The San Francisco Chronicle acknowledged that "taking . . . this man from the officers and summarily executing him is a grave violation of the law"; but, the paper added, "few, if any, deprecate it."[16] No mob had yet done anything to Tarpey when the *Chronicle* printed those words; in essence, the newspaper called for his death. When a mob did hang him, the *Chronicle* hailed the work as "ORDERLY" and an "UPRISING OF THE PEOPLE." The *Chronicle* had already reported Tarpey's crime, but with his hanging editors needed to reiterate its heinous nature. "No event," the paper cried, "that has ever occurred in this valley has created so intense an excitement as the shocking murder of Mrs. Sarah Nicholson. . . ." Race had nothing to do with this endorsement of mob violence. Tarpey, the paper reported, had a fair complexion; the problem was his "fierce and ungovernable temper." He was a "brawling, profane, cowardly ruffian." Women must be protected from such characters, many believed. After the mob hanged him, the *Chronicle* reassured its readers that Mrs. Nicholson had been avenged. The *New York Times* repeated the *Chronicle* story.[17] At least by 1882 mobs had begun to place placards on their victims that declared "we will protect the female sex," or a similar message.[18]

Twenty years later, when white Southern males claimed to act on behalf of their women, Wells refuted this with evidence that only about a third of lynchings actually involved charges of rape. In the 1870s only a quarter of lynching incidents reported in the *New York Times* involved rape; but lynchers nonetheless believed they acted, at least in part, to protect women. The notion that lynchers protected women subsumed racism. Black newspapers acknowledged the necessity of defending women outside the law.[19] A fairly slim majority of the alleged rapists the *New York Times* reported as lynched in the 1870s were black (twenty-seven of forty-one); certainly the ratio reported allowed the impression that crowds singled out rapists regardless of their color. Furthermore, as the Tarpey lynching demonstrated, hanging a rapist was not the only way to protect women. Male lynchers (and newspapers described lynchers as almost entirely male) said they protected their women, even when they charged the men they lynched with killing other men. Murderers described as having generally bad characters (Tarpey was a "desperado," a not uncommon description) probably threatened female society even if their proximate crime involved the death of another man.[20]

Newspapers only occasionally entertained doubt about the guilt of persons hanged or burned by mobs. Many "neutral" newspaper articles actually silently justified the lynching by focusing on the guilt of the lynched victim. Many of these assertions of guilt were entirely gratuitous. The *New York Times* described one Alabama lynching victim as "a fiend in human shape," and a "wretch," guilty of raping a little white child, just four years old. At the end of the article, the reporter almost dared any reader to express sympathy for the "fiend," writing: "The injured child is very low and . . . is not expected to live."[21] In Arkansas "AN INHUMAN MONSTER," a "negro named Johnson," married a woman with a four-year-old child. Annoyed by his new daughter, Johnson held the child in front of the fireplace until the heat roasted the four-year-old to death. Officers were in pursuit of the fugitive, the press said, predicting that "if he is captured he will be lynched."[22] Even when lynching victims had not gone before any formally constituted jury or received any due process of law, the New York Times routinely described lynching victims as guilty criminals—just as guilty as if they had been convicted by a jury of their peers with all the due process protections found in courts of law. One reporter declared the evidence against a lynched person "as clear and connected as that on which many have been made to ascend the scaffold."[23] Such prejudice went beyond provincial reporters. Times editors wrote headlines that declared "A BRUTAL NEGRO LYNCHED," "THREE MURDERERS LYNCHED IN TENNESSEE," and "A MURDERER HANGED WITHOUT TRIAL."[24]

In the 1870s, the New York Times's prejudices sometimes went beyond headline writing. In 1870, the Times noted editorially that the murder of a New Yorker named Townsend in front of his children had outraged the whole community. Worse, the murderer showed no sign of penitence for his crime and, in fact, bragged that he did it "for a spree" because he knew he would not be seriously punished. "Hanging for murder," the Times quoted the man as saying, "is played out in New-York." Fearing this might be true, the New York Times thought it "high time for the citizens of New-York to act." If people did take the law into their own hands, the Times observed, negligent authorities could hardly complain. Observing that police held the alleged murderer at a police station on Leonard Street, the Times demanded: "This Leonard-street Station House—is it impregnable?" Lynching violated the law, the paper conceded, "but sometimes it is palliated by many circumstances."[25]

UNREASONING ANGER

The second stage in the narrative process involved the outrage of the community where the crime occurred. Wells articulated this when she identified "unreasoning anger" as an element in the justification for lynching. Anger was an appropriate response to a terrible crime, an ordinary reaction. What was not appropriate was sentimentality. The New York Times warned that slow-moving courts promoted "morbid sentimentality" and even invested the defendant with "a spurious kind of heroism."[26] This was no new complaint. In 1855, when Wisconsin mobs hanged two prisoners, some observers complained that the lynchings had occurred because "sickly sentimentalists" in the state legislature had abolished capital punishment.[27] In 1886, an anonymous Memphis citizen's complaint about the cruelty of Arkansas chain gangs prompted a rebuke from J. S. Carruthers, who accused the anonymous writer of sentimentality and mocked him as "the kindhearted gentleman." Should desperate and hardened criminals be "shocked with tie vines and locked with a buttonnaire by some fair hand?"[28] Newspapers did not anticipate murderers and rapists to elicit a sentimental response. Such "fiends" should expect anger and public outrage, not sympathy.

When sensational crimes occurred, like the Tarpey case, newspapers did not wait for lynch mobs to form before reporting the anger and outrage that could legitimize and even promote mob violence. The press described villages as "wild with excitement" at reports of rapes or murders, especially when the criminal struck a child.[29] In Illinois, "unknown parties" attempted to murder Georgia Aldridge in 1886. "Intense excitement prevails," the papers reported, "and if the guilty party is found he will be dealt with in a summary manner." Ironically, the would-be murderers of Aldridge had tried to hang her.[30]

This crowd excitement went a long way toward explaining lynchings, or so the press believed. The vocabulary used to describe the crowds was small; they were "infuriated," "enraged," "outraged," or "excited." Racism is a kind of rage or outrage, and certainly racial hatred excited nineteenth-century whites. And, at times, the press recognized that race did infuriate white crowds. Near the town of Loudon, in eastern Tennessee, reports that a black man had attempted to rape and then had murdered a housewife infuriated the entire section where the crime occurred, sending citizens into "a frenzy of excitement."[31] Through the 1870s, though, community agitation did not always flow from race. When a Wisconsin white man named Ludwig Neher murdered a popular young man in 1871, his crime so infuriated a crowd that the mob punched and kicked him as officers escorted him to jail. The officers managed to get him behind bars, but could not protect him from a mob so crazed with anger. Journalists reported that the "infuriated crowd" could not be prevented from battering down the jail door, seizing Neher, and hanging him.[32]

LAX COURTS

Journalists did not believe that horrible crimes, even when followed by intense excitement, automatically justified lynching. Hardly anyone endorsed mob violence as an appropriate response to every horrible crime. Excitement alone did not excuse crowd violence, but a brutal crime, followed by popular agitation in a place with no effective court system, was another matter. Newspapers saw the state of criminal justice as a key index of whether the people should act outside the law against criminality. Lynch law, the *Times* explained in an editorial, is "practiced on the border and in territories where the institutions of justice are feeble in motion and difficult to access."[33] In 1875, the *Times* sarcastically remarked that "we are under the impression that local courts in Louisiana must be very lax. . . . If this were not so, we must presume the people would not be compelled to get up at night and hang suspected persons."[34] Five years later, the press justified the hanging of an alleged rapist by insisting that "the fact must be admitted that the quips and quirks of the law afford so many obstacles to the speedy punishment of criminals . . . that public sentiment quite generally indorses this resort to border law."[35]

When the courts clearly did function, and were not "lax," the *Times* criticized lynchers excited by horrible crimes. In 1878 the *Times* announced its disapproval of a lynching near Lexington, Kentucky, "where the machinery of the courts is supposed to be in full operation."[36] When Ohioans lynched a man named Schell, the *Times* complained that "there was no pretense that Schell would not have had a fair trial and been surely punished if he were guilty."[37] Even while it condemned the Schell lynchers, the paper made it clear that had a trial not been certain, then the lynching might have been justified. Southern papers did not disagree on this point. The *Atlanta Herald* forcefully repudiated lynch law, but added, "except when the courts are known to be corrupt or venal."[38]

Unanimous Public Support

When horrible crimes occurred, exciting public opinion in places without effective courts, many believed popular sovereignty gave mobs the right to override jailers and sheriffs. In 1887, California historian Hubert Howe Bancroft articulated this idea most clearly in a book entitled *Popular Tribunals*. When misbehavior outraged a community, Bancroft explained, citizens could and should rise up "in their sovereign privilege" to smite the malefactors. Factional violence, carried out to advance some narrow interest, differed from popular violence widely supported by the community. A mob that genuinely represented most people, according to Bancroft, was no mob at all but the People. The People made the law, and nothing they could do contradicted their own law. A mob, by contrast, was "*mobile vulgus,*" a riotous faction acting against the common good.[39]

Many journalists subscribed to Bancroft's popular sovereignty theory. When an Abilene, Kansas, crowd seized a man identified only as Elsizer from jail and hanged him for murder, the *New York Times* observed that "there

is something to be said in extenuation of the people's art." The *Times* reviewed Abilene's turbulent history of murder and violence, unleashed every
time the full tide of Texas cowboys rolled through town. The *Times* thought
such violence would lead any reasonable person to ask why the people did
not rise en masse and thrust out the evildoers. The only reason they did not,
according to the *Times,* was that the criminals vastly outnumbered the non-
criminals.[40] Good people certainly had the right to rise up—when crime was
outrageous, criminals thwarted justice, and the (good) people unanimously
favored extralegal action.

To be legitimate, journalists insisted that support for extralegal violence
be nearly unanimous. Judging community support was complicated by the
fact that officials often jailed criminals in county seats, away from crime
scenes. Thus, lynch mobs from where the crime occurred sometimes represented united communities, but not the same communities where the lynching occurred. In 1876 the *Times* noted that "strangers to the people of the
town and even to the sheriff" filled the streets at the time of the mobbing.[41]
Press accounts sometimes described invading mobs fending off curious or
hostile local crowds. In one town the locals nearly thwarted a lynching by
ramming a fire engine into the mob. The crowd hastily bashed in the head of
their prisoner with a sledgehammer.[42]

Mobs often brought sledgehammers and other tools to lynchings, just in
case authorities refused to unlock the doors. When newspapers reported that
officers offered only limp resistance when confronted by a mob, this provided
some implicit testimony to the community's determination to lynch. Heroic
and determined sheriffs and jailers unable to resist lynch mobs better proved
the power of popular sovereignty. In the face of enraged citizens, officers
seemed so overwhelmed, so often, that stories of their brave but futile resistance seemed further evidence that the people could not be thwarted. This
was the real meaning of officers' failed resistance. And newspapers sometimes
did offer stories of impressive determination and bravery on the part of officers confronting mobs. In 1888, Birmingham, Alabama, Sheriff Joseph S.
Smith organized forty armed guards to resist a mob of two thousand. When
the mob approached his jail, the young sheriff called on the crowd to stop.
The would-be lynchers surged ahead anyway and Smith ordered his men to
fire directly into their approaching fellow citizens. They did and then fired a
second fusillade. Eleven fell dead and the crowd seemed stunned for a moment, amazed that their own sheriff would fire on them.[43] In Pennsylvania,
one stubborn detective tried to fend off a mob with his pistol. When that did
not work, and the crowd put its noose around his prisoner's neck, the detective wrapped the rope around his own arm only to be jerked off his feet when
the crowd drew the rope up.[44] Sheriffs sometimes boldly confronted mobs at

the jail door or hid prisoners, moving them to more secure jails. Some sheriffs spent days in cat-and-mouse games with lynchers, maneuvering prisoners from one refuge to another in apparently sincere attempts to thwart lynchers. Others seemed merely to go through the motions. One officer declared he would fight to the death, only to have a lyncher coolly reach into his pocket, extract the keys, and say "No you won't."[45]

In determining a mob's representativeness, size mattered. Sometimes reporters counted only ten or twenty lynchers, but they often expressed awe at the "immense" size of the crowd. Even in the 1870s, some crowds sometimes reached proportions that might be called spectacular. In 1872, newspapers reported that three thousand showed up for a lynching in little Celina, Ohio, which had a population of less than nine hundred.[46] In New Jersey, "every" able bodied man in the vicinity turned out when a nineteen-year-old white girl accused Sam Johnson, a black man, of rape. When officers arrested Johnson, they could hardly get him to jail for the crowd that surged around them, attempting to wrest their prisoner away. Officers jailed Johnson, but the mob broke him out and hanged him.[47] Perhaps three thousand people did not really fill the streets of little Celina; perhaps not quite "every" able bodied man hanged Johnson. The reality does not matter so much as the fact that the newspapers had incorporated the idea of lynching as spectacular displays of popular sovereignty into their reporting and into readers' consciousness. And enough people lynched Johnson to make the community stolidly resistant to inquiring New York reporters and even to their own courts.[48]

There were times when the press said that public sentiment did not support crowd violence. In fact, through the 1870s and 1880s, the *New York Times* found public support "unanimous" only 15 percent of the time.[49] In January 1886, newspapers reported that a Louisiana black man named Joe Flowers had killed a white man in self-defense after being attacked. The dead man's friends found Flowers, seized him near Ruston, and made plans to hang him only to see their plans thwarted when Flowers escaped, running for the local sheriff. The sheriff jailed him to save him from the lynch mob. When a mob tried to break Flowers out of jail, the sheriff released him, not to the mob, but out a backdoor. The *Memphis Appeal* sided with the sheriff because "much feeling exists among all classes of citizens against the mob."[50] This last sentence came at the bottom of the article, the reporter's final judgment, giving the impression, at least, that in this instance the local community determined the mob's lack of legitimacy.

Newspapers saw the participation of leading citizens as another sign that a lynching enjoyed unified public support, just as Hubert Howe Bancroft used class to measure mob legitimacy in his book, *Popular Tribunals.* A violent crowd composed of respectable, intelligent people deserved more respect than some "tumultuous rabble" or "movable common people."[51] This idea was not invulnerable to ridicule. After West Virginia citizens hanged the alleged murderer of a little girl, the *New York Times* headlined its story, "HOW THE DEVOUT AND RESPECTABLE CITIZENS OF MARTINS-BURG, W.VA. SHOWED THEIR RESPECT FOR THE LAW."[52]

Newspapers thought that black participation in lynchings was crucial evidence of wide public support. In the 1870s, the *New York Times* reported nine incidents where blacks either actively joined white lynchers or cheered from the sidelines. Perhaps this alleged black participation in lynch mobs helped convince Ida B. Wells to see lynching as reasonable through the 1870s and 1880s. The *Charleston (South Carolina) News and Courier* claimed that black members of one lynch mob wanted to burn alive three black men accused of murder. Their white colleagues balked, insisting on hanging the trio instead.[53] The *Daily Memphis Avalanche* closed its account of the extralegal hanging of Emmet Key and Nat Forbes with the line that "both white and black are implicated in the lynching."[54] When a crowd hanged a black man named John Gillespie for the murder of a white woman, Mrs. Thomas Gray, the newspaper claimed that "leading negroes assisted in the lynching."[55] In 1886, the *Memphis Daily Appeal* assessed public sentiment, "among the whites, and blacks as well," to show universal support for lynching a black man accused of bludgeoning to death an aged white man in Arkansas.[56] In 1886, one Memphis paper thought the "most noticeable feature about the lynching" was that large numbers of blacks joined in the mobbing or "boldly indorsed it."[57] Stories of a labor war in Arkansas included reports that "several colored men" joined the posse whites organized to put down an uprising among black laborers.[58] Perhaps blacks really did willingly participate, or whites forced them to do so, or maybe they did not play any role. The point is that journalists felt it necessary to say blacks joined lynching parties, suggesting that the lynchings would not have been legitimate had all the rioters been white.

In the Gilded Age leading newspapers thought lynching could be legitimate, if it was not racially motivated. In this period before the meaning of lynching had been racialized, even the Southern press, at least the large urban papers, agreed that a crowd of racist whites killing a black person was not a legitimate lynching because it suggested a divided rather than a united community. The *Memphis Daily Appeal* scoffed at reports that a Texas detective and deputy sheriff had rightly shot and killed three black persons. "The remarkable feature of the tragedy is that neither of the officers received a scratch," the *Appeal* noted, though they claimed to have killed the three blacks in a gun battle. The *Appeal* revealed to its readers that "a new and horrible theory" had emerged, suggesting that the killings were entirely unprovoked.

Wells made no mention of this incident in her diary, and the *Chicago Tribune* did not count it as a "lynching" for that year. While some twentieth-century lynching opponents argued that police violence should be included in lynching counts, few in the nineteenth century thought so.[59] Similarly illegitimate killings occurred elsewhere as well. In Tennessee, law enforcement officers organized a posse that chased and killed two alleged burglars. When the posse examined the two white men's bodies, they found not a pair of ruffians but fashionably dressed gentlemen wearing valuable jewelry. They just did not look like criminals. The *Appeal* reported that no one could identify the two dead men as the burglars, and "the impression is gaining ground that undue haste was exercised by the officers."[60]

In the 1870s, the newspapers' standard narrative dictated that a lynching preceded by a horrible, shocking crime that infuriated the neighborhood when no court functioned effectively could be legitimate if the public universally supported it. In the 1870s even Easterners were well versed in the on-going process of moving west. Newspapers and other publications taught them that migrants traveling in territories where courts had yet to be established sometimes had to punish criminals on the spot. Although western migration validated the concept, journalists applied the formula to all geographic regions. Journalists thought Southerners always resorted to crowd violence more often than other parts of the country, but anyone reading the newspapers through the 1870s would have been struck by the large number of lynchings carried out in Western and Northern states. Many of the persons lynched were white, as were many of the lynchers. The Ku Klux Klan rode all through the period, but racial violence did not define what newspapers called lynching. In the 1870s, a newspaper reader simply could not think all lynchings occurred in the South or that all lynchings involved the killing of a black person by white persons. In fact, in several years there were more incidents journalists chose to label lynchings outside the South than inside. And more whites than blacks died at the hands of lynch mobs—according to the press.

BLACK RESPONSE

Black protest against white racial violence ultimately redefined the meaning of lynching. At first, black journalists protested racial violence as a continuation of Ku Klux Klan violence, *vigilance* rather than *lynching*. In 1874, a black newspaper called the *Louisianian* warned against "the cruelties and folly of the White Leagues" that continued the violence of the Ku Klux Klan. According to the *Louisianian*, lawless whites filled the ranks of the White League, which had compiled a record of "utter lawlessness, of murder and outrage in the in-terior parishes of Louisiana."[61] In Mississippi white mobs attacked and broke up black political meetings. It is impossible to know how many politically ac-tive blacks perished in these attacks.[62] In 1874, the Texas governor reported the murder of seven black men near Bryan, four black men in Wharton County, and nine prisoners confined in the Bolton County jail. Not men-tioned was another "score or more" of instances where mobs broke into or burned jails. In addition, the governor said, "There has been a pretty liberal killing of Mexicans in our southwestern counties." The governor saw this vi-olence as part of a trend that began before the Civil War, when courts "com-menced to cede their functions to irresponsible mobs."[63] In 1880 the *People's Advocate* published an article that characterized white violence, "midnight raids," assassinations, murders, carried out by "the Ku Klux Klans, Rifle Clubs, White Liner and Regulators," as responsible for whites' political suc-cess. The so-called Solid South came from the Ku Klux Klan, the *People's Ad-vocate* alleged.[64] The *People's Advocate* complained of white "outrages," the same language used in Reconstruction. So did Congressional investigators. "The magnanimity of this Government toward the Southern traitors is bearing its fruits," one black Pennsylvania editor wrote bitterly after reporting on Con-gressional testimony that sounded the same as similar evidence collected in the 1870s or the 1860s.[65] As late as 1881 the *People's Advocate* still decried "hor-rible outrages," "blood-thirsty mobs," but not lynchings.[66]

While the *People's Advocate* did not like the word lynching, T. Thomas For-tune may have used it from the beginning of his career. In the earliest sur-viving issues of Fortune's paper, the *New York Globe,* he blasted Southern "lynch-law."[67] In January 1883, Fortune applauded the *New York Evening Post* for its criticism of white Southerners' tendency toward homicide. The *Post* complained that in the South, business disputes too often turned murderous. Fortune's *Globe* agreed, but insisted the *Post* did not go far enough in con-demning the South. "There is another class of southern homicides," For-tune's *Globe* declared, "homicides not growing from any business disputes, but homicides actuated simply by the inborn depravity and insolence of a [poor] class of southern whites." These homicides, Fortune thought, should be called *lynchings.*[68]

Lynchings, Fortune decided, justified violent resistance. On March 17, 1883, Fortune predicted that white lynchers would not always find Southern blacks servile or acquiescent. A few months later, Fortune urged blacks to fight vi-olence with violence, holding that whites themselves had created the logic of black violent resistance to oppression. The Supreme Court had decided the federal government had no role in protecting citizens' rights. The states ac-tively supported racial violence. Fortune fervently advocated constitutionalism, but no constitutional avenues were left open. Lynchers, he declared, should be lynched.[69]

Though closely allied with Booker T. Washington, Fortune agitated for revolution. Fortune came too early to leave filmed images of himself appealing to his audiences, and text alone can be misleading. When Wells met Fortune she expected a "strong, sensible, brainy man" and instead found him a "dude," with long hair and spectacles.[70] Dude or not, Fortune had a reputation as a powerful orator; the surviving texts of his speeches suggest that, even with his curling hair and glasses, he knew how to sway an audience. In one speech, Fortune derided "the fashion to hoot" racial questions out of Northern political discussion, allowing the country to "drift" back into antebellum states' rights doctrines. This "drift" contradicted the Constitution, Fortune declared. "I affirm it to-night," he said, "that the citizen of the United States is greater than the citizen of the state; that the laws of the United States are more sovereign than the laws of the states." Fortune went on to further link his call to the nation's organic law. "I appeal to the Constitution of the United States," he declared, before quoting the Fourteenth Amendment in ringing words that dared his audience or anyone else to suggest that the Constitution did not empower Congress to protect American citizens. Having established the legitimacy of his call for black rights, Fortune said—he must have shouted—"Let us agitate! *agitate!* AGITATE!" Fortune called for "Liberty! Fraternity! Equality!" This was revolutionary language because he understood that if ordinary black Americans mobilized themselves for their constitutional rights, the effect would be revolutionary.[71]

As early as the 1870s, black newspaper editors had urged that lynchers be met with violent resistance, pointing out that neither the federal government nor the state governments could be counted on to resist whites' violence. In 1878, the *Topeka (Kansas) Colored Citizen* exhorted its readers to burn the homes of offending whites surreptitiously rather than appeal to the law for help. "The brutes" should be burned while "sleeping with their families around them dreaming of the terror they have scattered among the colored people."[72] A year later the same paper declared, "We believe in papers that will tell our people to stand up like men. . . . We have been poor whining beggers for protection, long enough."[73] Such militancy circulated widely among black newspaper editors at the end of the 1870s. In 1879, the *Colored Citizen* observed that only two or three colored papers were not militant enough.[74]

While the *New York Times* worried that continued reports of white Southerners' criminality might convince voters that the Republican party's Reconstruction program had failed, Fortune fretted that a decline in newspaper

reports of white violence might fool readers into thinking that Southern violence was a thing of the past. Fortune had a ready answer for those among
his critics who insisted that whites were not so violent as he claimed. Any list
of lynchings, Fortune lectured the Boston Herald from the pages of his own
newspaper, disproved suggestions that lawlessness was a thing of the past in
the white South. Fortune suspected that because the owners of the Herald had
invested in Southern enterprises, they thought it "good policy to make it appear that 'all is quiet on the Potomac.'"[75] In 1885, Fortune stoutly denied reports that race relations had become "friendly." He complained that
Southern newspapers and rigged Southern courts had fooled Northern
newspapers into believing that blacks committed more crimes than whites.[76]

Fortune's crusade against lynching ran into resistance from within the
black community. It is very likely that most black Americans did not agree
with Fortune. Many blacks saw the real solution for white racism in self-improvement. Fortune completely agreed that Southern blacks needed to work
harder, educate themselves, and acquire property.[77] After the Civil War,
blacks had not been prepared to take advantage of their new liberty, he conceded. "Social and civil disabilities of the race" had to be overcome.[78] Fortune
nonetheless chided those who thought education and wealth were somehow
the "panacea" for deflecting white racist violence.[79] Fortune ran into his
most intransigent opposition from those who had achieved middle-class status. They pursued the politics of respectability, hoping to win deference from
white America.[80] In 1894 one black political leader declared that "a rep-
utable or respectable negro has never been lynched, and never will be. Only
outlaws have suffered such a fate. It was right and just that they should be
outlawed for their crimes."[81] Fortune's benefactor and ally, Booker T. Washington, promoted self-improvement as the only protection from white lynch
mobs. The politics of respectability runs as a theme through the works of
many black memoirists. Class divisions within the black community meant
that many African Americans had little trouble accepting the white argument that only truly guilty criminals need fear lynch mobs. These middle-
class folk signed petitions for laws against lynching and opposed lynching,
but they knew that "Decent and intelligent coloured people," "self-respect-
ing Negroes," not only had little to fear from lynchers, but also should not
even have to associate with the kind of people likely to be lynched.[82] The author of Heir of Slaves, William Pickens, pictured himself as successful through
self-discipline. "From early boyhood I was laughed at among my fellows
for . . . totally abstaining from strong drink and tobacco."[83] Another writer
remembers "enter[ing] the school-room for the development of my race."[84]
Another author writes that "I know my people would have been better off
had they let the white man's beer and liquor alone. My people remind me of

the monkey in this respect; they don't know when to stop."[85] "White people," another memoirist explained, are not entirely to blame for their racial violence. "Rowdy Negroes . . . full of bad liquor," he wrote, caused the trouble.[86] Much of this reflects class divisions that split the black community just as surely as race split American society. Middle-class African Americans thought themselves well above likely targets of lynch mobs.

Whether the views of black middle-class memoirists fairly represented the attitudes of the mass of black Southerners is a nice academic question. In general, they certainly did not, but on this point it is worth noting that black leaders like T. Thomas Fortune believed such attitudes pervasive and worried that overcoming them would be no easy task. In January 1884, Fortune described Mississippi blacks as "browbeaten, intimidated."[87] A year later, Fortune published a letter from J. Gordon Street criticizing North Carolina blacks as "miserable cowards" who run like dogs. After a local white bully had jostled two black professors, a mob formed and one of the professors landed in jail. Many African Americans saw what happened, but did not dare intervene. A majority fled. "Shame on them!" Street exclaimed.[88]

In the 1870s, even Northern newspapers like the New York Times saw lynching as sometimes justifiable. Militant African Americans resisted the logic of this argument, but even among blacks this argument made slight headway.

By the 1880s, whites had convinced not only themselves but also many blacks that truly horrific crimes that excited or infuriated the public might, in some cases, justify lynching. One crucial variable was the state of the criminal justice system. Ineffective or "lax" courts made it more reasonable for a united population to rise up and hang without trial suspected criminals. This formula allowed neighborhoods and communities to imagine that they had the right, as popular sovereigns, as the ultimate makers of law, to police their courts, watching for signs of softness toward criminals.

Northern newspapers, and Southern newspapers as well, looked for signs of racial division. Black participation in a lynching signaled a truly united population, one of the elements in a legitimate lynching. When lynching violence sparked "a war of the races," it lost its legitimacy.

Nonetheless, the press had done a good job of establishing a model for lynching that allowed local people to assess the success of their courts in dealing with the criminal element. Many black journalists failed to refute the model. When white Southerners decided that the courts could not effectively deal with black criminals, they did not deviate dramatically from the established American paradigm for mob violence.

CHAPTER SIX

"Threadbare Lies"
MAKING LYNCHING RACIAL

On March 18, 1886, Ida B. Wells wrote in her diary that "the daily papers bring notice this morning that 13 colored men were shot down in cold blood yesterday." The killings took place in Carrollton, Mississippi.[1] Despite her wide reading, and despite her later fame as a fighter against lynching, this was Wells's first comment on racial violence in her diary for 1886. Throughout the year, she wrote about only two episodes of whites' racial violence.

Wells was working as a Memphis schoolteacher when she noticed the Carrollton massacre, six years before she became an international leader in the fight against racial violence. Bored with teaching, she diligently pursued her craft as a writer, outlining a novel, preparing articles for religious journals, corresponding with editors, and reading avidly. She read black newspapers, including the *Indianapolis Freeman* and the *Washington Bee,* and she subscribed to T. Thomas Fortune's *New York Freeman* (successor to the *New York Globe*.) She also read the "home papers," the Memphis dailies, continuing her subscriptions even when journeying to California in the summer of 1886.

Wells got her information about Carrollton from the *Memphis Daily Appeal* and its rival, the *Daily Memphis Avalanche.* When assessing the legitimacy of the Carrollton killings, both papers tested them against standards journalists had been following for years in judging the legitimacy of crowd violence. The story Wells read described the killings as "a terrible tragedy" and explained that fifty men rode into the Mississippi town of Carrollton, invaded the courthouse, and shot thirteen black men inside. This initial report described the affair as a feud between small numbers of black and white citizens. The white newspaper editors in Memphis did not think the affair qualified as a lynching. No horrid crime had aroused the community and, for that reason, the killers seemed cold blooded rather than driven by their excited outrage over some shocking crime. According to the reports reaching Memphis from Mississippi, the killings "grew out of the attempted assassination of James Liddell, a prominent citizen, who was shot and seriously wounded by these negroes several weeks since." By claiming that "these negroes" shot Liddell, the story made it sound as if all thirteen of the dead had been involved in the attempt to kill Liddell.[2] Wells did not question this account: "It was only because they had attempted to assassinate a white man (and for just cause I suppose)."[3] Wells called the Carrollton murders, aptly, a "massacre." In the privacy of her diary, she wailed, "O, God when will these massacres cease."[4]

On another key point the Carrollton killings failed to qualify as lynchings. For at least fifteen years major newspapers had been rehearsing the notion that the persons lynched had to be truly guilty for the killers to have any claim to legitimacy. In Carrollton, only one of the thirteen killed had, in fact, even been accused of committing any crime. Twelve of the dead had been spectators at a trial, shot only because they happened to be present when whites stormed the building. On March 19, the *Appeal* and *Avalanche* both admitted that "a few innocent colored people were drawn into [the] fuss."[5] This incident of racial violence, which attracted Wells's attention when many others did not, did not fit whites' formula for justified popular violence. What happened in Carrollton was not legitimate according to the standards promulgated by whites themselves. Wells pioneered no new ground when she condemned Carrollton.

While Wells remained true to the standard formula, some whites tried to figure out ways to excuse what happened in Carrollton. By March 19, the *Avalanche* sounded more defensive than the *Appeal*. The *Avalanche* headline over its story admitting that innocent people had died charged that the "Negroes Incited to Riot by Vicious Leaders of their Own Race" while the *Appeal* said simply, "THE CARROLLTON HORROR: ADDITIONAL DETAILS OF THE MISSISSIPPI TRAGEDY." The article both papers ran claimed that the trouble started with an impudent African American named Ed Brown, who had smeared and poured molasses on Robert Moore, friend of J. M. Liddell, Jr., of Greenwood. After Liddell intervened to chastise Brown, Brown armed himself and recruited his neighbors to ambush Liddell. In the resulting shootout, Liddell and Brown each shot each other, though neither was fatally injured. Whites took Brown before a magistrate who bound him over for trial. The white papers accused Brown of continuing his insulting and "impudent" behavior even while on bail, awaiting trial. Brown brought charges against Liddell, a fact that the papers reported without comment but that many white readers probably thought constituted still more intolerable black "impudence."

Even defenders of the Carrollton killers could not call what happened a "lynching." Only once, in a headline, did the Memphis papers use that word to describe the Carrollton killings.[6] The number killed could not have been determinative; when Texas Confederates hanged forty-four in 1862, no one called it a "massacre." That event became the "Great Hanging" and a "lynching."[7] Like Wells, the *Appeal* called the Carrollton killings "a massacre" and reported that the shootings paralyzed Carrollton blacks with fear, a fact designed to evoke some sympathy for the plight of the blacks. Later the *Appeal* supplied "revolting details" drawn from a St. Louis paper that put the blame even more squarely on Carrollton whites. In this account, Liddell interfered in a trivial altercation between Brown and Moore, and the white killers acted without provocation. "It is alleged," the *Globe-Democrat* said, "that one of the prisoners began firing when the mob entered the room, but it is hardly reasonable to suppose that men arraigned for trial were permitted to retain their weapons. . . ." The paper went on to say that the victims met their fate unarmed, "without the least chance of self-protection."[8]

The *Avalanche* tacked in a different direction. That paper relied on James K. Vardaman, later famous as a demagogic Mississippi governor and lynch law proponent, for its most detailed information. While the *Appeal* thought the Carrollton killers had plotted mass murder, Vardaman saw this as a case where black criminality had infuriated the attacking whites. In other words, he labored mightily to wrestle the bloody Carrollton affair into the journalistic conventions of a legitimate lynching. It was tough work and required Vardaman to argue that the "recent collision" did not flow from "any wanton and reckless spirit" on the part of whites. So many "exciting and exasperating" insults came from Carrollton blacks that the "best [white] men" in town came to believe that "terrible as the issue was, the necessity to meet it by short, sharp, and decisive action was imperative."[9] Based on Vardaman's account, the *Avalanche* editor concluded that "the negroes were at first greatly in the wrong."[10] Further, unlike the *Appeal,* the *Avalanche* never doubted that Brown fired on the whites as they crowded into the courtroom.

Vardaman, in other words, argued that under the terms of the formula, whites acted legitimately in killing the thirteen blacks. A "gang of negroes" had been insulting white persons, elbowing them off the pavement, defying the mayor. Such misconduct enraged whites so much that they could not fail to act. In the 1870s, major newspapers established the idea that gross criminality could propel a community to violence. Vardaman racialized the formula. Black criminality, he said, enraged whites. It was the old idea, one largely accepted by Northerners, and even by many blacks, but with a new, more racial slant, than the original iteration. Soon Southern whites fashioned a rhetoric arguing that a black tendency to rape justified lynching.

Vardaman insisted on the legitimacy of the Carrollton massacre even though no black person supported it. This was an important point, one that shows that while Vardaman used the old formula in some ways, he dramatically altered it by racializing it. Through the 1870s, whites viewed black support for lynching as one measure of its legitimacy. Blacks clearly did not support the Carrollton massacre. Indeed, the *Memphis Appeal* published resolutions passed at a meeting of "colored" Memphis ministers condemning the "savage butchery" of "innocent and unoffending men." Even in the face of such evidence of white racism and violence, the ministers did not challenge the formula justifying crowd violence, acknowledging that "under strong provocation and amid great excitement caused by some shocking crime" a community might be provoked to lynch some terrible criminal. This, they emphasized, was not such a situation. The ministers accused the Carrollton killers of cold-blooded murder.[11] The killing of randomly chosen blacks, men accused of no crime, was not right and not a lynching.

While Vardaman became the strongest spokesman on behalf of the white killers, T. Thomas Fortune emerged as the most ardent black voice against the massacre. He ran stories about the "MISSISSIPPI CUT-THROATS" in Carrollton until April 17. Carroll County whites, Fortune alleged, had a history of mobbing and shooting black men and women. "The whole thing was a base, dastardly and cowardly murder," he wrote. Fortune called on Mississippi blacks to assert themselves. "Colored men of Mississippi," he demanded, "are you cowards? Are you going to allow this butchery to go on unnoticed?"[12] Fortune did not think the Carrollton slaughter represented anything new at all. At least some of his readers agreed. One wrote to say that it was the same old story, "always the same, only more and more horrible and outrageous."[13]

The Carrollton massacre was the first act of racial violence Wells discussed in her Memphis diary. The silence seems strange, especially because Wells used her diary to try out ideas for articles and save information for later use. In 1886, the year covered by her extant diary, the press reported many other violent episodes before March 18. The *Chicago Tribune* counted twenty-eight lynchings between January 1 and March 17. The Memphis papers did not report all of these, but they did publish stories on fourteen, plus another three the *Tribune* missed. The Carrollton massacre undoubtedly attracted Wells's attention because of the large number killed. In one afternoon, Carrollton whites killed nearly as many blacks as the total the Memphis papers had reported lynched since January. But there had been earlier massacres, some with even larger body counts.[14]

If the Carrollton massacre had been a lynching—one or two guilty criminals hanged by a community infuriated by real crime—it is unlikely Wells would have taken notice. As a massacre, it arrested her attention because it seemed more wanton, more cold-blooded, than the lynchings that preceded it. Though the earliest reports implicated the dead in a murder conspiracy, Wells could easily see that the killings resulted from a feud rather than any real assertion of popular justice. The killers were not "infuriated" or "excited" or "outraged." They calculated the murders before carrying them out.

After Carrollton, Wells's 1886 diary is silent on racial violence until September. On September 4, Wells wrote that she had penned "a dynamitic article . . . almost advising murder!" She did so after learning that Jackson, Tennessee, whites had stripped a black woman naked and hanged her, riddling her body with bullets. The whites had accused the woman of poisoning a white woman. "The only evidence being that the stomach of the dead woman contained arsenic & a box of 'Rough on Rats' was found in this woman's house."[15]

Wells did not name the woman killed in Tennessee, but the *Appeal* reported on August 19 that Jackson whites had killed Eliza Woods for poisoning Mrs. J. P. Wooten. Unlike the Carrollton massacre, in this case "Great excitement prevailed." This was not a wanton, cold-blooded act. "It was," journalists said, "impossible to reason with the infuriated mob at the jail." The *Appeal*'s account came from the paper's stringer in Jackson. "It is due our fair city to say that everything in reason was done to prevent the lynching, but the masses were fully determined to kill a black female devil." The Jackson writer trotted out all the signs journalists usually relied on to justify lynchings, including the claim that many local blacks supported the act.[16]

In both Carrollton and Jackson, the innocence of the persons killed excited Wells's sympathy. In neither instance did she go outside the formula that deemed lynching legitimate. In Carrollton, the standard excuses did not fit, despite Vardaman's efforts to argue otherwise. The Eliza Woods killing did not obviously violate the standards for a legitimate lynching. In all likelihood, the death of a woman attracted Wells's sympathy, leading her to scrutinize skeptically the evidence against Woods. But none of this required new thinking. Routine newspaper writing allowed for innocents lynched in error; white newspaper readers had long been trained to sympathize with innocent persons lynched by mistake. Newspapers' stories about innocent people erroneously lynched were a mainstay of mid-nineteenth-century journalism. The most compelling evidence that these cases had little impact on Wells's thinking comes from Wells herself. Wells never claimed that anything before 1892 contributed to her change of heart. In her autobiography, Wells writes that not until the 1892 lynching of three friends did she change her thinking about whites' racial violence.

Wells's change of heart came when a Memphis mob killed Thomas Moss, Calvin McDowell, and Henry Stewart. The Memphis papers still relied on the old narrative, but Wells thought it misused in this case. Moss had saved his money and started a little grocery in a district already served by a white man's grocery. The white press conceded that the killings resulted from an economic rivalry between competing grocers. The white grocer, W. T. Barrett, threatened Moss. Hearing that whites threatened to mob their grocery, Moss, McDowell, and Stewart organized an armed defense. When the armed guards shot three white intruders, the local papers ran sensational headlines accusing Moss of running "a low dive." The police arrested and jailed many blacks, including Moss, McDowell, and Stewart. A mob "was admitted to the jail, which was a modern Bastille," Wells wrote. The crowd took the three men to the city limits and shot them to death.[17]

Having admitted that Barrett instigated the trouble, Memphis journalists, in stories reprinted around the nation, nonetheless characterized Moss, McDowell, and Stewart as "bad niggers," "recognized as such by respectable people of both races."[18] This lie did not prevent inquiries from flooding into Memphis from journalists all over America and Europe. Newspapers headlined the news that Memphis blacks seemed on the verge of retaliation. The funeral home displayed the bodies in open caskets, so that mourners could see how they had been mutilated. Hundreds turned out for the services. White journalists worried that the "unthinking and dangerous classes" among blacks were "ready for bloody vengeance."[19]

Wells knew that none of the lynched men was a "bad nigger." She was godmother to Moss's daughter. "He and his wife," Wells wrote, "were the best friends I had in town." Wells began to concentrate her energies on whites' racial violence, disparaging arguments that a black tendency to rape justified violence. No one had accused Moss, McDowell, or Stewart of rape. Their real crime, Wells said, was economic success. Wells fashioned a rhetoric attacking whites' rape rhetoric that became the centerpiece of her campaign against lynching. Rather than arguing that even guilty people deserve a fair trial, Wells insisted on the innocence of lynchers' victims.[20]

Wells changed her mind about the nature of lynching at the same time as many blacks made a similar shift in their thinking. In the 1870s and 1880s, whites occasionally feared that local blacks would retaliate for racially motivated lynchings.[21] In 1883, Birmingham blacks deeply resented the lynching of Louis Houston, accused of attempted rape. "The colored people," the *Birmingham Iron Age* reported, "seeming to believe the victim of the lynchers was innocent, were indignant, and protested, though among themselves, against the swift work of the mob." The *Iron Age* stressed that black protest occurred only "among themselves" and attempted to calm things down by asserting that no evidence existed that blacks intended to molest anyone in Birmingham. Nonetheless, whites rioted and authorities called on the Alabama militia to maintain order.[22]

If press accounts can be trusted, black outrage at whites' violence escalated around 1891. On June 14, the *New York Times* noted that after a lynching in Bristol, Tennessee, "there is intense feeling to-night among the colored people, though," the *Times* hastily added, "some of them openly approve the course of the mob."[23] In August, Kentucky lynchers broke into a jail and hanged a black prisoner inside, ignoring two jailed white men charged with murder. This blatant prejudice in the selection of lynching victims enraged local blacks. Mysterious fires erupted and black men frightened whites by clustering on street corners, talking in low, angry tones.[24] Whites voiced similar fears after lynchings in Virginia and Texas.[25]

Black protest against white mobs centered on mobs' racial prejudice rather than on a blanket condemnation of mob attacks. Western whites continued to lynch Mexicans with little notice from Wells or other black protesters.[26] Nor did lynchings of Italians attract Wells' attention. In what one historian has called "the Worst Lynching in America," a New Orleans mob killed eleven Italian-Americans jailed for the assassination of the police chief. Newspapers approved and a grand jury justified the mob action as well. Henry Cabot Lodge pointed to these New Orleans lynchings as proof that America needed more restrictive immigration laws to keep out people likely to be lynched.[27] With America increasingly aroused to the problem of racial violence directed toward blacks, this evidence of a generalized impulse toward extralegal violence seemed almost beside the point.

Nor did Wells question the right of mobs to kill the guilty. She merely doubted that blacks were as invariably guilty as whites claimed. She did not so much question the old lynching formula as challenge Vardaman's racialized version. Shortly after Moss, McDowell, and Stewart died, Wells traveled to Tunica County, Mississippi, just south of Memphis, where the Associated Press had reported that the rape of a seven-year-old child had prompted a lynching. In Tunica County and elsewhere, Wells found such claims to be bogus.[28] After these research trips, Wells published an editorial entitled "Eight Men Lynched" in her own newspaper, the *Free Speech,* on May 21, 1892. She pointed out that eight black men had been lynched by whites in Arkansas, Alabama, Louisiana, and Georgia since the last issue of *Free Speech* had been published. In this editorial, Wells denounced the justification for lynching most favored by whites, that black men raped white women, as an "old threadbare lie" that "nobody in this section of the country believes."[29] This article so enraged Memphis whites that it forced Wells into exile. She took a job as a writer for T. Thomas Fortune's newspaper, the *New York Age*. Later in the same year she wrote her first pamphlet, *Southern Horrors: Lynch Law in all its Phases*, published by the *New York Age*, selling it for fifteen cents a copy. *Southern Horrors* drew on her May 21 editorial and on articles she had published in the *New York Age*, even repeating her "old threadbare lie" line. She cited specific cases to prove that "there are white women in the South who love the Afro-American's company even as there are white men notorious for their preference for Afro-American women."[30]

CHANGING PERCEPTIONS

Near the end of her life, Wells argued that lynching permanently declined after 1893 in response to her decision to embarrass white Americans by taking her message to England. Wells sailed for England on April 5, 1893, where she stayed for a year, writing as a correspondent for the *Chicago Inter-Ocean*.

Just a few months before her departure, white Texans burned Henry Smith. The Southern newspaper reports hit the familiar notes. Smith, "a burly negro," had committed a particularly heinous crime by raping and murdering a four-year-old child, "the most atrocious murder and outrage in Texas history." Thousands turned out to torture and kill Smith, thrusting red-hot irons against his body and down his throat. The mob then burned him, with the crowd cheering his every contortion.[31] This widely reported savagery primed Wells' English audiences for her message. The *New York Times*'s London correspondent grumbled that "it would be difficult to exaggerate the evil mischief this steady stream of low sensationalism or worse is working among all classes of English readers."[32]

Wells's trip attracted considerable press attention in England, which in turn sparked a defensive reaction from the white press in America. In April 1894, the *New York Times*'s London correspondent noticed Wells, predicting that "this young woman, if she keeps her head, may create a great furor in these islands." The correspondent intended no compliment. Salacious revelations, he explained, excited English "busybodies."[33]

In the United States, some blacks denounced Wells's campaign as well.[34] But most of the criticism Wells received came from whites. As she toured Europe, the *New York Times* dogged her journey, criticizing her message, questioning her motives, and challenging her integrity.[35] The governor of Alabama responded to British antilynchers, and the *Times* headlined its story "LESSONS FOR BUSYBODIES." While the governor and the *Times* claimed little sympathy for lynching, "theoretically," they had even less for British "fanatics."[36] The *Times*'s London correspondent confidently reported that the governor's letter circulated widely in England, where it was well received by the "big majority of sensible Englishmen who resent the meddlesome antics of a little and noisy minority."[37]

Even before Wells sailed for England, Northern newspapers had begun to report more black deaths at the hands of lynchers. One possibility is that, at the same time as Wells went to England, whites actually began killing more blacks. This was, after all, the decade when whites worked most vigorously to oust blacks from suffrage, and whites had historically used violence to keep blacks from voting. More Southerners lived in towns and villages than ever before, not-quite-urban places where whites saw blacks as more threatening than in rural landscapes. Moreover, once blacks lost the right to vote, they retreated into positions more politically defenseless. The 1898 Wilmington, North Carolina, race riot came immediately after the Democrats had waged a successful white supremacy campaign. The foremost historian of disfranchisement cannot link racial violence to specific political developments, but suspects that, somehow, there is a connection.[38] When segregation began is a matter of scholarly debate, but some historians argue that whites imposed a new and stricter segregation regime in the 1890s. Even if segregation existed long before the 1890s, intensified black resistance might have provoked more white violence.[39]

Another theory holds that whites' style of violence changed in the 1890s. Some now argue that "spectacle lynchings" emerged from industrialization. In the 1870s and 1880s, business expanded as new technologies mass produced products and an expanded railway network allowed these new, cheaper products to reach a national market. National manufacturers began to replace the neighborhood craftsman as the primary producers of goods. This transformation changed the thinking of ordinary people. Lynching in a consumer culture differed from lynching in a neighborhood-based market, or so the theory goes. Proponents of this view point to the 1893 Henry Smith lynching in Texas. In fact, mob violence had always drawn big crowds. Newspapers reported lynchings in the 1870s with crowds of a thousand or more. In 1878, newspapers claimed three thousand persons turned out in Mount Vernon, Tennessee, for the extralegal hanging of Dan Harris, Jim Good, William Chambers, Jeff Hopkins, and Ed Warren, all accused of rape and murder. Perhaps this pales in comparison with the "surging mass of humanity 10,000 strong" the *New York Times* claimed watched Smith die in 1893. The Texas mob placed Smith on a carnival float, "in mockery of a king upon his throne." Ten thousand is more impressive than three thousand, but the change should not be described as a shift from surreptitious vigilantism to blatantly public rituals.[40]

Factors other than actual behavior may have swayed journalists' perceptions of mob violence. The *New York Times* once sought to limit lynching reports for fear of making their party's Reconstruction policies appear unsuccessful. That was in 1870.[41] After the Republicans won control of Congress and the presidency in 1888, they redoubled their efforts to pass stronger legislation to protect black citizens. They had new political reasons for telling voters just how violent white Southerners could be. With nothing but a Southern filibuster standing between Congressional Republicans and victory, the *New York Times* and the *Chicago Tribune* more vigorously reported mob violence in the South.[42]

While Republican politics probably influenced newspaper reporting, it may also be that the long campaign begun by Fortune and continued by Wells to influence white American journalism bore fruit. In the 1890s, this campaign energized black protest, a protest that attracted the attention of newspaper editors and, at the same time, launched a white backlash. In the 1890s, the *New York Times* presented mob violence as more racist and less justified than it had in the past. This was precisely what Fortune and Wells had been saying for years. More importantly, a leading Republican newspaper began a campaign to document lynchings. Few historians today accept the *Chicago Tribune*'s statistics as exactly accurate, yet the *Tribune* established the chronology. Racial lynching "began" in 1882, when the *Tribune* launched its statistical reporting.

The *Chicago Tribune* began publishing its annual compilation of lynchings ten years before Wells went to England. Editor and owner Joseph Medill made the *Tribune* strongly Republican and conservative. Medill hated socialists, "boodlers, bummers, and taxeaters." At the same time, Medill believed in popular democracy and insisted that the common man, properly educated and informed, would move society in the right direction.[43] Medill's belief that his paper should educate the masses to his way of thinking led him to publish an annual statistical review of life in America.

The *Tribune* began the endeavor that led to its famous annual compilation of lynchings out of a spirit of boosterism and civic patriotism combined with faith in social science. On January 1, 1875, just months after Medill took control, the *Tribune* announced that improvements in business required a new style of writing. This "new style" amounted to a phalanx of facts, numbers, and tables: what a later generation would call scientism. At first, the *Tribune* confined itself to reporting business statistics. Prepared by the *Tribune*'s commercial editor, Elias Colbert, the *Tribune*'s 1875 review of business statistics for 1874 launched a long-running tradition. By 1883 the paper boasted of having achieved new levels of truly objective science without "bombast or brag." The facts, Colbert declared, would speak for themselves.[44]

The *Tribune* soon went beyond business statistics to include counts of suicides, train wrecks, shipwrecks, embezzlements, murders, legal executions, and epidemics. In joining the annual review, lynchings came in as a subset of "hangings." The first tabulation, for 1882, included 86 incidents. Most of these incidents involved the lynchings of white persons. Even so, the *Tribune* included a larger percentage of blacks (44 percent) in its tabulation than did the *New York Times* in its news reporting.[45] Though the *Tribune*'s count is incomplete, because the paper tried to tabulate lynchings rather than choose those worthy of a news article, the *Tribune*'s count may come a bit closer to reality than the *New York Times*. Nevertheless, both papers thought most persons lynched before 1886 were white.[46]

This soon changed. In 1885, the *Tribune* reported ninety-seven whites lynched, seventy-eight "colored," and six "Chinamen." The next year, the *Tribune* found only sixty-two whites lynched and seventy-one blacks. The following year, 1887, more blacks were lynched than whites by a nearly two-to-one margin—forty-three to eighty.[47] By 1888, *Tribune* editors had begun pointing out that most lynchings occurred in the South. In 1890, the same year the *Tribune* endorsed the Lodge Bill or the "Force Bill," designed to punish Southern states for denying black citizens of their right to vote, the *Tribune*'s annual report on "Judge Lynch's Work" carried "How the Colored Man Has Suffered" as a sub-headline.[48]

Though motivated by social science, the *Tribune*'s editors employed less than rigorous methods. The *Tribune* never provided its readers with anything like a definition for lynching. It is not possible to know what criteria the editors used to exclude some events and include others. It is likely the editors simply never thought about the problem very much. It is also likely that black victims formed an increasingly large proportion of reports of Judge Lynch's victims because the *Tribune*'s editors, and the editors of other, contributing papers, unconsciously adapted to changes in understandings of what constituted a lynching. The *Tribune* relied on an exchange system where the *Tribune* swapped copies of its own paper for copies of smaller papers. If the papers that supplied the *Tribune* with its information called a homicide a lynching, then it became one in its tallies. Nor did the *Tribune* have any way of allowing for newspapers that chose not to report lynchings. And the *Tribune* added to the problems of its sources, failing to replicate the smaller papers' information accurately. Two sociologists who have traced the *Tribune* statistics back to the original newspapers found a daunting universe of error in the *Tribune* tabulations. The *Tribune* sometimes reported the same lynching twice, putting one victim in two different locations, or listed a victim by his real name and then again under his alias. The *Tribune* reported false rumors of lynchings as fact. In some cases attempted lynchings, in which the victim did not die, were reported as actual lynchings. The *Tribune* inconsistently reported killings by legally constituted posses, sometimes counting such killings as "lynchings" and sometimes not. In some cases legal executions became lynchings in the *Tribune's* columns.[49] The *Chicago Tribune's* annual lynching count ultimately only monitored a Northern white newspaper's *perception* of lynching at a particular point in time.

The *Tribune* revised its own count in 1895 when it printed a table that summarized its statistics for previous years. A comparison of the 1895 summary with the original reports reveals that the *Tribune* had silently "corrected" its earlier reporting, sometimes finding more lynchings than originally reported, sometimes less.[50]

In 1895 Wells published *A Red Record: Tabulated Statistics and Alleged Causes of Lynchings in the United States, 1892–1893–1894*. Despite its title, only a small portion of this pamphlet actually provides tabulated statistics on lynchings in 1892, 1893, and 1894. Most of the pamphlet is a catalog of horrors, accounts of brutal racial violence. The statistical portion of the pamphlet, Wells told her readers, came directly from the *Chicago Tribune*. She corrected the *Tribune's* figures. Wells found 241 lynchings in 1892 while the *Tribune* found 236, corrected by the *Tribune* to 235 in 1895. In 1893, she found fewer lynchings of blacks than the *Tribune*, 159 rather than 200. In 1894 she found seven more, 197 rather than 190.[51]

Like the *Tribune,* the *New York Times* changed its thinking about lynching in the 1880s and early 1890s. Throughout the 1870s, the *New York Times* had denounced lynching as too likely to kill innocent persons, especially African Americans.[52] In the 1880s, the *Times* began to argue editorially that even guilty persons had inalienable rights to due process.[53] Change came more subtly to the news columns. In the 1880s, 39 percent of the lynching incidents reported involved black victims, almost exactly the same percentage as in the 1870s. The *Times* seemed impressed with the level of community support for the lynchers 23 percent of the time. Over half the *Times* articles pronounced the person who was lynched guilty. Nonetheless, there was a change in the 1880s. In the 1870s, lynching stories concentrated on the horrific violence of the crime that drove the local population into a maddened hunt for vengeance. This happened in the 1880s as well, but more often reports focused on the details of the actual lynching, giving less detail about the crime that inspired the lynching. The following *New York Times* accounts of two white lynchings illustrate the shift.

1874

Kansas papers give accounts of the lynching of a man named John R. Pearce, who had murdered his father-in-law in the little village of Jacksonville, Neosho County, Kan. The cause of the murder was a family feud. Pearce having met his father-in-law, Anthony Amend, in the village store, and accused him of having circulated a report that he abused and maltreated his wife. Mr. Amend denied the accusation, but in the interview with his son-in-law, told him that he knew such was the fact although he had given no publicity to his knowledge. Pearce instantly grew indignant, and drawing a revolver . . . discharged . . . his revolver. . . . [54]

1884

At 9 o'clock on Thursday morning Judge Pinney sentenced John Heith to confinement in Yuma Penitentiary for life for complicity in the Bisbee murders. Twenty-four hours later the dead body of Heith dangled from the cross bar of a telegraph pole near the foot of Toughnut-street, where it was suspended by a rope. The following are the particulars of the occurrence as near as can be gathered: About 8:30 yesterday morning a crowd of men, mostly miners, numbering about 150, proceeded to the Court-house. Arriving there they detailed seven of their number from Bisbee, who entered and demanded that John Heith be turned over to the mob. . . . [55]

By making Pearce's murder of his father-in-law the focus of the 1874 article, with the news that a crowd killed Pearce buried at the end of the story, the writer makes the lynching seem a natural and normal consequence of the original crime, exhibiting how, in the 1870s, most *New York Times* lynching articles focused on the crime that supposedly justified the lynching, not the lynching itself.

The 1884 article, by contrast, contained virtually no information about Heith's crime. Local papers certainly had carried coverage of Heith's trial, supplying the missing details, but the *New York Times* article only describes the lynching, and it does so in detail. The *Times* still asserted that the locals thought Heith deserved his fate, but this seems less convincing for coming in the midst of a story detailing the lynching rather than the crime.

Such evidence that the *New York Times* shifted in the 1880s does not mean that Southerners rejected the lynching formula. They continued it, albeit in an increasingly racialized form. In 1880, the Charleston, South Carolina, *News and Courier* confidently boasted that white Southerners need not fear criticism from Easterners or Westerners. "They know how it is themselves, and do as the South Carolinians have done."[56] In 1880, it was still possible for newspapers to report that "the entire male population" joined in a manhunt and mean blacks as well as whites.[57] In the 1890s, when Southern papers reported horrific crimes, committed by "black fiends," that filled the woods with searchers, everyone understood that only whites joined the manhunt.[58] In 1897, white Southern columnist Bill Arp sounded defensive when he wrote that "lynching for crime is the law of nature, and will go on." He added: "When juries are organized to try hyenas and wolves and gorillas, maybe these brutes in human form will be tried, but not before."[59]

Throughout the 1880s the *Times'* lynching articles thought almost a quarter of lynching incidents had community support, but in the 1890s the *Times* very rarely found community support sufficient to make a lynching explicable: They found community support worthy of comment in only 5 percent of incidents reported. In the 1880s, the *Times* thought the person lynched was certainly guilty 52 percent of the time. In the 1890s, the lynched person seemed guilty only 21 percent of the time. And in the 1890s, the percentage of blacks lynched jumped dramatically. In the 1880s, only 38 percent of lynching incidents reported by the *New York Times* involved the killing of a black person. In the 1890s, 54 percent of lynching incidents in the *Times* involved whites lynching blacks. The overall number of lynching incidents the *New York Times* reported did not change much. There were 177 in the 1870s and 170 in the 1890s.

CONTINUED WHITE RESISTANCE

More journalistic attention for racial lynchings did not mean that ordinary white people had changed their minds on the question of racial violence. Most whites, Northern and Southern, simply ignored Wells, continuing to argue that a black propensity to rape justified lynching as though the things Wells had said or written meant nothing. In 1916, one Georgia judge advised that "the best way to stop lynchings is to stop the crimes that provoke the lynchings." He meant rape and simply repeated an argument whites had been making for decades.[60] Even whites who accepted Wells's statistical proof that few lynchings really involved accusations of rape could still reject the thrust of her argument. In 1926, a Tennessee prosecutor named George W. Chamlee (who would later serve as International Labor Defense attorney for the Scottsboro Boys) pronounced himself opposed to mob violence in all cases and was instrumental in preventing four lynchings. He readily conceded that most lynchings involved no accusation of rape. Despite his genuine opposition to racial violence, Chamlee still insisted that rape underlay most lynchings, even lynchings in which the persons being lynched had not raped anyone. "I suspect," he wrote, "that underneath all such outbursts there smolders the lurking, ever present fear of violation (legal or forcible) of white womanhood by the Negro."[61] Whites saw any violent black man as a threat to their women.

One sign that white America was not yet ready to spurn lynching even after Wells's English tour occurred in 1893, when the mayor of Roanoke, Virginia, called out the Roanoke Light Infantry to guard Thomas Smith, a black man charged with beating and robbing a white woman. Mayor Henry S. Trout's decision sparked a night of rioting that killed eight Roanokers and did not prevent rioters from killing Smith.[62]

One year later, in Ohio, the Fayette County sheriff asked Governor William McKinley for troops to protect a young black prisoner charged with "atrociously maltreat[ing]" a white woman. The troops came down to Washington Court House from Columbus and so zealously guarded the prisoner that they shot dead three would-be lynchers and injured twenty-four more. Public indignation against the militia and their commanding officer, Colonel A. B. Coit, ran so high that authorities had to convene a court of inquiry and then a murder trial. Hostile witnesses from Washington Court House claimed the militia and their officers were drunk.[63] Other observers reported that the crowd of three thousand pressing against the courthouse planned to dynamite the building with the soldiers and their prisoner inside. A jury acquitted Coit. The black man he guarded went to prison for twenty years. Years later older Washington Court House citizens still remembered the soldiers as reckless. To this day the courthouse door in Washington Court House remains riddled with the soldiers' bullets.[64] A similar controversy erupted in 1897, when Ohio guardsmen killed two Urbana citizens. In contrast to Washington Court House, the Urbana mob ultimately triumphed. Popular indignation raged so much against the soldiers that the local militia lost its nerve and fled. The mayor sided with the mob, turning back a troop train with reinforcements, telling them they were not needed. At the same time, fifty deputy sheriffs switched sides, joining the mob. The absence of soldiers allowed rioters to break into the jail without opposition and hang the prisoner. In the wake of this lynching, the public and press called for court martials of the soldiers. There was no attempt to prosecute members of the mob.[65] In both Washington Court House and Urbana, the Ohio soldiers ran into trouble because they seemed to have acted contrary to the theory of popular sovereignty. What they did proved more controversial than the actions of the mob.

South of Ohio, whites' commitment to their right to lynch continued. With the 1896 election of William McKinley as president, the Republicans again controlled the government but did so at a time when America seemed to back away from racial issues. McKinley had once supported black rights, but, as president, emphasized sectional reconciliation over racial issues. But not entirely. McKinley appointed some blacks as postmasters in the South, and every appointment angered white postal patrons. In 1898 a South Carolina mob murdered Frazier B. Baker, the Lake City postmaster, and his two-year-old child, burning his house and post office, and shooting his wife and three other children as they fled the flames. Postal inspectors, aided by a private detective, found that Lake City whites had plotted the crime for some time, holding meetings to discuss how to rid themselves of their black postmaster. The inspectors learned that while the murders outraged South Carolinians generally, whites around Lake City would not cooperate with investigators. Few whites sympathized with efforts to prosecute the killers of black people, and those inclined to talk received death threats. The postal inspectors tried to arrange for witnesses to leave the Lake City area with financial support from the government. Prosecutors persuaded two of the conspirators to confess and testify against their fellow participants.[66] In April 1899, a federal grand jury in South Carolina returned indictments for the lynching of Frazier B. Baker. The grand jury charged the men with violating the Reconstruction-era Enforcement Act of 1870. When the case went to trial, the U.S. prosecutor, Abial Lathrop, was pleased with the jury selected. They were, he thought, representative businessmen from all over South Carolina. Lathrop felt confident that he could win convictions. As the trial unfolded, Lathrop found he could not make a case against three of the indicted men (they were acquitted), but thought he proved conclusively the guilt of eight. Nonetheless, the jury could not agree on a verdict, and the eight men went free. One lawyer employed by the government may have exaggerated a bit when he concluded that the evidence was so strong that in any state other than South Carolina, conviction would have been certain. Or perhaps he really thought South Carolina's tolerance for violence exceeded that in Georgia, Mississippi, and other Southern states.[67] The killing of a postmaster really angered federal officials. As late as 1908, the attorney general would not agree to drop the cases, but, in 1911, the government finally surrendered, ceasing prosecution against all the accused lynchers.[68]

The Lake City case outraged Northerners. William Lloyd Garrison II, son of the famed abolitionist, raised money for the surviving members of the Baker family. African Americans in Boston organized rallies to speak against the atrocity. The Colored National League organized protests. While others quarreled over what to do, Lillian Clayton Jewett, an unknown aspiring novelist and a white woman, secretly journeyed to South Carolina and smuggled the Bakers out, bringing them to Boston. In Boston, Jewett and the Bakers became celebrities, extensively interviewed by the Boston press and appearing before large rallies. For a moment, Jewett attained national fame, even earning the opprobrium of Ben Tillman. Southern newspapers made her name a watchword for Northern deviltry.[69]

Between April 13 and April 23, 1899, as government investigators and prosecutors prepared to bring the Lake City case to trial, white Georgians hunted down and killed a black man, named Sam Hose or Sam Holt, charged with murdering a white man and raping his wife. Atlanta newspapers so sensationalized the crime that it seems better to rely on the reports of a white detective named Reverdy C. Ransom, hired by a black activist to inquire into the affair. Wells also researched the affair. Ransom and Wells both found that Hose had quarreled with his white employer, Alfred Cranford, killing him only when Cranford threatened to shoot him.[70]

While the narrative published in the *Atlanta Constitution* bore little resemblance to what Ransom and Wells learned, it faithfully followed the standard lynching narrative. According to the *Constitution* story, Hose assassinated Alfred Cranford and then "assaulted" (raped) his wife. The first story announced "there is no possible doubt" about Hose's guilt and reported that white citizens "are wrought up to an unusual degree." Hose's crime, then, was terrible enough to mobilize the entire population. Atlanta journalists reassured readers after the Hose ordeal that their society had not plunged into anarchy. In the Hose case, the mob acted because a ghastly crime had been committed.[71]

It took white searchers long enough to find Hose that the local press had time to create an elaborate narrative/justification for his torture and death. The *Constitution*'s first story, appearing April 14, predicted that pursuing whites would capture Hose in a few hours, adding, confidently, that "news from the pursuing mob is hourly expected."[72] A day later the *Constitution* still thought capture imminent, but the delay allowed the crime Hose had committed to become more horrible in the minds of the *Constitution*'s editors and writers than first reported. The paper also began to argue that the public solidly supported the lynching. The posses searching for Hose included leading citizens. Women urged their husbands, sons, and fathers to participate in the lynching.[73] By April 18, the *Constitution* made it sound as if all the people in middle Georgia had joined in the continuing search for Hose. The paper added that black people aided "as much as possible."[74] When Hose continued to elude his pursuers, the *Constitution* reported that excitement remained intense, "though manifested in a different sort of way from the mad frenzy" exhibited at first. Now the "excitement" appeared as grim determination.[75]

After the pursuing whites captured Hose and put him to death, burning him and then clawing through his smoldering remains for souvenirs, the *Constitution* redoubled its efforts to justify what had happened. Again, the editors and reporters turned to the standard narrative, presenting Hose's crime as so horrible that it justified his savage torture and death. The *Constitution* beseeched its readers to "Keep the Facts in View." The "facts," of course, related to Hose's crime, a crime so awful that it drove the population into a frenzy. According to the paper, Hose had approached his unsuspecting victim from behind and sank his axe into Alfred Cranford's brain. He roughly tore Cranford's child from its mother's arms and flung it aside. He then seized and choked Mrs. Cranford, throwing her onto the floor where he raped her in a pool of her husband's blood. "Remember the facts!" the *Constitution* cried, "remember that shocking degradation which was inflicted by the black beast, his victim swimming in her husband's warm blood as the brute held her to the floor!" Such a crime "dethroned the reason of the people."[76]

The *Constitution,* and white Georgians generally, felt themselves in a rhetorical war with Northern papers. The *Constitution* ran a page of critical editorials from Northern papers. When lynchers hanged Hose's supposed accomplice, they placarded his body with a sign that read "N.Y. Journal: We Must Protect our Ladies."[77] The *Constitution* editor had reason to take personally the criticisms of the Hose killing. The *Constitution* paid a reward to the man who captured Hose, J. B. Jones. And Jones gave the *Constitution* credit as well, giving the paper a testimonial saying he would not have known to look for Hose or known what he looked like, had it not been for the *Constitution*'s detailed description.[78]

Southerners continued to argue that black criminality drove whites, and "good" blacks, berserk. In the midst of its coverage of the Hose killing, the *Constitution* published a symposium looking at the problem of how to protect women and girls in the country districts.[79] The most prominent white spokesman on behalf of white women and their need for protection was South Carolina Senator Ben Tillman. His argument for lynching reprised arguments cultivated by Northern newspapers through the 1870s: Some crimes drive whole communities into a violent rage. When black brutes attack a white woman, Tillman said on the floor of the U. S. Senate, "Our brains reel under the staggering blow and hot blood surges to the heart. Civilization peels off us, any and all of us who are men, and we revert to the original savage type whose impulses under any and all such circumstances has always been to 'kill! kill! kill!'"[80] In Tillman's fevered world, black criminality drove whites to violence. They did not choose to peel off civilization; it just happened as their brains reeled and their hearts pumped. Many dismissed Tillman as a ranting fool for his reckless rhetoric. Some of his fellow senators expressed dismay at his remarks. But many also found the core of his argument hard to resist. Tillman merely continued the same argument advanced by Vardaman after the Carrollton massacre. And Vardaman had only reiterated, and racialized, an argument for popular violence that the newspapers had followed for years. The *New York Times* and other papers continued to assume that community sanction somehow justified mass violence. Instead of directly refuting Tillman's argument, opponents of lynching began to argue that most lynchings had nothing to do with rape. This almost conceded that rapists deserved extralegal punishment.[81]

In 1912, South Carolina Governor Cole Blease sounded equally reckless when he said: "Whenever the constitution of my state steps between me and the defense of the virtue of white womanhood, then I say to hell with the Constitution!"[82] Again, many in America shook their heads in disbelief at Blease's intemperance. Yet his speech cannot be dismissed as the eccentric rantings of a marginal character. Blease was so confident of the widespread appeal of his endorsement of lynching that he had campaign posters printed with the slogan "A Governor Who Lauds Lynching" and promised never to call the militia against white racist mobs.[83]

Popular culture also continued to promote extralegal violence. Western writer Owen Wister reiterated key elements in the old argument for lynching in his 1902 novel *The Virginian*. In his novel, Wister did distinguish Western from Southern lynchings. Wister's fictional Molly confronts Judge Henry, demanding to know: "Have you come to tell me that you think well of lynching?" Henry replies that he does not approve of publicly burning Southern blacks. Hanging thieves in private, though, did meet his approval. "You perceive there's a difference, don't you?" he asks. Molly does not and Henry goes on: "I consider the burning a proof that the South is semi-barbarous, and the hanging proof that Wyoming is determined to become civilized. We do not torture our criminals when we lynch them. We do not invite spectators to enjoy their death agony." Henry then continues with the classic lyncher's defense. The people made the law in the first place, and they have the right to take it back when necessary. When citizens lynch, "they only take back what they once gave."[84]

Wister wrote this passage with the brutal Henry Smith lynching in mind. White Texans' torture of Smith genuinely repulsed Wister, but the novelist argues that in particular circumstances lynching is necessary and legitimate. Wister wrote *The Virginian* against the backdrop of Wyoming's notorious Johnson County War, when wealthy cattlemen lynched small-time ranchers as "rustlers." He sided with the cattle barons, with the use of extralegal violence to protect property. The cattlemen, and Wister, believed they had a right to act outside the law because the courts would not decisively punish "rustling" by small-time homesteaders. Wister's defenders insist that his Southerner, *The Virginian,* should not be compared to the Southern lynchers of Sam Hose. But Wister's novel advanced the old Western argument that

American citizens have the right to act outside the law when they perceive their courts to be ineffectual.[85]

Wister's The Virginian proved powerfully influential, the prototype for countless western novels, films, and television programs. The Virginian went through thirty-five printings, sold two million copies, and became a Broadway play before translation into films and a television series. Among white Americans, Wister's influence for lynching in defense of property proved far more powerful than Wells's campaign. Through the twentieth century Americans forgot Wells; countless television programs and movies repeated Wister's paean to extralegal cowboy violence.[86]

This mentality penetrated academia. In 1907, the eminent historian William Archibald Dunning justified the post–Civil War Ku Klux Klan on grounds similar to those advanced by Tillman and Blease. White Southerners turned to violence after the Civil War when the federal government illegitimately "interfered" in their political affairs. Dunning described Ku Klux Klan violence as "the inevitable extra-legal protest."[87] Dunning chose to describe the "protest" as "inevitable" to convey the notion that white men backed to the wall could hardly control themselves. They had to fight back and claim the political power that was rightfully theirs. Dunning did not use the inflamatory language Tillman favored. Brains did not reel and hearts did not pump hot blood in Dunning's prose, but the point was the same. Whites not only had a right to violent oppression of blacks, they did so inevitably and not even by conscious choice.

THE FAME OF IDA B. WELLS

Even though at the end of her life Wells may have claimed too much for her England trip in terms of its impact on white people, there is evidence that, at the time, she recruited more blacks than whites to her fight against lynching. Wells did not seem much interested in white sentiment when she published her pamphlet praising the black killer of four New Orleans white policemen as a hero. In 1900, Robert Charles killed a police officer, and then killed more police officers as they tried to arrest him. Charles made his last stand on Saratoga Street, holding off a mob the New York Times and the Chicago Tribune claimed numbered twenty thousand. The New Orleans Times-Picayune estimated the crowd at five thousand, not counting the police and a company of militia. Wells quoted the larger figure. Even the Times-Picayune admitted that a crowd of thousands, "armed with shotguns, rifles, and pistols of every description, all waiting for the negro to show his head," could not "overawe" Charles. Wells praised Charles's courage and called him "the hero of New

Orleans." It is hard to believe Wells expected whites to read her pamphlet. As Wells acknowledged, whites saw Charles as a "desperado," the murderer "who has been the cause of all the rioting." The *Times* charged that the "Black Fiend Deliberately Murdered a Praying Boy." Labeling someone a "black fiend" clearly made a racial argument. Calling an outlaw a "desperado" seemed more racially neutral, placing the person beyond the pale of all civilized society, hopeless and impossible to rehabilitate. According to the white press, respectable New Orleans blacks repudiated Charles and offered their services in running down the "desperado." In praising Charles, Wells made the same argument Fortune had made thirty years before, when he called on Southern blacks to arm themselves to resist illegitimate white authority.[88]

Her pamphlet on Charles reveals Wells as fully a race woman. She did not want to see the race torn asunder along class lines, nor, for that matter, along gender lines. Blacks must learn, she lectured her readers, that support for crowd violence against any segment of "the race" endangered all black people.

Wells had her most powerful impact on black Americans. Just going to England won her greater respect among black newspaper editors. In 1894 H. C. C. Atwood, a former United States consul and currently secretary of the National Negro Democratic League, inadvertently documented Wells' success when he complained that she had been "gathering notoriety."[89] When the *Inter-Ocean* published her account of a Kentucky lynching, the paper reminded its readers that "Miss Wells is the young colored woman whose addresses in England last Spring attracted so much attention and excited so much comment."[90] The *National Baptist World* identified Wells as the voice that "aroused so many countrys[*sic*]."[91] When Wells returned to England the following year, the *Wichita People's Friend* and the *Kansas City American Citizen* tracked her progress.[92] In August, the *People's Friend* still felt Wells was not famous enough as to need no introduction. The *Chicago Inter-Ocean* still had to remind its readers who she was as late as March 1895.[93] By the end of August, though, the *American Citizen* thought that "any man, woman, or child who has not heard of Miss Ida B. Wells is not up with the times."[94]

Whites promoted her fame by attacking her. The governor of Virginia, Charles T. O'Farrell, accused Wells of organizing a conspiracy to retard the South's progress.[95] Many black Americans perceived Wells as standing alone against a great enemy. She was, some thought, in over her head. The black press began referring to Wells as "the noble little lady" and the "brave little lady."[96] One female commentator, signing herself "Mrs. H. Davis," hailed Wells, but thought her success showed that the race now needed "a savior" or "a Moses"—a man. Wells had stepped out of the female sphere, "from behind the curtain of joy" to "stand pleading" for peace and liberty. "In the days of the prophets," this writer explained, when men needed a great king, "a virgin like the first Eve, stepped forth into the world and brought forth a savior, and through him came redemption." Davis had some pleading of her own to do. Through Wells, Davis wrote, "may we find a savior of our race among our men." She called on black men of strength to wake up to their duty. "We cannot afford to let her stand and battle so long alone," Mrs. H. Davis concluded.[97]

Even at the end of the nineteenth century, many black leaders did not want to join Wells. Many still accepted the argument that lynching victims brought their punishment on themselves. In the South, blacks hardly dared condemn lynching without also denouncing black rapists. Atlanta blacks organized an antilynching campaign, but one that carefully condemned Northern outrages as well as the Southern variety and called for an end to assault on women as well as lynchings.[98] Similarly, the National Race Council at Nashville discussed the problem both of rape and of lynching. One speaker declared: "Let us hurl all the power of being against the fiend who, in violation of God's holiest law, and contrary to the laws of the land"—not against lynchers, but against villains who "rob women of the most precious jewel given by heaven to earth." This speaker promised that "negroes of this land will . . . hunt down and strike down this crime and those criminals."[99]

Nonetheless, there were signs that some black leaders were now ready to follow Wells. In 1897 African Methodist Episcopal Bishop Henry M. Turner announced that he had for years wanted to denounce lynchings, but had hesitated to do so. Now, though, Turner said, he would "speak it, preach it, tell it, and write it." Bishop Turner had been radicalized. "Get guns, negroes!" he cried, "get guns, and may God give you good aim when you shoot."[100] Two years later, the National Afro-American Council of the United States declared June 2 a day of fasting and prayer to denounce lynching.[101] T. Thomas Fortune had tried the same thing twenty years before, but now black outrage against lynching reached into the mainstream. In 1899, even Booker T. Washington spoke against lynching. Washington could not do so without conceding "there is too much crime among us" growing "out of the idleness of our young men and women," but he earnestly appealed to white Southerners to value human life.[102] This widespread arousal of black protest eventually led to the formation of powerful institutional opposition to lynching: the National Association for the Advancement of Colored People (NAACP) and the Tuskegee Institute.

Black anger joined—and helped fuel—the longstanding rhetoric that accused white Southerners of a barbaric bent toward mob violence. The biographers of Ben Tillman and Ida B. Wells have both claimed that their subjects helped paint the South as prone to bloodshed. Rhetoric, not culture, crafted an image of the white South as reflexively violent. Tillman promoted an image of white Southerners as savages, people whose violent urges must be tolerated or excused for being uncontrollable. Similarly, Wells marketed the notion that the white South was not fully civilized. It may be that the South's uncivilized nature resulted not from centuries-old culture but rather from skillful oratory and journalism announcing that Southerners could not help themselves.[103]

Even as Americans came to see lynching as racial and Southern, nonracial lynching continued unabated. In 1906, one lynch mob chartered a train from Monroe, Louisiana, to the Tallulah jail cell of a white man named Robert T. Rogers. Rogers's conviction for murdering Jesse Brown had been reversed by Louisiana's supreme court. At 8:30 P.M. on May 28, 1906, men with lanterns, ropes, chains, sacks, and guns began scrambling out from under boxcars and mounting the chartered train. The train stopped along its way to Tallulah, allowing additional lynchers to climb aboard. Passing through the car, one railroad employee noticed that some of his passengers carried guns. The railroad periodically rented its trains to baseball clubs, theatrical companies, and wedding parties. This was not one of those: "I suspicioned [sic] something," the worker, A. A. Madden, recalled later. The train stopped right in front of the courthouse and the mob dismounted, attacking the jail with sledgehammers and pry bars. People living in Tallulah could hear Rogers shrieking as the crowd hauled him out of his cell. The train's headlight caught Rogers's still twitching body as he died, swinging from a telegraph pole. Members of the mob stayed around to be interviewed by reporters, telling the journalists that they feared that legal "technicalities" would prevent the courts from properly punishing Rogers.[104]

Lynchings of white men perhaps even accelerated in the World War I era. In the anticommunist hysteria called the first Red Scare, mobs harassed German citizens and their sympathizers. An Illinois mob forced Robert Praeger to kiss an American flag and then hanged him. In Mississippi, a wealthy planter named William A. Hunter narrowly escaped an extralegal hanging. He was tarred and feathered instead and forced to leave the state. Western vigilantes regularly went after striking workers, especially the Industrial Workers of the World (IWW). Newspapers reported the formation of these vigilante organizations as self-help efforts. In 1917 IWW opponents killed Frank Little, a labor organizer charged with treasonable utterances. The San Francisco-based Communist party newspaper *Western Worker* charged that through the 1920s and into the 1930s police often joined with vigilante mobs to lynch or threaten to lynch strikers. In 1924 the IWW produced photographic evidence that "a mob of armed thugs" dipped children caught at an IWW meeting in boiling coffee, leaving "their little limbs . . . practically cooked to the marrow."[105]

Such nonracial lynchings seemed more legitimate than the antiblack variety. After Little died, the mainstream *Boston Transcript* claimed to know "millions of people who, while sternly reprehending such proceedings . . . will nevertheless be glad, in their hearts, that Montana did it." The *Chicago Tribune* thought protests against the Little lynching "will find no echo in any reasonable heart."[106] Even the great lawyer Clarence Darrow once told an NAACP meeting: "Personally, I don't object to lynching." He only complained when lynchers harbored racial bias. If lynching could be applied equally to whites and blacks, Darrow said, it would be better than "the slower processes of the courts."[107]

Newspaper coverage of crowd violence before lynching came to be perceived as mostly Southern and racial reveals that most Americans, like Darrow, understood lynching as authorized by popular sovereignty under certain conditions. Before the South sanctioned popular violence, crowds took to the streets all over America. Journalists wrote the script for the South's defense of its tendencies to violence well before white Southerners knew they needed such a script. White Southerners claimed they must lynch blacks because the courts could not effectively control African American criminality and because blacks' crimes were so savage and brutal. In the face of horrible crime, the public's passions rage beyond control, white Southerners alleged. Every element in the lynching apologia had been established by Northerners and Westerners well before Southerners had any special need to defend themselves from critics.

CHAPTER SEVEN

Tuskegee, the NAACP, and the Definition of Lynching, 1899–1940

Early in the twentieth century an antilynching activist named Jessie Daniel Ames campaigned for a lynch-free year. Ames was looking for—or trying to create—a sign that white America had turned a corner. If America seemed to be moving away from racial violence, maybe it really would. The lynch-free year idea proved a clever slogan and caught on among journalists. Though it seemed straightforward, Ames's slogan carried important implications. First, she believed white newspapers to be the key to ending community-sanctioned racial violence. She saw lynching as racial, a relatively new idea, and as community sponsored, a very old notion. Newspaper editors could persuade specific towns, neighborhoods, and sheriffs not to sanction lynchings. Second, she assumed, and then insisted, that lynching could be precisely defined. To eliminate the behavior of racial violence, Ames needed to spell out exactly what was to be eradicated. She did not aspire to end every incident of racial violence or the larger problem of racism. Ames's opponents accepted neither her assumptions nor the implications in her effort. They saw American racism as nationally pervasive and not correctable by "fixing" particular communities. In Ames's lifetime, the National Association for the Advancement of Colored People (NAACP) and other organizations began to reshape their understanding of lynching, no longer seeing it as the act of particular towns and communities. Thus, Ames's campaign for a lynch-free year went to the heart of the ideological struggle that dominated efforts to end lynching in the first decades of the twentieth century.

Even as Northern newspapers became less sympathetic to crowd violence, some white Southern editors continued to exhort readers to lynch blacks. In 1899, one Georgia newspaper called lynching "necessary" and explained that rapists had to be lynched because the courtroom is "no place for a decent woman." Since the white female rape victims should not be called to testify, lynching offered the best way to punish rapists. This is a white man's country, the paper said, and "if it takes violence to implant this truth in the minds of the colored brother, let it come." Syndicated columnist John Temple Graves described "lynching as the remedy for rape." He thought this "fixed and unchangeable law [had been] written in the heart of a race that reveres its women next to God."[1] Such attitudes continued into the twentieth century. In 1903 one Georgia newspaper called lynching "necessary and proper."[2] In 1920 another Georgia newspaper editorialized that it was "gratifying" to know that blacks would be lynched for raping white women.[3]

It should not be assumed that every white Southern opinion leader automatically promoted lynching. In 1906 and 1907 the former governor of Georgia, William J. Northern, barnstormed his state, trying to build opposition to lynching. Northern had disparaged criticism of mob violence as early as 1899, but the 1906 Atlanta race riot alarmed him. He was particularly influenced by letters published and endorsed by the *Atlanta Constitution* criticizing whites for not better mentoring blacks as a Christian duty. A paternalistic racist committed to the defense of women, Northern nonetheless came to see mob violence as a menace to law and constitutionalism.[4]

Many newspaper editors denounced Northern, but not all. In Mississippi, one conservative steadfastly and without compromise opposed lynching. Like Northern, John Gordon Cashman was a Confederate veteran. He had edited the *Vicksburg Evening Post* as a "Redeemer" and a conservative Democrat since May 4, 1883. Politically, he championed Grover Cleveland and condemned William Jennings Bryan. Cashman saw it as "conservative" to criticize mob violence. Although he once killed a rival editor (in self-defense), Cashman was a law-and-order man through and through.[5] In 1903, he ran a headline that read "NO SYMPATHY FOR LYNCHERS" and described an Attala County lynching as "unprovoked and unnecessary."[6] Cashman praised governors willing to stand up to mobs,[7] and heaped scorn on those unwilling to act.[8] Cashman entitled one editorial "No Excuses for Lynching," and lectured his readers that an appeal for law and order was not the same as endorsing criminality. "There is nothing in common between the two," Cashman said.[9] Where other editors weaseled, saying they opposed lynching, "except where the provocation is great,"[10] Cashman was forthright: "No crime, however revolting, justifies lynching."[11] Some editors criticized the criminal justice system, arguing that "legal impediments and technical barriers" led to mob law.[12] By contrast, Cashman consistently supported the courts over mob law. He once declared that "lynching does not reduce crime."[13] On another occasion he said, "Nothing but evil can come from mob rule. There is no safety outside of the law."[14] Later, Cashman quoted another editor who had sarcastically written, "Mobs intent upon lynching should at least make reasonably sure that they have selected the right men for victims before proceeding to the final act." Cashman added that such mistakes "are by no means rare," as mobs act on suspicion rather than evidence.[15] Cashman denounced a lynching in Corinth as "like a chapter of some occurrence in the 'dark ages.' It was a piece of savagery."[16]

Josephus Daniels of the *Raleigh News and Observer* was a more typical editor. In his memoirs, Daniels remembered publishing strong editorials against lynching.[17] And in fact the *News and Observer* ran editorials under such headlines as "LYNCHING MUST BE STOPPED AT ANY COST," and declared that lynching is "a crime for which there is no paliation or defense." Daniels understood that newspapers shaped public opinion and believed that public sentiment could end lynching.[18] The *News and Observer* sometimes tried to instruct smaller newspapers on how to dampen the lynching spirit.[19]

Unfortunately, Daniels's opposition to mob law sometimes wavered. Inadvertently or by design, he allowed ordinary reporting to promote mob violence. It was nearly impossible for a white newspaper editor not to print accounts of black criminality. Such newspaper reports amounted to a rhetorical edifice from which lynchers could defend themselves. Even journalists such as Daniels who were "opposed" to lynching sometimes helped promote it through such reporting. The *News and Observer* described blacks accused of crimes as "Negro Maniacs" and "Beasts in Black." The paper warned against "maudlin sentimentality" for criminals.[20] And while Daniels disparaged lynching, he also believed such violence understandable when a terrible crime enraged a neighborhood and the lynchers managed to act before the accused criminal had been arrested. However, Daniels thought lynch mobs insulted law and justice when they broke open a jail, overpowering the sheriff. Seizing and killing a criminal before he could be arrested posed less of an affront to the law.[21] The *News and Observer* made it clear that, while it opposed lynching, it had no sympathy whatsoever for black persons lynched. As the paper declared after a 1902 lynching, "The negro who perished deserved nothing better."[22] In the end, Daniels's racism overwhelmed his commitment to law.[23]

Some white journalists deliberately manipulated news of black criminality if they saw it as politically advantageous. In 1897, Daniels, desperate to
mobilize white voters to regain power for his party, concocted what one historian has called "a rape scare." In one typical story, the *News and Observer*
headlined "A RAPE AT KITTRELL" where "The Black Brute Accom-
plishes His Purpose."[24] Daniels used these reports to political advantage. "Ignorant and mean negroes," he explained, "feel that when the 'Publican party
is in power they have license that they do not enjoy when the party of their
white neighbors is in control of government."[25] White people, in other
words, should vote for the Democrats. Daniels may be the best example of a
journalist manipulating the news in this way, but he was not the only one. In
Georgia, Tom Watson warned against impudent black men who assaulted
"fair young girlhood" in the name of "social equality." In 1906 Atlanta newspapers reported rape after rape in extra editions until white mobs finally
erupted. Thereafter, white racist Democrats won the election.[26] For whites,
reports of black crime could be politically lucrative; they became invested in
the reports' accuracy.

The truth of newspaper accounts of black criminality became so important that even white reformers sensitive to the plight of Southern blacks
could not resist "the truth" of black criminality. And so they sometimes inadvertently contributed to the climate of sympathy for lynching. By almost
any criteria, Episcopal clergyman Cary Breckenridge Wilmer should be
classed as a progressive. A white man born in Virginia, he served on the National Child Labor Committee and worked with black children for ten years
as superintendent of the Lynchburg, Virginia, Colored Orphan Asylum.
Nonetheless, Wilmer argued that when Northerners criticized lynchings,
saying nothing about the black crime that prompted it, "the great mass of ignorant, blinded Negroes take that as a quasi-endorsement of crime."[27]

White efforts to justify lynching through reports of black crime put some
African Americans on the defensive. In 1910 Booker T. Washington favored prohibition in Alabama chiefly because he thought it lessened crime
among blacks, "especially rape." White people, one Washington aide reported, "have attained a certain amount of self-control" and would not
abuse drink even without prohibition. A black man, on the other hand, "will
abuse his privileges"; and increased drunkenness results in increased crime
among blacks, more so than among whites, this researcher reported.[28] Ten
years later, another writer felt compelled to concede, "I don't condone
crime among my people in the least," before pleading, "but since we have a
law, shouldn't it be allowed to take its course?"[29] Two years after that, Ara
Lee Settle wrote Warren G. Harding, "I admit that there are some lawless
Negroes in America . . . but, Mr. President, what good does lynching do?"[30]

To a considerable extent, the effort to combat lynching centered on rolling back the kind of thinking Wilmer expressed. Journalists wielded great influence, making it easier for lynchers to act. Opponents of lynching understood they had to reform the white news media as a prerequisite for ending the killing. Ida B. Wells called on the white press to stop "brand[ing blacks] as a race of rapists." She complained that newspapers promoted lynching by suppressing the truth and printing slanders.[31]

Those hoping to continue Wells's work defined lynching as community-sanctioned murder, just as she did. Wells and those who followed her agreed that the cure for lynching involved changing white communities' attitudes. As one newspaper explained, "The people of a community in the last analysis are responsible for a lynching."[32] Sociologist James Cutler gave this definition scholarly legitimacy in 1905 when he published *Lynch-Law.* "In the course of this investigation," Cutler concluded, "it has become evident that there is usually more or less public approval, or supposed favorable public sentiment, behind a lynching." Popular justification, Cutler added, was the sine qua non of lynching, distinguishing it from murder, assassination, or insurrection.[33]

For many, the first step toward ending public approval of lynching lay in persuading educated Southern whites to denounce it. Lynching opponents hoped to use influential men to dissuade established and would-be lynchers. Rank-and-file lynchers, some theorized, did not so much calculate their purpose as suffer from "a contagious social disease." Jessie Daniel Ames had this in mind when she held the environment, not individuals, responsible for lynching.[34] Delegates to the 1901 Alabama Constitutional Convention blamed lynching on "the moral sentiment of a community." When the community turns against lynching, some delegates believed, "then the thing practically ceases."[35] In 1916 the University Commission on the Southern Race Question, composed of eleven representative Southern college professors, met in Durham, North Carolina, and called on Southern college men to reject lynching.[36] To cure the contagion or change the environment, leaders had to be persuaded to stop their habitual exhortation to violence.[37] The importance lynching opponents attached to winning over community leaders explains the cries of alarm that greeted California Governor James Rolph, Jr., in response to his 1933 endorsement of a lynching in his state. Lynching opponents feared that statements by such a prominent political leader would encourage lynchers in thinking of their actions as legitimate. A Columbia University psychologist thought Rolph's remarks had launched a fresh "craze for lynching," a cycle not easily broken. The *New York Times* reported that Rolph had set back years of effort in the South to end lynching.[38] In a fit of hyperbole, the Communist party press in California credited Rolph with introducing lynching to the Golden State.[39]

A YEAR WITHOUT LYNCHING

Based as it was on a strict definition of lynching, Jessie Daniel Ames's campaign for a lynch-free year had its roots in Alabama, at the Tuskegee Institute. There, Monroe Work became a leader in the crusade to reverse the attitudes Rolph and others like him expressed. A minister and 1898 graduate of Chicago Theological Seminary, with two degrees from the University of Chicago Sociology Department, he developed a faith in the reform possibilities of sociology. Work joined the Tuskegee Institute in 1908, hoping to combat lynching with scientific information. At this time, only the *Chicago Tribune* collected lynching statistics. Other papers sometimes ignored the *Tribune's* findings because they did not want to credit a rival source. Work felt sure that he could persuade white Southern newspapers to publish figures on the number of reported lynchings each year if the data came from an independent authority. Work gathered his information from newspapers, in some cases corresponding with informants. Each year he produced a numerical compilation free of editorial comment. In a sense, though, Work's annual summaries reflected his own personality. He gave up his career as a minister when he discovered that worshippers did not like his speaking style: a thoughtful monotone delivered through barely moving lips. His unembellished factual reports won over the white Southern press, which accepted his reports as accurate and presented them as a true picture of Southern lynching.[40]

Jessie Daniel Ames's antilynching organization also had religious roots, growing out of Methodist missionary societies and the Commission on Interracial Cooperation (CIC), organized by Will Alexander in 1919. The Interracial Commission aspired to soften and humanize segregation by establishing interracial committees throughout the South. The commission appears to have been the first major white organization to permit real black participation in its decision-making. A former Methodist minister, Alexander dedicated himself to bettering Southern public opinion. While he studiously avoided advocacy of "social equality" (many of his followers thought the National Association for the Advancement of Colored People too radical), Alexander favored better educational facilities, sanitary housing, and economic justice for blacks. Alexander also opposed lynching, but at first the problem seemed likely to disappear without his intervention. He acted when the number of reported lynchings shot up dramatically after the 1929 stock market crash. Alexander recruited a sociologist from North Carolina named Arthur F. Raper to prepare an anecdotal analysis of lynching and its origins.

In 1930, Ames organized an autonomous women's organization to fight lynching called the Association of Southern Women for the Prevention of

1. The 1856 San Francisco Vigilance Committee printed elaborate documents like this. The iconography in the margins argues that masculine lynchers (see the figure on the left) protected feminine guardians of moral power, pictured on the right. Bancroft Library, University of California, Berkeley.

left   2. Atlanta antiques dealer James Allen collected images of lynchings which caused a sensation when exhibited in New York. This picture shows a Waco, Texas mob in the act of burning Jesse Washington in 1916. Allen-Littlefield Collection, Special Collections Division, Robert W. Woodruff Library, Emory University.

above   3. The last full-scale history of lynching appeared in 1905, authored by sociologist James E. Cutler. Case Western Reserve University Archives, Cleveland, OH.

LYNCHING IN THE UNITED STATES—1889-1922

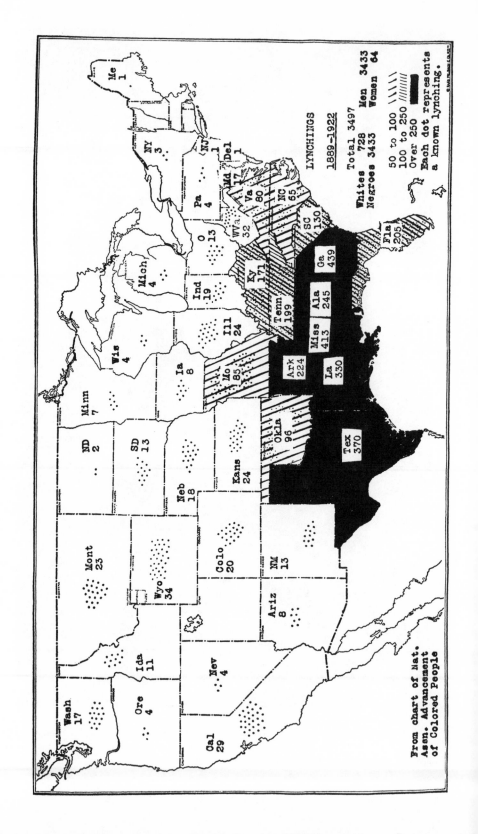

LYNCHINGS
1889-1922

Total 3497
Whites 728   Men 3433
Negroes 3433   Women 64

\\\\ 50 to 100
//// 100 to 250
■   Over 250
⚐   Each dot represents
      a known lynching.

From chart of Nat.
Assn. Advancement
of Colored People

Me 1
NY 3
NJ 1
Ind 17
Del 1
Pa 4
Va 80
NC 65
WVa 32
SC 130
O 13
Ky 171
Ga 439
Mich 4
Ind 19
Tenn 199
Ala 245
Fla 205
Ill 24
Miss 413
Ark 224
La 330
Wis 4
Ia 8
Mo 85
Okla 96
Tex 370
Minn 7
ND 2
SD 13
Kans 24
Neb 18
Colo 20
NM 13
Mont 23
Wyo 34
Ariz 8
Ida 11
Nev 4
Ore 4
Wash 17
Cal 29

FRANK LITTLE
VICTIM OF ANACONDA COPPER COMPANY
THUGS DIED AUG. 1 1917 BUTTE MONT

left 4. The NAACP designed maps like this to suggest a scientific, objective basis for describing lynching as largely confined to one region, the South, and almost entirely directed against African Americans. Author's personal collection.

above 5. In 1917 IWW opponents killed Frank Little, a labor organizer charged with treasonable utterances. The *Boston Transcript* claimed to know "millions of people who, while sternly reprehending such proceedings . . . will nevertheless be glad, in their hearts, that Montana did it." The *Chicago Tribune* thought protests against the Little lynching "will find no echo in any reasonable heart." Courtesy of the Labor Archives and Research Center, San Francisco State University.

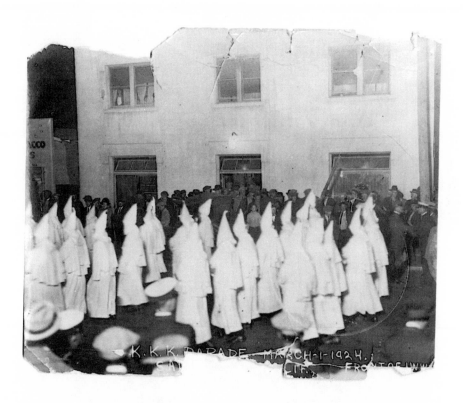

6. In the 1920s, the Ku Klux Klan became pervasive. This picture shows a Ku Klux Klan parade in San Pedro, California, March 1, 1924. The Klansmen are marching in front of the Industrial Workers of the World Headquarters. Courtesy of the Labor Archives and Research Center, San Francisco State University.

7. Young girl injured in a 1924 mob attack on IWW headquarters in San Pedro, California. This was "not" a lynching. Courtesy of the Labor Archives and Research Center, San Francisco State University.

above   8. At the Emmett Till trial officials segregated all blacks in attendance. This picture, taken by Ernest Withers, shows L. Alex Wilson, standing at left in light-colored jacket, and Emmett Till's mother seated below the window. Rayfield Mooty is seated to the right of Till's mother.
Copyright Ernest C. Withers. Courtesy Panopticon Gallery, Waltham, MA.

right   9. Emmett Till's uncle, Mose Wright, testified against the murderers of his nephew.
Copyright Ernest C. Withers. Courtesy Panopticon Gallery, Waltham, MA.

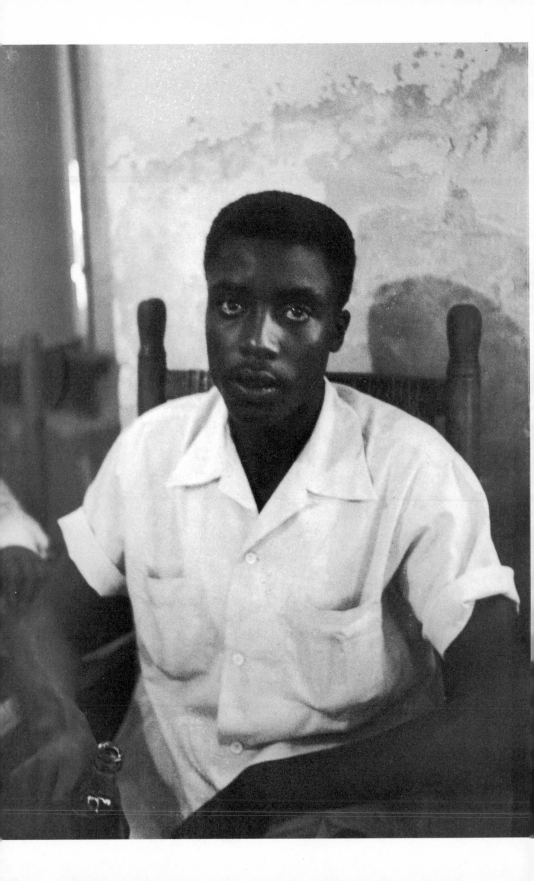

left 10. The son of a sharecropper, Willie Reed testified that he saw the murderers of Emmett Till transport their victim in a pickup truck. Later he could hear them beating Till inside a barn. Copyright Ernest C. Withers. Courtesy Panopticon Gallery, Waltham, MA.

above 11. Influenced by H. L. Mencken, William Bradford Huie wrote about racial violence throughout his life. Photograph by Bachrach. Courtesy Martha Huie.

12. Lynching rhetoric continues. In 2000, as Texas authorities prepared to execute Shaka Sankofa (or Gary Graham) for murder, Pennsylvania officials moved ahead with plans to execute Mumia Abu-Jamal, convicted in 1982 for murdering a Philadelphia police officer. (A federal judge threw out Abu-Jamal's death sentence in December 2001.) This poster protests the legal proceedings against both men as lynchings, language designed to depict the legal processes as racially biased and failing to follow true due process. Mumia Abu-Jamal by Key Martin. Shaka Sankofa by Johnnie Stevens. Courtesy International Action Center.

Lynching (ASWPL).[41] Ames herself had risen from obscurity by campaigning for female suffrage. Before joining the CIC she directed the Williamson County, Texas, Equal Suffrage Association and served in the Texas League of Women Voters. Rank-and-file women in her organization primarily came from Southern evangelical churches. As Ames's biographer explained, for most middle-class white women the church encouraged female solidarity. Evangelical religion justified crossing racial lines. The South's first region-wide women's organization came from the Methodist Church: the Methodist Women's Foreign Mission Society, organized in 1878. By 1911 white Methodist women had begun to experiment in interracial cooperation.[42]

Southern Methodists prized their regional autonomy and such ideas may have helped convince Ames that lynching could best be ended by changing the attitudes of the white South from the inside. She doubted outsiders could turn Southern men away from racial violence.[43] Ames and her association worked to persuade white Southerners that black men did not cause lynching by raping white women.[44] Ames feared that emphasizing white Southern brutalities might encourage rather than discourage racial violence. Far better, she thought, to underscore the positive. When she found a sheriff heroically resistant in the face of a threatening mob, Ames urged her followers to write flattering letters directly to the sheriff.[45] She tried to influence newspaper reporting by corresponding with influential editors. She warned editors that their editorials denouncing lynchings did little good when they printed news stories highlighting black venality. She warned papers against relying on stringers, regional correspondents mired in local prejudice working part time for larger newspapers.[46] Ames also urged the Tuskegee Institute to report foiled lynchings as well as the successful variety. She explained that "we are doing almost as much with prevented lynchings now as we are with lynchings." Ames wanted to create an impression that lynching was in decline; every report of a thwarted mob promoted that idea.[47]

Ames's campaign against lynching represented a reversal of the position more commonly associated with Southern white women. Rebecca Latimer Felton, born to a Georgia planter family in 1835, presented the more common view. Politically active, she energetically spoke across Georgia for the Woman's Christian Temperance Union. She lobbied for higher education for women and defended wage earning women in a debate published widely in Georgia. Felton charged that white Southern men had failed to protect their women. This fact led her to agitate for woman's suffrage. It also prompted her to advocate lynching. "If it needs lynching to protect woman's dearest possession," she famously cried, "I say 'lynch' a thousand times a week if necessary."[48]

It was to combat such thinking that Ames pushed for a lynch-free year, and she had her frustrations. Some years could be heartbreakers. In 1936 Ames suffered "a spell of depression" when a lynching occurred in Mississippi. "Our hopes had grown so high," Ames wrote, consoling herself that at least Texas had stayed clear. In July 1938 Ames and the Tuskegee Institute announced that six months had passed without a lynching, the first half-year without a lynching since the *Chicago Tribune* began counting lynchings in 1882. Some white Southern newspapers rushed to hail the news as evidence that no federal antilynching law was needed. But within days of Ames's press release, a Cordele, Georgia, mob burned alive John Dukes for murdering the town marshal.[49]

THE NAACP

The National Association for the Advancement of Colored People began its campaign against lynching with a script not so different from that of Work or Ames. In 1916, the NAACP appealed to Boston philanthropist Philip G. Peabody for money to fight lynching. The NAACP's application leaned heavily on the traditional definition of lynching as murder sanctioned by the community. A successful fight, the NAACP declared, "must start with the recognition that popular justification is the *sine quo non* of lynching." The difference between ordinary murder and lynching, the NAACP explained, is that lynchers have some degree of community support behind them.[50]

The NAACP proposed gathering and publishing data, preparing model antilynching bills and organizing local committees to identify and prosecute lynchers. Peabody ultimately decided not to award the NAACP the money because, he said later, he realized his small sum would hardly make a dent in such an immense problem. Though the NAACP failed to persuade Peabody to make the grant, writing the grant proposal helped convince officials they should make lynching their top priority.[51]

For several years, the NAACP proved at least as conservative as Work in tabulating lynchings. In 1919 the NAACP's count of lynchings was actually lower than Work's. The disputed lynchings were in Arkansas, where the NAACP tabulated seven and Tuskegee twelve. Work included the murders of Elihu, Louis, Gibson, and Leroy Johnson in Elaine, Arkansas, on the basis of local press accounts. Public opinion, Work argued, must be respected when determining whether a murder should be counted as a lynching or not. The Johnson brothers should be included because local newspapers had accepted their deaths as lynchings.[52] The NAACP capitulated on the Johnson brothers, but insisted that a white man burned by a mob after he committed suicide must not be counted as a lynching.[53] In 1920 Work once again listed more lynchings than did the NAACP, including some that the Northern organization had overlooked.[54]

The campaign for a federal antilynching law also shows the NAACP's initial conservatism in defining lynching. The elements of the legislation favored by the NAACP appeared in 1918 when Republican Congressmen Leonidas Dyer and Merrill Moores introduced an antilynching bill in the House. This bill defined a lynch mob as three or more persons, promised to guard the lives of American citizens denied protection by their states, punished state officials who refused to protect citizens, and fined entire counties or cities where lynchings occurred. This last provision had a long history. Eleven states had antilynching laws that penalized localities that sponsored lynchings. The amounts ranged from $1,000 (in Nebraska) to $10,000 (in Pennsylvania). Requiring entire communities to pay for murders committed by crowds fit well with the definition of lynching prevailing at the beginning of the twentieth century: murder by community.[55]

In one sense, the NAACP-backed bill proposed dramatic change. The NAACP wanted to transfer from the states to the federal government the power to prosecute a particular kind of murder. The Supreme Court had ruled at the end of Reconstruction that the Fourteenth Amendment did not allow federal murder prosecutions. That job remained in the hands of the states. The Supreme Court based its decision on the language of the Fourteenth Amendment ("No State shall"), which seemed to forbid certain state actions. The national government, under this doctrine, could act against wrongs committed by states but not against the private misdeeds of individuals.[56] The NAACP argued for a new rule: when states and localities refused to prosecute racially motivated murders, that amounted to a failure to protect citizens equally and justified federal intervention.[57]

In another sense, the proposed legislation broke no new ground. While constitutionally revolutionary in that it would have transferred powers traditionally held by local authorities to federal courts, the NAACP's idea of community responsibility followed old understandings. The organization wanted federal authorities to punish counties that refused to punish lynchers rather than going after the actual lynchers directly. English common law had suppressed rioting in the same fashion for centuries.

By the end of the 1920s, the NAACP had moved away from its understanding of lynching as violence endorsed by specific towns or communities. A few years after its Peabody proposal and after it first endorsed a federal law against lynching, the NAACP dramatically loosened its definition, no longer regarding community support as the sine quo non of lynching. By 1928 the

NAACP pressed Tuskegee to count as lynchings a broader range of deaths. The NAACP counted twenty-one lynchings for 1927, while Work counted only sixteen. The five killings marked as lynchings by the NAACP but not by Tuskegee included a Los Angeles incident where prisoners in a jail beat to death a fellow inmate, killings by posses in Tennessee and North Carolina, and a Florida drowning, in which the crowd threw its victim into the Suwannee River.[58]

Politics and not changes in the behavior of Southern whites explains the NAACP's shift. One reason the NAACP loosened its definition can be found in rivalries between the NAACP and its competitors on the left. In the Great Depression the American Communist party and the International Labor Defense (ILD) recruited thousands of new members, taking people who might have joined the NAACP in earlier years. In 1931 the NAACP lost a major public relations battle with the ILD. In the celebrated "Scottsboro case," where Alabama whites accused black youths of rape, the ILD publicly bested the NAACP in a competition for the right to represent the defendants. Many in the NAACP saw their fight against lynching as a trump card. When cornered, the NAACP could always present itself as the preeminent opponent of lynching; and in the 1930s, the NAACP leadership certainly felt cornered. The NAACP's antilynching campaign had been a low priority for years, but with its back to the wall, the organization revived the fight.[59]

The NAACP's rivals did not ignore the lynching issue. Indeed, they took the offensive on that as well, hammering the NAACP for its overly narrow definition of lynching. In 1932, the Associated Negro Press called for a loose rule defining lynching as "any death to an individual or individuals inflicted by two or more privately organized citizens, who impose such violence with correctional intent."[60] Focused on the class dimension to lynching, the Communist League of Struggle for Negro Rights included labor violence in its annual tally of "lynchings." Some in the black community found the League's analysis appealing. The *Baltimore Afro-American* thought it made sense to include such murders: "Inasmuch as a mob of white outlaws is organized for the purpose of murdering all Negro firemen on Southern railroads, why shouldn't it be termed lynching?"[61] While the NAACP had remained true to the old idea of lynchings as murders carried out by a mobilized populace, the Communists pushed for a law that punished individuals as lynchers.[62]

Individuals, not mobs, killed black railway workers. Critics of the NAACP charged that when it failed to include lynchings carried out by small groups, the association missed an important dimension of racial violence. In 1933 the League of Struggle for Negro Rights claimed to have detected a change in the character of lynchings, which no longer sprang from spontaneous expressions of lynch mania. Instead three or four well-organized men acted at the behest of white businessmen and public officials. Increasingly, sheriffs, deputies, and police officers carried out lynchings, the League alleged. Assassinations of black railroad workers must be counted as lynchings, the League insisted, because the killers acted on behalf of organized white elites. The League accused the NAACP of deliberately soft-pedaling crimes by the white ruling classes, conspiring to deceive "the Negro masses."[63]

Such charges were baseless, but they had the effect of pushing the NAACP toward the League's looser definition. The NAACP tally for 1930 included another prisoner murdered in his cell and a Shreveport, Louisiana, man who had been seized by a mob for killing two cops but had died before the mob could "lynch" him. Although the NAACP itself had once insisted that dead bodies could not be "lynched," the organization now wanted to count the Louisiana case. Two years later the issue came up again when the NAACP counted as a lynching the burning of a body; the victim had died before the mob could burn him.[64]

The character of the NAACP itself may have preordained a shift away from the Tuskegee approach of narrowly defining, counting, studying, and exposing lynching preparatory to its elimination. Unlike Work and Ames, the NAACP did not focus exclusively on lynching. Formed after the 1908 race riot in Springfield, Illinois, the NAACP drew support from outside the South, building a constituency to combat discrimination of all types. For the NAACP, lynching became the symbol of a broader problem, not the problem itself. As one writer explained, "lynching became the wedge by which the NAACP insinuated itself into the public conscience."[65] While Work and Ames looked forward to the day when they could declare victory over lynching, the NAACP challenged a long-term, deeply rooted enemy. NAACP founders expected their organization to be permanent. If lynching came to an end, the NAACP would face an intractable foe, white racism, without its most effective propaganda tool. If Ames and Work eliminated lynching by defining it as some particular kind of murder, they would not have abolished the prejudice, brutality, and violence that lynching represented.

The character of the people leading the NAACP also predisposed the organization against rigidly defined abstract statistics. Men disenchanted with positivism dominated the NAACP leadership. By the time the NAACP came into existence, W. E. B. Du Bois and other leaders had abandoned social science and sociology as appropriate vehicles to attack lynching. In 1894 Du Bois had begun a career in social science, applying scientific law to society. Laws of science, he thought, ruled the world, directing even human society toward greater accomplishment and civilization. In 1899 he published *The Philadelphia Negro: A Social Study,* a relentlessly empirical compilation of facts about Philadelphia's mostly black seventh ward. The same year Du Bois published his social science magnum opus, lynchers murdered Sam Hose, exhibiting his severed knuckles at the grocery store on Atlanta's Mitchell Street. This murder so outraged Du Bois that it shook his faith in social science. Calm, cool, detached science was not the correct response to such horrors. Du Bois never forgot the value of science as rhetoric, but he chose a more openly polemical approach. Just four years after *The Philadelphia Negro* appeared, Du Bois published *The Souls of Black Folk*,[66] which took a "linguistic turn," understanding language as a malleable tool that can be shaped to persuade, a tool that never merely neutrally describes.[67]

One NAACP leader experienced his declension while in the organization. John R. Shillady, appointed NAACP executive secretary in 1918, headed the NAACP when it published *Thirty Years of Lynching in the United States, 1889–1918*. A statistical compilation, *Thirty Years of Lynching* proved what Wells had already proven: that lynchers rarely accused their victims of rape, despite their insistence that rape justified lynching. Shillady lost faith in numerical research when an Austin, Texas, mob, which included a judge and a constable, assaulted him. Instead of denouncing the beating, the governor of Texas took the opportunity to scold the NAACP, criticizing interfering outsiders. Shillady realized facts and figures could not deter such crazily wrong-headed logic. This episode broke Shillady's faith that lynching statistics could reform white Southerners. Not long after, he left the NAACP.[68]

Du Bois and Shillady were not the only NAACP leaders disenchanted with social science positivism. After he joined the NAACP, Walter White wrote a novel about an African American doctor who travels South, where he learns that a life devoted to pure science is impossible.[69] Having turned away from objective science, Du Bois and White launched a frankly polemical attack on racial violence, relying on statistics only when rhetorically useful.

Although the NAACP collected and tabulated data along with the other antilynching organizations, its real contribution to the debate came in the form of investigative reports. In 1915 Roy Nash traveled to Georgia, where he collected information on lynchings in Dawson and Forsyth counties. His report appeared in the NAACP's magazine, *The Crisis*. In 1918, NAACP leaders sent Walter White south to get inside information on lynchings. His accounts created "a gratifying sensation" that replenished the NAACP's empty treasury with contributions from blacks and whites who were shocked by the details he provided.[70] In 1929 White published *Rope and Faggot: A Biography of Judge Lynch*. White's book made a statistical argument that Ida B. Wells would have recognized. He reported, for example, that lynchers had murdered 1,665 persons between 1890 and 1900, and included a lengthy appendix replete with tables.[71] He counted the number of victims burned alive and those burned after death. But White also tried to unravel lynchers' mentality. In White's view, Southern society had "stunted" the "mental and moral growth" of "generation after generation of Southern whites."[72] Looking at the lynchers' psyches, White decided that lynching emerged from poor law enforcement, "human love of excitement," and "the human unwillingness to form new ideas." White added that an over-emphasis on sex, resulting from "the dullness of life and the lack of such diversions as theatres," in lynching states contributed to the violence.[73]

When White associated lynching with Christianity, he struck at the basic foundations of white Southern society. He charged that the church had tacitly approved lynchings and that evangelicals had generated the kind of fanaticism that encouraged racial violence. White must have intended his criticism of the church as a dig at his rivals, knowing, of course, that Work had been a minister and that Ames had been active in the Methodist women's movement. The same Christianity White attacked as promoting lynching had produced his competitors. More significantly, the difference between White and Ames and Work on this issue shows the more radical nature of the NAACP. White wanted to change the structure of Southern society dramatically. For him, lynching was merely a symptom of a depraved culture. Ames and Work, by contrast, believed that the basic structure—and they considered their churches to be the basic structure—of the South was sound.[74]

Setting for himself the task of changing the underpinnings of white Southern society, White had little reason for confidence. He only occasionally tempered *Rope and Faggot* with optimism. After seven chapters outlining the social and economic forces that stunted white Southerners' culture, White announced himself relieved to report evidence of improvement and praised Southern newspapers opposed to lynching and especially his own organization, the NAACP, for its work. But he returned to more familiarly grim terrain in his next and final chapter. The South's "discouraging picture," he declared, is "encouraging only by comparison with previous years."[75] Without a federal law, he concluded, lynching will not end in "the backward states." Without such federal action, White predicted, "sad and terrible days . . . for all of America, seem inevitable."[76]

Newspaper reaction to the NAACP's bid to broaden the definition of lynching split along racial lines. Black newspapers found the NAACP position not only rational but also inescapable. They observed that any count of lynchings could never be more than an estimate, as murders of plantation field hands, labor camp peons, and chain gang convicts could never be fully included. In some cases, state executions amounted to "legal lynchings" and should be included as well.[77]

White Southern newspapers suspected that the NAACP inflated the number of lynchings. At least by the 1930s, many white newspaper editors sincerely opposed lynching. For the most part, they had absorbed the lessons taught by Wells, Work, and Ames. Southern communities had to reform their thinking, and, as community leaders, newspaper editors had the duty to lead the effort. Robert Latham, editor of the *Asheville Citizen-Times,* wrote privately that "too often there is a public sentiment behind the lynchers. This is what we have all been trying to break down."[78] Nonetheless, white journalists, committed to statistics and social science positivism, found all-inclusive lynching definitions unsettling. For many, the NAACP represented an outside force, one hostile to the South, and many more found the NAACP insistence on a loose definition puzzling if not suspicious. Newspaper editors sometimes wrote the NAACP directly asking how Tuskegee could produce such different tabulations.[79]

Journalists pressured all the organizations to square their lists, and at least as early as 1920 Monroe Work and the NAACP exchanged lists of lynchings. They swapped lists in the following year as well, when they again came up with different tallies.[80] But this effort at reconciliation disenchanted Work. He complained that NAACP officers wanted to manipulate his statistics for their own advancement. They did not want accuracy, he charged; they wanted propaganda.[81] In 1933, Work tried to persuade White not to count the "lynching" of Doc Rogers in Pender County, North Carolina. Rogers had been shot by police officers after he engaged them in a gun battle. A mob seized Rogers' dead body and shot it again, mutilating it. Work pointed out that under the proposed federal law—backed by the NAACP—shooting a dead body would not count as a lynching.[82]

"Black Legion" killings in Michigan led to another dispute between Work and the NAACP. The nature of the killings perpetrated by the Black Legion makes Work's reluctance to count them as "lynchings" seem odd and misplaced. Although based in the North, the Black Legion closely resembled the Klan. The Legion, in fact, began in 1925 as an arm of the Klan when an Ohio Grand Cyclops, Dr. William Jacob Shepard, designed black costumes for a faction of his followers. The black outfits proved so popular that Klan leaders feared Shepard might be building his own empire. They revoked Shepard's charter, which had the effect of making real their worst fears. Shepard started the Black Legion, his own version of the Klan that preached a similar litany of prejudice against foreigners, Catholics, and Jews. Shepard's nativist organization quickly spread across Michigan and Indiana, where recruiters used anticommunist rhetoric to attract disaffected workers into their organization. In May 1936 the *Detroit News,* the *New York Times,* and other periodicals headlined the news that a "Vigilante Society Is Exposed." Over six years the Black Legion had committed fifty-seven murders in one area of Michigan alone. The Legion's murder of a young Works Progress Administration worker named Charles Poole led to its exposure. A crowd of Legionaires had confronted Poole, accused him of beating his wife, and then shot him to death. The official investigation of Poole's death led to sixteen arrests and revelations of violent racism in the North. One member later testified that Black Legion leaders sometimes ordered Legionaires to "get a colored guy" for them.[83]

Newspaper reporting of the Black Legion killings makes it clearer why Work, always respectful of local journalists' judgments, might want to exclude such murders from his list. *New York Times* editors studded their headlines with quotes, making clear their sensitivities to the language they used. "SEVEN 'VIGILANTES' ACCUSED OF MURDER," the *Times* headlined, adding "Detroit Officials say Four of the 'Black Legion' Admit 'Executing' Man as Wife Beater." In later articles the *Times* described Black Legion members as "night riders" or "terrorists," never as "lynchers."[84] The *Chicago Tribune* thought they were "ROBED SLAYERS," night riders, and vigilantes.[85] The *New Orleans Times-Picayune* characterized them as "Self-Appointed Guardians of Morals." "Ganglike," they "slew" but did not lynch anyone.[86] Newspaper editors had decided these Northerners were vigilantes, not lynchers.

Work's policy of deference to the journalists dictated that he follow suit. In February 1937, he wrote White to insist that the Black Legion killings should not be classified as lynchings. Work echoed the *Times-Picayune*'s depiction of the Legion as "ganglike," writing that the murders sounded like "racketeer killings" not sanctioned by the community. Southern whites had long argued that Northern big-city organized crime assassinations should be counted as "lynchings."[87] In the 1930s racketeering was understood to be strong-arm tactics associated with organized crime and extortion. Loan sharks using violence to collect debts were "racketeers." Lynching meant racially inspired violence, while racketeering meant murder or violence for profit. Money motivated racketeers; race motivated lynchers. But just as the label "lynching" could be manipulated for political gain, so, too, could "racketeering."[88]

Work misunderstood the Black Legion killings, which were undoubtedly prompted by race and nativism more than money. Unlike Work, the NAACP no longer felt constrained by newspaper classifications. The association wanted to impose its own labels on racial killings regardless of what journalists wrote. NAACP leaders probably felt that they had little choice. If killings by Klanlike groups in the North were "executions" performed by vigilantes, and not lynchings, then Klan killings in the South could be dismissed in the same fashion. Lynching was too powerful a word to be surrendered so easily. The NAACP promptly responded that such "racketeer killings" as those carried out by the Black Legion should be seen as lynchings. "To fail to classify these as lynchings and to draw a fine line of demarcation by calling them racketeer killings would be to give an inaccurate picture of the lynching situation." By any definition, the NAACP asserted, Black Legion killings qualified as lynchings.[89]

Another issue involved killings carried out by law enforcement officers. For years Communist organizations insisted that such deaths must be included in lynching tallies. At first both Tuskegee and the NAACP had resisted. In 1936, the Tuskegee Institute still made the same argument, explaining that it did not want to count as lynchings killings perpetrated by police officers while making arrests. In some cases police shot criminals who were resisting arrest, and Tuskegee did not think such cases should be intermingled with the sometimes innocent victims of lynch mobs. Making the distinction required drawing a fine line. Police officers and sheriff's deputies sometimes led or participated in lynch mobs. Some posses composed of civilians and police officers closely resembled mobs in the way they hunted down and executed fugitives.[90]

Dwindling numbers of lynchings intensified tensions between Tuskegee, the ASWPL, and the NAACP. In 1939 Ames, who relied on Tuskegee for her statistics, felt close to a lynch-free year and escalated her inquiries into purported lynchings. Most often disputes over whether particular murders should be counted as lynchings or not pitted the ASWPL and Tuskegee against the NAACP, but now Ames argued that both the NAACP and Tuskegee exaggerated the numbers of lynchings. She charged that "statistical agencies" wanted to include *any* murder of black by white as a lynching.[91] In February the NAACP reported a lynching in El Dorado, Arkansas. Suspicious, Ames made inquiries and found that a man named Walter Frazier had been shot by two people in a car after he tried to rob them. Since that did not meet the standards promoted by the NAACP in its proposed federal legislation, which required three or more murderers, Ames refused to count Frazier as lynched.[92] On April 1 newspapers called the murder of Miles W. Brown in Panama City, Florida, a lynching. Four or five masked men removed Brown from a jail after he had been convicted of murder. "Four or five masked men" came perilously close to not meeting the "three or more" standard the NAACP had accepted in its proposed federal law. The *New York Times* avoided describing the incident as a "lynching" but Tuskegee included it.[93]

Ames understood the power of journalists to stamp a murder with the lynching label and accordingly kept a sharp eye on the press. On April 29

Daytona Beach lawmen arrested Lee Snell after his taxi struck and killed a child. The child's two brothers shot and killed Snell while he sat in a constable's car. The Daytona Beach murder would not have qualified as a lynching under the NAACP's proposed law, and Ames blamed the Associated Press (AP) for calling it one. No one called the killing a lynching except the AP, Ames charged, and she urged one of her subordinates to speak with the Associated Press.[94] When she heard a rumor the next month of another lynching, Ames again called the Associated Press. The AP contacted the sheriff, who denied that any lynching had occurred. When Ames asked an assistant to contact local blacks, they agreed with the sheriff.[95]

Ames succeeded in erasing one incident from the record after Tuskegee first reported it as a lynching. Tuskegee had announced four lynchings in the first six months of 1939, including the murder of Charlie Williams in Screven County, Georgia, which was reported in a black Savannah newspaper. Since she disliked relying on stories published in "negro newspapers, unconfirmed by white persons," Ames contacted a Methodist minister in Savannah, asking him to visit Screven County and confirm the report. The minister, J. O. J. Taylor, contacted a local minister, interviewed white journalists in Savannah, and questioned railroad crews passing through Screven County. On July 26, he reported to Ames that no lynching had occurred.[96] In this initial letter Taylor reported he could not find Williams, but within days Savannah police had located the very-much-alive lynching "victim." Southern newspapers printed Williams's picture and quoted Williams as saying: "I heard I was lynched but didn't pay any attention to it 'cause I knew I was living." The quote delighted whites, as did Williams's statement that "white folks have always been my best friends."[97] All over the South white newspaper readers delightedly enjoyed a laugh at Tuskegee's expense.[98] White Georgians rejoiced that their state had been "cleared" of the one lynching alleged against it. The NAACP and the ILD refused to strike the Williams "lynching" from its list, merely changing the name of the victim from Williams to "Identity unknown (Negro)."[99]

On May 8, 1939, a person or persons in Canton, Mississippi, tortured and killed Joe Rodgers after Rodgers had quarreled with his white landlord. When officials pulled his body from the Pearl River, they found his feet and hands had been bound. Work counted Rodgers as a lynching, though no one saw how many persons had killed him. Work calculated that several must have been involved, as one killer could not have tied up Rodgers. Ames objected, insisting that a single murderer could have both tied and murdered his victim.[100] Nonetheless, newspapers widely accepted the Rodgers homicide as a lynching, the last lynching of 1939.

As months rolled by after Rodgers's death, the press reported no new lynchings. Ames began to look forward to her lynch-free year and the NAACP moved to rebut her claim. To do this they again changed their understanding of what qualified as a lynching. Before Ames closed in on her goal of a lynch-free year, the NAACP had counted killings by mobs as lynchings, counting seven in 1938, for example.[101] Now the organization embraced the position staked out by the ILD and the League of Struggle for Negro Rights years earlier, explaining that Southern lynchers had changed tactics, hiding their work by delegating the killings to small committees. The Rodgers killing was actually a good example of the "new" style of lynching.[102] By the end of 1939, some newspapers reported the "startling" information from the NAACP of hitherto unknown lynchings.[103] Walter White issued press releases charging that twenty Mississippi lynchings had gone unreported. In the midst of this perception of an upsurge in new lynching violence, the NAACP again called on Tuskegee to urge coordination and comparison of lynching records. NAACP charged that recent Tuskegee underestimates had heartened the proponents of lynch law.[104]

The NAACP changed its definition to meet Ames's challenge, but the organization had a point. Some Ku Klux Klan klaverns certainly did secretly brutalize people, black and white, and literally did rely on "committees" to carry out the work. In the Atlanta area, the East Point Klan, for example, maintained a Klokan, or investigative, committee. Only the chairman's identity was known to the other Klansmen. Since the chairman of the committee could recruit whomever he wanted for particular jobs, the membership of the committee shifted from time to time. This committee investigated new members and the morality of current members. In addition, the Exalted Cyclops organized "wrecking crews" to whip persons outside the Klan. At times Georgia Klansmen patroled public roads at night to break up illicit trysts between lovers. Wrecking crews whipped sellers of liquor or men who had "bigged a girl" outside marriage. Klansmen flogged husbands when their wives complained of their abuse or drunkenness. Often Klansmen impersonated law enforcement officers, sometimes displaying badges and brandishing fake warrants. On other occasions, real police officers accompanied Klan "wrecking crews." When asked why he did not arrest a lawbreaker instead of threatening him with violence, one sheriff's deputy answered, "How could I? I was enrobed."[105]

When Atlanta Klan "wrecking crews" murdered three white people, Sarah Rawls, Benton Ford, and Ike Gaston, the news media did not call the killings "lynchings." Klansmen caught Rawls and Ford parked on a "lovers' lane." The Klan beat Gaston to death after his wife lodged a complaint that she and her children had no groceries or coal and that Gaston, a barber, had been drinking instead of providing for his family.[106] In all three cases, the killers used a leather belt, which the *New York Times* compared to "a medieval torture instrument." These murders attracted considerable attention, with *The Nation* publishing an article entitled "The Klan Rides Again" and *American Mercury* calling its article "The Klan Kicks Up Again." *The Nation* and *American Mercury* articles traced the history of the Atlanta Klan, describing nightridings and floggings without using the word "lynching." The *New York Times* also did not describe the "night-riding band of flogging terrorists" as "lynchers." The investigation inspired by the murders of Rawls, Ford, and Gaston prompted many victims of Klan violence to step forward. *The Nation* estimated that "hundreds" of floggings—but not lynchings—had occurred in the previous year. *American Mercury* put the number more conservatively at fifty over two years.[107]

THE LYNCH-FREE YEAR

With the press reporting "floggings" but no lynchings in Georgia or anywhere else by May 8, 1939, Ames impatiently anticipated the first official lynch-free year in American history. By January Ames and her followers were counting the days. In August Ames described herself as holding her breath for fear that Tuskegee might find another lynching that had occurred before May 8.[108] Finally the great day arrived. Two months after the three Georgia murders, Ames issued a press release based on Tuskegee data announcing that for the first time in American history a year had passed without a single lynching.[109]

Within days Walter White fired back with a letter that the *New York Times* headlined "Lynching Still Goes On."[110] One NAACP officer described himself as "inexpressibly shocked by Tuskegee's statement."[111] The NAACP's Oswald Garrison Villard expressed astonishment.[112] Thurgood Marshall thought the fight against lynching had been set back. He made the argument that lynchers had merely adopted "the subcommittee technique," operating in secret.[113] One newspaper reported "on good authority" that whites conspired to silence newspaper reports of lynchings, wanting to quiet demand for a federal antilynching law.[114]

Some African Americans concluded that Tuskegee and Ames had sold out. The *Nashville Globe and Independent* criticized Tuskegee for "explanations which do not explain." The paper thought it could detect the taint of abject apology for the lynchers.[115] The secretary of the Brevard County, Florida, branch of the NAACP, Harry T. Moore, wrote that it was unfortunate that Tuskegee had been too optimistic. "We ourselves," Moore wrote, "should never try to help the white man cover up his misdeeds in dealing with our race."[116]

White lectured the president of Tuskegee, Frederick Douglass Patterson, that "you and I know from personal experience that strenuous efforts are being made to keep the news of lynchings out of the papers and away from public attention. . . ." The best example of this, he added, was Ames's refusal to include the three Atlanta Klan killings. Walter White probably suspected Patterson played a role in the "strenuous efforts" he criticized. Patterson had become head of Tuskegee in 1935, after serving as director of the school of agriculture. His philosophy of race relations remained in the Booker T. Washington tradition. Two years after he became president, Patterson launched a school for domestic service at Tuskegee.[117]

Ames responded to White's criticism by agreeing that Southerners sometimes secretly murdered blacks and whites. She disputed the NAACP implication that this amounted to a new kind of lynching, pointing out that such individual murders had been going on for many years. In fact her own research had long ago identified certain places in Georgia, Mississippi, Texas, and Louisiana where "putting Negroes away quietly was part of the custom of the communities." The federal law proposed by the NAACP, Ames pointed out, could not prevent such murders. That could be done only by reforming the attitudes of Southern whites.[118]

Southern white newspapers rallied to Ames' defense, challenging some of the murders the NAACP insisted should be counted as lynchings. In 1933 the *Wilmington (North Carolina) Morning Star* articulated the definition that most newspapers accepted. "In the usual sense," the newspaper explained, "a lynching occurs when a mass of citizenry outraged by a real or fancied grievance takes the law into its own hands and visits summary vengeance upon the object of its wrath."[119] Such a definition did not cover Ike Gaston. The *Richmond Times-Dispatch* chastised the NAACP for calling that killing a lynching.[120] The *Atlanta Daily World* understood that one way to challenge the NAACP was to demand a strict definition. Such a demand seemed reasonable to most readers and would result in the perception of fewer lynchings.[121] The *Jacksonville (Florida) Times-Union* wrote that the Tuskegee records must be trusted, adding that Southern women fought lynching more effectively than did the NAACP.[122] Famed Virginia newspaper editor Virginius Dabney offered the most articulate repudiation of the "lynching goes underground" argument. Dabney wrote that he hesitated "to accept the undocumented statement that 'underground' lynchings claim 'countless' victims annually." He doubted "that this species of barbarism is more prevalent to-day than formerly; it may, in fact, be definitely on the wane. . . ."[123]

The NAACP had a point when it reported that whites carried out considerable racial violence in secret. Extant documentation from the East Point Klan makes it clear that white racists literally did appoint committees and subcommittees to carry out acts of covert violence against African Americans. But Dabney had a point as well. If secret assassinations carried out by Klan klaverns and Klanlike groups should be counted as "lynchings," then no one can identify a statistical trend line or central tendency in the data. When the NAACP announced that lynching had "gone underground," it acted in response to political pressures, not the realities of racial violence. Since covert acts are by definition not public, surreptitious beatings and killings of blacks may or may not have been more extensive in the past than in the 1940s. It is impossible to know.

SUMMIT CONFERENCE

Ames's lynch-free year ran from May 1939 to May 1940, based on Tuskegee's reporting of lynchings. The NAACP tried to spoil Ames's celebration early, by undermining Tuskegee's credibility. On July 3, 1939, Walter White chastised Tuskegee in a blistering telegram. "Tuskegee," he said, "should either establish machinery to get facts completely and accurately or stop issuing lynching figures."[124] Patterson responded to White's telegram by suggesting that the two organizations should meet "in an effort to make a clean-cut statement as to what properly constitutes a lynching." Patterson proposed meeting in September.[125]

It took longer than two months for the two organizations to agree on protocols for the meeting. White and Patterson had agreed to broaden the conference to include people not connected with either the NAACP or Tuskegee. They disagreed over just who the extra conferees should be. White urged "the addition of a few more Negroes," while Tuskegee wanted to invite white journalists. White wrote that he did not mean to impugn the integrity of the white editors whom Patterson proposed inviting, but he believed white Southerners would subconsciously lean toward minimizing lynching. Patterson responded by saying that all different points of view must be represented.[126] The extant correspondence seems cordial, but negotiations between Tuskegee and the NAACP became so strained the two sides agreed to a preliminary conference, a meeting before the actual conference, where differences about the main meeting could be ironed out.[127]

Tuskegee officials carried to the meeting a lynching definition designed to exclude murders carried out in secret or committed by lawmen. A lynching, according to Tuskegee, was "an activity in which persons not officers of the law, in open defiance of the law, administer punishment by death to an individual for an alleged offense or to an individual with whom some offense has been associated."[128]

White predicted that the conference would focus on Tuskegee's refusal to include as lynchings secret assassinations and killings by law enforcement officers. These, White said, were dangerous exclusions.[129] Thurgood Marshall agreed and told White that NAACP negotiators must stick to its definition. It was imperative as well, Marshall emphasized, to include secret lynchings carried out even without the approval of any committee.[130]

On December 14, 1940, the NAACP and other antilynching organizations met at Tuskegee. Just as NAACP leaders had feared, the white journalists in attendance rallied to the side of Ames and Tuskegee. McClellan Van der Veer, a Birmingham journalist, joined Jessie Daniel Ames to argue in favor of a precise and narrow definition for lynching. Journalists, Van der Veer insisted, would not accept an overly broad definition; they wanted "reality." Van der Veer argued that accurate information on lynching, carefully defined, would do more to fight racial violence than overt propaganda. Ames renewed her appeals for a narrow definition. She thought that a corpse and a court record should actually exist before a homicide could be counted as a lynching. Ames asserted that misclassifications of murders as lynchings had actually hurt the antilynching effort.[131] Both Van der Veer and Ames repeated their arguments that frequent reports of lynchings hardened whites to racial violence, explaining that a steady stream of headlines reporting "NEGRO TREADS AIR," or "NEGRO MURDERER GIVEN SHORT SHRIFT," or "DRAGGED FROM JAIL TO DIE BY THE ROPE" encouraged lynchers by making lynching appear to be routine.[132] Accurate information would "create the feeling that lynchings are not to be expected." Ralph Davis of the Tuskegee Institute proposed Tuskegee's narrow definition, which followed the lines Van der Veer and Ames urged.[133]

Walter White, Arthur Raper, and Ira Reid of Atlanta University opposed Van der Veer and Ames, pushing the NAACP position instead. White, Raper, and Reid argued for a wide definition of lynching. White began by claiming that the NAACP used the same definition of lynching as in proposed federal antilynching bills, but admitted that his organization often counted as lynchings murders that did not fit the federal definition. Raper warned the conference not to "drive lynching out of the picture by definition." Implicit in his warning was the concern that such a powerful rhetorical device as the lynching label should not be sacrificed on the altar of science. Raper warned that murders organized by officers of the law must be counted as "lynchings." Reid insisted that he did not want lynchings restricted to acts in defiance of the law, nor did he want officers of the law excluded. The Tuskegee definition would not count as lynchings the surreptitious killings the NAACP called "quiet lynchings."[134]

Seeking to reconcile these competing views, those at the meeting agreed on four criteria. First, before an incident could be declared a lynching, there had to be a dead body. Second, the corpse had to have met death illegally. Third, the murderers had to be a group. Participants debated the meaning of "group," some urging for the definition used by several states in their antilynching statutes: three or more people. Others thought that number too limiting. The membership of the conference never agreed, so "group" remained undefined. Last, conferees did agree that the murderers must have acted under pretext of service to justice, race, or tradition for their murder to count as a lynching.[135]

At least some newspapers described the conference as an unconditional NAACP victory. The *Nashville Globe and Independent* explained to its readers that the two sides would exchange information to get better statistics. More meaningfully, the *Globe and Independent* reported that killings by police would be counted—just as the NAACP had insisted going into the conference.[136] The NAACP also succeeded in derailing Tuskegee's requirement that only killings carried out in open defiance of the law be counted as lynchings. Under the definition worked out at the conference, killers need only believe they acted in "service to justice, race, or tradition" to qualify as lynchers. Just as Ames feared, this requirement would not rule out any racially motivated killings.

Ames ultimately rejected the conference's compromise definition, writing that the new definition "could be made to convert into a lynching the death of every Negro at the hands of white persons." For instance, the new definition included two 1941 murders in which authorities promptly and successfully prosecuted the killers. Josephus Daniels wrote that including such murders threatened to reduce lynching statistics into silliness.[137] And, in fact, even after the conference, the NAACP and Tuskegee still produced contradictory counts of lynchings.[138] The NAACP remained doggedly determined to maintain the broadest definition of lynching possible. In 1953, Marguerite Cartwright wrote in the NAACP's journal that "lynching has become a symbol and should be so understood." With startling candor, she admitted that reports of declines in lynchings threatened NAACP fund raising. "I was once refused an NAACP contribution by a wealthy acquaintance as he cited the decline in lynching," Cartwright complained. Instead of a "technical and doctrinaire" definition, Cartwright urged, lynching should be understood as a "technique of racial exploitation,—economic, cultural and political."[139]

Although the NAACP and other antilynching organizations found the 1940 definition inadequate, historians have rallied around it. Scholars writing about lynchings routinely invoke the 1940 definition, even when using data collected before 1940.[140] In fact there is no way to control the definition of lynching, the product of decisions made by many local editors and their correspondents. The *Chicago Tribune* pointed out in 1890 that "How many unrecorded victims have been lynched" in the South "will never be known."[141] A Kentucky newspaper, the *Boone County Recorder*, described an 1894 lynching as the eighth in the county, even though earlier issues of the paper only mentioned three.[142]

The most important fact about the 1940 summit conference is what it did *not* accomplish. The antilynching organizations did not reach a common understanding about the meaning of lynching. The NAACP's own staffers did not share a clear understanding of what constituted a lynching. In the years after the 1940 summit conference, America nationalized talk about lynching. No longer neighborhood talk, conversation about racially motivated lynchings became a topic of the national debate about race. These changes, described in the next chapter, happened with no common agreement about the meaning of lynching.

CHAPTER EIGHT

"High-Tech Lynchings"
MAKING THE RHETORIC NATIONAL

Nineteenth-century Republicans had tried and failed to nationalize concerns about racial violence. At the end of the nineteenth century, most Americans still viewed racial violence as a neighborhood concern. In the twentieth century powerful forces finally worked to nationalize understandings of lynching as racial and wrong. The NAACP and other institutional opponents of lynchings had worked toward that end early in the century. Technological advances in news gathering and dissemination helped the press to achieve much of what the NAACP sought.

The man whose name will forever be linked to lynching illustrated this reality by exploiting it. In 1991 Clarence Thomas told members of the U. S. Senate Judiciary Committee that he had been *lynched.* The committee had released to the press unsubstantiated stories that the Supreme Court nominee had once sexually harassed a former assistant. In another context, the victim of such leaks might accuse the leakers of character assassination. But Thomas had more devastating language available. In words that stunned the white senators assembled in front of him, Thomas charged that broadcast of such accusations amounted to a "high-tech lynching."[1]

Had Thomas tried to redefine lynching, to make the word mean something people could not recognize, he would not have been nearly so successful. Rather, he skillfully manipulated Americans' existing conceptions about lynching. While Americans cannot agree on a definition of lynching, through newspapers, radio, and television they can imagine what lynchings should look like. These images center on the notion that white men lynch black men who have usually been accused of some sexual crime by a woman. The press disseminates such accusations, whipping up public opinion against the man to be lynched. Thomas called up all these images, which were stored in the head of almost every American.[2]

In three words, Thomas captured the two most important developments in twentieth-century lynching. At least from the 1830s, technology worked to integrate once-isolated communities into a national news market by breaking down obstacles to the spread of words, images, slogans, and ideas. "High-tech" refers to the national news media, the power of popular culture to reach consumers across a continent immediately. The word *lynching* had carried a political punch since it first appeared in the American oral culture; high-powered communications technology immeasurably increased its political power.

And because Thomas made his charge before a committee of the U. S. Senate, his words called to mind twentieth-century changes in the meaning of lynching. At the end of the nineteenth century, white authorities complicated the meaning of lynching, working to drive lynching indoors by making the criminal justice system more efficient, capable of delivering punishment so swiftly that no "lynching" need occur. One governor proposed placing judges on call, to be summoned immediately to crime scenes for faster trials and quicker executions.[3] The states made rape a capital crime, giving juries the power to put rape defendants to death. In other words, all-white, all-male juries got to pick which rapists lived and which ones died. This was supposed to forestall "lynching" by substituting the power of the state for the mob.[4] It blurred the line between lynching and execution. By 1991, Thomas could plausibly describe himself as "lynched" by the supposed lynchers: members of the U. S. Senate. Thomas defended himself with an image derived from nearly a century of "lynchings" carried out by courts and other legal institutions.

Some would say that what came nine years later, on June 16, 2000, was a real lynching, nothing like the metaphorical lynching Thomas claimed for himself. On that day, in Kokomo, Mississippi, Raynard Johnson's father came home from work to find his seventeen-year-old son's body hanging from a pecan tree in the front yard. News of his discovery spread much like Thomas's metaphorical lynching. The major newspapers and the television networks hurried to Mississippi to cover the story. Jesse Jackson flew to Kokomo, trailed by a crowd of journalists. New York's Al Sharpton announced plans to go to Mississippi. Attorney General Janet Reno met with Raynard Johnson's mother and promised a federal investigation.[5] Coverage of Johnson's death was just as "high-tech" as the television reporting of allegations against Clarence Thomas. ABC News broadcast the story on its news magazine program *20/20*. CBS and NBC carried the story on their evening news broadcasts, and CNN organized panels of experts to discuss the hanging throughout July.[6]

After July the story disappeared. Raynard Johnson's "lynching" may have been no more "real" than Thomas's. For all the attention his death received, Raynard Johnson may have hanged himself. Two autopsies, one sponsored by the Johnson family, failed to find evidence that Johnson had been lynched.[7] Given the uncertain nature of Johnson's death, the notice it received is remarkable. The unresolved death of a teenager, either by suicide or murder, seldom attracts such national attention. But in a "high-tech" news environment, a plausible lynching charge packed a global wallop. Thomas had deftly put his finger on the central reality in lynching. Lynching was a word with the power to influence an audience and, at the same time, a word that can be made to mean many things. As technology allowed news outlets faster access to larger markets, lynching became more broadly powerful, attracting crowds of journalists from all over the nation to the scenes of reported lynchings. Lynching became a word that could more obviously reshape the thinking of a nation.

LOW-TECH LYNCHINGS

Throughout the nineteenth century and for much of the twentieth, young black men like Raynard Johnson died with little notice. Lynchings were still "low tech," generally attracting only muted attention outside the neighborhood where they occurred. Many Americans had trouble seeing lynching as illegitimate in their war against crime. Crime was such a serious problem that even members of the Supreme Court believed it best not to inquire too closely into just how neighborhoods controlled crime. Perhaps the most extreme example of this thinking appeared in 1903, when Justice David J. Brewer published an article in *Leslie's Weekly* urging elimination of all appeals in criminal cases. This, Brewer theorized, would cure the lynching problem.[8] Brewer's article did not necessarily typify the thinking of lawyers or judges.

Yet, while the other justices did not want to go quite as far as Brewer, they did see crime fighting as primarily a matter of neighborhood concern. The Leo Frank case makes this clear. In 1913, the police, the courts, and the press trampled over Leo Frank's due process rights. If ever a case begged for federal intervention to protect a citizen's rights from mob-dominated neighborhood justice, this was it. The Atlanta, Georgia, police began their botched investigation on April 27, 1913, when they recovered Mary Phagan's body from the National Pencil Company factory. Missing the real murderer, police instead arrested the Jewish factory superintendent, Leo Frank. Local newspapers vied with each other to see who could run the most hysterical headline, who could best sentimentalize Phagan, and who could most

graphically demonize Leo Frank. Frank went on trial in a courthouse surrounded by a mob. His lawyers called over 100 character witnesses and put
Frank himself on the stand. To the cheers of the crowds outside, the jury
brushed all this aside and delivered a guilty verdict. The judge sentenced
Frank to death.[9]

What happened to him might be called a "legal lynching," though that
term was not common in 1913. His lawyers petitioned the United States
Supreme Court for a writ of habeas corpus, a procedure that would have
forced state officials to justify their handling of the case before a federal
judge. The justices were divided over whether to allow states to short-circuit
due process. Most thought they could. Justice Mahlon Pitney wrote the
opinion of the Court, rejecting the whole idea of using federal writs of
habeas corpus to scrutinize state criminal trials. The states, Pitney declared,
had the job of controlling crime and the federal government should not dare
interfere in such critical work. Holmes wrote a scathing dissent. The court
that convicted Frank, Holmes said, had been openly hostile to the defendant.
For Holmes, the presence of the mob was enough to show that Frank had
been denied his due process rights. The mob terrorized the jury, frightening
them into giving the verdict the mob demanded. Such a procedure, Holmes
said, obviously demolished real due process.[10]

It may be ironic that the Supreme Court's decision in the Leo Frank case
led to a "real" lynching. In 1915, Governor John M. Slaton commuted Frank's
sentence and ordered the prisoner be shipped to the state prison farm in
Milledgeville. Across the country, newspapers hailed Slaton as a hero. In
Georgia, the commutation ignited hatred that boiled just below the surface.
A mob broke into the prison, seizing and hanging Frank.[11] Seventy years
later, a witness to the murder confirmed that the prosecution's chief witness
against Frank had actually committed the murder, not Leo Frank.[12]

Though they thoroughly understood the commercial news value of grisly
crime stories, newspaper editors largely agreed with the Supreme Court that
controlling crime was a neighborhood matter, not something outsiders should
be overly interested in. When authorities found Mary Phagan's body in the
pencil factory, Atlanta papers covered their front pages with the news. Papers
in Chicago and New York ignored the story, if they even knew about it.[13]

This remained true in 1916, when newspapers outside Texas only paid
slight attention when Texas authorities charged a black youth named Jesse
Washington with murder after he had allegedly assaulted and raped his landlord's wife. Washington went on trial in Waco, where the courthouse was
surrounded by a screaming mob. During the entire trial, Washington's attorney asked only a single cross-examination question. The transcript fills a
mere seven typewritten pages. The state called just eight witnesses, mostly to

authenticate Washington's confession.[14] In that environment, no juror would have dared vote "not guilty" and none did. Even that was not enough. As the judge wrote the verdict in his official record, the mob stormed into the courtroom, seizing Washington. Hustling Washington outside, the mob stripped and castrated him before chaining him to an automobile to be dragged through the streets. At the end of the dragging, the crowd built a fire and dangled his writhing body over the flames by a chain wrapped around his neck. Waco high school children left their lunches to watch the show. Women watched, laughing and chatting as they did so. Even after being dragged through the streets, Washington was still alive as he hung over the fire, his hands frantically clawing for the chain.[15]

Journalists wrote articles about Waco on a rhetorical battlefield where the armies of localism fought nationalization. Texas papers expressed shame and worried that outsiders might blame the whole state. The *Nation* and the *New Republic* denounced the affair, as did the *New York Times.* In the reporting of the Waco story, though, the localists easily turned back efforts to make the Waco lynching a national scandal. The *New York Times* ran its news story on Washington's horrifying death on page four, a five-paragraph article under a headline that emphasized the size of the crowd, estimated at 15,000. The *San Francisco Chronicle* put its similar story on page three, pushed down the page by more important stories on the city budget and a photograph promoting the German Relief Bazaar. Other large metropolitan papers ran similarly small stories. By banishing Waco to a small story on their inside pages, the *New York Times,* the *San Francisco Chronicle,* and other papers conceded that even the most brutal lynchings remained primarily a matter for local concern.[16] And the story had no staying power. After the *New York Times,* the *Chicago Tribune,* and other large metropolitan papers had reported the burning, with no state trial or inquiry to follow, there really was little else to say.

Even with the criminal courts and the press indifferent, Judge Lynch's victims had legal recourse: torts. In 1907, the widow and children of Robert T. Rogers, a white man lynched in Louisiana the previous year, sued a railroad company for transporting the mob that killed her husband. The leader of the mob had chartered a special train from Monroe to Tallulah, loading it with the lynch mob. In 1911, when Rogers's widow, Annie May Rogers, finally got her case to court, Judge Henry C. Niles threw out her evidence and directed the jury to acquit. Rogers had been unable to prove, Niles announced, that the railroad had knowingly carried the lynch mob. The testimony had been contradictory, with the railroad's top executives insisting they had not known why the train had been chartered and would not have knowingly allowed one of their trains to be used to kill someone. Lower ranking employees conceded they "thought something was up, something wrong."[17]

When Annie May Rogers appealed her defeat to the Fifth Circuit Court of Appeals, she won. "Corporations," the three-judge panel ruled, "are liable in damages for torts, and in proper cases may be convicted of conspiracy." As for Judge Niles's doubts about Rogers's proof that the railroad knowingly furnished the means for the mob to gather, "these questions can only be answered by a jury."[18] At her second trial, Rogers presented the same contradictory testimony as before, bolstered by insurance agents' testimony estimating the value of her husband's life. This time the train engineer testified, denying that he knew anything about the train's mission, but other witnesses disagreed.[19] The judge remained as skeptical as before and, while he allowed the case to go to the jury, gave a charge hostile to the plaintiffs.[20] Rogers lost. Nonetheless, the Fifth Circuit had affirmed the principle that the families of lynching victims could sue lynching conspirators for damages.

Few such suits occurred. With their deep pockets, railroads were the most obvious targets of such prosecutions. Lawyers would risk representing even paupers like Annie May Rogers, and go to the expense of collecting numerous depositions from railroad employees scattered all over the southeast, in hopes of scoring a profitable win. Newspapers observed that railroad executives showed up for the Rogers trial, obviously concerned about their liability.[21] They must have been alarmed when Rogers's attorneys charged that even if the railroad had not known its train transported a mob, it should have known and had a duty to know.[22] The Fifth Circuit did not disagree with this reasoning. There were fewer reports of special trains chartered for lynchings after the Rogers appeal. There may have been few such suits because railroads stopped chartering their trains so freely.

With torts not really an option, black Americans had little recourse but to seek protection from the federal government. And they did, bombarding presidents and their attorneys general with letters demanding and begging for federal help in the face of terrible racial violence. The Toussaint Louverture branch of the Savannah Chapter, American Red Cross, sent a telegram to President Woodrow Wilson describing themselves as shocked and frightened by whites' racial violence. These women, representing the "Negro womanhood of Georgia," called on Wilson to use the power of his office to punish the perpetrators of such violence.[23] Some correspondents could see clearly that racial violence against American citizens violated their constitutional rights. They could not understand why the federal government did not protect their rights against such violations.[24] John R. McChord of Claxton, Georgia, asked his president, "will you all please do something about these white folks Down hear [sic] and the southern States"?[25] The federal government remained indifferent to these pleas for help. The case of Will Moore, lynched in Mississippi, sparked a flicker of interest when an anonymous writer claimed Moore had been an active-duty soldier when killed. Finding that Moore had been a civilian, and, in fact, had been a bootlegger, Justice Department officials decided that Moore, like all other American citizens, deserved no federal protection.[26]

Technology and the News Business

The Washington lynching occurred as the news business was changing in America. Intellectual currents ran against localism, with some advanced thinkers like the legal philosopher and professor Hans Kelsen already promoting globalism and international justice over provincialism.[27] In the United States, the greater challenge to parochial, neighborhood newspapers characteristic of the nineteenth century came from demographic changes in the American population. Between 1910 and 1930, the U. S. population grew by thirty million, much of this growth taking place in the cities: the urban population alone increased by twenty-five million. During the same two decades, daily newspaper readership nearly doubled, from twenty-two to forty million. Those forty million newspaper readers had fewer newspapers to choose from. As the population increased dramatically, the number of newspapers decreased by 258. More and more people read fewer newspapers. Twentieth-century newspapers had to appeal to wider audiences to survive. For newspapers, neutral, "objective" reporting became the order of the day.[28]

At the same time, some publications, especially magazines, appealed to national audiences with muckraking journalism, investigative reporting that fed progressive causes by printing lurid accounts of corruption and horrors of the time. Muckrakers could keep a story in the news even with no trials or legal proceedings. The muckrakers' investigations themselves became the news, published in magazines with national circulations. Though the muckrakers went after a variety of social ills and injustices, they generally ignored racism and lynching. *Colliers,* a magazine famous for its muckraking, protested racially motivated violence until the Spanish-American War. Thereafter, *Colliers* dropped the subject of lynching from its pages. Most muckraking magazines did not even do as much as *Colliers.*[29]

In 1905, muckraker Ray Stannard Baker did briefly take an interest in lynching, though he did little to end racial violence. In two articles published by *McClure's,* a leading muckraking journal, Baker explained that two types of "negroes" inhabit the South. The "home negro" generally wins the affection of respectable white people. The "so-called 'worthless negroes',," in contrast, did not. "Worthless negroes," Baker wrote, menaced white society, floating from town to town, doing rough work. Ignorant and lazy, such "floating, worthless negro[es] caused most of the trouble." Once criminally excited, these floaters attacked "with almost animal-like ferocity." In a murderous rage, they could not seem to stop themselves from reverting to a savage state, bruising and battering their victims "out of all semblance to humanity." When whites told Baker that poor law enforcement made lynching necessary, he believed them. Baker informed his readers that in the North as well as the South, lynching occurred in places where authorities failed to vigorously enforce the law.[30] The only muckraker to look at lynching took the white side almost entirely.

The NAACP tried to turn the muckraking technique into a weapon against lynching, starting its own journal, *The Crisis: A Record of the Darker Races,* in 1910. The *Crisis* appeared under the auspices of the NAACP, but the great civil rights organization could offer its editor, W. E. B. Du Bois, only office space. He immediately dedicated his magazine to racial uplift and the struggle against violence, editorializing against a Florida lynching of two Italians in the first issue. Within a year, 10,000 subscribers read Du Bois's reports of lynchings and racial violence.[31]

NAACP officers Joel Spingarn and Oswald Garrison Villard thought the Waco lynching justified the first nation-wide campaign against lynching and used the *Crisis* to launch their effort. A suffragist named Elizabeth Freeman, already in Texas, hurried to Waco and spent ten days collecting information. Her report filled eight pages in the *Crisis*. The sheriff had moved Washington three times to avoid a lynching, Freeman reported. But then, facing reelection, Freeman charged, the sheriff covertly allowed the mob to finally take Washington in hopes of garnering votes on election day.[32] The NAACP struggled to make the Waco horror a national story, sending its supplement to 700 newspapers, to every member of Congress, and to ordinary citizens.[33]

Other black journalists also participated in the trend toward more national readerships, but did not see neutral reporting as the path to more readers. Robert S. Abbott founded the *Chicago Defender* in 1905, printing 300 copies of the first issue. Born in Georgia in 1868 to freed slaves, Abbott had graduated from law school but found he could not successfully practice law on account of his race. For four years, Abbott operated the *Defender* on a shoestring, doing the reporting, editing, and printing himself, and personally peddling his papers. In these early years, the *Defender* resembled many nineteenth-century black newspapers, seeming to be a neighborhood gossip sheet. In 1909, Abbott discovered muckraking, attacking sex, drinking, and white proponents of such behavior. Sensational stories about Chicago's red-light district, Abbott discovered, sold papers. By 1910, the *Defender* claimed a circulation of 25,000. That year, Abbott hired J. Hockley Smiley as his managing editor, forging an alliance that created the modern *Chicago Defender*. With Smiley as editor, the *Defender* became even more dedicated to "yellow" journalism, playing the latest racial atrocity in screaming red headlines. By 1915, when Smiley died, the *Defender*'s sensationalism carried its distribution down the Mississippi Valley and across the South, the first national black newspaper in American history. Sixty-seven thousand copies circulated nationally every week, two-thirds of which was distributed outside Chicago. In Mississippi, where the paper had an especially large circulation, copies sold out the day they arrived, the issues passing from hand to hand until they wore out. One prominent African American in Louisiana reported that "negroes grab the *Defender* like a hungry mule grabs fodder." Abbott inspired the massive migration of black Southerners to Chicago known as the Great Migration. The *Defender* called on Southern blacks to abandon their cotton fields for the North, contrasting lynching horrors with sanguine views of the North. "Millions Prepare to Leave the South Following Brutal Burning of Human," Abbott headlined. Abbott cleverly created an impression of a mass movement North before the migration really became massive. That the trickle northward turned into a torrent testified to Abbott's influence. So, too, did governmental efforts to suppress the *Defender*. During World War I Southern whites complained to the government about *Defender* "disloyalty," offering as evidence its report about a lynching headlined "Southern Stunts Surpass Hun." Government agents investigated Abbott and his paper, scrutinizing its columns for such disloyal statements.[34]

Government agents could not prevent the *Defender* corporation from expanding its power, as it bought black papers in other cities, publishing *Defenders* in New York, Detroit, and Memphis. These regional newspapers shared stories, often publishing the same story in all the *Defender* papers. *Defender* editors and reporters worked to bring neighborhood atrocities against blacks to the attention of a national readership. Stories that white papers relegated to the inside pages, as of chiefly local interest, appeared under banner headlines on the *Defender*'s front page. The *Defender* implicitly argued that when white neighborhoods oppressed individual blacks, all African Americans should care.[35]

Just as newspapers nationalized the news in new ways, the motion picture industry aspired to help construct a national ethos. Filmmakers created an image of their nation, an American myth that tied the country together, uniting through common experience audiences from the North and South, both rural and urban. In 1915, D. W. Griffith created a racist image that white Southerners could rally behind in *The Birth of a Nation*. Black filmmaker Oscar Micheaux countered with *Within our Gates,* a film that includes a grisly lynching set in Vicksburg. Whether it produced a racist product or not, the movie industry endangered the isolation of rural neighborhoods and communities.[36]

The invention and mass production of radio also challenged once-secluded neighborhoods. The first scheduled radio broadcast came in 1920, and between August 1921 and May 1922, 286 radio stations began broadcasting. By the late 1920s two networks controlled most of the programs Americans heard on their new radios. The NBC program "Amos 'n' Andy," with white actors mocking blacks, proved so popular that radio makers boosted production to meet demand. In part because African Americans made up such an insignificant portion of the radio audience (14 percent in the cities, 3 percent in the country), national white broadcasters did not hesitate to rely on racial stereotyping. But regional radio stations would broadcast "black" music, and whites sometimes found they liked it.[37]

Changes in law enforcement made America a bit less local as well. Though Prohibition is often presented as an effort to preserve neighborhood values against outside forces, efforts to enforce its ban on alcohol challenged neighborhood autonomy. In Alabama, the state legislature passed a "little Volstead Act" that "charged the governor with supervising and directing the enforcement of the laws of the State for the promotion of temperance." The legislature gave the governor sweeping new powers to command officers all over the state and created a new, though very small, police force under the governor's personal command. The new force was to "perform their functions and pursue their activities anywhere and at all times throughout the State, irrespective of local political subdivisions."[38] Such language seemed designed to strike fear in the hearts of local politicians, used to ruling their counties through courthouse rings with little or no outside influence. Often these local leaders had worked out corrupt alliances with local moonshiners. Some saw efforts to control liquor as a threat to local autonomy. The *Birmingham Age-Herald* complained that the governor's officers had "been running about the state wherever they saw fit to go and more or less messing into the affairs in the several counties." Sometimes the governor's officers broke up lynch mobs as well as stills.[39] Prohibition left the country, especially its law enforcement procedures, a bit less decentralized.

In the midst of these revolutionary changes, the Supreme Court turned away from its earlier toleration of neighborhood justice. In theory, changes in newspaper reporting and the popular culture should have had little impact on the federal courts. The Constitution insulates Supreme Court justices from the clamor and tumult of everyday politics. Nonetheless, in 1923, just as changes in news reporting and radio challenged the barriers around formerly isolated communities, the Supreme Court revised its thinking as well. One landmark case grew out of a 1919 Arkansas race riot and a state trial in which whites convicted the black victims of their rioting. Arkansas newspapers published inflammatory articles accusing blacks of plotting an insurrection, a race riot. Officials used tainted evidence to prosecute black defendants for murder in courthouses dominated and terrorized by mobs. The defendants appealed their convictions to the U. S. Supreme Court, where Oliver Wendell Holmes, already on record as saying the mob-dominated courts could deliver no justice, still sat.[40]

In the Leo Frank case, Holmes could not convince a majority of the justices to agree with his views. But since 1915, the Court had changed substantially, reflecting shifts in the nation's thinking. George Sutherland, Edward Sanford, Louis Brandeis, William Howard Taft, and Pierce Butler had all joined the Court since its Leo Frank decision. Sutherland and Butler would gain fame as half of the fearsome "Four Horsemen," reactionary opponents of the New Deal. Sanford and especially Brandeis brought more progressive thinking to the Court. Their influence gave Holmes the majority he needed to write the opinion of the Court in the Arkansas riot case. The federal judiciary, Holmes ruled, must step in when states allow public passion to overwhelm counsel, jury, and judge.[41]

Holmes did not talk about lynching directly, though the Arkansas riots could be called attempted lynchings. What he accomplished, though, had a direct impact on thinking about Southerners' racial violence. Holmes insisted that when Southern communities mistreated their black citizens, all of America should take notice and right the wrong.

And yet, despite Holmes's plea and increased national attention, local traditions stubbornly persisted. Even in 1930, to take one example of many, lynchers in Marion, Indiana, extricated from jail and hanged two black men accused of raping a young white woman. The governor of the state and the president of the United States snubbed the NAACP when it brought the case to their attention. Only the Indiana attorney general took action, dispatching two deputy attorneys general to Marion to investigate and prosecute members of the mob. Witnesses and local authorities refused to cooperate; strangely, local law officers looked right at the Marion mob and could not recognize anyone. When the two lawyers took two men to trial, juries refused to convict.[42]

LEGAL LYNCHING AS NATIONAL SPECTACLE

In the first decades of the twentieth century the number of times white men *lynched* black men decreased at just the time when the numbers of legal executions of black men skyrocketed. Such numbers, of course, come from newspaper reporting and so the exact number of nineteenth-century legal executions is probably as unknowable as the real number of lynchings. But the perception of increasing executions and decreasing lynchings was very real. Legal executions operated much as lynchings in the public mind. The actual ritual attached to the executions mattered less than the patterns disseminated in the press. Novelist and journalist Rebecca West would later compare trials dominated by race to opera; the expected players assumed their predictable roles. The 1931 Scottsboro Boys case in Alabama was a prime example. Knowing her part, Victoria Price falsely accused nine black youth of rape both in the press and in court. In 1982, Price told a reporter, "I was tellin' the whole truth and nothin' but the truth. . . . I was stickin' to my race." When she told her truth in 1931, local newspapers leapt at the bait with incendiary headlines, charging that the nine "brutes" had committed the "unspeakable" crime.[43]

The opera in Scottsboro became a cause celebre because there was an audience primed for the performance. In the 1920s, New York achieved cultural preeminence and power. Hundreds of thousands of blacks brought their talents to New York, energizing the culture there. Sophisticated urbanites, regardless of their color, took an increasingly jaundiced view of rural America. *Time, The New Republic,* and the other national magazines looked more critically at the South. H. L. Mencken sneered at Rotarians and Methodists. His magazine, *American Mercury,* included a regular column chronicling the antics of Southern mobs. In a famous 1917 essay, he derided Southerners' anti-intellectualism, their hostility to literature and the arts.[44] Mencken had enormous influence on the culture, and Southern writers found his hard-nosed, unsentimental criticism of the region's lack of intellectualism hard to resist. His Southern admirers included such journalistic greats as Grover C. Hall and Virginius Dabney. In Hartselle, Alabama (population 2,204 in 1930), William Bradford Huie translated north Alabama's traditional hostility toward "Big Mules" or wealthy planters into a lifelong skepticism of prevailing culture along the lines of his hero, Mencken. Huie's high school chums thought him brilliant, and reading Mencken was something brilliant people did. Once, while working as a reporter for the *Birmingham Post,* Huie encountered Alabama Governor Bibb Graves, who could not understand how any Alabama man could admire the South-hating Mencken. Why, Graves demanded of Huie, do you write those scurrilous stories? Don't you know about harmony? Huie, of course, enjoyed knowing that he had upset the governor of Alabama.[45]

This new generation of sophisticates relished instances of rural foolishness. Mencken printed small caliber examples of this throughout the 1920s.

Erskine Caldwell published *Tobacco Road,* which caricatured "poor white trash" Southern characters in 1932. Caldwell's book became a bestseller and a Broadway play. The urban North had become a ready market for a nonfiction cause célèbre of rural Southern misbehavior. If the International Labor Defense (ILD) did not understand this better than the NAACP, it at least proved itself better able to exploit the opportunity when it arrived.[46] First reports claimed that Alabama gave the Scottsboro defendants fair trials. The ILD nonetheless contacted the defendants, persuading them to sign an agreement making ILD lawyers their counsel.

Almost immediately, the Communist party press dubbed the Scottsboro proceedings a "legal lynching."[47] For some years the Communist party newspapers reported more legal lynchings than the extralegal kind. Capitalist courts rendered "lynch verdicts."[48] In 1933, the *Western Worker* warned that capitalists were engineering "Lynch Rule" for the entire country. Communist journalists assumed Southern judges belonged to the Ku Klux Klan and deserved to be branded as "chief lynchers."[49] At one point the *Western Worker* asserted that the Scottsboro Boys "knew there is no real difference between lynching and . . . legal murder."[50]

The Communist party used the mothers of lynching victims to combat lynching apologists' rape rhetoric. The ILD featured the mothers of the condemned prisoners in its New York rallies and some of the mothers toured the country. By the time the ILD attorneys carried the Scottsboro Boys case to the U. S. Supreme Court, it was no ordinary appeal; it was the cause célèbre consumers of news all over the nation, but especially in New York, wanted.[51] The nation cheered when the Court threw the convictions out.[52] The Communist party press attributed the great victory, "one of the greatest victories ever won by the American workers," to pressure applied by the American laboring classes.[53]

When Alabama retried the defendants, the *New York Times,* both wire services, and the Birmingham papers all sent reporters to watch the new proceedings. Western Union rented extra space across the street from the courthouse to accommodate the extra press attention. Larger urban newspapers in the South began to question the guilt of the accused.[54] ILD defense attorney Samuel Leibowitz became the star of the new performances; a loud and aggressive New Yorker, he was the worst possible choice—if the ILD really wanted to woo Alabama jurors to acquit the defendants. By accident or design, Leibowitz irritated rural Alabamans with his big-city tactics. If, by contrast, the ILD's real goal was to put Alabama on trial before a national audience, Leibowitz may have been the very best choice possible. He forced Alabama to defend its all-white jury system on an international stage. As Northern journalists watched, scribbling notes for their stories, Leibowitz called the jury commissioners, exposing their ignorance about Alabama law, showing that they chose jurors not through the procedures from law books but through blind prejudice. Leibowitz also called upstanding black citizens to the witness stand, men clearly qualified for jury service but who had never been called and could never be called under the existing system. Leibowitz could not possibly have hoped that the judge would integrate the jury pool based on this testimony; but he certainly could expect the world to see the corrupt and biased nature of jury selection in Alabama.[55]

NATIONAL POWER

Though a sensation, the Scottsboro Boys case had only a limited long-term impact on the American psyche. The ILD could not even hold the interest of its constituency through all their trials. The ILD managed to organize a protest parade in December 1933, but it proved a wan effort, with a smaller attendance than earlier rallies.[56] In 1934, when the Supreme Court blocked another legal lynching, this time in Mississippi, the case attracted little attention. After torturing the three into confessing, Mississippi had sentenced Ed Brown, Henry Shields, and Arthur Ellington to death for the murder of their landlord.[57] The U. S. Supreme Court threw out the convictions, ruling for the first time that coercing a confession from a defendant violated the Constitution.[58]

The Court's decision came without the mass protests the ILD staged for the Scottsboro Boys, but there were other forces at work. The Great Depression and the New Deal encouraged the Court's willingness to sanction federal protection of individual rights over states' rights. In 1937, a year after its decision in the Mississippi case, the Supreme Court handed down a series of decisions upholding the power of the National Labor Relations Board, which had the effect of greatly expanding the power of the federal government in labor relations.[59] In effect, the Supreme Court's decisions broadly shifted power from the states to a newly energized federal government.

This shift of power had its limits. In 1937, the NAACP very nearly—but not quite—achieved victory in its long-term effort to pass a federal anti-lynching law. Southern congressmen could usually thwart reformers in the House of Representatives, but on the morning of April 14, just as the House assembled to vote on the NAACP-sponsored bill, the press reported a particularly grisly Mississippi lynching. Members of Congress picked up their morning papers to read that Duck Hill whites tortured two men to death with blow torches. Whites accused the pair of murder, but even some Mississippi papers doubted their guilt. Southern representatives read this as they prepared to urge their fellow congressmen to vote against the proposed law because lynching was no longer a problem in America. The NAACP dispatched an investigator named Howard Kester to gather details about the killings, and Kester discovered that the local sheriff colluded with the mob and found also that the citizens of Duck Hill "seemed rather well pleased with themselves." But nothing the NAACP could do matched the impact of the original news reports, published just as the House prepared to vote on the bill.[60]

Mississippi newspapers did not spare their readers the details. According to the *Jackson Daily News,* "Spitting a hot blue flame, the brass torches were pressed against the quivering flesh of the negroes."[61] Confronted with blue flame against quivering flesh, some Mississippi whites decided the Duck Hill "tragedy" proved that the nation needed a federal law against lynching.[62] Others, though, remained unimpressed and insisted again that "as long as Southern blood is hot," whites would react violently to Negro criminality just as they always had. Like many other Mississippi whites, one Baptist minister saw a sinister link between the proposed antilynch law and Franklin Roosevelt's plan to "pack" the Supreme Court with justices more sympathetic to his New Deal. Pastor W. A. Sullivan glumly predicted Congress would pass the antilynch law and then authorize the Court-packing scheme, allowing the Court to declare constitutional the usurpation of states' rights. An Indiana man thought the Court-packing plan and the antilynching law similarly "communistic."[63] White Southern women urged their representatives to defeat antilynching bills, "to see to it that the South—*that the women of the South*—are not sold down the river by the partisan advocates of this political expediency piece of legislation."[64] Such extreme views, however, probably did not reflect the thinking of most Southern whites. According to one journalist, most whites stood between the "rather large pro-lynching fringe" on one side and "the smaller anti-lynching fringe on the other." This means, of course, that the bulk of Southern whites did not absolutely oppose lynching.[65]

Sullivan need not have been so melancholy. While the House passed the antilynching law, Southern senators successfully filibustered the bill to death, as they did when the proposal came back in following years. Southerners in Congress found it politically impossible to favor a federal law against lynching. A New Deal liberal like Alabama's Hugo Black smoothly justified his opposition by depicting the measure as antilabor. Striking workers, Black said, might face prosecution as a lynch mob. Black put his finger on the bill's weak spot: The authors of the various antilynching bills could never figure out how to define lynching so as to exclude violence that had nothing to do with race. In Alabama, governors linked to the coal industry had denounced striking miners as prone to lynching black strikebreakers.[66]

Still, Black's argument was more than a bit disingenuous. In Alabama, union men did not lynch so much as suffer at the hands of lynchers. A law against lynching would have curbed night-riding Ku Klux Klansmen when they terrorized union men. The only actual lynching in Alabama's 1920 coal strike came when the Alabama National Guard broke into the Walker County jail and lynched Willie Baird after a shooting incident involving a soldier and a miner. Again, a federal law against lynching would have been felt on the antiunion side, not by the strikers.[67] Further, Black knew full well that for years white Southerners had complained that the NAACP defined lynching regionally and racially, rejecting the sins of Northerners. Black also knew that no fair definition could be written that defined lynching as purely racial and only Southern, even though that was what the authors of the antilynching bill had in mind.[68]

Among Southern senators arrayed against the bill, Mississippi's Theodore G. Bilbo may have been the most crudely intemperate; if crafty Hugo Black slipped a stiletto to antilynchers, Bilbo beaned them with a sledgehammer. He bluntly told his constituents that the proposed law was "damnable, undemocratic, unconstitutional, unrighteous, and un-American." Bilbo insisted he opposed lynching—just as he opposed rape, he always pointedly added— and proposed his own "antilynching" measure. Bilbo wanted to end lynching by "repatriating" African Americans to Africa. Bilbo claimed that over two million black Americans had congratulated him for making the proposal and endorsed his "repatriation" plans.[69]

Some blacks really did favor Bilbo's proposal, though the number came closer to two than two million. Far more African Americans protested white racial violence. Singer Billie Holiday turned away from the commercial success she craved to record "Strange Fruit" in 1939. A white school teacher named Abel Meeropol wrote the lyrics, describing lynching victims as a "strange and bitter crop." The song became permanently associated with Holiday; Meeropol (who wrote the song as "Lewis Allan") became far more famous for adopting Ethel and Julius Rosenberg's orphaned children than for the song. Most Americans never heard Meeropol's words. Few radio stations ever played it; some crowds heckled Holiday when she sang it. Holiday refused to sing the song for some audiences, fearing they would misunderstand it. Columbia Records refused to record it. Even so, some have called the impact of Holiday's anthem "revolutionary." Meeropol's words and Holiday's music so moved the New York Theatre Arts Committee that it sent a copy of the song to every member of the U. S. Senate in 1939. Journalists not used to reporting on pop music acknowledged Holiday's influence. *Time* magazine published a portion of the lyrics with the singer's photograph. A columnist for the *New York Post* thought "Strange Fruit" had a powerful impact. "It hits, hard." Studs Terkel recalls hearing it in 1942, as he was about to join the army. "The voice goes up—crah-ah-OP!—like a scream," he remembered later. Terkel thought Holiday's singing resembled the Edvard Munch painting of a screaming figure, "only in this case you hear it. She leaves the last note hanging. And then—bang!—it ends." According to Terkel, when he heard the song the entire audience wept.[70]

As black protest became a part of popular culture, some white Southerners began to turn against lynching. While Bilbo's constituent mail documents white Southerners' continued determination to teach "meddlesome yankees" to mind their own business,[71] the voters back home sometimes surprised and unsettled him by favoring federal efforts to end lynching.[72] Journalists understood that change was afoot. In 1941, Virginius Dabney reminded newspaper columnist John Temple Graves that in 1935 Graves had claimed to have many letters from intelligent white Southerners favoring lynching. "I should like to know," Dabney wondered, "whether you get as many nowadays."[73]

The same year Dabney wondered if white Southerners' thinking had not changed, William Bradford Huie published an article entitled "The South Kills Another Negro." After graduating from the University of Alabama, Huie used his experiences working for the *Birmingham Post* to create a fictionalized account of the trial and execution of a black man falsely accused of raping a white woman. In Huie's narrative, the Alabama National Guard encircled a courthouse where authorities hastily rushed a black man charged with rape to a guilty verdict and a death sentence. The hard-boiled, unsentimental story, published in *American Mercury*, held up Southern localism to national scrutiny. More significantly, Huie described his own metamorphosis, presenting himself as initially indifferent to the black defendant's fate but slowly won over by the man's essential humanity.[74] Huie's article documented a shift occurring across the South, albeit among a limited segment of the population.

Huie was not the only white American to make the leap. The same intellectual environment that nourished Huie as he wrote "The South Kills Another Negro" encouraged Attorney General Frank Murphy to create the Civil Liberties Unit, later called the Civil Rights Division, within the Department of Justice. A former governor of Michigan, Murphy had long been interested in the rights of laborers and challenges to labor organizers' rights of free speech and assembly.[75] His decision also came in at the outset of World War II. Americans experimented with accusing Nazis of *lynching* Jews, but the bigger problem was to defend America itself against such accusations. As the whole country mobilized for total war against the Axis, the U. S. government positioned itself as the worldwide champion of freedom, an image difficult to put forth because of lynching and peonage at home.[76]

And racial violence continued at home. In 1942, a Texas mob seized Elbert Williams and killed him after blacks around Brownsville attempted to vote.[77] In the same year, a Sikeston, Missouri, mob burned alive Cleo Wright, an accused rapist. Blacks called on each other to "Remember Pearl Harbor— and Sikeston, Missouri."[78] Throughout World War II, black American families sent their young men off to war, just as white families did. But black families had worries not shared by white families. Often, black families that had migrated North to escape racial violence saw their sons shipped to Southern army camps. As the army trained for war in the Pacific and Europe, gossip spread that white soldiers lynched black GIs.[79] The *Chicago Defender* reported that rural Illinois whites lynched a black soldier named Hollie Willis.[80] One false rumor held that whites at a Mississippi military post had massacred as many as 1,200 black U.S. Army soldiers.[81]

At Nashville's Fisk University, Charles S. Johnson, an African American sociologist, launched a journal with the unwieldy academic title of *A Monthly Summary of Events and Trends in Race Relations.* Johnson's journal collected news reports of racist violence. The first issue appeared in August 1943 and included a column headed "Soldier Violence." Johnson attributed the frequency of violence against black soldiers to whites' anger over uniformed African Americans and the spirit of resistance military service kindled in the minds of black GIs. Johnson reported violent incidents camp by camp and continued such reports throughout the war, building an academic record of violent white racism even as whites fought Nazism.[82]

Black newspapers had a far more popular impact. Writing more bluntly than Johnson, black journalists charged that lynchings inside or outside the army promoted the Axis cause. The *Defender* papers described racist whites as a "fifth column" engaged in "a relentless fight in many ways against our war effort." Fomenting lynchings, the *Defender* explained, aided the Axis.[83] The *Negro Labor News* was more direct: "THE LYNCHING OF NEGROES HELPS HITLER."[84]

The Roosevelt administration absorbed some of this thinking. Roosevelt saw himself as leading the nation in a war for freedom around the world. FDR specified four kinds of freedom, each illustrated by a Norman Rockwell painting: freedom of speech, freedom of religion, freedom from want, and freedom from fear. After the Sikeston lynching, the Justice Department issued a press release explaining that when the country fought for democracy around the world, "lynching has significance far beyond the community, or even the state, in which it occurs."[85] When a federal grand jury looked at the Sikeston lynching and determined that no federal law had been broken, the head of Roosevelt's Civil Rights Division, Victor Rotnem, protested that the grand jury got it wrong—the killers had, in fact, violated federal law. He made no effort to conceal his motives. "Lynching," Rotnem wrote, "cannot be tolerated in a land engaged in carrying the Four Freedoms abroad."[86] Federal officials did not quit after the setback in Sikeston. In Mississippi, federal officials convinced a grand jury to indict five Jones County lynchers in 1943. Although the trial jury needed only fourteen minutes to acquit all the defendants, just getting the case past a grand jury and before a trial jury was an achievement. Newspapers headlined the case as the first federal lynching trial in forty years.[87] Under Roosevelt not only federal prosecutors, but the president himself, acted. FDR created the Fair Employment Practices Committee to stave off a threatened march on Washington by A. Philip Randolph and, perhaps, as many as one hundred thousand African Americans. And individual blacks petitioned the president, the first lady, and the FBI for help when they had been assaulted by racist whites.[88]

In popular culture, World War II accelerated a critique of mob law that had begun in the 1930s. In 1936, Hollywood had probed lynching twice, once in *Fury,* with Spencer Tracy as the lynching victim, and again in a Warner Brothers movie entitled *Black Legion.* Although Hollywood's Production Code blunted the industry's censure of Judge Lynch by forbidding all references to racial lynching or vigilantism in the South, moviemakers delivered their toughest attack on lynching with a film based on a novel by Walter Van Tilburg Clark. Clark's 1940 book, *The Ox-Bow Incident,* takes place in Nevada in 1885, and depicts a mob lynching three innocent men for rustling and murder. While Clark's Western setting cloaked his real concerns about extralegal justice, critics easily recognized his novel as more than just a cowboy story. Some reviewers (and Clark himself) saw the novel as a warning against Nazism. At the end of the book, Clark lectures his readers that law is "a lot more than words you put in a book." Law, Clark writes, is "everything people ever found out about justice and what's right and wrong. It's the very conscience of humanity."[89]

World War II had some influence on American thinking, but such propaganda did not really unseat deeply felt racial passions. The impact of *The Ox-Bow Incident* can be measured in dollars and cents. Henry Fonda starred in the movie version of *The Ox-Bow Incident* and considered it one of his best pictures, a "prestige picture" he could be proud of. When Fonda urged that more such movies be made, Darryl F. Zanuck sourly made him look at the red ink in his ledger.[90]

INCREASING FEDERAL INVOLVEMENT

In the 1940s, the federal government began to move against neighborhood violence in new ways. One of the most important instances of this came in

Georgia. On January 29, 1943, Sheriff M. Claude Screws of Baker County arrested a young black man named Bobby Hall for stealing a tire. No tire had been stolen. The quarrel between Screws and Hall really involved a pearl-handled pistol belonging to Hall but confiscated by the sheriff. Screws did not think any of the "damn negroes" in his jurisdiction should have a pistol; Hall hired a lawyer to get his gun back.[91] A Newton City Police officer told a friend later that he and Screws beat Hall to death because "the negro acted so damn smart and went before the Court in some way trying to make them give it back."[92] Screws claimed later that Hall, though handcuffed, had tried to attack the sheriff and two other officers with a shotgun. Screws admitted later that he "went to work on him with my fists, and one of the deputies struck him with a black-jack." Screws sent Hall to a hospital, where the young black man died.[93]

Perhaps Screws hoped the South's traditional neighborly isolation would shield him from scrutiny and, in fact, he must have felt relieved when only a few local newspapers covered the incident. But by February 3 the NAACP branch in Albany had heard of the killing and contacted its headquarters in New York. At the NAACP Thurgood Marshall and Walter White briefly debated whether the killing of Hall should be called a lynching or not. Deciding that it should, Roy Wilkins wrote Victor Rotnem, head of the Civil Rights Division. Wendell Berge, an assistant attorney general, answered, reporting that the FBI had already been asked to investigate. Berge also urged that the NAACP not publicize the case, arguing that publicity might impede the FBI's investigation. Use of such an inflammatory word as "lynching" to describe the killing worried Rotnem. "It is believed advisable," Berge told the NAACP, "to have a definite understanding as to the use of this word, and it is suggested that the next time Mr. Walter White or Mr. Thurgood Marshall are in Washington they, or either of them, call upon Mr. Rotnem to discuss this matter."[94] When a killing was called a lynching, it attracted news coverage, publicity—precisely what Rotnem sought to avoid as the investigation proceeded. Perhaps he worried that federal judges and the Supreme Court might hesitate to affirm the federal prosecution of a *lynching* after Congress refused to make such an offense a federal crime. If Rotnem did have such a concern, he was right to worry.

The NAACP sometimes found the FBI's lack of interest in civil rights cases frustrating.[95] In this case, though, the FBI moved quickly. Agents Marcus B. Calhoun and William H. Crawford hurried to Newton from the FBI's Atlanta office on February 20. The two immediately interviewed Screws and the two other officers accused of aiding in the beating, Frank Jones and Jim Bob Kelley. Working diligently, Calhoun and Crawford picked apart Screws's story piece by piece, proving the sheriff a murderer and a liar. Witnesses saw and heard the beating. Screws had forged the warrant accusing Hall of theft. The sheriff had been drunk the night of the shooting.[96]

By prosecuting Screws, the Civil Rights Division pushed to use federal law in a new and imaginative fashion. A federal grand jury indicted the three officers for violating Hall's civil rights, basing its charge on a law originally passed by Congress in 1870 that forbade state officers from violating civil rights "under color of law."[97] This indictment amounted to an effort to test Rotnem's hypothesis, expressed in his law review article, that existing federal law could be used to protect black citizens' civil rights. This would be the first time the Supreme Court tested the constitutionality of the 1870 law in a case not involving an election. By calling on the Supreme Court to convert the 1870 Enforcement Act into a federal antilynching law, Rotnem really asked the justices to do what Congress could not accomplish. Two writers later said that a government victory would be "a libertarian's dream of by-passing a filibustered Congress."[98]

Federal officials tried Screws and his two codefendants at the federal courthouse in Albany. Calhoun and Crawford had done their work well. A jury convicted all three and the court of appeals upheld the convictions. Screws and the other defendants appealed to the U. S. Supreme Court, arguing that the Court should hear the case because "there is a special division of the Department of Justice of the United States commonly known as the Civil Rights Division whose personnel is militant in seeking to expand the law by the prosecution of state officers for assaulting prisoners." The Supreme Court, Screws's lawyers concluded, should settle the question of whether federal courts can punish violently racist state officers like Screws.[99]

Few Supreme Court justices harbored much sympathy for the Civil Rights Division's efforts. In their inner sanctum, Hugo Black and Robert Jackson warned their fellow justices that failing to overturn Screws's conviction would, in essence, by-pass Congress to turn an archaic law into a modern antilynching statute. Jackson insisted that problems involving local justice must be left to the communities, not transferred to federal authorities. Jackson disliked the Reconstruction civil rights laws and called Reconstruction "a shameful era" in American history. Hugo Black thought the civil rights law so vague that it violated due process. Citizens have a right to know exactly what the law prohibits, he pointed out. Felix Frankfurter wrote a number of decisions outlawing police brutality, but in this case he wanted to throw out Screws's conviction. Police misconduct that corrupted due process offended Frankfurter, but prosecution efforts to push the Supreme Court into making a new law worried him more. "I would like to see [the conviction] reversed," he told his fellow justices, "if we could put it on grounds we could stomach."[100]

One justice saw no problem with the Civil Rights Division's prosecution of Screws. Elevated to the Supreme Court, Frank Murphy, founder of the Civil Rights Division, urged that Screws's conviction be affirmed. Murphy's argument might be called noble or eloquent, but its nontechnical nature probably undermined his influence by reinforcing a common view among the Court justices that Murphy was ill-prepared for his duties, overly dependent on his clerks for help with legal nuances. His biographer doubts Murphy wrote even one of his own opinions in its entirety.[101]

William O. Douglas wrote the Court's opinion for Screws, upholding a federal right to prosecute such violent racists as Screws, but limiting that power by finding also that federal prosecutors had to prove defendants' racial malice. Screws, in other words, could only be convicted if prosecutors could prove that he knowingly ("willfully") violated Hall's civil rights and did so because Hall was black. And this rule would apply not just to Screws but to all future defendants charged under the 1870 enforcement act. The Screws case would hamstring Justice Department efforts to prosecute violators of citizens' civil rights for decades. Documenting malefactors' state of mind proved an almost impossible hurdle for the prosecution to cross. One writer went so far as to call it "an unpleasant echo of Dred Scott" because it made it so difficult for the government to protect the rights of African American citizens.[102]

While the Screws precedent devastated civil rights law, it had little impact among ordinary citizens. At least as late as 1946, the New York Times still relegated lynchings to small articles on its back pages. In Minden, Louisiana, a mob murdered a black army veteran named John C. Jones on August 8, 1946. An energetic U. S. Attorney identified five of the killers and put them on trial, though a jury acquitted them. The Minden paper complained of "false accusations by outside interests" and ignored the affair. Nor did Jones get much coverage from the New York Times. One college professor complained that the Times gave more prominent coverage to an aircraft downing over "Yogoslavia" than it did to the Minden case. The professor's protest that the lynching "seems to me as important as the Yogoslavia incident" signaled that some readers now understood the national significance of neighborhood mobs. It also shows that the Times editors did not yet agree.[103]

The Screws incident also failed to attract editors' attention because it was "not" a lynching. Leading newspapers carried an article reporting the Supreme Court decision and its significance, but provided little detail on the actual killing or the people involved in the case. Few newspapers outside of Georgia reported on the testimony, leaving the Court's decision a technical legal precedent more than a human drama. Three officers beating a black man to death in the name of white supremacy certainly qualified as a lynching under the so-called NAACP definition. Yet, because of Rotnem's decision not to build public support for his prosecution by calling the crime a lynching, the killing itself attracted little attention.

Incidents that seemed to journalists to "be" lynchings sometimes attracted more attention. In 1945, when Jesse James Payne disappeared from his Florida jail cell, national news magazines smelled a lynching and published stories about the affair. Payne's trouble had started when he quarreled with his landlord. The landlord and his sons seized Payne and tried to intimidate him by snapping a gun at his head. Payne managed to scramble away, escaping into the woods. The landlord organized a posse, which included the sheriff, telling local whites that Payne had raped his five-year-old daughter. The posse captured Payne and loaded him in a local jail. On October 11, Payne disappeared from the jail, his body turning up along a dirt road, blasted with buckshot.[104]

Most of the definitions of lynching debated throughout the 1940s attached considerable importance to the number of persons involved in the killing. Since no one stepped forward to say how many persons kidnapped Payne from the jail, it was technically impossible to determine whether a mob or an individual killed Payne. The governor of Georgia tried to exploit this uncertainty. When the press called the Payne killing a lynching, Governor Millard F. Caldwell disagreed, insisting that Jesse James Payne had been *murdered.* Journalists thought Payne's death so obviously a lynching that Caldwell must have been whitewashing the crime. The governor dispatched an investigator to look into the Payne killing. After reading his agent's report, Caldwell announced that the sheriff had acted stupidly, but had not knowingly aided in a lynching. When a researcher for the *Encyclopedia Britannica* called on Caldwell, the governor again insisted that Payne's death did not fit any recognized definition of lynching. In a speech, Caldwell complained that national news writers had besmirched Florida when they called the murder a lynching. Caldwell worsened his situation by explaining later that whites turned to lynching only to protect white females from black lust.[105]

It required courage to stand up to a governor willing to file a libel suit. When *Time* magazine denounced Caldwell, the governor complained to the magazine's publisher, Henry R. Luce, and *Time* backed down, apologizing. This respite from journalistic scrutiny proved short lived, however. A short time later, *Colliers* criticized Caldwell, using almost exactly the same language as *Time.* Unlike Luce, the publishers of *Colliers* would not back down. Caldwell filed suit in federal district court.[106]

Caldwell's suit went to trial in 1948. A jury heard the evidence, deliberated for two hours, and produced a verdict awarding Caldwell $237,000 in damages. After an appellate court ordered a new trial, Caldwell's case went to a second trial and jury. This time the jury offered Caldwell $100,000.[107]

Although Jesse James Payne attracted a flurry of media attention, he never became the subject of national debate the way later acts of racial violence would. Perhaps the killing of a sharecropper by white landlords was still too routine to attract special attention. Or perhaps Caldwell's legal strategy actually worked. In any case, after the Payne affair, lynching remained locked in neighborhood isolation. But there would be more assaults on neighborhood autonomy. A far more sensational national challenge came in 1947, after Greenville, South Carolina, police found the body of Willie Earle shot, battered, and stabbed. The governor did not hesitate to label this killing a "lynching" and called out the state police (then called the state constabulary) to investigate the crime.[108]

The killers of Willie Earle acted after he had been arrested for stabbing Thomas W. Brown, a Greenville taxi driver. The other taxicab drivers went to the jail, removed Earle, and killed him. The governor of South Carolina was a young, energetic D-Day veteran, Strom Thurmond. Unlike Caldwell, who maladroitly tried to cover up racial violence in his state, Thurmond successfully courted the press with pledges that he would use "every resource at my command to apprehend all persons who may be involved in such a flagrant violation of the law."[109] Thurmond did not even object when FBI agents joined the investigation. Within four days, investigators had identified thirty-one taxi drivers as members of the lynch mob.[110] Thurmond hoped that by appearing cooperative and forthright, he could fend off national threats to states' rights. Thurmond represented a new generation of Southern governors, committed not to old island communities, but to states' rights. Lynching threatened his plan to keep power in the states.

In Greenville, the press depicted formidable forces lined up to convict the lynchers. Thurmond appointed Sam R. Watt as the special prosecutor to try the case. If Thurmond intended Watt's appointment as a gesture to impress Northern journalists, the trick worked. The New York Times and other papers reported that Watt had convicted all but 2 of the 473 defendants he had prosecuted the previous year.[111] By 1947, any Southern lynching trial would have drawn a crowd of press reporters. The trial of 31 lynchers, billed as the biggest lynching trial in history, drew a potent press contingent. Time, Life, Newsweek, and the New Republic all ran first-person accounts of the trial.[112]

Defense lawyers worked hard to circle the wagons against outsiders. One lawyer called on jurors to reject "Northern meddling" while another lawyer pointed out FBI agents in the courtroom and reminded jurors that the

North had invaded the South in the Civil War as well. "Willie Earle is dead," one lawyer thundered, "and I wish more like him were dead." The judge admonished the attorney, but the reprimand had slight effect. "You might shoot a mad dog and be prosecuted," the same lawyer continued, "but if a mad dog were loose in my community, I'd shoot the dog and let them prosecute me."[113]

The most detailed examination of the trial appeared in the New Yorker and was written by Rebecca West. Harold Ross, the New Yorker's editor, had sent West to report on the trials of World War II Nazi leaders and traitors like William Joyce, also known as "Lord Haw-Haw." West perfected her technique during these trials, mercilessly transcribing every twitch the defendants made, reading their crimes into their faces and bodies. Hermann Goering appeared "like a madam in a brothel," West sneered, while another resembled a governess and another looked like a dirty old man. West's prose seemed to flow effortlessly from her typewriter onto the pages of the New Yorker; Ross did not hesitate to caricature Nazis.[114]

West's words did not flow out of South Carolina so easily. Ross did not believe in printing "bitter" articles "about this race business."[115] Even after he published West's article, Ross grumbled that the "damned colored question" should not be allowed in "every other story, verse, etc."[116] With the exception of the lawyers, West liked everyone she met in Greenville. She thought the jurors looked attractive, the jailer who had turned over Earle to the mob seemed reasonable, and the defendants "quite good-looking." Greenville blacks seemed a bit mysterious: They sat in shadowy silence, sullen, she guessed, but not really communicative to an English journalist. Though he showed no concern for Southern blacks, Ross wanted to make sure his author treated white Southerners fairly. Ross hired Northern and Southern lawyers to go over West's manuscript and a Greenville journalist to check her facts. Even that was not enough. "I had to sit up with Harold Ross," West told a friend, "till four in the morning while he cross-examined me on the proofs."[117] At the NAACP, Walter White circulated a copy of West's essay. White thought West "overkind" in her description of white South Carolinians and too quick to judge Earle guilty, but generally liked the article and wanted to reprint it.[118]

The press viewed the whole affair very optimistically, even after the not-guilty verdicts. Not only the capitalist press, but the Communist press as well, thought the South Carolina trials signaled a new wind blowing across the South, a wind that would soon sweep away lynchings.[119] Fresh attention for what Americans increasingly saw as a national problem even influenced the president of the United States. The same year Rebecca West reported on the taxi-cab lynchers' trial, President Harry S. Truman began to break down

Southern isolationism and assert federal power over neighborhood justice. The president appeared before the NAACP annual conference (just showing up was something no previous president had done) and declared that the nation must no longer tolerate racial bias. A few months later, Truman's Committee on Civil Rights issued *To Secure These Rights,* a report calling for the elimination of segregation, a federal law against lynching, and other actions designed to end the discrimination that horrified white Southerners of the sort Truman grew up with in his native Missouri. Truman's speech and the committee report represented a real conversion, a presidential change of heart. White Southerners had good reason to assume they could count on the new president from Missouri to hold the line against the NAACP and other civil rights advocates. A descendant of slave owners and Confederate sympathizers, Truman cheerfully described his parents as "violently unreconstructed." Truman himself exhibited little sympathy for blacks. In those unguarded moments when he revealed his private thoughts, Truman habitually called blacks "niggers" and "coons." Racial violence—acts called lynchings—changed Truman's sensibilities. In 1946 he learned of a black army sergeant who was blinded when a South Carolina police officer poked his eyes out with a night stick. In Georgia, whites killed the only black man to have voted in his area. In Walton County, Georgia, whites killed four blacks. By one account, Truman's face went "pale with horror" when he learned of these violent acts. "My God," he exclaimed, "I had no idea it was as terrible as that. We've got to do something!"[120]

In the words of one historian, Truman's conversion on the question of race "changed the nation forever."[121] Perhaps, but Mississippi's treatment of a black man named Willie McGee documents the limits of that change. No listing of lynchings will ever include McGee, executed by the state of Mississippi after three trials and repeated appeals to state and federal appeals courts. In 1945, Jones County, Mississippi, authorities had hastily convicted McGee of rape, a capital crime in Mississippi since the end of Reconstruction. Mississippi and other Southern states made rape a capital crime in an attempt to substitute the state for the lynch mob. McGee's court-appointed lawyers appealed on several grounds, including the fact that the threat of lynching had shattered McGee's nerves so much he could not coherently assist in his own defense. The Mississippi Supreme Court ordered a new trial, judging that he should have been granted a change of venue.[122] After a second trial in Hattiesburg, McGee's lawyers complained that he had been convicted by all-white juries, and the Mississippi Supreme Court awarded him yet another trial.[123] After this second reversal, state authorities again put McGee on trial, this time with a black man in the pool of prospective jurors, the first integrated jury panel in Jones County since Reconstruction. At this third trial, McGee charged that he had been tortured into confessing by a cabal of local officials that included the police chief, the sheriff, a state highway patrol officer, and the county prosecutor. The judge was openly skeptical, and the jury convicted McGee for a third time. This time the Mississippi Supreme Court saw no reason to reverse the conviction.[124] McGee's lawyers began to petition the federal courts for help.

At this point public opinion began to shift against McGee. *Time* magazine complained that communists had distorted the facts of the case. *Life* labeled McGee a rapist and criticized his communist "friends" as persons always on the lookout for some new symbol.[125] When members of the Civil Rights Congress tried to persuade the governor to grant McGee clemency, one local paper asked, "Why go to Korea to shoot Communists when the hunting is good on home grounds?"[126] Although individual justices issued various stays of execution, the entire Supreme Court refused to hear the case. On May 8, 1951, Mississippi authorities finally electrocuted McGee in Laurel, Mississippi. After his death, young Carl Rowan went to Laurel, where he interviewed blacks who believed that McGee's "victim" had actually welcomed his advances. The witnesses had not testified for fear of their lives, Rowan reported.[127] The state of Mississippi had, essentially, lynched Willie McGee.

TURNING POINT: LYNCHING BEFORE AND AFTER BROWN

Mississippi's trials and execution of Willie McGee marked no turning point in the national public's perception of lynching and racial violence; nor did the 1951 bombing of the house of Florida NAACP leader Harry T. Moore, whose life and death involved lynching. Moore investigated reports that Florida whites tortured and killed blacks. He took special interest in reports that Sheriff Willis McCall led a posse that killed one rape suspect and tortured three others. Florida tried and convicted the three tortured suspects in a trial so dominated by mob tumult that the Supreme Court ordered a new trial. Before a new trial could be conducted, Moore learned that Sheriff McCall had shot and killed one of the defendants and seriously injured a second. Moore watched as McCall became famous and his shooting played on the front pages of newspapers all over America.[128]

On Christmas night, 1951, a powerful dynamite blast ripped through Moore's house as he and his wife lay in their bed. His death attracted national attention, and the FBI made a sincere and exhaustive effort to crack the case. J. Edgar Hoover personally supervised the investigation, sending detailed telegrams from Washington directing his agents to pursue leads.

Despite the publicity the murder generated, Moore soon faded from public consciousness.[129] Hoover's commitment was not enough to solve the crime.

Moore fought lynching and died at the hands of lynchers before the Supreme Court changed the nature of the national debate about racism with its *Brown v. Board of Education* decision. The Supreme Court's decision in the famous school desegregation case came on May 17, 1954. Thereafter white America saw racial violence differently. The conversation about neighborhood-sanctioned violence went national.

White Southerners reacted to the Court's decision by escalating their racial violence. Whites had brutalized black people for many years, but after 1954 it became even more obvious that such attacks did more than injure African Americans. Now the bombings and the beatings seemed part of a war against the law as laid down by the Supreme Court. In *Brown v. Board of Education,* the Court ruled that the most local and most community-based institution in American society, the neighborhood school, had to adhere to national standards. And it did so in the midst of the Cold War, when Americans fought for freedom and democracy around the world. That local folk resisted such "interference" with a profoundly local institution comes as no surprise. But resistance to desegregation increasingly seemed a doomed enterprise.

The lynching case that came right after *Brown v. Board of Education,* the case that would capture the attention of the world like no other murder before it, differed little from scores of racially motivated killings that had gone on for generations. The murder of Emmett Till did not itself signal that things had changed, but the reaction to the murder did. Emmett Till, a fourteen-year-old Chicagoan, had traveled to Mississippi to visit his uncle and cousins. When J. W. Milam and Roy Bryant took Emmett Till from his uncle's house, shot him, and dumped his body in Mississippi's Tallahatchie River, they may well have thought that they were defending their community against outside powers. Till had offended a white woman, Carolyn Bryant, Roy's wife. Like South Carolina's Strom Thurmond, Mississippi Governor Hugh White vigorously denounced the crime and pledged a spirited prosecution of the killers. Many or most white Mississippians found the brutal killing of a child outrageous and demanded swift justice.[130]

In a technique pioneered by the Communist party, Till's mother emerged as the central figure in opposition to white Mississippi. Whites had long justified lynching by sentimentalizing rape victims. By the mid-twentieth century, after the Scottsboro Boys and other less notorious cases, the organizers of protests against lynching routinely looked to the victim's mother to arouse public support.[131] Till's mother, Mamie Bradley, staged a massive funeral for her son, one with an open casket, exposing Till's horribly bloated and mutilated face to public inspection. At least ten thousand people walked by his casket. Mamie Bradley's decision to open the casket helped propel the Till case from an ordinary murder to a national situation. Mrs. Bradley insisted that she made this decision alone. Ernest Withers, who covered the trial as a photographer for the *Memphis Tri-State Defender,* agrees that Bradley's role transformed the case, but he has a different explanation for Bradley's decision to open the casket. Withers remembers that Bradley's cousin, Rayfield Mooty, president of a CIO steelworkers' union in Chicago, influenced Till's mother to show her son's face to the public. Mooty, who accompanied Bradley to Mississippi for the trial, expected her to mobilize Chicago blacks, who were long reluctant to join labor unions.[132]

The Till murder caught the public's attention. One hundred journalists turned up for Milam and Bryant's trial. The three television networks flew planes daily into a nearby airfield to ferry film back to their evening news broadcasts. Reporters from *Life, Time, Newsweek, Jet, Ebony,* the *Chicago Sun-Times,* the *New York Daily News* and the Associated Press traveled to Sumner, Mississippi, population 550, for the trial. The Communist party press sent a journalist named Rob F. Hall to Mississippi to report on the trial firsthand.[133] Black journalists hurried to Mississippi to attend the trial. The *Chicago Defender* followed the story even before authorities recovered Till's body and when it was located, they announced its discovery under a page-one banner headline. L. Alex Wilson of the *Memphis Tri-State Defender* journeyed to Sumner, as did James Hicks of the *New York Amsterdam News.* Hicks's paper published the grisly picture of Till's battered head on its front page. The most stunning documents of the trial, though, came from Withers, the Memphis photographer covering the trial for the *Tri-State Defender.* Allowed to move freely about the courtroom, Withers photographed the defendants, the other black journalists, the witnesses, the town, and the crowds around the courthouse. He captured the dramatic moment when Mose Wright pointed out the defendants as the men who had kidnapped his nephew, saying "Thar he." He photographed Willie Reed, the son of a sharecropper who testified that he saw Till in the back of a pickup truck and heard him wailing and crying from the barn where he was beaten.[134]

Heightened press coverage turned locals' sympathy away from young Till and toward the two men on trial. It did not help that the NAACP falsely claimed that no leading whites in Mississippi had denounced the crime or that Roy Wilkins alleged that all of white Mississippi favored murdering children to maintain segregation. "You're making a mountain out of a molehill," one man shouted at reporters. "The NAACP," he added, "is really making you work."[135] Whites harassed the black journalists, tailing them as they drove to Clarksdale, where they were staying. A deputy sheriff arrested one reporter for passing a school bus, even though the journalist's car had been parked in front of the courthouse all day. Officers beat up and arrested James Hicks for spitting on a sidewalk.[136]

White Southerners in the 1950s still jealously guarded their neighborhoods from "outside" interference. Local newspapers often cooperated in this effort, often by not reporting killings or carefully reporting racial violence as ordinary homicide. They knew that Northern newspapers often depended on their initial judgments to determine if small-town murders warranted national exposure.

When the jury acquitted Milam and Bryant, newspapers around the world carried the story. The most important reporting came in January 1956, when *Look* published William Bradford Huie's interview with Roy Bryant and J. W. Milam. Acquitted, and therefore immune from further prosecution, the two freely admitted to having killed Till. Huie's article proved the most influential document to come out of the affair—for white Americans.[137]

The *Chicago Defender* continued its coverage of the Till case even after the jury acquitted Milam and Bryant. In October the *Defender* headlined the news that Mississippi whites had jailed Levy "Too Tight" Collins and Henry Lee Loggins to keep them from testifying that they had washed blood out of Milam's truck. In a first-person account, the editor of the *Tri-State Defender,* L. Alex Wilson, described his "mission" to Mississippi as "four harrowing, danger-filled days." Making contact with Mississippi blacks, the "Mississippi underground," Wilson found and transported Collins out of the state. Even after Wilson took him safely out of Mississippi, Collins proved uncooperative. In a lengthy interview with the *Defender,* he denied knowing anything about the Till case at all. Collins even opined that Milam had not killed Till, as "he was too nice a man to do it."[138] Collins had family in Mississippi and insisted on returning home. Thereafter the *Defender* lost track of him for a few days, headlining the news when Wilson again found his witness, employed in a Mississippi sawmill.[139]

Even after the Till story, whites continued to intimidate blacks with lynching rhetoric. Newspapers reported no lynchings when nine young black children desegregated Little Rock's Central High School in 1957. No statistical study of lynching is ever likely to include Little Rock. Nonetheless, the children felt almost constantly in fear of lynching throughout the school year. Perhaps more significantly, local whites maintained faith in the power of mob violence. Little Rock whites really believed they could maintain segregation through mob violence. In her memoir of that horrible year, Melba Pattillo Beals describes whites as violently determined to oust her and the other black students from the school, convinced that they could thwart the will of the federal courts with mob violence.[140]

In the last half of the twentieth century, there was no full-fledged debate over the meaning of lynching, as there had been in the first few decades. Nonetheless, the meaning of lynching remained confused and uncertain. In 1959 a gang of Mississippi whites murdered a young black man named Mack Charles Parker, who was accused of raping a white woman. A white Mississippian wrote privately that he had "seen a few Linchings [*sic*] in Mississippi by white men," and the Parker killing did not qualify. C. L. Wilson could not believe that a killing carried out in secret by eight or ten men could be a lynching. In Mississippi, when white people lynched, Wilson said, "it was from 100 to 5000 with no masks and after the victim was dead he was taken to some PUBLIC place and hung where all could see him." Wilson concluded that Parker must have been killed by some skulking Negroes; whites just did not lynch like that.[141]

Invited by Mississippi's governor, FBI agents came to Poplarville and launched an extensive investigation in the face of a hostile local reaction. Agents identified a candidate for sheriff, John Pershing Walker, as a lyncher; he was likely to win the election because he had helped kill Parker. Walker's campaign workers promised voters that once Walker became sheriff he would run the FBI out of town.[142] Locals harassed out-of-town journalists as well, pushing and shoving a CBS cameraman.[143] When the Department of Justice decided to defer to the local grand jury, announcing that no federal law had been violated, congressmen protested. An official from the American Bar Association wrote Attorney General William P. Rogers to correct his understanding of the law. The mob, Arthur J. Freund wrote, clearly violated the Reconstruction-era civil rights laws. Freund suggested that Rogers read Victor Rotnem's old article, "The Federal Right Not to be Lynched."[144] In the end, the local grand jury refused to act and, when the Department of Justice relented and did submit the facts to a federal grand jury, nothing happened there either.[145]

As the Department of Justice pursued the Parker case, some Americans complained that the government defined lynching as a racial killing carried out by white Southerners. No Northern killing qualified.[146] A year after Parker's death, Huie published an article accusing Newbury, Vermont, citizens of lynching a white man named Orville Gibson, "a hard working farmer, accused of many things—particularly success." Huie demanded to know why the FBI had not investigated the Gibson lynching as it had the Parker killing. "The FBI bolts into action when a Negro rapist . . . is thrown into the Pearl River." It "bolts in the opposite direction when an innocent, honorable, white farmer is . . . thrown into New Hampshire's Connecticut River." By almost any definition, Huie was right: The Gibson killing qualified as a lynching. The killers acted because Gibson had beaten Eri Martin, his hired hand, in 1957. The community killed Gibson, imposing extralegal justice on their victim. But, as Huie pointed out, the press did not follow the definition of lynching, preferring instead to call the killing a vigilante action.[147]

Huie had a variety of motives for traveling to Vermont to investigate the Gibson "lynching." Huie made a career out of puncturing the balloons of hypocritical people with power and of debunking prevailing "wisdom." When *Life* magazine called Emmett Till's father a war hero, Huie published an article detailing Till's wartime record as a murderer and rapist.[148] When, after the cases of Emmett Till and Mack Parker, the nation seemed settled on the idea that equated white Southerners with lynching, Huie headed for Vermont. "I'm only Southern-trained in lynching," Huie wrote tongue-in-cheek,[149] as he tried to torpedo the notion of lynching as purely Southern. Huie understood that the meaning of lynching had changed, having become more regional and racial, and he wanted to change it back. By the 1950s, Americans could not believe that a white mob of Northerners could lynch another white Northerner. That had to be vigilantism or something else. Such killings had once fit within the meaning of lynching, but not any more.

On October 11, 1991, Clarence Thomas seated himself before fourteen white U. S. senators. At times during his emotional testimony, he seemed on the verge of giving up ("no job is worth it"), but in the end polling showed that most Americans found his testimony persuasive. The Senate confirmed his nomination, and Thomas became a Supreme Court justice. Scholars became fascinated with the Thomas-Hill hearings, publishing books and articles complaining that Thomas could make his voice heard while Anita Hill's voice disappeared, "erased."[150] The power of lynching rhetoric seemed to catch historians and other scholars by surprise. One of Hill's scholarly allies decided that Hill could not be heard because what she said did not fit into existing rhetorical conventions in any fashion that made her look good. Thomas fit himself into a convention: black man as lynching victim betrayed by a woman. Even as he criticized his opponents for stereotyping him, Thomas brilliantly met the expectations of his audience, portraying himself as the classic lynching victim.

Scholars were ill prepared for Thomas's language because they did not properly understand lynching. For decades sociologists had studied lynching as a behavior, something concrete that could be precisely defined and quantified. There is no single behavior that can be called "lynching." Any attempt to impose a definition on such a diverse, subtle, and complex reality will inevitably miss the point. Lynching is a word with power, a rhetoric that can move an audience. The history of lynching is profoundly rhetorical—the politics of meaning and definition.

For a hundred years scholars have insisted on a positivist approach to the study of lynching, calculating numbers of persons lynched as a way of persuading people not to lynch. At a recent history conference, one scholar recognized the impossibility of defining lynching and yet pressed ahead, insisting that the number of Mexicans lynched must be calculated or Mexicans would not be taken seriously as a victimized segment of the population.[151]

The history of the changing definition of lynching reveals that the twentieth century fragmented and confused the meaning of lynching. There is no consensus today on the meaning of this important word that describes such a vital subject. It is clear that community support has long been a touchstone. When reformers call a particular killing a *lynching,* they do so as a way of criticizing some larger entity, the neighborhood, the community, the society. To call a killing a lynching asks: *How can you—all of you—tolerate such violence? What will you do about it?*

At the same time as the meaning of lynching became more confused, the debate over racial violence went national. This is the most important development in the history of twentieth-century lynching rhetoric. There was pressure to break moral judgments about particular acts of violence out of isolated neighborhoods all throughout the nineteenth century. Nonetheless, it was not until the advent of "high-tech" news operations, and the *Brown v. Board of Education* court case, that a national public exploded the isolation of neighborhoods determined to legitimize their violence on their own terms. Never again would the nation acquiesce as some secluded neighborhood group killed a person and called it justice. Never again, that is, unless we change our minds.

And this does matter. This history is implanted in the minds of most ordinary Americans. It is the national consciousness, the country's conscience. When a crowd of "good" citizens captures a "bad" person, they sometimes must decide on the spot just how much punishment they can legitimately inflict. As they wrestle their miscreant to the ground, they must calculate their confidence in the criminal justice system. Can the courts be trusted to punish a dangerously guilty person, or is this a time for self help? History supplied the answer. In the twentieth century we learned that even the most local, the most isolated neighborhood must answer to a national audience, not just to themselves.

Hate Crimes

The most important news story about the Emmett Till slaying came in the January 24, 1956, issue of *Look*. William Bradford Huie paid Milam and Bryant roughly four thousand dollars to describe for *Look* their crimes against young Till. Both Milam and Bryant met with Huie, though Milam did most of the talking. They detailed the story, telling Huie what they had never admitted in court and had not even told their own lawyers.

According to Huie, Milam and Bryant painted themselves as motivated by their community. The world they lived in drove them to murder. Huie wrote that once Roy Bryant knew that young Till had harassed his wife, "in his environment, in the opinion of most white people around him," he had little choice but to do something. In their conversations with Huie, the pair admitted to having kidnapped Till, claiming they only meant to frighten him. Their plans turned deadly only when Till unexpectedly defied and taunted them.[1] According to Milam, even as the two white men beat him, Till mocked them: "You bastards, I'm not afraid of you, I'm as good as you are, I've 'had' white women. My grandmother was a white woman." Milam recounted this language, and perhaps made it up, to justify his actions. "What else could we do?" he asked Huie. "He was hopeless."[2] Milam thought that any white person hearing what Till had said would sympathize with his killers.

Milam was not wrong. The sheriff sabotaged prosecution efforts at the trial. Jurors and all the attorneys later admitted that they went into the trial knowing there was no chance of conviction. No white man could be convicted for defending his wife against Negro aggression. One official asked the jury to wait a while before returning their verdict, to make it "look good." A resident of Tallahatchie County remembered later that the acquittal of Milam and Bryant seemed "to place a stamp of approval on the murder, and to encourage harassment of Negroes in the county." White teenagers felt liberated to ride through "Negro town" and hurl firecrackers into black homes.

One group of white teenagers composed a song that celebrated the power whites had to kill "a jig" and still count on acquittal.[3]

At the same time, it may be that Milam's need to make this argument signaled that local whites had already begun to turn against him. They did not have far to turn. Even before they killed Till, many local whites saw Milam and Bryant as marginal people, petty criminals, "white trash," or "peckerwoods."[4] Milam and Bryant's attempt to justify themselves through Huie failed. A year later, Huie returned to Mississippi and again interviewed Milam. The two killers had been ostracized. "I had a lot of friends a year ago," Milam wistfully told Huie, but now, "everything's gone against me." In what Milam took to be a calculated insult, the sheriff ordered him to stop carrying his gun. Bryant's store, where the incident occurred, failed—unsurprisingly since most of its customer base had been black. Out of a job, Milam had no choice but to sharecrop. Even finding that kind of work proved difficult. No landlord in all of Tallahatchie County would rent him land. Banks refused him a loan. He had been poor before the murder, owning neither a television nor a car. Huie now found him sharecropping in neighboring Sunflower County in a house without running water. Milam was pathetic: "My wife and kids are having it hard," he told Huie.[5] Ultimately, Bryan and Milam both migrated to Texas.[6]

In large part, the changing form of the kind of violence often called lynching—extralegal violence and racially motivated crimes—reflects larger cultural trends. Antebellum sentimentalism gave rise to sympathy for the persons lynched at Vicksburg and made lynching seem to some a great social evil. After the Civil War, lynching thrived because such sentimental empathy with the victims declined. In the twentieth century, another national mood swing changed the nature of racial violence. Just as politicians and pundits diagnosed Americans as increasingly socially isolated and disengaged, lynchings began morphing into hate crimes. After World War II, Americans not only bowled alone, they also perpetrated their racial violence alone or at least in smaller groups.[7]

The term "hate crime" did not exist in 1957 and would not exist until the 1980s. Nonetheless, Mississippi's transformation of Milam and Bryant from defenders of white civilization into ostracized and impoverished sharecroppers illustrates the difference between a lynching and a hate crime. A hate crime is an alienated individual's offense against society. Huie's *Look* articles document the ambiguity of Milam and Bryant's position. They acted in an environment that almost required them to "do something" about Till, Huie wrote. And Till acted in a way that Milam thought required a violent response, a response any white man would have performed, according to Huie. Milam persistently argued to Huie that he was a lyncher representing his community and not an individual acting against his neighbors. He may have been telling the truth, but the image Huie created was that of an individual isolated from his community.

Journalists and scholars have largely supported Milam in his quest to make himself the quintessential Mississippi white man. This support comes largely in the form of efforts to find other white people involved in the killing. L. Alex Wilson of the *Chicago Defender* tried and failed to do this by interviewing "Too Tight" Collins. Scholars have scrutinized evidence presented at the trial, openly skeptical that Milam and Bryant could have acted alone. This issue is a historical flash point only if the involvement of three or four or five persons rather than two really implicated the entire community. If three killers make a lynching, then positive proof that just one more killer had joined Milam and Bryant in the act makes the Till killing not a hate crime but a lynching.

In the nineteenth century, Americans understood lynching to mean an action committed by a whole community, one not necessarily racially motivated. In some cases, a large portion of the whole neighborhood actually participated in the killing. Alternatively, individuals or a small group carry out the murder with the approval of the larger population. Often this approval takes the form of recalcitrant witnesses and obstructionist judges, prosecutors, and juries. Defenders of lynchings deny that the word "crime" should be applied to lynchings at all. Such a crime, condoned by the people, cannot be a crime, since people make the law.

Hate criminals are motivated by their prejudices, as lynchers often are, but in an age of declining civic engagement and social connectedness, society defines its most awful race crimes as individuals' crimes against the public, rather than condoned by the public. Laws against hate crimes seek to isolate the persons charged, separating them from the larger society, holding them up as a model of what is not tolerable. When Milam and Bryant killed Till, they thought they acted with the approval of the community. While they did nothing that generations of Southern whites had not done before, the hostility they faced after the verdict showed that things had changed or at least had begun to change. Whites in Mississippi moved to cut Milam and Bryant out of the fabric of society.

On June 11, 1963, Byron De La Beckwith shot and killed Medgar Evers. Like Milam and Bryant, Beckwith expected his fellow whites to cheer his act. And they did. One Mississippi town held a celebratory parade for Beckwith. Fan mail poured into his jail cell. He wrote many letters from jail, some of them incriminating. "He was almost in a state of glee over this whole situation," a friend remembered later. He referred to his plight as "the cause."[8]

At the same time, even in 1963, Mississippi whites realized Beckwith was not quite one of them. The prosecutor, a champion of segregation named William Waller, petitioned the court for a sanity hearing. A storm of defense objections made it difficult for Waller to get his witnesses' testimony on the record, but he did document Beckwith's peculiarly violent disposition, including a tendency to beat and humiliate his wife. His former wife later said, "It was just like De La, he'd rather be accused of murder than have anybody question his sanity. That alone shows he was crazy." Even by 1963 Mississippi standards, the killer of Medgar Evers was arguably out of his mind. Therefore, it took some doing for Beckwith to wriggle out of questions about his sanity. But he managed to pull it off—with the assistance of lawyers and judges.[9]

The legal definition of insanity is often given as an inability to tell right from wrong. What the law does not allow, but history understands, is that the meaning of right and wrong is socially constructed, peculiar to particular historical circumstances. The legal definition fits Beckwith, who was caught in the nation's transition away from tolerance for racially motivated violence. Beckwith literally could not tell right from wrong because he came from a culture where killing a misbehaving black man was not "wrong." Unfortunately for him, he outlived his own time, living into an age in which white America, even white Mississippi, began to question that sort of thing.[10] Beckwith went on trial twice in 1964; both times jurors could not agree to acquit him. This turned out to be an important victory for the prosecution as well as a monument to the uncertainties beginning to creep into the white mind.

In 1994, prosecutor Bobby DeLaughter reopened Beckwith's case. Much had changed since 1964, though Beckwith had not changed at all. Mississippi blacks voted, and in 1986 Mike Espy had become Mississippi's first twentieth-century black congressman. Vicksburg elected a black mayor. A white reporter named Jerry Mitchell energetically investigated Mississippi's racist past. From DeLaughter's point of view in the 1990s, Beckwith seemed even crazier than he had in 1963. Looking at a letter Beckwith wrote to prosecutors, DeLaughter thought, "This guy is crazier than a shit-house rat."[11] Put on trial a third time, one journalist thought the 1994 jurors eyed Beckwith like an especially distasteful bug.[12]

America in the 1990s found Beckwith fascinating, his eccentricities evidence of how different the old racist was from modern America. Beckwith's retrial generated books published by major publishers. Journalists Maryanne Vollers, Reed Massengill, and Adam Nossiter all visited Beckwith in jail, writing about their encounters as if they were scientists viewing some strange and frightening specimen caught on a petri dish. Vollers found a joke-cracking racist, cackling about a "petrified nigger." Beckwith exploded when Nossiter came for a visit. "You're a damn Jew. Get out. Get out!" Massengill's visit was the most frightening of all. His *Portrait of a Racist* described Beckwith as feeding on his own hate, gathering strength as he progressively grew more agitated. After half an hour, Beckwith began ranting and shouting, making frightening threats. "I have more power in jail than you have out there," he warned.[13] For all three authors, Beckwith seemed a frightening specter from Mississippi's past, a very bad individual, manifestly not a "normal" person, someone different and peculiar. At the same time, all three authors made it a central point of their books to ask if remnants of Beckwith's old approval still lingered in Mississippi's present. All three wanted to know: Just how much of an isolated individual is Beckwith?

White Americans very much wanted Beckwith and his ilk to be or become an aberration. After 1980, virtually every state and the U. S. Congress passed hate-crime laws, statutes aimed at punishing individual bigots like Beckwith. These laws either required longer sentences for crimes motivated by hate or bias or they directed officials to keep records of hate crimes. Congress began debating a hate-crime law in 1985, when John Conyers, Barbara Kennelly, and Mario Biaggi sponsored a bill called the "Crime Statistics Act." Congress passed this bill in 1990 and then passed a law calling for longer sentences for hate-motivated criminals in 1994. The 1990 law required the Department of Justice to keep a tally of crimes motivated by hate based on race, religion, ethnicity, or sexual orientation. The 1994 law ordered the U. S. Sentencing Commission to increase the penalities for certain designated hate crimes.

The purpose of hate-crime laws goes beyond punishing hateful individuals. The goal is to reform society. Proponents argue that hate-crime laws champion equal rights and racial democracy, values the laws must assert rather than defend. Proponents of hate-crime laws sometimes claim that a hate-crime epidemic has seized the country. It is the opponents of hate-crime law who argue that civil rights and racial harmony already exist. When Beckwith's third jury convicted him of murder, one courthouse observer declared: "This poison and hate will end here, with this old man. It ends here, today."[14] The advent of laws against hate crime marks the advent of an attempt to redefine and isolate racial violence into some new category. Hate-crime laws represent a new phase in lynching rhetoric.

In the hate-crime era, Americans have made several efforts to atone for their sins of racial violence. Some of these efforts to make things right evolved from bombings and riots in which whites killed blacks, but these were incidents the press did not choose to label "lynchings." In 1976, Alabama Attorney General William Baxley launched a new investigation of the Ku Klux Klan bombing of Birmingham's Sixteenth Street Baptist Church in 1963. Baxley's effort resulted in the conviction of Robert "Dynamite Bob"

Chambliss, a long-time bomber who could more easily be called a serial killer than a lyncher. Baxley wanted to put other Klansmen on trial for the bombing, but did not, thwarted, he said later, by FBI recalcitrance.[15] In 1994, the Florida legislature voted to spend 2.1 million dollars to compensate former residents of Rosewood. Seventy years earlier, Florida whites had destroyed the town of Rosewood, killing black residents.[16] In 1997, Oklahoma organized a Tulsa Race Riot Commission to investigate the 1921 Tulsa race riot. The commission's historian, Scott Ellsworth, told reporters that whites may have hunted down and killed as many as 300 black Tulsans. The commission, after finding that as many as 10,000 white rioters destroyed 35 blocks of homes and businesses, called for reparations.[17]

The commission's call for reparations provoked a skeptical response in Oklahoma. And opponents of hate-crime laws generally doubt such legal efforts can promote healing. Instead, they charge them with promoting "identity politics." According to these critics, laws passed to protect the rights of particular groups invest those groups in their own oppression. Once tangible benefits are attached to minority status, groups compete for that status. The original federal hate-crime law covered only "prejudice based on race, religion, sexual orientation, or ethnicity." Senator Jesse Helms of North Carolina, fearing that this language somehow endorsed homosexuality, insisted on adding a second section, a Congressional "finding," declaring that the American family is the foundation of "American society."[18] Subsequently, lobbyists for the disabled insisted that the 1990 law be amended to include the word "disability" after "religion."[19] When Congress passed its law directing the sentencing commission to stiffen penalities for hate crimes, it defined "hate crime" as "a crime in which the defendant intentionally selects a victim . . . because of the actual or perceived race, color, religion, national origin, ethnicity, gender, disability, or sexual orientation."[20] Critics insist that such changes in the crimes covered show the political nature of hate crimes. Groups are included based on the strength of their ability to lobby Congress, not because their particular group naturally fits into some immutable standard for prejudice.

The new hate-crime rhetoric met its most serious test in 1998. Three white Texans picked up a disabled black man named James Byrd, Jr., beating and kicking him before dragging him to his death behind their pickup truck. Murder by dragging looked very much like a lynching. Some journalists pointed to the Byrd killing as disturbing evidence that nothing had changed in America. Journalists probed Jasper, Texas, the scene of the crime, interviewing defensive Texans who insisted they lived in a "good" town despite what had happened. One newspaper ran a headline over a column by Clarence Page that read: "The era of lynchings has not ended."[21]

As the trials of the three accused men progressed, attention increasingly focused on the three killers' biographies, not on Jasper. Journalists noticed that the police arrested the three almost immediately and law enforcement did not "lose" evidence or fail to locate critical witnesses. Newspapers ran biographical sketches of the three killers, John William King, Shawn Allen Berry, and Lawrence Russell Brewer, trying to understand how these individuals could go so horribly wrong.[22] Many in the press judged the three to be stereotypical hate criminals, "three troubled men out riding and drinking on a Saturday night." King came off particularly badly as "a foulmouthed convicted burglar."[23] Many concluded that King's prison experiences, rather than his residence in Jasper, had triggered his violent hatred. King had wanted to form his own hate group, the Texas Rebel Soldiers Division of the Confederate Knights of America; the very name sounded lunatic, the product of an individual's troubled mentality.[24] Harvard sociologist Orlando Patterson thought the murder of James Byrd resembled a lynching because more than one person committed the crime and hatred motivated the killers. But Patterson also saw stark differences between a lynching and the Byrd murder. In Jasper, citizens expressed outrage at the killing; lynchers acted with community support.[25] Juries ordered that two of the three men be put to death.[26] Ultimately, Americans decided King, Brewer, and Berry had committed a hate crime, not a lynching. America did not define itself, or any part of itself, as ultimately responsible. Three individuals had committed the crime.

This does not mean that the "era of lynching" has ended. Words do not often die, especially powerful words that can change minds. Lynching belongs to a powerful rhetoric, too good a tool to be discarded. There will be future lynchings because rhetoricians, like Clarence Thomas, will find the word irresistibly useful.

Notes

1. Interview with Ernest Withers, June 14, 2001. I did not taperecord my conversation with Withers and, therefore, will not use quote marks around my recollections of what he said.
2. Christopher Waldrep, *Roots of Disorder: Race and Criminal Justice in the American South* (Urbana: University of Illinois Press, 1998).
3. W. Fitzhugh Brundage, in *Lynching in the New South: Georgia and Virginia, 1880–1930* (Urbana: University of Illinois Press, 1993), 292, concedes that all definitions of lynching are "arbitrary." Philip Dray, in *At the Hands of Parties Unknown: The Lynching of Black America* (New York: Random House, 2002), viii, writes that the term has "always been somewhat ambiguous."
4. Stewart E. Tolnay and E. M. Beck, *A Festival of Violence: An Analysis of Southern Lynchings, 1882–1930* (Urbana: University of Illinois Press, 1995), 260.
5. Annotation by "TM" on Walter White memorandum to Marshall and Wilkins, December 16, 1946, box A407, group II, NAACP Papers (Library of Congress, Washington, D.C.); annotation by "TM" on Ferle Hoffman memorandum to White and Marshall, December 23, 1946, ibid.
6. Julia E. Baxter to legal department, June 4, 1947, box A407, group II, NAACP Papers; Marian Wynn Perry to Walter White, June 11, 1947, ibid.
7. Julia E. Baxter to Walter White, January 3, 1948, box A407, group II, NAACP Papers.
8. For the sexual or patriarchal control argument, see Joel Williamson, *The Crucible of Race: Black-White Relations in the American South Since Emancipation* (New York: Oxford University Press, 1984); Walter White, *Rope and Faggot: A Biography of Judge Lynch* (New York: Knopf, 1929); Glenda Elizabeth Gilmore, *Gender and Jim Crow: Women and the Politics of White Supremacy in North Carolina, 1896–1920* (Chapel Hill: University of North Carolina Press, 1996); Martha Hodes, *White Women, Black Men: Illicit Sex in the 19th-Century South* (New Haven: Yale University Press, 1997); Jacquelyn Dowd Hall, *Revolt Against Chivalry: Jessie Daniel Ames and the Women's Campaign Against Lynching* (New York: Columbia University Press, 1993).

   For the economic or social control argument, see John Dollard, *Caste and Class in a Southern Town* (1937; revised ed., Garden City: Doubleday, 1957); Brundage, *Lynching in the New South: Georgia and Virginia, 1880–1930*; Stewart E. Tolnay and E. M. Beck, *A Festival of Violence*; Carl Hovland and Robert R. Sears, "Minor Studies of Aggression: Correlation of Lynchings with Economic Indices," *Journal of Psychology* 9 (May 1940): 301–310; Alexander Mintz, "A Re-Examination of Correlations Between Lynchings and Economic Indices," *Journal of Abnormal and Social Psychology* 41 (April 1946): 154–165.

9. Tolnay and Beck, *A Festival of Violence*.

10. Trudier Harris, *Exorcising Blackness: Historical and Literary Lynching and Burning Rituals* (Bloomington: Indiana University Press, 1984), 1–28; Leon Litwack, *Trouble in Mind: Black Southerners in the Age of Jim Crow* (New York: Knopf, 1998), 285.

11. Harry K. Thaw, *The Traitor: Being the Untampered With, Unrevised Account of the Trial and All that Led to It* (Philadelphia: Dorrance and Co., 1926), 11, 141–145; *Vicksburg Evening Post*, February 20, 1907.

12. Harris, *Exorcising Blackness*, 69–94, (quotation from 70).

13. Shirley Wilson Logan, *"We Are Coming": The Persuasive Discourse of Nineteenth-Century Black Women* (Carbondale: Southern Illinois University Press, 1999), 1–22, 70–97; Ericka M. Miller, *The Other Reconstruction: Where Violence and Womanhood Meet in the Writings of Wells-Barnett, Grimke, and Larsen* (New York: Garland, 2000), 1–56; Gavin Jones, "'Whose Line is it Anyway?' W. E. B. Du Bois and the Language of the Color-Line," in Judith Jackson Fossett and Jeffrey A. Tucker, eds., *Race Consciousness: African-American Studies for the New Century* (New York: New York University Press, 1997), 19–34; Jacquelyn Dowd Hall, *Revolt Against Chivalry*, 150.

14. James H. Madison, *A Lynching in the Heartland: Race and Memory in America* (New York: Palgrave, 2001).

15. *CNN Breaking News*, transcript, September 11, 2001; *All Things Considered*, National Public Radio, September 11, 2001.

16. Peter Novick, *The Holocaust in American Life* (Boston, New York: Houghton Mifflin, 1999), 3–7, 127–133; Jon Petrie, "The Secular Word 'Holocaust': Scholarly Sacralization, Twentieth Century Meanings," http://www.berkeleyinternet.com/holocaust/; David P. Boder, *I Did Not Interview the Dead* (Urbana: University of Illinois Press, 1949); Donald L. Niewyk, *Fresh Wounds: Early Narratives of Holocaust Survival* (Chapel Hill: University of North Carolina Press, 1998), 1–23.

17. National Center for Health Statistics, "International Comparative Analysis of Injury Mortality: Findings from the ICE on Injury Statistics," http://www.cdc.gov/nchswww; *1998 Demographic Yearbook* (New York: United Nations, 2000), 482–505; *Crime in the United States: Uniform Crime Reports* (Washington: U.S. Government Printing Office, 2000), 13.

18. Spencer C. Tucker, ed., *Encyclopedia of the Vietnam War: A Political, Social, and Military History* (Santa Barbara: ABC-Clio, 1998), 3:1093.

19. Richard Maxwell Brown, "Legal and Behavioral Perspectives on American Vigilantism," *Perspectives in American History* 5 (1971): 95–144; idem, *Strain of Violence: Historical Studies of American Violence and Vigilantism* (New York: Oxford University Press, 1975); David Hackett Fischer, *Albion's Seed: Four British Folkways in America* (New York: Oxford University Press, 1989); Bertram Wyatt-Brown, *Southern Honor: Ethics and Behavior in the Old South* (New York: Oxford University Press, 1982); Kenneth S. Greenberg, *Honor and Slavery: Lies, Duels, Noses, Masks, Dressing as a Woman, Gifts, Strangers, Humanitarianism, Death, Slave Rebellions, the Proslavery Argument, Baseball, Hunting, and Gambling in the Old South* (Princeton: Princeton University Press, 1996); Edward L. Ayers, *Vengeance and Justice: Crime and Punishment in the 19th-Century American South* (New York: Oxford University Press, 1984); Grady McWhiney, *Cracker Culture: Celtic Ways in the Old South* (Tuscaloosa: University of Alabama Press, 1988); Dickson D. Bruce, Jr., *Violence and Culture in the Antebellum South* (Austin: University of Texas Press, 1979); David T. Courtwright, *Violent Land: Single Men and Social Disorder from the Frontier to the Inner City* (Cambridge: Harvard University Press, 1996); James Elbert Cutler, *Lynch-Law: An Investigation into the History of Lynching in the United States* (1905; reprint ed., Montclair: Patterson Smith, 1969).

20. Richard Maxwell Brown, *No Duty to Retreat: Violence and Values in American History and Society* (New York: Oxford University Press, 1991).

21. Ironically, police officers sometimes create communities where extralegal violence is tolerated and even expected. One retired officer remembered that "one rule I learned was that any suspect who assaulted a police officer in any way was never supposed to be able to walk into the station house on his own. He was supposed to be beaten so badly that he couldn't walk." Police officers who did not follow this rule were admonished by colleagues and sometimes by superiors. Lieutenant Arthur Doyle, "From the Inside Looking Out: Twenty-Nine Years in the New York Police Department," in Jill Nelson, ed., *Police Brutality: An Anthology* (New York: Norton, 2000), 173.

CHAPTER ONE

1. *San Francisco Chronicle,* August 1, 2001; *London Independent,* November 26, 2000; *London Daily Telegraph,* February 6, 2001. For lynching outside its American context, see Roberta Senechal de la Roche, "The Sociogenesis of Lynching," in W. Fitzhugh Brundage, ed., *Under Sentence of Death: Lynching in the South* (Chapel Hill: University of North Carolina Press, 1997), 51.

2. Haller Istvan, "Lynching Is Not a Crime: Mob Violence Against Roma in Post-Ceauscescu Romania," *European Roma Rights Center Newsletter* (Spring 1998): http://www.netsoft.ro/proeuro/HRO/Roma.htm.

3. William Beik, *Urban Protest in Seventeenth-Century France: The Culture of Retribution* (Cambridge: Cambridge University Press, 1997), 2–6.

4. *Virginia Gazette* (Purdie and Dixon), January 26, 1769.

5. Roberta Senechal de la Roche, "Why is Collective Violence Collective?" (paper presented at the Annual Meeting of the American Society of Criminology, San Diego, November 1997).

6. Francis J. Grund, *The Americans in their Moral, Social, and Political Relations* (1837; reprint ed., New York: Johnson Reprint, 1968), 178–180.

7. Hubert Howe Bancroft, *Popular Tribunals* (San Francisco: History Co., 1887), 1:1–2.

8. Bancroft, *Popular Tribunals,* 6–7; James Elbert Cutler, *Lynch Law: An Investigation into the History of Lynching in the United States* (1905; reprint ed., New York: Negro Universities Press, 1969), 13–17.

9. Bancroft, *Popular Tribunals,* 1:2–7. Although Bancroft cited the extensive history of extralegal violence to justify lynching, he was not necessarily wrong in reporting its extent. Early-twentieth-century opponents of lynching commonly held that only Americans *lynched,* when, in fact, crowd violence of the sort usually labeled *lynching* was hardly limited to the United States. Without using the term, Ancient Romans and Greeks *lynched,* as have Africans, Chinese, and Native Americans. *Lynching* as a practice was truly a worldwide phenomenon. Senechal de la Roche, "The Sociogenesis of Lynching," in W. Fitzhugh Brundage, ed., *Under Sentence of Death,* 51. See also Bancroft, *Popular Tribunals,* 2–6.

10. *The National Cyclopedia of American Biography* (New York: John T. White, 1962), 45:119.

11. Cutler, *Lynch Law,* 13–15, 267.

12. Cutler, *Lynch Law,* 268–269.

13. Jefferson to William Campbell, July 3, 1780, in Thomas Jefferson, *The Papers of Thomas Jefferson,* ed. Julian P. Boyd (Princeton: Princeton University Press, 1951), 3:479.

14. "Lynch's Law," *Southern Literary Messenger* 2 (May 1836): 389; "Lynch Law," *Harper's Monthly* 18 (May 1859): 795.

15. Louise Phelps Kellog, ed., *Frontier Retreat on the Upper Ohio, 1779–1781* (Madison: Wisconsin Historical Society, 1917), 24.

16. William Preston to Thomas Jefferson, March 1780, in Kellog, ed., *Frontier Retreat on the Upper Ohio,* 143. For William Preston, see Emory G. Evans, "Trouble in the

Backcountry: Disaffection in Southwest Virginia During the American Revolution," in Ronald Hoffman, Thad W. Tate, Peter J. Albert, eds., *An Uncivil War: The Southern Backcountry during the American Revolution* (Charlottesville: University Press of Virginia, 1985), 179–212.

17. Jefferson to Preston, March 21, 1780, in Jefferson, *The Papers of Thomas Jefferson,* 3:325. For treason, see David James Kiracofe, "Treason and the Development of National Identity in Revolutionary America, 1775–1815" (Ph.D. diss., University of Connecticut, 1995), 1–36.

18. Arthur Campbell to William Edmiston, June 24, 1780, in Kellog, ed., *Frontier Retreat on the Upper Ohio,* 195–196.

19. Walter Crockett to William Preston, August 6, 1780, in Kellog, ed., *Frontier Retreat on the Upper Ohio,* 236.

20. William Preston to Thomas Jefferson, August 8, 1780, in Kellog, ed., *Frontier Retreat on the Upper Ohio,* 241.

21. Thomas Walker Page, "The Real Judge Lynch," *Atlantic Monthly* 88 (December 1901): 731–743. Though ignored by historians of lynching, scholars of the Revolution in Virginia have done an excellent job documenting Revolutionary-era discontent and the extralegal reaction to it. See especially Evans, "Trouble in the Backcountry," 179–212; John E. Selby, *The Revolution in Virginia, 1775–1783* (Williamsburg: Colonial Williamsburg Foundation, 1988), 219–221; H. J. Eckenrode, *The Revolution in Virginia* (1916; reprint ed., Hamden: Archon, 1964), 232–260.

22. Charles Lynch to William Preston, August 17, 1780, in Kellog, ed., *Frontier Retreat on the Upper Ohio,* 250.

23. Bedford County Court Order Book 6, 288–290 (microfilm, Library of Virginia); William Waller Hening, *The Statutes at Large: Being a Collection of all the Laws of Virginia* 13 vols., (Richmond, 1809–1823), 10:268; Preston to Jefferson, August 8, 1780, in Kellog, ed., *Frontier Retreat on the Upper Ohio,* 242.

24. Bedford County Court Order Book 6, 295–305 (microfilm, Library of Virginia).

25. Nancy Devereaux to William Preston, August 1780, in Kellog, ed., *Frontier Retreat on the Upper Ohio,* 252; for pleas of guilty to high treason, see Bedford County Court Order Book 6, 295–303 (microfilm, Library of Virginia).

26. See Kellog, ed., *Frontier Retreat on the Upper Ohio,* 252–256. Emory Evans imagines the scene: exhausted, frightened men trying to respond at gunpoint to shouted questions. Evans, "Trouble in the Backcountry," 201–202.

27. Jefferson to Charles Lynch, August 1, 1780, *Papers of Thomas Jefferson,* 3:523.

28. Jefferson to Charles Lynch, August 1, 1780, *Papers of Thomas Jefferson,* 3:523.

29. Jefferson to Charles Lynch, August 1, 1780, *Papers of Thomas Jefferson,* 3:523.

30. Arthur Campbell to Colonel Davies, June 5, 1782, in William P. Palmer, ed., *Calendar of Virginia State Papers and Other Manuscripts* (1883; reprint ed., New York: Kraus, 1968), 3:190. Later Lynch's fears that the victims of lynch law might sue led him to call on the Virginia legislature to legitimate his activities. Maud Carter Clement, *The History of Pittsylvania County, Virginia* (Lynchburg: J.P. Bell, 1929), 178–179; Page, "The Real Judge Lynch," 731–743; Hening, *The Statutes at Large,* 11:134.

31. Herman Belz, "New Left Reverberations in the Academy: The Antipluralist Critique of Constitutionalism," *Review of Politics* 36 (1974): 265–283; Hendrik Hartog, "The Constitution of Aspiration and 'The Rights that Belong to us All,'" *Journal of American History* 74 (December 1987): 1013–1034.

32. Clement, *The History of Pittsylvania County,* 178–179; Page, "The Real Judge Lynch," 731–743; Hening, *The Statutes at Large,* 11:134.

33. Thomas Jefferson to Virginia Delegates in Congress, October 27, 1780, in William T. Hutchinson and William M. E. Rachal, eds., *The Papers of James Madison* (Chicago: University of Chicago Press, 1962), 2:153; Frances Hallam Hurt, *An Intimate History of the*

American Revolution in Pittsylvania County, Virginia (Danville: Womack Press, 1976), 97–110.

34. Pittsylvania County Court Order Book 4, 283, 287, 372–373 (microfilm, Library of Virginia).

35. David Jameson to James Madison, November 25, 1780, in *Papers of James Madison,* 2:201.

36. Catherine Van Cortlandt Mathews, *Andrew Ellicott, His Life and Letters* (New York: Grafton, 1908), 220–222; Silvio A. Bedini, "The Survey of the Federal Territory: Andrew Ellicott and Benjamin Banneker," *Washington History* (Spring/Summer 1991): 77–95.1

37. Rachel N. Klein, *Unification of a Slave State: The Rise of the Planter Class in the South Carolina Backcountry, 1760–1808* (Chapel Hill: University of North Carolina Press, 1990), 47–77.

38. George Washington, "Sixth Annual Address," November 19, 1794, in James D. Richardson, comp., *A Compilation of the Messages and Papers of the Presidents* (Washington: Bureau of National Literature and Art, 1903), 1:163; Christian G. Fritz, "Legitimating Government: The Ambiguous Legacy of the People's Sovereignty, 1776–1860" (unpublished manuscript), chapter five. For "club law," see *Niles Register* 22 (June 1, 1822), 224.

39. Mathews, *Andrew Ellicott,* 220–222.

40. "Lynch's Law," *Southern Literary Messenger* 2 (May 1836): 389. Poe left the *Messenger* in 1837. In 1839, when the *Messenger* returned to the theme of lynching, Thomas Willis White edited the journal. This time, in an article entitled "Recollections of a Retired Lawyer," the *Messenger* repudiated lynching. The retired lawyer conceded that he had once applauded lynchings as they seemed to work well with brutish husbands and other miscreants. But as time passed the old lawyer realized the danger of lynch law: It naturally spread to cover more and more "crimes." "Recollections of a Retired Lawyer," *Southern Literary Messenger* 5 (March 1839): 218–219; Robert D. Jacobs, "Campaign for a Southern Literature: The Southern Literary Messenger," *Southern Literary Journal* 2 (fall 1969): 66–98.

41. Recently the charter Poe published has been cited as evidence that William Lynch really was the first lyncher. John Ross, "At the Bar of Judge Lynch: Lynching and Lynch Mobs in America" (Ph.D. diss., Texas Tech University, 1983), 16–22. But Poe was a notorious prankster, once fooling the U. S. Senate into thinking that his bogus "Journal of Julius Rodman" genuinely described an expedition across the Rockies. On another occasion he sold to the *New York Sun* a false account of a transatlantic balloon flight. He once ridiculed the Gold Rush by publishing a fictitious report that chemists could change lead into gold. Kenneth Silverman, *Edgar A. Poe: Mournful and Never-Ending Remembrance* (New York: HarperCollins, 1991), 62, 147, 225–226, 402; Andie Tucher, *Froth and Scum: Truth, Beauty, Goodness, and the Ax Murder in America's First Mass Medium* (Chapel Hill: University of North Carolina Press, 1994), 47–48. It may be best to allow William Lynch's charter to remain dormant.

42. David Crockett, *Narrative of the Life of David Crockett* (Baltimore: E. L. Carey and A. Hart, 1834), 135.

43. David K. Jackson, "A Poe Hoax Comes Before the U. S. Senate," *Poe Studies* 7 (1974): 47–48; Linda Miller, "Poe on the Beat," *Journal of the Early Republic* 7 (Summer 1987): 147–165.

44. Population increase for Ohio, Indiana, Illinois, Maryland, Alabama, Mississippi, Louisiana, Tennessee. See *Historical Statistics of the United States, Colonial Times to 1957* (Washington, 1960), 13. Morris Birkbeck, *Notes on a Journey from the Coast of Virginia to the Territory of Illinois* (1817; rev ed., London, 1818), 34; Malcolm J. Rohrbough, *The Trans-Appalachian Frontier: People, Societies, and Institutions, 1775–1850* (New York: Oxford University Press, 1978), 157–217; Charles D. Lowery, "The Great Migration to the Mississippi Territory, 1798–1819," *Journal of Mississippi History* 30 (1968): 173–192.

45. Tyrone Power, *Impressions of America During the Years 1833, 1834, and 1835* (London: P. Bentley, 1836), 300.

46. Calculated from John Frederick Dorman, *Virginia Revolutionary Pension Applications* (Washington, D.C., 1958-), vols. 1–13. Since Dorman compiled his material in alphabetical order, this means I have used the applications of veterans through Peter Butler.

47. Henry Rowe Schoolcraft, *Rude Pursuits and Rugged Peaks: Schoolcraft's Ozark Journal* (Fayetteville: University of Arkansas Press, 1996), 70.

48. James Flint, *Letters from America,* ed. Reuben Gold Thwaites (Cleveland: Clark, 1904), 199–200.

49. John James Audubon, *Delineations of American Scenery and Character* (New York: G. A. Baker, 1926), 19–22.

50. Adam Hodgson, *Letters from North America Written During a Tour in the United States and Canada* (London, 1824), 188; An English Gentleman [William Newnham Blane], *An Excursion Through the United States and Canada During the Years 1822–23* (1824; reprint ed., New York: Negro Universities Press, 1969), 233–236.

51. Arthur Singleton, *Letters from the South and West* (Boston, 1824), 106.

52. Godfrey T. Vigne, *Six Months in America* (London: Whittaker, Treacher, 1832), 68–76.

53. Tyrone Power, *Impressions of America During the Years 1833, 1834, and 1835,* 297.

54. William Faux, *Memorable Days in America: Being a Journal of a Tour to the United States, Principally Undertaken to Ascertain, by Positive Evidence, the Conditions and Probable Prospects of British Emigrants.* . . . (London, 1823), 304.

55. James Hall, *Letters from the West* (1828; reprint ed., Gainesville: Scholars' Facsimiles, 1967), 291.

56. James Stuart, *Three Years in North America* 2 vols. (rev. ed., Edinburgh, 1833), 2:179, 267.

57. Washington Irving, *A Tour of the Prairies,* ed. John Francis McDermott (1835; reprint ed., Norman: University of Oklahoma Press, 1956), 33.

58. David W. Newton, "Voices Along the Border: Language and the Southern Frontier, *Guy Rivers: A Tale of Georgia,*" in John Caldwell Guilds and Caroline Collins, eds., *William Gilmore Simms and the American Frontier* (Athens: University of Georgia Press, 1997), 118–139; William Gilmore Simms, *Guy Rivers: A Tale of Georgia* 2 vols. (New York: Harper and Bros., 1834), 1:64–65.

59. Flint, *Letters from America,* 198–199.

60. Otto A. Rothert, *The Outlaws of Cave-in-Rock* (Cleveland: Arthur H. Clark, 1924), 60–142, 142 (quotation); W. D. Snively, Jr., and Louanna Furbee, *Satan's Ferryman: A True Tale of the Old Frontier* (n.p.: Frederick Ungar, 1968), 46–56.

61. James M. Denham, *"A Rogue's Paradise": Crime and Punishment in Antebellum Florida, 1821–1861* (Tuscaloosa: University of Alabama Press, 1997), 153–154.

62. Irving, *A Tour of the Prairies,* 33; [Joseph Holt Ingraham], *The Southwest* 2 vols. (New York: Harper and Brothers, 1835), 2:186.

63. Hall, *Letters from the West,* 291–292.

64. Stuart, *Three Years in North America,* 2:179.

65. Stuart, *Three Years in North America,* 2:179.

CHAPTER TWO

1. "Lynch Law," *Harper's New Monthly Magazine* 18 (May 1859): 794; J. L. McConnell, *Western Characters or Types of Border Life in the Western States* (Redfield, 1853), 171–175.

2. For 1834, see Carl E. Prince, "The Great 'Riot Year': Jacksonian Democracy and Patterns of Violence in 1834," *Journal of the Early Republic* 5 (Spring 1985): 1–18. David Grimsted calls 1835 the "Year of Violent Indecision" in David Grimsted, *American Mobbing, 1828–1861: Toward Civil War* (New York: Oxford University Press, 1998), 3–32.

3. *New York Sun,* July 2, 1834.

4. *Niles' Register,* April 12, May 3, August 23, 1834, January 24, 1835; *New York Evening Post,* June 12, 1835; *New York Sun,* December 3, 1833, March 25, July 24, June 24, 1834, January 17, February 2, 27, April 28, 1835.

5. *New York Sun,* June 25, 1835.

6. *Galena (Illinois) Galenian,* June 16, 1834; Eliphalet Price, "The Trial and Execution of Patrick O'Conner at the Dubuque Mines in the Summer of 1834," *Palimpsest* 1 (1920): 86–97.

7. *St Louis Republican* quoted in *Niles' Register* 45 (October 5, 1833): 87.

8. *Niles' Register,* January 31, 1835; Bertram Wyatt-Brown, *Southern Honor: Ethics and Behavior in the Old South* (New York: Oxford University Press, 1982), 462–493; Col. James R. Creecy, *Scenes in the South and other Miscellaneous Pieces* (Washington: Thomas McGill, 1860), 52–56.

9. *Louisville Advertiser,* July 11, 1835,

10. *Vicksburg Register,* July 9, 1835.

11. *Vicksburg Register,* July 9, 1835.

12. William Gilmore Simms, *Guy Rivers: A Tale of Georgia* (New York: Harper and Bros., 1834), 1:65; Simms, *Guy Rivers: A Tale of Georgia,* new and revised ed. (Chicago: Belford, Clarke & Co., 1887), 69–71; Charles S. Watson, *From Nationalism to Secessionism: The Changing Fiction of William Gilmore Simms* (Westport: Greenwood Press, 1993), 80–83; Christopher Morris, *Becoming Southern: The Evolution of a Way of Life, Warren County and Vicksburg, Mississippi, 1770–1860* (New York: Oxford University Press, 1995), 121–122.

13. *Vicksburg Register,* July 9, 1835.

14. *Vicksburg Register,* July 9, 1835; *Natchez Courier,* July 10, quoted in *Boston Liberator,* August 8, 1835.

15. *Louisiana Advertiser,* July 11, quoted in *Boston Liberator,* August 1, 1835.

16. *Louisiana Advertiser,* July 11, quoted in *Boston Liberator,* August 1, 1835; *New Orleans American* quoted in *Niles' Register* 48 (July 25, 1835): 363.

17. *Louisiana Advertiser,* July 13, 1835, quoted in *Portland (Maine) Daily Evening Advertiser,* August 1, 1835.

18. *Louisiana Advertiser,* July 13, 1835, quoted in *Portland (Maine) Daily Evening Advertiser,* August 1, 1835; William Taylor, *Cavalier and Yankee: the Old South and American National Character* (Cambridge: Harvard University Press, 1979), 300–313; George M. Frederickson, *The Black Image in the White Mind: The Debate on Afro-American Character and Destiny, 1817–1914* (New York: Harper and Row, 1971), 30–34; Herbert Ross Brown, *The Sentimental Novel in America, 1789–1860* (New York: Pageant, 1959), 358–370; Helen Waite Papashvily, *All the Happy Endings: A Study of the Domestic Novel in America, the Women who Wrote it, the Women who Read it, in the Nineteenth Century* (New York: Harper, 1956); E. Douglas Branch, *The Sentimental Years, 1836–1860* (New York: Hill and Wang, 1962), 191–223.

19. James Stuart, *Three Years in North America* (Edinburgh, 1833), 2:241–267.

20. *Louisiana Advertiser,* December 16, 1834; January 14, February 3, 1835.

21. *Charleston Courier* July 22, 1835.

22. *Sangamo Journal,* July 25, 1835.

23. *Chicago Democrat,* August 15, 22, 29, 1835.

24. *Boston Daily Advertiser and Patriot,* July 27, 1835.

25. *Portland (Maine) Daily Evening Advertiser,* July 28, 1835.

26. *New York Evening Post,* July 27, 1835; *Boston Daily Advertiser and Patriot,* July 27, 1835; *Morning Courier and New-York Enquirer,* July 27, 1835.

27. *New York Sun,* July 27, 1835.

28. *New York Sun,* July 31, 1835.

29. *Wheeling Gazette,* quoted in *Boston Daily Advertiser and Patriot,* August 4, 1835, in the *Chicago American,* August 22, 1835, and in the *Nashville Republican,* August 13, 1835.

30. *Boston Daily Advertiser and Patriot,* August 4, 1835.

31. *Chicago American,* September 5, 1835.

32. *Vicksburg Register,* July 23, 1835.

33. *Niles' Register* 48 (August 1, 1835): 381.

34. James Burns Wallace diary, January 13, 1836, (Louisiana State University Library); Richard Wynkoop to H. S. Wynkoop, October 1, 1836, reprinted in *Vicksburg Herald,* December 27, 1912; Harriet Martineau, *Retrospect of Western Travel* (London, New York: Harper and Brothers, 1838), 17; G. W. Featherstonhaugh, *Excursion through the Slave States* (London: J. Murray, 1844), 250–254.

35. David Ray Papke, *Framing the Criminal: Crime, Cultural Work and the Loss of Critical Perspective, 1830–1900* (Hamden, Conn.: Archon Books, 1987), 33–53; Frank M. O'Brien, *The Story of the New York Sun, 1833–1928* (New York, London: D. Appleton, 1928), 1088; James L. Crouthamel, *Bennett's* New York Herald *and the Rise of the Popular Press* (Syracuse: Syracuse University Press, 1989), 19–55; Michael Emery, Edwin Emery, and Nancy L. Roberts, *The Press and America: An Interpretive History of the Mass Media,* ninth ed. (Boston: Allyn and Bacon, 2000), 97–107; Ronald J. Zboray, *A Fictive People: Antebellum Economic Development and the American Reading Public* (New York: Oxford University Press, 1993), 3–16.

36. Dan Schiller, *Objectivity and the News: The Public and the Rise of Commercial Journalism* (Philadelphia: University of Pennsylvania Press, 1981), 110–113.

37. *New York Sun,* August 22, 1835.

38. *New York Sun,* September 2, 3, 14, 21, 29, 1835; *New York Herald,* September 24, 1835.

39. *New York Herald,* September 9, 1835.

40. Crouthamel, *Bennett's* New York Herald, 19–55.

41. *Louisville Advertiser,* July 29, 1835; Alan D. Watson, "The Lottery in Early North Carolina," *North Carolina Historical Quarterly* 69 (1992): 365–387; Lewis L. Laska and Severine Brocki, "The Life and Death of the Lottery in Tennessee, 1787–1836," *Tennessee Historical Quarterly* 45 (Summer 1986): 95–118.

42. *Niles' Register* 45 (October 5, 1833): 87.

43. Frederick Hawkins Piercy, *Route from Liverpool to Great Salt Lake Valley,* Fawn M. Brodie, ed. (1855; new ed., Cambridge: Harvard University Press, 1962), 81; Karen Halttunen makes this point in *Confidence Men and Painted Women: A Study of Middle-Class Culture in America, 1830–1870* (New Haven: Yale University Press, 1982).

44. John M. Findlay, *People of Chance: Gambling in American Society from Jamestown to Las Vegas* (New York: Oxford University Press, 1986), 65–69; Ann Fabian, *Card Sharps, Dream Books, and Bucket Shops: Gambling in 19th-Century America* (Ithaca: Cornell University Press, 1990), 33–37; *Niles' Register* 48 (August 8, 1835): 402; Halttunen, *Confidence Men and Painted Women,* 1–55.

45. *Niles' Register* 46 (March 15, 1834): 35; ibid., (April 5, 1834): 85; ibid., (April 12, 1834): 100–101; ibid., (April 26, 1834): 130; ibid., (May 3, 1834): 147, 152–153; ibid., (May 24, 1834): 210; ibid., (June 21, 1834): 291; ibid., (June 28, 1834): 300; ibid., (July 12, 1834): 332; ibid., (July 19, 1834): 346, 357; ibid., (July 26, 1834): 365; ibid., (August 16, 1834): 413; ibid., (August 23, 1834): 426, 435; ibid., (August 30, 1834): 444; ibid., 47 (September 6, 1834): 15; Grimsted, *American Mobbing, 1828–1861: Toward Civil War,* 3–32.

46. *Chicago American,* August 29, 1835.

47. *Chicago American,* September 5, 1835.

48. *Chicago American,* October 17, 1835.

49. *Chicago American,* October 24, 1835. This story appeared in the *New York Sun* originally.

50. Thomas F. Schwartz, "The Springfield Lyceums and Lincoln's 1838 Speech," *Illinois Historical Journal* 83 (Spring 1990): 45–49.

51. Lincoln, "Address Before the Young Men's Lyceum of Springfield, Illinois," January 27, 1838, in Abraham Lincoln, *The Collected Works of Abraham Lincoln* ed. Roy P. Basler,

(New Brunswick: Rutgers University Press, 1953), 1:108–115; Neil Schmitz, "Murdered McIntosh, Murdered Lovejoy: Abraham Lincoln and the Problem of Jacksonian Address," *Arizona Quarterly* 44 (Autumn 1988): 15–39.

52. Allan Nevins, ed., *The Diary of Philip Hone, 1828–1851* (1927; reprint ed., New York: Kraus, 1969), 1:167; Grimsted, *American Mobbing*, 3; James M. Denham, *A "Rogues Paradise": Crime and Punishment in Antebellum Florida, 1821–1861* (Tuscaloosa: University of Alabama Press, 1997), 186.

53. William Gilmore Simms, *Mellichampe, A Legend of the Santee* (New York: Harper and Bros., 1836), 312; Simms, *Border Beagles: A Tale of Mississippi* 2 vols. (Philadelphia: Carey and Hart, 1840), 336; Simms, *The History of South Carolina* (New York: Redfield, 1860), 144–146; Watson, *From Nationalism to Secessionism*, 25–145.

54. Editors of the *National Police Gazette*, *The Life and Adventures of John A. Murrell, the Great Western Land Pirate* (New York: H. Long and Brother, 1847).

55. Alfred Huger to Samuel L. Gouverneur, August 1, 1835, in Frank Otto Gatell, ed, "Postmaster Huger and the Incendiary Publications," *South Carolina Historical Magazine* 64 (October 1963): 194–195; Bertram Wyatt-Brown, *Lewis Tappan and the Evangelical War Against Slavery* (Cleveland: Case Western Reserve University Press, 1969), 143–163; Lewis Tappan, *The Life of Arthur Tappan* (1871, reprint ed., Westport: Negro Universities Press, 1970), 243–252; James Brewer Stewart, *Holy Warriors: the Abolitionists and American Slavery* (New York: Hill and Wang, 1976), 33–65; W. Sherman Savage, *The Controversy Over the Distribution of Abolition Literature, 1830–1860* (n.p.: Association for the Study of Negro Life and History, Inc., 1938), 13–26.

56. Defensor, *The Enemies of the Constitution Discovered, or, an Inquiry into the Origin and Tendency of Popular Violence, Containing a Complete and Circumstantial Account of the Unlawful Proceedings at the City of Utica, October 21st, 1835; The Dispersion of the State Anti-Slavery Convention by the Agitators, the Destruction of a Democratic Press, and of the Causes which Led Thereto, Together with a Concise Treatise on the Practice of the Court of His Honour Judge Lynch* (New York: Leavitt, Lord & Co., 1835), 11.

57. Howard Alexander Morrison, "Gentlemen of Proper Understanding: A Closer Look at Utica's Anti-Abolitionist Mob," *New York History* 62 (1981): 61–82; Benjamin Sevitch, "The Well-Planned Riot of October 21, 1835: Utica's Answer to Abolitionism," *New York History* 50 (1969): 251–263; Defensor, *The Enemies of the Constitution Discovered*, 54–104; Samuel J. May, *Some Recollections of Our Antislavery Conflict* (Boston: Fields, Osgood, & Co., 1869), 162–169.

58. Defensor, *The Enemies of the Constitution Discovered*, 104–122.

59. *Lexington (Kentucky) True American,* June 3, November 25, 1845,

60. *Chatham (Canada West) Provincial Freeman,* February 23, 1856. For other abolitionist attacks on the Southern tendency to lynch, see, for example, *New York Colored American,* June 20, 1840; *Washington National Era,* April 3, 1851; *Chatham (Canada West) Provincial Freeman,* June 7, 1856, June 20, 1857.

61. Congress, Senate, Senator Foote speaking against a bill for the Protection of Property in the District of Columbia, 30th Cong., 1st sess., *Congressional Globe* (April 20, 1848), appendix, 502.

62. For this debate, see *Congressional Globe* (April 20, 1848), appendix, 500–510. For the Revolutionary War, see Congress, Senate, Senator Thompson speaking against a bill for the Protection of Property in the District of Columbia, 30th Cong., 1st sess., *Congressional Globe* (April 21, 1848), 659.

63. Richard Hildreth, *Despotism in America: An Inquiry in the Nature, Results, and Legal Basis of the Slave-Holding System in the United States* (Boston: John P. Jewet, 1854), 252.

64. Grimsted, *American Mobbing*, 85–113. For a different view, see Paul A. Gilje, *Rioting in America* (Bloomington: Indiana University Press, 1996).

65. *Boston Liberator,* September 27, 1834.

66. *Rochester Union* reprinted in *Kansas City Enterprise,* October 25, 1856.

67. *New York Times,* September 14, July 27, 1853, March 8, 1854, June 2, 1855, September 1, 1856.

68. "The Vigilantes, Nebraska's First Defenders," *Nebraska History Magazine* 14 (January-March 1933): 3–18.

69. *Milwaukee Sentinel* reprinted in *St. Louis Missouri Republican,* August 13, 1855.

70. *St. Louis Missouri Republican,* April 23, June 4, July 1, 19, 25, 1857.

71. *St. Louis Missouri Republican,* February 18, 1856; *Vicksburg Daily Whig,* March 6, 1856, August 20, 1857; *New York Times,* September 1, 1856.

72. *Boonville Observer* reprinted in *New York Times,* July 27, 1853; *Columbia Statesman* reprinted in *New York Times,* September 14, 1853. Historians disagree over the continuity of white fears of black rapists. For continuity, see Peter Bardaglio, "Rape and the Law in the Old South: 'Calculated to Excite Indignation in Every Heart,'" *Journal of Southern History* 60 (1994): 749–772. Martha Hodes argues for discontinuity; see *White Women, Black Men: Illicit Sex in the 19th-Century South* (New Haven: Yale University Press, 1997), 125–208.

73. *Boston Liberator,* October 2, 1857.

74. See, for example, *Boston Liberator,* October 27, 1848, April 13, May 11, 1849. For "Vicksburg Lynch law," see October 5, 1849.

75. *Boston Liberator,* September 26, 1835.

76. *Boston Liberator,* July 2, 1836.

77. *Boston Liberator,* December 17, 1841, July 25, 1851.

78. *Mississippi Free Trader* reprinted in the *New York Times,* March 8, 1854.

79. *Boston Daily Advertiser and Patriot,* August 20, 1835.

80. *Morning Courier and New-York Enquirer,* September 8, 1835.

81. *Boston Daily Advertiser and Patriot,* July 30, 31, 1835.

82. Quoted in *Boston Daily Advertiser and Patriot,* August 7, 1835.

83. *Morning Courier and New-York Enquirer,* August 28, 1835.

84. *New York Herald,* September 9, 29, 1835.

85. Abraham Lincoln, *The Collected Works of Abraham Lincoln,* ed. Roy P. Basler (New Brunswick: Rutgers University Press, 1953–1955), 4:262–271; Phillip Shaw Paludan, *"A People's Contest": The Union and Civil War, 1861–1865* (New York: Harper and Row, 1988), 3–32.

86. Looking at the South, Dickson Bruce identified a fear of passion amongst nineteenth-century Americans. This seems congruent with my findings of a more general fear of excitement or disorder. See Bruce, *Violence and Culture in the Antebellum South* (Austin: University of Texas Press, 1979).

87. For various examples of this, see the Senate's debate over the bill for the Protection of Property in the District of Columbia, 30th Cong., 1st sess., *Congressional Globe* (April 20, 1848), 500–510.

88. *Lexington (Kentucky) Intelligencer* reprinted in *Boston Daily Advertiser and Patriot,* August 7, 1835.

89. David Grimsted, "Rioting in Its Jacksonian Setting," *American Historical Review* 77 (April 1972): 361–397, 380–382 (quotation).

90. *Boston Liberator,* May 21, 1836; Florence Doll Cornet, "The Experiences of a Midwest Salesman in 1836," *Missouri Historical Society Bulletin* (July 1973): 227–235; David Grimsted, *American Mobbing,* 103–104.

91. *Cincinnati Daily Evening Post* quoted in *Narrative of the Late Riotous Proceedings Against the Liberty of the Press in Cincinnati* (Cincinnati, 1836), 47; Birney to Charles Hammond, November 14, 1835, Dwight L. Dumond, ed., *Letters of James Gillespie Birney, 1831–1857* (1938; reprint ed., Gloucester: Peter Smith, 1966), 1:263–264; *Cincinnati Philanthropist,* May 13, 1836.

92. *New Richmond (Ohio) Philanthropist*, April 8, 1836.

93. *Cincinnati Philanthropist*, April 22, 1836.

94. *Cincinnati Philanthropist*, July 15, 22, 1836.

95. *Narrative of the Late Riotous Proceedings Against the Liberty of the Press in Cincinnati with Remarks and Historical Notices Relating to Emancipation*, 19; Michael Kent Curtis, "The 1837 Killing of Elijah Lovejoy by an Anti-Abolition Mob: Free Speech, Mobs, Republican Government, and the privileges of American Citizens," *UCLA Law Review* 44 (April 1997): 1126–1128.

96. Stephen Ellingson, "Understanding the Dialectic of Discourse and Collective Action: Public Debate and Rioting in Antebellum Cincinnati," *American Journal of Sociology* 101 (July 1995): 100–144.

97. *Cincinnati Philanthropist*, June 12, 1838.

98. *St. Louis Observer*, November 19, 1835, July 14, 1836.

99. Curtis, "The 1837 Killing of Elijah Lovejoy," 1136–1138.

100. *Alton Observer*, December 28, 1837.

101. *New York Emancipator*, October 21, 1841; Congress, Senate, Senator Stephen A. Douglas speaking on a bill for the Protection of Property in the District of Columbia, 30th Cong., 1st sess., *Congressional Globe* (April 20, 1848), appendix, 506; *New York Times*, June 2, 1855.

102. Charles Lynch, Inaugural Address, January 7, 1836, published in *Clinton Gazette*, January 16, 1836.

103. *Norfolk American Beacon*, August 8, 1835.

104. *Norfolk American Beacon*, August 15, 1835.

105. *Nashville Republican*, September 3, 1835.

CHAPTER THREE

1. For antebellum Northerners' racial attitudes, see Jean H. Baker, *Affairs of Party: The Political Culture of Northern Democrats in the Mid-Nineteenth Century* (Ithaca: Cornell University Press, 1983), 212–258; Noel Ignatiev, *How the Irish Became White* (New York: Routledge, 1995); Eugene H. Berwanger, *The Frontier Against Slavery: Western Anti-Negro Prejudice and the Slavery Extension Controversy* (Urbana: University of Illinois Press, 1967), 30–59.

2. The most complete account of San Francisco vigilantism endorsed the extralegal violence. Hubert Howe Bancroft, *Popular Tribunals*, 2 vols. (San Francisco: History Co., 1887). Twentieth-century historians have been more critical. Richard Maxwell Brown, *Strain of Violence: Historical Studies of American Violence and Vigilantism* (New York: Oxford University Press, 1975), 134–143, documented the political nature of the 1856 Vigilance Committee. Joseph M. Kelly, "Shifting Interpretations of the San Francisco Vigilantes," *Journal of the West* 24 (1985): 39–46; and Kevin J. Mullen, *Let Justice Be Done: Crime and Politics in Early San Francisco* (Reno: University of Nevada Press, 1989), find crime far less rampant than claimed by the vigilantes. Robert M. Senkewicz, *Vigilantes in Gold Rush San Francisco* (Stanford: Stanford University Press, 1985); David A. Johnson, "Vigilance and the Law: The Moral Authority of Popular Justice in the Far West," *American Quarterly* 33 (Winter 1981): 558–586, treats the vigilantes' "moral authority" as fleeting and ephemeral.

3. See, for example, David Crockett, *Narrative of the Life of David Crockett* (Philadelphia: E. L. Carey and A. Hart, 1834), 133–135.

4. James E. Davis, *Frontier Illinois* (Bloomington: Indiana University Press, 1998), 214–217; Randall Parrish, *Historic Illinois: The Romance of the Earlier Days* (Chicago: McClurg, 1906), 400–413; Nicole Etcheson, "Good Men and Notorious Rogues: Vigilantism in Massac County, Illinois, 1846–1850," in Michael Bellesiles, ed., *Lethal*

Imagination: Violence and Brutality in American History (New York: New York University Press, 1999), 149–169; James A. Rose, "The Regulators and Flatheads in Southern Illinois," *Transactions of the Illinois State Historical Society for the Year 1906* (Springfield: Illinois State Journal, 1906), 108–121; Alice Louise Brumbaugh, "The Regulator Movement in Illinois" (M.A. thesis, University of Illinois, 1927).

5. John Phillip Reid, *Policing the Elephant: Crime, Punishment, and Social Behavior on the Overland Trail* (San Marino: Huntington Library, 1997), 139, 157–158, 195–197; Malcolm J. Rohrbough, *Days of Gold: The California Gold Rush and the American Nation* (Berkeley: University of California Press, 1997), 216–229.

6. *Washington Southern Press,* May 9, 1851.

7. J. L. McConnell, *Western Characters or Types of Border Life in the Western States* (New York: Redfield, 1853), 175; Richard Hildreth, *Despotism in America: An Inquiry in the Nature, Results, and Legal Basis of the Slave-Holding System in the United States* (Boston: John P. Jewet, 1854), 252.

8. Richard Slotkin, *The Fatal Environment: The Myth of the Frontier in the Age of Industrialization, 1800–1890* (Middleton: Wesleyan University Press, 1985), 51–136; James Hall, *Letters from the West; Containing Sketches of Scenery, Manners and Customs* (1828; reprint. ed., Gainesville: Scholars' Facsimiles, 1967), 290–292; Charles S. Watson, *From Nationalism to Secessionism: The Changing Fiction of William Gilmore Simms* (Westport: Greenwood Press, 1993), 25–81.

9. Johnson, "Vigilance and the Law," 558–586.

10. *Richmond Whig,* reprinted in *Greensborough (North Carolina) Patriot,* September 12, 1856.

11. *Alta California* reprinted in *Charleston (South Carolina) Courier,* May 21, 1851.

12. *St. Louis Missouri Republican,* July 18, 1856.

13. Congress, Senate, Senator Stephen A. Douglas of Illinois speaking on Admission of California as a state, 30th Cong., 2nd sess., *Congressional Globe* (January 11, 1849), 193.

14. Alfredo Mirande, *Gringo Justice* (Notre Dame: Notre Dame University Press, 1987), 51–75; *Los Angeles Star,* June 4, 11, 18, 1864.

15. Rodolfo Acuna, *Occupied America: A History of Chicanos,* 3rd ed. (New York: Harper and Row, 1988), 28.

16. William B. Secrest, *Juanita* (Fresno: Sage-West, 1967), 7–26.

17. Major Horace Bell, *Reminiscences of a Ranger or Early Times in Southern California* (Santa Barbara: Wallace Hebberd, 1927), 8–43.

18. Maurice H. Newmark and Marco R. Newmark, eds., *Sixty Years in Southern California, 1853–1913: Containing the Reminiscences of Harris Newmark,* 3rd ed. (Boston: Houghton Mifflin, 1930), 141.

19. Statement of William T. Coleman, not dated, William T. Coleman Papers, (Bancroft Library, University of California, Berkeley); Bancroft, *Popular Tribunals,* 1:179–214.

20. Mullen, *Let Justice Be Done,* 161–208; Bancroft, *Popular Tribunals,* 1:208–213; William T. Coleman statement, William T. Coleman Papers.

21. *San Francisco Evening Bulletin,* November 20, 1855.

22. *San Francisco Evening Bulletin,* January 22, 1856.

23. *San Francisco Evening Bulletin,* January 23, 1856.

24. *San Francisco Evening Bulletin,* May 15, 1856.

25. Joseph B. Crockett to his wife, May 19, 1856, Joseph Bryant Crockett Papers, (Bancroft Library, University of California, Berkeley); *San Francisco Evening Bulletin,* May 19, 1856.

26. Crockett to wife, May 19, 1856, Joseph Bryant Crockett Papers.

27. *San Francisco Evening Bulletin,* May 20, 1856.

28. *San Francisco Evening Bulletin,* May 20, 1856.

29. Calhoun Benham and John McDouglas to J. Neely Johnson, May 28, 1856, John Neely Johnson Papers (Bancroft Library, University of California, Berkeley); Johnson to D. Scannell, June 2, 1856, ibid.; David Scannell to Johnson, June 2, 1856, ibid.; Johnson,

Proclamation, June 3, 1856, ibid.; Johnson to William T. Sherman, June 3, 1856, ibid.; Charles Lindley to Johnson, June 5, 1856, ibid.

30. *San Francisco Evening Citizen,* June 23, 1856; Bancroft, *Popular Tribunals,* 2:374–377.

31. William C. Kibbe to Johnson, July 5, 1856, and William C. Kibbe to Johnson, July 8, 1856, both in John Neely Johnson Papers.

32. *San Francisco Evening Bulletin,* June 26, 1856. Johnson may have had similar concerns about Terry. On June 10 Johnson had cautioned Terry to exercise caution, warning that "a conflict at this juncture . . . would be suicidal in the extreme." Johnson to Terry, June 10, 1856, John Neely Johnson Papers.

33. *San Francisco Evening Bulletin,* July 31, 1856.

34. *Missouri Republican,* September 19, 1856; Bancroft, *Popular Tribunals,* 2:466–486.

35. *New York Herald,* June 11, 1856; *New York Times,* June 13, July 15, 1856; *Judges and Criminals: Shadows of the Past, History of the Vigilance Committee of San Francisco, Cal.* (San Francisco: Privately printed, 1858), 9–37; Bancroft, *Popular Tribunals,* 1:201–406, 2:69–547; Herbert G. Florcken, "The Law and Order View of the San Francisco Vigilance Committee of 1856," *California Historical Society Quarterly* 14 (December 1935): 350–374; ibid., 15 (March 1936): 70–87; ibid., 15 (June 1936): 143–162; ibid., 15 (September 1936): 247–275.

36. William Tecumseh Sherman, *Memoirs of General William T. Sherman* (1875; reprint ed., New York: Library of America, 1990), 150.

37. *San Francisco Evening Bulletin,* November 6, 1856.

38. *San Francisco Herald* reprinted in *New York Times,* February 14, 1856.

39. Johnson to President Franklin Pierce, June 19, 1856, John Neely Johnson Papers.

40. *Vicksburg Weekly Whig,* May 14, 1851.

41. *San Francisco Evening Bulletin,* May 20, 1856.

42. *San Francisco Evening Bulletin,* January 23, May 19, 20, 1856; *Washington Southern Press,* April 12, 1851.

43. William Johnson to Neely Johnson, June 9, 1856, John Neely Johnson Papers.

44. *St. Louis Missouri Republican,* July 18. 1856.

45. Frank Soule, John H. Gihon, James Nisbet, *The Annals of San Francisco* (New York: D. Appleton & Co., 1855), 315.

46. William Johnson to Neely Johnson, June 9, 1856, John Neely Johnson Papers.

47. Crockett to wife, September 4, 1856, Joseph Bryant Crockett Papers.

48. *New York Times,* June 14, 1856.

49. William Johnson to Neely Johnson, June 9, 1856, John Neely Johnson Papers.

50. *New York Herald,* July 15, 1856.

51. *San Francisco Evening Bulletin,* May 18, 1856.

52. *St. Louis Missouri Republican,* July 18, 1856; *San Francisco Evening Bulletin,* June 3, 1856.

53. Soule, Gihon, and Nisbet, *Annals of San Francisco,* 351–352.

54. *St. Louis Missouri Republican,* November 20, 1857.

55. *Nashville Republican Banner and Whig,* April 18, March 1, 1851; *St. Louis Daily Missouri Republican,* April 7, 1851.

56. *Greensborough Patriot,* May 3, 1851, quoting the *Richmond Whig.*

57. *Wilmington Herald* quoted in *Greensborough Patriot,* August 9, 1851.

58. *Baltimore Sun* quoted in *Savannah (Georgia) Daily Morning News,* July 19, 1856.

59. *New York Times,* August 4, 1856; *St. Louis Missouri Republican,* August 20, 1856, October 22, 1856; *Washington (D.C.) Southern Press,* April 12, 1856; Edward McGowan, *Narrative of Edward McGowan* (San Francisco: privately published, 1857).

60. *Vicksburg Daily Whig,* September 19, 1856.

61. *Mobile Daily Register,* April 7, 1851, July 9, 1856.

62. *Savannah (Georgia) Daily Morning News,* July 19, 1856; *Alta California* reprinted in *Vicksburg Weekly Whig,* August 27, 1851; *Vicksburg Daily Whig,* July 31, 1856.

63. *San Francisco Evening Bulletin,* December 2, 1856.

64. *New York Herald,* July 6, 1856.

65. *Kansas City (Missouri) Enterprise,* July 26, 1856; *Charleston Courier,* August 11, 1851.

66. Secretary of State to Johnson, July 19, 1856, folder 56, John Neely Johnson Papers; William Blanding to C. Cushing, September 19, 1856, box 1, letters received, California Land Claims, Records of the Attorney General's Office, Department of Justice, RG 60 (National Archives, College Park, Maryland).

67. Secretary of State to Johnson, July 19, 1856, folder 56, John Neely Johnson Papers; Crockett to wife, September 4, 1856, Joseph Bryant Crockett Papers.

68. Sherman, *Memoirs of General William. T. Sherman,* 150; Florcken, "The Law and Order View," 71.

69. *New York Times,* June 2, 1855.

70. *New York Commercial Advertiser,* May 9, 1870.

71. *Washington (D.C.) National Era,* July 10, 1856.

72. *Milwaukee Daily Sentinel,* August 3, 1855.

73. *Milwaukee Daily Free Democrat,* August 10, 1855.

74. *Milwaukee Daily Free Democrat,* August 8, 1855.

75. Sherman to John T. Doyle, January 4, 1884, William T. Sherman Letters (North Baker Research Library, California Historical Society, San Francisco).

76. *Savannah (Georgia) Daily Morning News,* July 18, 1856.

77. *Atchison (Kansas) Squatter Sovereign,* March 13, 1855.

78. *St. Louis Missouri Republican,* August 22, 1856.

79. *St. Louis Missouri Republican,* October 2, 1856.

80. *Kansas City Enterprise,* August 23, 1856.

81. *Kansas City Enterprise,* August 2, 23, 1856.

82. *Atchison Squatter Sovereign,* July 1, 1856.

83. William Phillips, *The Conquest of Kansas by Missouri and Her Allies* (Boston: Phillips, Sampson, and Co., 1856), 38–39.

84. Boston *Liberator,* July 6, 1855; Phillips, *The Conquest of Kansas by Missouri and Her Allies,* 58, 61–62.

85. *Herald of Freedom,* September 29, 1855.

86. *Kansas Free State,* August 8, 1857.

87. *Washington (D.C.) National Era,* July 10, 1856; *Kansas Free State,* August 8, 1857.

88. *Atchison Kansas Freedom's Champion,* May 8, 1858.

89. Edgerton, 36th Cong., 1st sess., *Congressional Globe,* March 2, 1860 930; Gregory Aydt, "A Radical Cure: Thomas Dimsdale, Radical Republicanism, and the Montana Vigilantes During the Civil War" (M.A. thesis, Eastern Illinois University, 1999), 29–56.

90. Dimsdale's book went through over 20 editions, including a 1965 Italian version. Almost immediately, Dimsdale's account became the standard source for the lynchings. In 1868, the magazine *All the Year Round* summarized Dimsdale's book in four pages, praising the vigilantes for "maintaining right with the strong hands of honest men." "Vigilance of the Far West," *All the Year Round* (June 27, 1868): 61. In 1871, Mark Twain endorsed Dimsdale's account as "thrilling" and "bloodthirstily interesting" in a book entitled *Roughing It.* Other writers and journalists followed, retelling Dimsdale's story and presenting the vigilantes as honest men in a struggle against evil. In an 1890 book entitled *Vigilante Days and Ways,* Nathaniel Pitt Langford repackaged Dimsdale's arguments and again defended the extralegal hangings as necessary. Aydt, "A Radical Cure," 2–4; Thomas J. Dimsdale, *The Vigilantes of Montana* (Virginia City: Tilton, 1866); Nathaniel Pitt Langford, *Vigilantes Days and Ways* (Boston: Cupples, 1890). Most subsequent writers have merely reworked Dimsdale or Langford. J. W. Smurr, "Afterthoughts on the Vigilantes," *Montana* 9 (1958): 8.

91. The *Dictionary of American Biography* gives his occupation as "bandit." *Who Was Who in America* also lists him as "bandit" and repeats the vigilantes' implausible claim that his gang robbed or murdered 102 men in a few months. Defenders of Plummer recognize that he once went to prison for murder, but claim that by the time he became sheriff he was a changed man, softened by marriage. Hoffman Birney's nuanced 1929 book finds that Plummer's "every action" after his 1863 marriage "forces us to believe" that he had sincerely reformed. The "better element" in Bannack thought highly of Plummer. Nonetheless, even Birney ultimately does not dispute the vigilantes' judgment. He was the leader of a gang of robbers, Birney concluded. He "threw aside the garments of respectability that fitted him so poorly and definitely cast his lot with that of the Wild Bunch." And, for good measure, Birney alleges that Plummer was a "libertine." According to Birney, Plummer blubbered and groveled as he was about to be hanged. The morally dissolute, in nineteenth-century opinion, were unmanly and unable to control their fears any more than their appetites. Hoffman Birney, *Vigilantes* (Philadelphia: Penn Publishing, 1929), 97, 98, 124–125, 251.

   At least since 1958, historians have begun to question Dimsdale's work, a melodramatic author writing at a time when Westerners had begun to question the vigilantes and lynching in general. As J. W. Smurr recognized in 1958, Dimsdale's criticism of the miners as weak and easily persuaded amounted to an attack on the American jury system. Smurr, "Afterthoughts on the Vigilantes," 8–20. After Smurr's article, scholars began to scrutinize Dimsdale more critically. John H. Nesbitt, "Thomas J. Dimsdale," in Robert L. Gale, ed., *Nineteenth-Century American Western Writers* (Detroit: Gale, 1997), 87–92. And yet, Dimsdale's characterization of Plummer as unreformable, as evil incarnate, persists. *The New Encyclopedia of the American West,* published in 1998, still describes Plummer as using his sheriff's office as "the perfect cover for his other role" and as "a deep-dyed gold-camp desperado (an ex-convict and killer of four)." The lynchers' notion that truly evil people can never reform themselves is a powerful idea, one that resonates widely. Howard R. Lamar, ed., *The New Encyclopedia of the American West* (New Haven: Yale University Press, 1998), 893.

92. Dimsdale, *Vigilantes of Montana,* 25; Granville Stuart, "A Memoir of the Life of James Stuart," *Contributions,* I (1876), 56; James L. Thane, Jr., ed., *A Governor's Wife on the Mining Frontier: The Letters of Mary Edgerton from Montana, 1863–1865* (Salt Lake City: University of Utah Press, 1976), 52.

93. Dan Cushman, *Montana—Gold Frontier* (Great Falls: Stay Away Joe, 1973), 119.

94. Dimsdale, *Vigilantes of Montana,* 132.

95. R. E. Mather and F. E. Boswell, *Hanging the Sheriff: A Biography of Henry Plummer* (Salt Lake City: University of Utah Press, 1987), 35–36.

96. Jimmie Hicks, "The Frontier and American Law," *Great Plains Journal* 6 (Spring 1967): 60–61.

97. Eric Foner, *Reconstruction: America's Unfinished Revolution, 1863–1877* (New York: Harper and Row, 1988), 294–297.

98. Charles Stearns, *The Black Man of the South and the Rebels or the Characteristics of the Former, and the Recent Outrages of the Latter* (Boston: American News, 1872), 426.

CHAPTER FOUR

1. Allen W. Trelease, *White Terror: The Ku Klux Klan Conspiracy and Southern Reconstruction* (Baton Rouge: Louisiana State University Press, 1971), xxi, xliii, and passim; George C. Wright, *Racial Violence in Kentucky, 1865–1940: Lynchings, Mob Rule, and "Legal Lynchings"* (Baton Rouge: Louisiana State University Press, 1990), 19–60.

2. Historians date the start of the lynching era to some time in the 1880s. One historian writes that it began in 1889, claiming that as late as 1888 there was little hint of the coming wave. The best recent book on lynching concedes that Reconstruction violence "presaged" what came later, but differed significantly in that the Ku Klux Klan had a revolutionary intent while lynchers did not aim to overturn state governments. Joel Williamson, *The Crucible of Race: Black-White Relations in the American South Since Emancipation* (New York: Oxford University Press, 1984), 183–189; W. Fitzhugh Brundage, *Lynching in the New South: Georgia and Virginia, 1880–1930* (Urbana: University of Illinois Press, 1993), 6–7. For the revolutionary implications of Reconstruction, see also Eric Foner, *Reconstruction: America's Unfinished Revolution, 1863–1877* (New York: Harper and Row, 1988).

For the meaning of revolution, I draw theoretical inspiration from François Furet, *Interpreting the French Revolution,* trans. Elborg Forster (Cambridge: Cambridge University Press, 1981), 1–79; Keith Michael Baker, *Inventing the French Revolution* (Cambridge: Cambridge University Press, 1990), 1–58; William H. Sewell, Jr., *A Rhetoric of Bourgeois Revolution: The Abbe Sieyes and What Is the Third Estate?* (Durham: Duke University Press, 1994), 1–40; Linda Orr, *Headless History: Nineteenth-Century French Historiography of the Revolution* (Ithaca: Cornell University Press, 1990), 145–167.

3. For the persistence of Southern Antifederalist principles, see Donald Nieman, "Republicanism, the Confederate Constitution, and the American Constitutional Tradition," in Kermit L. Hall and James W. Ely, Jr., eds., *An Uncertain Tradition: Constitutionalism and the History of the South* (Athens: University of Georgia Press, 1989), 201–224. The classic account of Southern distinctiveness on this point remains Bertram Wyatt-Brown, *Southern Honor: Ethics and Behavior in the Old South* (New York: Oxford University Press, 1982); J. Mills Thornton, III, *Politics and Power in a Slave Society: Alabama, 1800–1860* (Baton Rouge: Louisiana State University Press, 1978), 3–162. For a nuanced account of Northerners' varied and conflicting notions of community, see Phillip Shaw Paludan, *"A People's Contest": The Union and Civil War, 1861–1865* (New York: Harper and Row, 1988), 3–102; Richard Franklin Bensel, *The Origins of Central State Authority in America, 1859–1871* (Cambridge: Cambridge University Press, 1990); John L. Brooke, *The Heart of the Commonwealth: Society and Political Culture in Worcester County, Massachusetts, 1713–1861* (Amherst: University of Massachusetts Press, 1989), 353–397.

4. Eric Foner has described Reconstruction-era Ku Klux Klan violence as a "wave of counterrevolutionary terror." Michael Fitzgerald has described the Klan as "a broad terrorist movement" dedicated to "systematic terror." Allen Trelease entitled his encyclopedic look at the Klan *White Terror.* Eric Foner, *Reconstruction,* 425, 427, 428–429, 431, 437; Michael W. Fitzgerald, "The Ku Klux Klan: Property Crime and the Plantation System in Reconstruction Alabama," *Agricultural History* 71 (Spring 1997): 186–206; Trelease, *White Terror.*

5. Frank Soule, John H. Gihon, James Nisbet, *The Annals of San Francisco* (New York: D. Appleton & Co., 1855), 318; John Phillip Reid, *Policing the Elephant: Crime, Punishment, and Social Behavior on the Overland Trail* (San Marino: Huntington Library, 1997), 139, 197.

6. *New York Times,* January 20, 1868; William C. Harris, *The Day of the Carpetbagger: Republican Reconstruction in Mississippi* (Baton Rouge: Louisiana State University Press, 1979), 172; Walter L. Fleming, *Civil War and Reconstruction in Alabama* (New York: Columbia University Press, 1905), 660–661; Alan Conway, *The Reconstruction of Georgia* (Minneapolis: University of Minnesota Press, 1966), 171; Richard Zuczek, *State of Rebellion: Reconstruction in South Carolina* (Columbia: University of South Carolina Press, 1996), 55–71.

7. Fitzgerald, "The Ku Klux Klan," 186–206; Harris, *Day of the Carpetbagger,* 173.

8. *Pulaski Citizen,* February 14, 1868.

9. Congress, House, *Joint Select Committee to Inquire into the Condition of Affairs in the Late Insurrectionary States,* 42nd Cong., 2nd sess., 6:280–281. Hereinafter cited as *KKK Report.*

10. *KKK Report,* 13:156–161, 230–233; *KKK Report,* 9:1037.

11. *KKK Report,* 5:1364, 1484, 1600–1603, 1691, 1924.

12. *KKK Report,* 9:1039; Trelease, *White Terror,* 363.

13. *KKK Report,* 9:1136–1139.

14. *KKK Report,* 9:742–743.

15. *KKK Report,* 6:50.

16. *Louisville Journal* quoted in *San Francisco Elevator,* October 6, 1865.

17. Nineteenth-century popular writers accused authority figures of "terrorism" when they acted in a dictatorial fashion. Judges, teachers, librarians, nurses, and even butlers were all capable of terror when they used their powers illegitimately. H. Graham, "Harrow School," *The Ladies' Repository* 4 (September 1869): 182; "Music and the Drama," *Appleton's Journal* 12 (October 24, 1874): 541; Will Williams, "Our London Letter," *Appleton's Journal* 13 (March 20, 1875): 330; A. F. Webster, "American Summer Resorts—Long Branch," *Appleton's Journal* 12 (October 3, 1874): 431; William Francis Dennehy, "Irish 'Outrages' in the Olden Time," *Catholic World* 35 (June 1882): 428. The *Presbyterian Quarterly and Princeton Review* urged preachers to avoid *terrorism* as "the mere appeal to fear." Thomas Nichols, "Preaching to the Conscience," *Presbyterian Quarterly and Princeton Review* (January 1875): 18.

    They more closely associated the term with illegitimate government power. James E. Worcester, *A Universal and Critical Dictionary of the English Language* (Boston: Wilkins, Carter, and Co., 1846), 732; *Oxford English Dictionary* (1897); *Zell's Popular Encyclopedia, a Universal Dictionary of English Language, Science, Literature, and Art* (Philadelphia: Zell, 1871), q.v. *terror*; Francis Leiber, ed., *Encyclopedia Americana* (Philadelphia: Thomas, Cowperthwait, & Co., 1840), q.v. *terror, reign of;* W. T. Brande, ed., *A Dictionary of Science, Literature, & Art* (London: Longman's Green and Co., 1865), q.v. *terror.*

18. *San Francisco Elevator,* October 23, 1868; J. William Snorgrass, "The Black Press in the San Francisco Bay Area, 1856–1900," *California History* 60 (Winter 1981–1982): 306–317.

19. Congress, House, *Papers in the Contested Case of Sheafe vs. Tillman in the Fourth Congressional District of Tennessee,* House Misc. Document 53, 41st Cong., 2nd sess., 214.

20. *KKK Report,* 10:1530–1532.

21. *KKK Report,* 7:1101.

22. September 11, 1868, November 21, 1868, David Schenck diary, Southern Historical Collection, University of North Carolina Library, Chapel Hill.

23. September 30, 1871, Schenck diary.

24. And Schenck's statements are confirmed by Michael Fitzgerald, "The Ku Klux Klan," 186–206.

25. Lou Falkner Williams, *The Great South Carolina Ku Klux Klan Trials, 1871–1872* (Athens: University of Georgia Press, 1996), 92–94, 114–115.

26. Otto H. Olsen, "The Ku Klux Klan: A Study in Reconstruction Politics and Propaganda," *North Carolina Historical Review* 39 (Summer 1962): 340–362.

27. Fred Lockley, *Vigilante Days at Virginia City* (Portland: privately printed, n.d.), 6.

28. *KKK Report,* 10:1567.

29. *KKK Report,* 2:3.

30. Albertus Hope testimony, *Proceedings in the Ku Klux Trials at Columbia, S.C., in the United States Circuit Court, November Term, 1871* (Columbia: Republican Printing Co., 1872), 169–173. (Hereinafter cited as *Ku Klux Trials.*)

31. Otto H. Olsen, *Carpetbagger's Crusade: The Life of Albion Winegar Tourgee* (Baltimore: Johns Hopkins University Press, 1965), 148.

32. Congress, House, *Papers in the Contested Case of Sheafe vs. Tillman in the Fourth Congressional District of Tennessee,* 241.

33. *KKK Report,* 2:3; Joel Williamson, *The Crucible of Race,* 11–119, argues that lynching resulted from "the particular conjunction of sex and race that seized the South in 1889" and that whites rarely commented on rape before that year.

34. *KKK Report,* 6:356–357.

35. *KKK Report,* 7:1208–1210.

36. *KKK Report,* 9:1271–1302; 10:1493, 1523–1524.

37. *KKK Report,* 12:1144. Martha Hodes has documented consensual sexual contacts between white women and black men. See *White Women, Black Men: Illicit Sex in the Nineteenth-Century South* (New Haven: Yale University Press, 1997).

38. *KKK Report,* 8:610.

39. *KKK Report,* 1:130–131.

40. Allen M. Gunn to Ulysses S. Grant, June 22, 1871, in John Y. Simon, ed., *Papers of Ulysses S. Grant* (Carbondale: Southern Illinois University Press, 1991), 22:15–16.

41. *KKK Reports,* 8:610; Jack Bass, *Taming the Storm: The Life and Times of Judge Frank M. Johnson, Jr., and the South's Fight Over Civil Rights* (New York: Doubleday, 1993), 7; Trelease, *White Terror,* 410.

42. *KKK Report,* 9:1082, 1100–1103; Kenneth C. Barnes, *Who Killed John Clayton? Political Violence and the Emergence of the New South, 1861–1893* (Durham: Duke University Press, 1998), 30; for the postbellum Whigs, see Dan T. Carter, *When the War Was Over: The Failure of Self-Reconstruction in the South, 1865–1867* (Baton Rouge: Louisiana State University Press, 1985), 66–68.

43. *KKK Report,* 6:67.

44. *KKK Report,* 2:3.

45. Charles W. Foster testimony, *Ku Klux Trials,* 200–213.

46. Osmond Gunthorpe testimony, *Ku Klux Trials,* 215–217.

47. Williams, *The Great South Carolina Ku Klux Klan Trials,* 19–39.

48. Senator Charles Sumner, *Congressional Globe,* 40th Cong., 1st sess., March 11, 1867: 50.

49. *Chicago Tribune,* November 2, 6, 10, 17, 23, 1876.

50. *Congressional Globe,* 41st Cong., 3rd sess., January 18, 1871: 570.

51. Manie White Johnson, "The Colfax Riot of April, 1873," *Louisiana Historical Quarterly* 13 (July 1930): 391–427; Joel M. Sipress, "The Triumph of Reaction: Political Struggle in a New South Community, 1865–1898" (Ph.D. diss., University of North Carolina, 1993), chapter 2; Indictment, December 5, 1876, *United States v. Harris,* case 1415, U.S. Circuit Court Papers, Memphis, RG 21 (National Archives, Atlanta Regional Archives Branch, East Point, Georgia).

52. Charles Fairman, *Reconstruction and Reunion, 1864–88, Part Two* (New York: Macmillan, 1987), 261–289; Robert J. Kaczorowski, *The Politics of Judicial Interpretation: The Federal Courts, the Department of Justice, and Civil Rights, 1866–1876* (New York: Oceana, 1985), 176–191.

53. Certificate of Division, February 5, 1878, *United States v. Harris,* case 8497, box 1187, U. S. Supreme Court Papers, RG 267, (National Archives, Washington, D.C.); *United States v. Harris,* 106 US 629 (1883); *Memphis Daily Appeal,* January 23, 1883; *New York Times,* January 23, 1883.

54. *KKK Report,* 8:57.

55. Albion W. Tourgée, *A Fool's Errand,* John Hope Franklin, ed. (Cambridge: Belknap Press, 1961), 281.

56. Tourgée, *Fool's Errand,* 281–282.

57. Tourgée, *Fool's Errand,* 230.

58. Tourgée, *Fool's Errand,* 298–299.

59. Tourgée, *Fool's Errand,* 296.

60. *KKK Report,* 9:767.

61. *KKK Report,* 9:702–704.

62. *San Francisco Elevator,* October 23, 1868, September 5, 1874.

63. *San Francisco Elevator,* October 10, 17, 24, 31, November 7, 14, 21, 1874.

64. Philip Hone, *The Diary of Philip Hone, 1828–1851,* ed. Allan Nevins (1927; reprint ed., New York: Kraus, 1969), 167–168; *Boston Liberator,* July 9, 1836, January 6, 1860; *Alton Observer,* December 28, 1837.

65. *Boston Liberator,* December 3, 1831.

66. *Boston Liberator,* January 28, 1842.

67. "We Are Not Yet Quite Free," address delivered at Medina, New York, August 3, 1869, Frederick Douglass, *The Frederick Douglass Papers,* ed. John W. Blassingame (New Haven: Yale University Press, 1991), 4:237–239. White Republicans did not always break the South into precisely the same categories as Douglass or express the same optimism as Lynch, but they agreed with the principal point. The U. S. Attorney for the northern district of Mississippi divided native-born whites into two classes. The larger class harbored bitter feelings toward Northerners, but this Mississippi Republican thought that the more respectable element desired harmony and treated Northerners with respect and kindness. *KKK Report,* 12:1148; Williamson disparages this as the "grit thesis," *Crucible of Race,* 292–295.

68. John Roy Lynch, *Reminiscences of an Active Life: the Autobiography of John Roy Lynch,* ed. John Hope Franklin (Chicago: University of Chicago Press, 1970), 139–144.

69. Allen M. Gunn to Ulysses S. Grant, June 22, 1871, in Simon, ed., *Papers of Ulysses S. Grant,* 22:16.

70. Governor Tod R. Caldwell to Ulysses S. Grant, April 20, 1871, in Simon, ed., *Papers of Ulysses S. Grant,* 22:362; Governor Robert K. Scott to Ulysses S. Grant, January 17, 1871, ibid., 21:259; Governor W. W. Holden to Ulysses S. Grant, March 10, 1870, ibid., 20:211.

71. Judge J. L. Henry to Ulysses S. Grant, April 27, 1871, in Grant, *Papers of Ulysses S. Grant,* ed. Simon, 22:364.

72. M. A. Smith to Ulysses S. Grant, January 16, 1871, in Grant, *Papers of Ulysses S. Grant,* ed. Simon, 21:410–411.

73. *New York Tribune,* January 23, February 23, March 10, 20, April 7, 1871.

74. *Supplemental Report of Joint Committee of the General Assembly of Louisiana on the Conduct of the Late Elections and the Condition of Peace and Good Order in the State* (New Orleans: A. L. Lee, 1869), iv–xl.

75. M. A. Smith to Ulysses S. Grant, January 16, 1871, in Grant, *Papers of Ulysses S. Grant,* ed. Simon, 21:411.

76. Tourgee, *Fool's Errand,* 246.

77. James A. Garfield, remarks on Southern outrages, *Congressional Globe,* 42nd Cong., 1st sess., March 16, 1871, 130; John Coburn, remarks on Southern outrages, *Congressional Globe,* 42nd Cong., 1st sess., March 16, 1871, 130–131; *Report of the Joint Select Committee to Inquire into the Condition of Affairs in the Late Insurrectionary States,* 42nd Cong., 2rd sess., 1:1–2.

78. Willard Warner, *Congressional Globe,* 41st Cong., 3rd sess., January 18, 1871: 570–572.

79. Stanley F. Horn, *Invisible Empire: The Story of the Ku Klux Klan* (1939; reprint ed., New York: Haskell, 1973), 183.

80. *KKK Report,* 10:1798–1799.

81. See, for example, James W. Garner, *Reconstruction in Mississippi* (1901; reprint ed., Baton Rouge: Louisiana State University, 1968), 345–353.

82. Horn, *Invisible Empire,* 17, 176, 183, 217, 232, 236.

83. Foner, *Reconstruction,* 412–421; Christopher Waldrep, *Roots of Disorder: Race and Criminal Justice in the American South, 1817–1880* (Urbana: University of Illinois Press, 1998); Gene

L. Howard, *Death at Cross Plains: An Alabama Reconstruction Tragedy* (University: University of Alabama Press, 1984), 61–74.

84. Michael Perman, *The Road to Redemption: Southern Politics, 1869–1879* (Chapel Hill: University of North Carolina Press, 1984), 147–177.

85. Cal M. Logue, "Rhetorical Ridicule of Reconstruction Blacks," *Quarterly Journal of Speech* 62 (December 1976): 400–409; Daniel W. Stowell, "Why Redemption? Religion and the End of Reconstruction, 1869–1877," paper presented at the Southern Historical Association, November 14, 1998; Tourgee, *Fool's Errand,* 177. Historians have examined Southern orators. See Waldo W. Braden, ed., *Oratory in the New South* (Baton Rouge: Louisiana State University Press, 1979); idem, "The Emergence of the Concept of Southern Oratory," *Southern Speech Journal* 26 (Spring 1961): 173–183. Cal M. Logue, "The Rhetorical Appeals of Whites to Blacks During Reconstruction," *Communications Monographs* 44 (August 1977): 242–243.

CHAPTER FIVE

1. Ida B. Wells, *Crusade for Justice: The Autobiography of Ida B. Wells,* ed. Alfreda M. Duster, (Chicago: University of Chicago Press, 1970), 64.

2. *New York Times,* August 27, 1874.

3. This is based on an examination of every article indexed under "lynching" in the *New York Times Index.* An "incident" is a lynching affair reported in the *New York Times,* including false reports. That is, it should be emphasized, an examination of news coverage, not a study of lynching as behavior. A count of incidents is not a body count. The report, for example, of 16 Negroes lynched in Tennessee in a single episode of mob law counts as one "incident." (*New York Times,* August 27, 28, September 2, 1874). By this measure, there were 170 incidents in the 1870s, 149 in the 1880s, and 170 in the 1890s.

4. *New York Times,* May 18, 1871; *San Francisco Chronicle,* May 18, 1871.

5. *New York Times,* December 4, 1878.

6. See, for example, Leon Litwack, *Trouble in Mind: Black Southerners in the Age of Jim Crow* (New York: Knopf, 1998), 285; William Blackstone, *Commentaries on the Laws of England* (1765–1769; reprint ed., Chicago: University of Chicago Press, 1979), 1:74–79.

7. *New York Times,* August 17, 1874; *San Francisco Chronicle,* May 18, 1871.

8. *New York Times,* April 30, 1882.

9. *New York Times,* July 28, 1880, June 27, 1883.

10. *New York Times,* December 12, 1880.

11. *New York Times,* July 22, 1877.

12. Later, Ida B. Wells investigated some instances of reported child rapes and found the actual age of the victims to be much older. See Wells, *A Red Record: Lynchings in the United States, 1892–1893–1894* (Chicago, 1895), reprinted in Jacqueline Jones Royster, ed., *Southern Horrors and Other Writings: The Anti-Lynching Campaign of Ida B. Wells, 1892–1900* (Boston: Bedford, 1997), 73–106.

13. *New York Times,* January 21, 1881.

14. Thomas J. Kernan, "The Jurisprudence of Lawlessness," a paper read before the American Bar Association, at St. Paul, August 30, 1906; Robert M. Ireland, "Insanity and the Unwritten Law," *American Journal of Legal History* 32 (1988): 157–172; idem, "Frenzied and Fallen Females: Women and Sexual Dishonor in the Nineteenth-Century United States," *Journal of Women's History* 3 (Winter 1992): 95–117; Newman Levy, "The Unwritten Law," *American Mercury* 35 (August 1935): 398–403.

15. Ireland, "Frenzied and Fallen Females," 95–117.

16. *San Francisco Chronicle,* March 17, 18, 1873.

17. *San Francisco Chronicle,* March 18, 1873; *New York Times,* March 26, 1873.

18. *New York Commercial Advertiser,* April 30, 1870; *New York Times,* June 13, 1882, July 28, 1882.

19. *San Francisco Elevator,* April 19, 1873; Linda O. McMurry, *To Keep the Waters Troubled: The Life of Ida B. Wells* (New York: Oxford University Press, 1998), 143.

20. *New York Times,* June 13, July 28, 1882.

21. *New York Times,* May 12, 1874.

22. *Memphis Daily Appeal,* February 6, 1886.

23. *New York Times,* February 18, 1880, July 14, 1881.

24. *New York Times,* July 28, September 16, 1880, March 25, 1878.

25. *New York Times,* February 1, 1870.

26. *New York Times,* July 28, 1880.

27. *Milwaukee Daily Sentinel,* August 10, 1855.

28. *Memphis Appeal,* August 14, 17, 1886.

29. *New York Times,* October 5, 1878.

30. *New York Times,* February 14, 1886.

31. *Memphis Daily Appeal,* March 18, 1886.

32. *New York Times,* June 9, 1871.

33. *New York Times,* July 28, 1880.

34. *New York Times,* October 18, 1875.

35. *New York Times,* July 28, 1880.

36. *New York Times,* January 18, 1878.

37. *New York Times,* September 26, 1875.

38. *Atlanta Herald,* quoted in *New York Times,* August 26, 1874.

39. Hubert Howe Bancroft, *Popular Tribunals* (San Francisco: History Co., 1887), 1:8–17.

40. *New York Times,* March 10, 1872.

41. *New York Times,* February 6, 1876.

42. *New York Times,* October 12, 13, 1882.

43. *Harpers Weekly* 32 (December 22, 1888): 988; Goldsmith B. West, *The Hawes Horror and Bloody Riot at Birmingham: A Truthful Story of What Happened* (Birmingham: Caldwell Printing Co., 1888); Jeff Northrup, "The Hawes Riot: All the News Unfit to Print," *Journal of the Birmingham Historical Society* 5 (January 1977): 16–25; idem., "The Hawes Affair: Part II," *Journal of the Birmingham Historical Society* 6 (January 1979): 15–23.

44. *New York Times,* December 28, 1880.

45. *New York Times,* September 28, 1883.

46. *New York Times,* July 9, 10, 1872; Francis A. Walker, comp., *A Compendium of the Ninth Census* (Washington: Government Printing Office, 1872), 298. The persons lynched were entirely innocent. See *New York Times,* March 26, 30, 1874.

47. *Memphis Daily Appeal,* March 7, 1886.

48. *New York Times,* March 7, 8, 9, 12, 16, 24, April 2, 20, 21, 1886.

49. Once again, this calculation is based on reported lynching incidents, not the actual number of persons lynched. In the 1870s, there were twenty-six episodes where the article published in the *New York Times* said or implied unanimous community support; there were twenty-three episodes in the 1880s.

50. *Memphis Daily Appeal,* January 17, 1886.

51. Bancroft, *Popular Tribunals,* 1:8, 14.

52. *New York Times,* August 26, 1874.

53. *New York Times,* December 12, 1880.

54. *Daily Memphis Avalanche,* January 9, 1886.

55. *Daily Memphis Avalanche,* March 19, 1886.

56. *Memphis Daily Appeal,* February 16, 1886.

57. *Memphis Daily Appeal,* August 19, 1886.

58. *Memphis Daily Appeal,* July 8, 1886.

59. *Memphis Daily Appeal,* January 31, 1886.

60. *Memphis Daily Appeal,* February 4, 1886.

61. *New Orleans Louisianian,* September 5, 1974.

62. *New Orleans Louisianian,* September 11, 1875.

63. *New Orleans Louisianian,* October 31, 1874.

64. *Washington (D.C.) People's Advocate,* April 10, 1880.

65. *Washington (D.C.) People's Advocate,* August 21, 1880; *Harrisburg (Pennsylvania) State Journal,* January 5, February 23, 1884.

66. *Washington (D.C.) People's Advocate,* March 19, April 21, 1881.

67. *New York Globe,* January 27, 1883.

68. *New York Globe,* January 27, 1883.

69. *New York Globe,* March 17, November 10, 1883.

70. Ida B. Wells, *The Memphis Diary: An Intimate Portrait of the Activist as a Young Woman,* ed. Miriam Decosta-Willis (Boston: Beacon Press, 1995), 52; Emma Lou Thornbrough, *T. Thomas Fortune: Militant Journalist* (Chicago: University of Chicago Press, 1972), 105–135.

71. *New York Globe,* January 19, 1884.

72. *Topeka Colored Citizen,* November 9, 1879.

73. *Topeka Colored Citizen,* August 30, 1879.

74. *Topeka Colored Citizen,* August 30, 1879.

75. *New York Globe,* February 9, 1884.

76. *New York Freeman,* July 11, 1885.

77. *New York Freeman,* April 25, 1885.

78. *New York Freeman,* May 30, 1885.

79. *New York Globe,* February 9, 1884.

80. See Glenda Gilmore, *Gender and Jim Crow: Women and the Politics of White Supremacy in North Carolina, 1896–1920* (Chapel Hill: University of North Carolina Press, 1996), 147–176; Evelyn Brooks Higginbotham, *Righteous Discontent: The Women's Movement in the Black Baptist Church, 1880–1920* (Cambridge: Harvard University Press, 1993).

81. *New York Times,* September 4, 1894.

82. James D. Corrothers, *In Spite of the Handicap* (New York: George H. Doran, 1916), 120–121.

83. William Pickens, *The Heir of Slaves* (Boston: Pilgrim, 1911), 138.

84. Elijah P. Marrs, *Life and History of the Rev. Elijah P. Marrs* (Louisville: Bradley and Gilbert, 1885), 77–78.

85. Frances Joseph Gaudet, *"He Leadeth Me"* (1913; reprint ed., New York: G. K. Hall, 1996), 52.

86. Corrothers, *In Spite of the Handicap,* 120–121.

87. *New York Globe,* January 5, 1884.

88. *New York Freeman,* June 27, 1885.

CHAPTER SIX

1. Ida B. Wells, *The Memphis Diary of Ida B. Wells,* ed. Miriam DeCosta-Willis (Boston: Beacon, 1995), 54.

2. *Memphis Daily Appeal,* March 18, 1886; *Daily Memphis Avalanche,* March 18, 1886. The other large Memphis daily published at this time, the *Memphis Scimitar,* is apparently no longer extant.

3. Wells, *Memphis Diary,* ed. DeCosta-Willis, 55.

4. Wells, *Memphis Diary,* ed. DeCosta-Willis, 55.

5. *Memphis Daily Appeal,* March 19, 1886; *Memphis Avalanche,* March 19, 1886.

6. *Memphis Daily Appeal,* March 26, 1886.

7. Richard B. McCaslin, *Tainted Breeze: The Great Hanging at Gainesville, Texas, 1862* (Baton Rouge: Louisiana State University Press, 1994), 82–83.

8. *Memphis Daily Appeal,* March 27, 1886.

9. *Daily Memphis Avalanche,* March 23, 1886.

10. *Daily Memphis Avalanche,* March 19, 1886. Though published before the paper printed Vardaman's account, the language in this editorial makes it clear that the editors were already relying on Vardaman's text.

11. *Memphis Daily Appeal,* April 7, 1886.

12. *New York Freeman,* March 27, 1886.

13. *New York Freeman,* April 10, 1886.

14. See, for example, *New York Times,* August 27, 1874, September 25, 1877, June 8, October 12, 1878, January 12, 1880, February 20, March 12, August 24, 1881, December 31, 1883.

15. Wells, *Memphis Diary* ed. DeCosta-Willis, 102.

16. *Memphis Daily Appeal,* August 19, 1886.

17. Ida B. Wells, *Crusade for Justice: The Autobiography of Ida B. Wells,* ed. Alfreda M. Duster (Chicago: University of Chicago Press, 1970), 47–51; Patricia A. Schechter, *Ida B. Wells-Barnett and American Reform, 1880–1930* (Chapel Hill: University of North Carolina Press), 75–77.

18. *New York Times,* March 10, 11, 1892.

19. *New York Times,* March 11, 1892.

20. Wells, *Crusade for Justice,* ed. Duster, 47–52.

21. *New York Times,* August 7, 1875.

22. *Birmingham Iron Age,* November 28, December 6, 20, 1883.

23. *New York Times,* June 14, 1891.

24. *New York Times,* August 30, 1891.

25. *New York Times,* October 19, 1891, February 21, 22, 1892.

26. In 1892 California newspapers reported the lynching of Francisco Torres, claiming that inadequate courts along with Torres's "brutal and savage" crime drove the people to violence. One paper even praised the killing as the "neatest and best executed job in the way of lynching ever performed in California." Jean F. Riss, "The Lynching of Francisco Torres," *Journal of Mexican American History* 2 (Spring 1972): 90–121. Texans lynched a Mexican citizen, Florentino Suaste, in 1895. Congress, Senate, *Lynching of Florentino Suaste,* Senate report 1832, 56th Cong., 2nd sess. Another Mexican perished at the hands of lynchers at Yreka, California, the same year. Congress, House of Representatives, *Indemnity to Relatives of Luis Moreno: Message from the President of the United States, Transmitting a Report from the Secretary of State with Accompanying Papers, Touching the Lynching in 1895, at Yreka, Cal., of Luis Moreno, a Mexican Citizen, and the Demand of the Mexican Government for Indemnity,* House Report 237, 55th Cong., 2nd sess.; William Dean Carrigan, "Between South and West: Race, Violence, and Power in Central Texas, 1836–1916" (Ph.D. diss., Emory University, 1999), 201–246.

27. Richard Gambino, *Vendetta: A True Story of the Worst Lynching in America, the Mass Murder of Italian-Americans in New Orleans in 1891, the Vicious Motivations Behind It and the Tragic Repercussions that Linger to this Day* (Garden City: Doubleday, 1977), 1–99; David A. Smith, "From the Mississippi to the Mediterranean: The 1891 New Orleans Lynching and Its Effects on United States Diplomacy and the American Navy," *Southern Historian* 19 (1998): 60–85; in 1896, residents of Hahnville, Louisiana, killed three Italian citizens, Salvatore Arena, Giuseppe Venturella, and Lorenzo Salardino. Congress, Senate, *Correspondence Regarding the Lynching of Certain Italian Subjects, Message from the President of the United States, transmitting, in Response to Resolution of the Senate of May 6, 1897, Calling for the Correspondence Regarding the Lynching in Louisiana of Certain Italian Subjects, A Report from the Secretary of State, with*

Accompanying Papers, Senate document 104, 55th Cong., 1st sess.; Congress, House of Representatives, *Heirs of Certain Citizens of Italy: Message from the President of the United States, Transmitting A Communication from the Secretary of State Relating to the Outrages Committed by Citizens of the United States Upon Citizens of Italy, and Recommending an Appropriation by Congress for the Relief of the Heirs of the Sufferers,* House document 37, 55th Cong., 1st sess.; Henry Cabot Lodge, "Lynch Law and Unrestricted Immigration," *North American Review* 152 (1890): 602–612.

28. Wells, *Crusade for Justice,* ed. Duster, 66.

29. Linda O. McMurry, *To Keep the Waters Troubled: The Life of Ida B. Wells* (New York: Oxford University Press, 1998), 146.

30. Ida B. Wells, *Southern Horrors: Lynch Law in all its Phases,* in Jacqueline Jones Royster, *Southern Horrors and other Writings: The Anti-Lynching Campaign of Ida B. Wells, 1892–1900* (Boston: Bedford, 1997), 49–72.

31. *New York Times,* February 2, 1893.

32. *New York Times,* February 5, 1893.

33. *New York Times,* April 29, 1894.

34. *New York Times,* April 30, September 4, 1894.

35. *New York Times,* May 13, 1894.

36. *New York Times,* October 15, 1894.

37. *New York Times,* October 7, 1894.

38. Alfred M. Waddell, "The Story of the Wilmington, N.C. Race Riots," *Collier's Weekly* 22 (November 26, 1898): 4–16; Edward L. Ayers, *The Promise of the New South: Life After Reconstruction* (New York: Oxford University Press, 1992), 55–80; Michael Perman, *Struggle for Mastery: Disfranchisement in the South, 1888–1908* (Chapel Hill: University of North Carolina Press, 2001), 268–269.

39. Ayers, *The Promise of the New South,* 67–68, 141–146; Leon F. Litwack, *Trouble in Mind: Black Southerners in the Age of Jim Crow* (New York: Knopf, 1998), 229–240.

40. Grace Elizabeth Hale, *Making Whiteness: The Culture of Segregation in the South, 1890–1940* (New York: Pantheon, 1998), 205–207. For 1870s lynchings with crowds estimated at a thousand or more, see *New York Times,* August 23, 1874, July 9, 1876, November 28, 1877, October 12, 13, 1878, July 9, 1879. For the Smith lynching, see *New York Times,* February 2, 3, 8, 1893.

41. *New York Times,* July 26, 1870.

42. Xi Wang, *The Trial of Democracy: Black Suffrage and Northern Republicans, 1860–1910* (Athens: University of Georgia Press, 1997), 220–252.

43. Lloyd Wendt, *Chicago Tribune: The Rise of a Great American Newspaper* (Chicago: Rand McNally, 1979), 247–281; David Paul Nord, "The Public Community: The Urbanization of Journalism in Chicago," *Journal of Urban History* 11 (August 1985): 411–441; idem, "The Paradox of Municipal Reform in the Late Nineteenth Century," *Wisconsin Magazine of History* 66 (Winter 1982–1983): 128–142 (quotation: 128).

44. *Chicago Tribune,* January 1, 1875, January 1, 1883, January 1, 1884.

45. *Chicago Tribune,* January 1, 1883.

46. *Chicago Tribune,* December 30, 1883, December 31, 1884.

47. *Chicago Tribune,* January 1, 1886, January 1, 1887, January 1, 1888.

48. *Chicago Tribune,* January 1, 1888, January 1, 1890.

49. Stewart E. Tolnay and E. M. Beck, *A Festival of Violence: An Analysis of Southern Lynchings, 1882–1930* (Urbana: Unversity of Illinois Press, 1995), 266–267.

50. *Chicago Tribune,* January 1, 1895.

51. Ida B. Wells, *A Red Record: Tabulated Statistics and Alleged Causes of Lynchings in the United States, 1892–1893–1894,* reprinted in Royster, ed., *Southern Horrors and Other Writings,* 73–157.

52. *New York Times,* March 17, 1871, September 26, October 18, 1875.

53. *New York Times,* December 25, 1880.

54. *New York Times,* April 4, 1874.

55. *New York Times,* February 24, 1884.

56. *Charleston News and Courier,* March 5, 1880.

57. *Charleston News and Courier,* March 2, 1880.

58. See, for example, *Raleigh News and Observer,* July 6, 7, 1897.

59. *Raleigh News and Observer,* July 11, 1897.

60. *Atlanta Constitution,* February 21, 1916.

61. George W. Chamlee, "Is Lynching Ever Defensible? The Motives of Judge Lynch," *Forum,* 76 (December 1926): 811–817.

62. Ann Field Alexander, "'Like an Evil Wind': The Roanoke Riot of 1893 and the Lynching of Thomas Smith," *Virginia Magazine of History and Biography* 100 (1992): 173–206.

63. *Annual Report of the Adjutant General to the Governor of the State of Ohio for the Fiscal Year ending November 15, 1894* (Columbus: Westbote Co., 1895), 18–20, 292–295; *New York Times,* October 18, 19, November 15, 23, 24, December 5, 1894.

64. *New York Times,* February 2, 1896; Jeff Phillips, "A Riots [*sic*] Events and Effects," (Washington Senior High School history paper, not dated).

65. *New York Times,* June 5, 6, 1897.

66. Abial Lathrop to Attorney General, March 5, 1898, box 1047A, year files (folded), Department of Justice Central Files, RG 60 (National Archives, College Park, MD); Lathrop to L. D. Melton, U.S. Marshal, March 30, 1899, ibid; John W. Bulla and H. T. B. Moye to Abial Lathrop, April 16, 1898, ibid.

67. Lathrop to Attorney General, April 24, 1899, box 1047A, year files (folded), Department of Justice Central Files, RG 60; Lathrop to Attorney General, January 10, 1899, ibid; B. W. Bell to Frank Strong, April 8, 1899, ibid.

68. Indictment, April 7, 1899, *United States v. Martin V. Ward,* et al., District Court of South Carolina in the United States Circuit Court (National Archives, East Point Georgia); *New York Times,* April 8, 13, 1899; Xi Wang, *The Trial of Democracy,* 253–266.

69. Roger K. Hux, "Lillian Clayton Jewett and the Rescue of the Baker Family, 1899–1900," *Historical Journal of Massachusetts* 19 (Winter 1991): 12–23.

70. Ida B. Wells, *Lynch Law in Georgia* (Chicago, 1899); Donald L. Grant, *The Way it Was in the South: The Black Experience in Georgia* (New York: Carol, 1993), 163.

71. *Atlanta Constitution,* April 14, 30, 1899.

72. *Atlanta Constitution,* April 14, 1899.

73. *Atlanta Constitution,* April 15, 1899.

74. *Atlanta Constitution,* April 18, 1899.

75. *Atlanta Constitution,* April 19, 1899.

76. *Atlanta Constitution,* April 24, 1899.

77. *Atlanta Constitution,* April 25, 1899.

78. *Atlanta Constitution,* April 25, 1899.

79. *Atlanta Constitution,* April 23, 1899.

80. Ben Tillman, January 12, 1907, United States Senate, *Congressional Record,* 59th Cong., 2nd sess., 1441.

81. See the *New York Times* coverage of the so-called corkscrew lynching in Doddsville, Mississippi. February 8, 1904.

82. Bryant Simon, *A Fabric of Defeat: The Politics of South Carolina Millhands, 1910–1948* (Chapel Hill: University of North Carolina Press, 1998), 32.

83. Simon, *Fabric of Defeat,* 33.

84. Roscoe L. Buckland, "Contrasting Views of Lynching in Two Wister Stories," *Wyoming Annals* 65 (Winter 1993–1994): 36–46.

85. For the Johnson County War, see John D. McDermott, "Writers in Judgment: Historiography of the Johnson County War," *Wyoming Annals* (Winter 1993–1994): 20–35; A. S. Mercer, *The Banditti of the Plains or the Cattlemen's Invasion of Wyoming in 1892* (1894;

reprint ed., Norman: University of Oklahoma Press, 1954); Helena Huntington Smith, *The War on Powder River* (Lincoln: University of Nebraska Press, 1966).

86. Owen Ulph, "The Virginian: Misbegotten Folk Hero," *Halcyon* (1983): 131–155.

87. William Archibald Dunning, *Reconstruction: Political and Economic, 1865–1877* (New York: Harper, 1907), 119.

88. *New Orleans Times-Picayune*, July 28, 1900; *New York Times*, July 25, 27, 28, 1900; *Chicago Tribune*, July 25, 26, 27, 28, 1900; Ida B. Wells-Barnett, *Mob Rule in New Orleans: Robert Charles and his Fight to the Death*, in Royster, ed., *Southern Horrors and Other Writings*, 158–208.

89. *New York Times*, September 4, 1894.

90. *Chicago Inter-Ocean*, July 25, 1893.

91. *Wichita National Baptist World*, October 5, 1894.

92. *The People's Friend*, June 22, 1894; *American Citizen*, July 13, 1894.

93. *Chicago Inter-Ocean*, reprinted in *Kansas City American Citizen*, March 29, 1895.

94. *Kansas City American Citizen*, August 24, 1894.

95. *National Baptist World*, September 28, 1894.

96. *Wichita National Baptist World*, September 28; August 31, 1894.

97. *Wichita National Baptist World*, October 5, 1894.

98. *New York Times*, August 27, 1897.

99. *New York Times*, September 3, 1897.

100. *New York Times*, March 17, 1897.

101. *New York Times*, May 4, 1899.

102. *New York Times*, June 22, 1899.

103. Stephen Kantrowitz, *Ben Tillman and the Reconstruction of White Supremacy* (Chapel Hill: University of North Carolina Press, 2000), 306–309; Gail Bederman, *Manliness and Civilization: A Cultural History of Gender and Race in the United States, 1880–1917* (Chicago: University of Chicago Press, 1995), 45–76.

104. A. A. Madden testimony, bill of exceptions, filed March 6, 1911, case number 251, *Annie M. Rogers et al., v. V. S.& P. R. R. Co.*, Circuit Court of the United States for the Western Division of the Southern District of Mississippi (National Archives, Southeast Region, East Point, Georgia); M. M. Bellah, testimony, ibid.; Ruben McCall testimony, ibid.; F. L. Bozeman testimony, ibid.; Deposition of Thomas F. Wright taken before Reginald H. Carter, esq., United States Commissioner, December 20, 1913, case number 295, *Annie May Rogers, et al., v. Vicksburg, Shreveport, and Pacific Railroad Co.*, United States District Court for the Western Division of the Southern District of Mississippi (National Archives, Southeast Region, East Point, Georgia); *State v. Rogers*, et al. 115 Louisiana 164 (1905); *Vicksburg Evening Post*, May 29, 1906.

105. *Vicksburg Evening Post*, April 5, 16, 1918; *San Francisco Chronicle*, June 26, 1934; *San Francisco Western Worker*, June 24, 27, July 1, August 5, 8, 1935; *The Bloodstained Trail* (Seattle: the Industrial Worker, 1927), 152–161; Christopher Capozzola, "The Only Badge Needed is Your Patriotic Fervor: Vigilance, Coercion, and the Law in World War I America," *Journal of American History* 88 (March 2002): 1354–1382.

106. "Lynch Law and Treason," *Literary Digest* 55 (August 18, 1917): 12–13.

107. Transcript of Darrow speech, Annual Conference Proceedings, 1910, Annual Conference, Part 1, reel 8, Papers of the NAACP.

CHAPTER SEVEN

1. Mary Louise Ellis, "'Rain Down Fire': The Lynching of Sam Hose" (Florida State University, Ph.D. diss., 1992), 24, 27–28.

2. W. Fitzhugh Brundage, *Lynching in the New South: Georgia and Virginia, 1880–1930* (Urbana: University of Illinois Press, 1993), 199.

3. *Washington (Georgia) News-Reporter,* July 2, 1920, reel 2, series A, Anti-Lynching Investigative Files, part 7, Anti-Lynching Campaign, Papers of the NAACP (microfilm, University Publications of America, Library of Congress). Hereinafter cited as NAACP Papers.

4. David F. Godshalk, "William J. Northern's Public and Personal Struggles against Lynching," in Jane Dailey, Glenda Elizabeth Gilmore, and Bryant Simon, eds., *Jumpin' Jim Crow: Southern Politics from Civil War to Civil Rights* (Princeton: Princeton University Press, 2000), 140–161.

5. *Vicksburg Evening Post,* May 4, 1983.

6. *Vicksburg Evening Post,* January 26, 1903.

7. *Vicksburg Evening Post,* November 10, 1902.

8. *Vicksburg Evening Post,* May 5, 1903, quoting the *Meridian Star.*

9. *Vicksburg Evening Post,* November 1, 1902.

10. *Greenwood Commonwealth,* February 27, 1904.

11. *Vicksburg Evening Post,* November 1, 1902.

12. *Nashville Banner,* March 4, 1904.

13. *Vicksburg Evening Post,* July 4, 1903.

14. *Vicksburg Evening Post,* October 29, 1902.

15. *Vicksburg Evening Post,* September 16, 1902.

16. *Vicksburg Evening Post,* September 30, 1902.

17. Josephus Daniels, *Editor in Politics* (Chapel Hill: University of North Carolina Press, 1941), 389, 401.

18. *Raleigh News and Observer,* June 19, 1902, August 29, 1905, August 11, 1902.

19. *Raleigh News and Observer,* March 4, 1905.

20. *Raleigh News and Observer,* July 12, February 3, 1905, December 5, 1902.

21. *Raleigh News and Observer,* August 26, 1902.

22. *Raleigh News and Observer,* August 26, 1902.

23. The *News and Observer* adamantly opposed black voting, November 16, 1904; expressed outrage (in an editorial entitled "Nigger in the Woodpile") when a political candidate hired a black printer to prepare his handbills, August 15, 1902; and published an article by Thomas Dixon, Jr., opposing Booker T. Washington's educational scheme as not servile enough, August 26, 1905.

24. Glenda Elizabeth Gilmore, *Gender and Jim Crow: Women and the Politics of White Supremacy in North Carolina, 1896–1920* (Chapel Hill: University of North Carolina Press, 1996), 91; *Raleigh News and Observer,* July 31, 1897.

25. *Raleigh News and Observer,* August 5, 1897; Gilmore, *Gender and Jim Crow,* 83–89.

26. Nell Irvin Painter, "'Social Equality,' Miscegenation, Labor, and Power," in Numan V. Bartley, ed., *The Evolution of Southern Culture* (Athens: University of Georgia Press, 1988), 47–67.

27. "W. E. B. Du Bois' Confrontation with White Liberalism During the Progressive Era: A *Phylon* Document," *Phylon* 35 (September 1974): 246.

28. Booker T. Washington to Monroe Nathan Work, November 19, 1910, in Booker T. Washington, *The Booker T. Washington Papers* eds. Louis R. Harlan and Raymond W. Smock (Urbana: University of Illinois Press, 1981), 10:452; Work to Washington, January 3, 1911, ibid., 525.

29. J. E. Boyd to Woodrow Wilson, November 19, 1920, file 158260, RG 60, Department of Justice numerical files (National Archives, College Park, MD).

30. Ara Lee Settle to Warren G. Harding, June 18, 1922, file 158260, RG 60, Department of Justice numerical files.

31. Ida B. Wells, *Crusade for Justice: The Autobiography of Ida B. Wells,* ed. Alfreda M. Duster (Chicago: University of Chicago Press, 1970), 71.

32. *Binghamton (New York) Sun,* May 3, 1923, reel 223, Tuskegee Institute News Clippings File (microfilm, Division of Behavioral Science Research, Carver Research Foundation, Tuskegee Institution).

33. James Elbert Cutler, *Lynch-Law: An Investigation into the History of Lynching in the United States* (London: Longmans, Green, 1905), 276.

34. *Independent,* February 7, 1916, in reel 221, Tuskegee Institute News Clippings File; Jessie Daniel Ames, "Editorial Treatment of Lynchings," *Public Opinion Quarterly* 2 (January 1938), 77–80. John Carlisle Kilgo made this argument in 1902. See Kilgo, "An Inquiry Concerning Lynchings," *South Atlantic Quarterly* 1 (January 1902): 4–13.

35. Stenographic report of debates at the Alabama Constitutional Convention, 1901, June 22, 1901, Association of Southern Women for the Prevention of Lynching Papers (microfilm, Atlanta University, University Microfilms International).

36. *New York Literary Digest,* January 22, 1916, in reel 221, Tuskegee Institute News Clippings File.

37. *Independent,* February 7, 1916, in reel 221, Tuskegee Institute News Clippings File.

38. *New York Times,* December 3, 1933; *Minneapolis Evening Tribune,* December 1, 1933; *Philadelphia Evening Public Ledger,* November 28, 1933, all in reel 227, Tuskegee Institute News Clippings File; Harry Farrell, *Swift Justice: Murder and Vengeance in a California Town* (New York: St. Martin's Press, 1992), 241–242, 271–279.

39. *San Francisco Western Worker,* June 11, 1934.

40. Linda O. McMurry, *Recorder of the Black Experience: A Biography of Monroe Nathan Work* (Baton Rouge: Louisiana State University Press, 1985), 118–134; Mark Tucker, "'You Can't Argue With Facts': Monroe Nathan Work as Information Officer, Editor, and Bibliographer," *Libraries and Culture* 26 (Winter 1991): 151–168.

41. Jacquelyn Dowd Hall, *Revolt Against Chivalry: Jessie Daniel Ames and the Women's Campaign Against Lynching* (rev. ed.; New York: Columbia University Press, 1993), 66, 159–161; Charles Kirk Pilkington, "The Trials of Brotherhood: The Founding of the Commission on Interracial Cooperation," *Georgia Historical Quarterly* 69 (Spring 1985): 55–80; Kathleen Atkinson Miller, "The Ladies and the Lynchers: A Look at the Association of Southern Women for the Prevention of Lynching," *Southern Studies* 2 (Fall and Winter 1991): 261–280.

42. Hall, *Revolt Against Chivalry,* 66–82.

43. Ames to Hatton Summers, July 9, 1937, ASWPL Papers; Ames to Hatton Summers, March 29, 1937, ibid.

44. Hall, *Revolt Against Chivalry,* 159–191.

45. Ames to members of the central council, October 11, 1940, reel 2, ASWPL Papers.

46. Ames, circular addressed to newspaper editors, reel 1, ASWPL Papers; George F. Melton to Ames, March 2, 1936, reel 1, ibid.; Ames to O. W. Riegel, October 15 1937, reel 2, ibid.; Ames, "Editorial Treatment of Lynchings," 77–84.

47. Ames to Work, July 14, 1936, reel 8, ASWPL Papers.

48. LeeAnn Whites, "Rebecca Latimer Felton and the Problem of 'Protection' in the New South," in *Visible Women: New Essays on American Activism* (Urbana: University of Illinois Press, 1993): 41–61; idem., "Rebecca Latimer Felton and the Wife's Farm: The Class and Racial Politics of Gender Reform," *Georgia Historical Quarterly* 76 (Summer 1992): 354–372; Rebecca Latimer Felton, *Country Life in Georgia in the Days of my Youth* (Atlanta: Index Printing Co., 1919).

49. *Atlanta Georgian,* July 3, 1938; *Daytona Beach News,* July 11, 1938; *Chattanooga Daily Times,* July 12, 1938, all in reel 231, Tuskegee Institute News Clippings File.

50. Roy Nash, "Memorandum for Mr. Philip G. Peabody on Lynch-Law and the Practicability of a Successful Attack Thereon," May 22, 1916, reel 1, NAACP Papers.

51. Robert L. Zangrando, *The NAACP Crusade against Lynching: 1909–1950* (Philadelphia: Temple University Press, 1980), 28–29.

52. Work to John R. Shillady, January 12, 1920, reel 2, NAACP Papers.

53. Shillady to Work, January 15, 1920, reel 2, NAACP Papers.

54. Monroe Work to John R. Shillady, January 12, 1920, reel 2, NAACP Papers; NAACP office secretary to Monroe Work, August 30, 1921, ibid.

55. Zangrando, *The NAACP Crusade against Lynching,* 43; James Harmon Chadbourn, *Lynching and the Law* (Chapel Hill: University of North Carolina Press, 1933), 48–57.

56. See, for example, *United States v. Cruikshank,* 92 U.S. 542 (1876); *United States v. Harris,* 106 U.S. 629 (1883).

57. Albert E. Pillsbury, "A Brief Inquiry into Federal Remedy for Lynching," *Harvard Law Review* 15 (March 1902): 707–713.

58. *Greensboro News,* January 10, 1928 in reel 3, NAACP Papers.

59. Zangrando, *The NAACP Crusade against Lynching,* 72–121.

60. *Norfolk Journal and Guide,* December 31, 1932, in reel 227, Tuskegee Institute News Clippings File.

61. *Baltimore Afro-American,* January 7, 1933, in reel 227, Tuskegee Institute News Clippings File. For the Communist League of Struggle for Negro Rights, see Mark D. Naison, "Communism and Black Nationalism in the Depression: The Case of Harlem," *Journal of Ethnic Studies* 2 (Summer 1974): 24–36.

62. Zangrando, *The NAACP Crusade against Lynching,* 99–101.

63. *Oklahoma City Black Dispatch,* February 2, 1933, reel 227, Tuskegee Institute News Clippings File.

64. *Macon (Georgia) News,* January 22, 1931, reel 4; Work to White, November 4, 1933, reel 5; Aline B. Loucheim to Roy Wilkins, October 26, 1936, reel 4; Roy Wilkins to Aline B. Loucheim, October 28, 1936, reel 4, all in NAACP Papers.

65. Zangrando, *The NAACP Crusade against Lynching,* 18–22, 210–216. For the NAACP's campaign for a federal anti-lynching law, see the *Crisis* generally, but especially Walter White, "The Costigan-Wagner Bill," *Crisis* 42 (January 1935): 10–11; George S. Schuyler, "Scripture for Lynchers," ibid., 12; "Can the States Stop Lynching?" ibid., 43 (January 1936): 6–7; "The New Federal Anti-Lynching Bill," ibid., 44 (March 1937): 72. See also Robin Bernice Balthrope, "Lawlessness and the New Deal: Congress and Antilynching Legislation, 1934–1938" (Ph.D. diss., Ohio State University, 1995), 133–201.

66. W. E. B. Du Bois, *The Autobiography of W. E. B. Du Bois: A Soliloquy on Viewing My Life from the Last Decade of its First Century* (n.p., International, 1968), 205, 221–222; W. E. B. Du Bois, *The Philadelphia Negro: A Social Study* (1899; reprint ed., New York: Schocken, 1967), 1–9; W. E. B. Du Bois, *The Souls of Black Folk: Essays and Sketches* (Chicago: A. C. McClurg, 1903); Dominic J. Capeci, Jr. and Jack C. Knight, "Reckoning with Violence: W. E. B. Du Bois and the 1906 Atlanta Race Riot," *Journal of Southern History* 62 (November 1996): 727–766; David Levering Lewis, *W. E. B. Du Bois: Biography of a Race, 1868–1919* (New York, 1993), 226–229, 333–337; Thomas C. Holt, "The Political Uses of Alienation: W. E. B. Du Bois on Politics, Race, and Culture, 1903–1940," *American Quarterly* 42 (June 1990): 301–323; Cornel West, *The American Evasion of Philosophy: A Genealogy of Pragmatism* (Madison: University of Wisconsin Press, 1989), 138–150.

67. Peter Novick, *That Noble Dream: The "Objectivity Question" and the American Historical Profession* (Cambridge: Cambridge University Press, 1988), 522–572; John E. Toews, "Intellectual History after the Linguistic Turn: The Autonomy of Meaning and the Irreducibility of Experience," *American Historical Review* 92 (October 1987): 879–907.

68. Zangrando, *The NAACP Crusade against Lynching,* 41, 52; Mary White Ovington, *Black and White Sat Down Together: The Reminiscences of an NAACP Founder* (New York: Feminist Press, 1995), 88–93.

69. Herbert Shapiro, *White Violence and Black Response From Reconstruction to Montgomery* (Amherst: University of Massachusetts Press, 1988), 63; Walter White, *A Man Called White: The Autobiography of Walter White* (1948; reprint ed., Athens: University of Georgia Press, 1995), 67.

70. White, *A Man Called White,* 52.

71. Walter White, *Rope and Faggot: A Biography of Judge Lynch* (1929; reprint ed., New York: Arno Press, 1969), 19, 227–269.

72. White, *Rope and Faggot,* 6.

73. White, *Rope and Faggot,* 8–11.

74. White, *Rope and Faggot,* 40–53; Hall, *Revolt Against Chivalry,* 19–128.

75. White, *Rope and Faggot,* 224.

76. White, *Rope and Faggot,* 226.

77. *New York News,* March 1, 1930, typescript in reel 3, NAACP Papers; *Greensboro (N.C.) News,* January 10, 1928, reel 3, NAACP Papers.

78. Robert Latham to Will B. Alexander, December 22, 1933, reel 1, ASWPL Papers.

79. P. Bernard Young to Walter White, July 18, 1936, reel 4, NAACP Papers.

80. Shillady to Monroe Work, August 30, 1921, reel 2, NAACP Papers.

81. McMurry, *Work,* 126.

82. Work to White, November 4, 1933, reel 5, NAACP Papers; *Rocky Mount Telegram,* September 4, 1933; *Burnsville (N.C.) Eagle,* September 1, 1933; *Raleigh News and Observer,* August 29, 1933, in reel 227, Tuskegee Institute News Clippings File.

83. Peter H. Amann, "Vigilante Fascism: The Black Legion as an American Hybrid," *Comparative Studies in Society and History* 25 (July 1983): 490–524; Michael S. Clinansmith, "The Black Legion: Hooded Americanism in Michigan," *Michigan History* 55 (Fall 1971): 243–262.

84. *New York Times,* May 23, 25, 27, 1936.

85. *Chicago Tribune,* May 23, 1936.

86. *New Orleans Times-Picayune,* May 23, 1936.

87. See, for example, *Forest City (N.C.) Recorder,* November 9, 1933, reel 227, Tuskegee Institute News Clippings File.

88. John V. Alviti and Mark H. Haller, "Loansharking in American Cities: Historical Analysis of a Marginal Enterprise," *American Journal of Legal History* 21 (1977): 125–156; Winston McDowell, "Race and Ethnicity During the Harlem Jobs Campaign, 1932–1935," *Journal of Negro History* 69 (Summer-Fall 1984): 134–146.

89. Work to White, February 17, 1937; White to Work, February 19, 1937, reel 5, NAACP Papers.

90. Roy Wilkins to Aline B. Loucheim, October 28, 1936, series A, part 7, reel 4, NAACP Papers. For an excellent discussion of this point, see Brundage, *Lynching in the New South,* 33–36,

91. *Tallahassee Democrat,* July 9, 1939, reel 231, Tuskegee Institute News Clipping File; *Macon Telegraph,* July 10, 1939, ibid.

92. Ames to Mrs. B. J. Reaves, June 19, 1939; Violett D. McKinney to Reaves, July 17, 1939, reel 5, ASWPL Papers; *New York Times,* December 31, 1939.

93. *New York Times,* April 2, 1939.

94. Ames to Jane Haves, May 24, 1939, reel 2, ASWPL Papers.

95. Ames to Mrs. C. E. Ellis, May 12, 1939, reel 6, ASWPL Papers.

96. *Savannah Morning News,* July 28, 1939, in reel 231, Tuskegee Institute News Clippings File.

97. *Savannah News,* August 4, 1939, in reel 231, Tuskegee Institute News Clippings File.

98. *Florence (South Carolina) Morning News,* August 4, 1939, *Greenwood (South Carolina) Index-Journal,* August 4, 1939, *Memphis Commercial Appeal,* August 4, 1939, *Greenville (South Carolina) News,* August 4, 1939, *Charleston (South Carolina) Evening Post,* August 4, 1939, *Montgomery (Alabama) Advertiser,* August 4, 1939, *Mobile (Alabama) Press,* August 4, 1939,

Tallahassee Democrat, August 4, 1939, *Huntsville (Alabama) Times,* August 4, 1939, *Charlotte (North Carolina) News,* August 7, 1939, all in reel 231, Tuskegee Institute News Clippings File.

99. ILD, "Tabulation of Recorded Lynchings in the United States," reel 231, Tuskegee Institute News Clippings file.

100. Ames to Mrs. Alex Spence, December 9, 1939; Ames to Bessie C. Alford, July 6, 1939, all in reel 6, ASWPL Papers.

101. "Can the States Stop Lynching?" *The Crisis* 46 (January 1939): 9.

102. *Chicago Bee,* November 5, 1939, reel 231, Tuskegee Institute News Clippings File.

103. *Chicago Bee,* December 19, 1939, reel 231, Tuskegee Institute News Clippings File.

104. White to Patterson, January 15, 1940, reel 28, NAACP Papers.

105. Confession of W. C. Bishop, March 24, 1940, box 60, Ralph McGill Papers (Special Collections, Robert W. Woodruff Library, Emory University, Atlanta); Richard H. Rovere, "The Klan Rides Again," *The Nation* 150 (April 6, 1940): 445. For the role of women in promoting Klan violence, see Nancy MacLean, "White Women and Klan Violence in the 1920s: Agency, Complicity, and the Politics of Women's History," *Gender and History* 3 (Autumn 1993): 285–303; Kathleen M. Blee, "Women in the 1920s' Ku Klux Klan Movement," *Feminist Studies* 17 (Spring 1991): 57–77; idem, *Women of the Klan: Racism and Gender in the 1920s* (Berkeley: University of California Press, 1991).

106. *New York Times,* March 12, 14, 17, 31, 1940; Confession of L. L. Trimble, April 4, 1940, box 60, Ralph McGill Papers (Special Collections, Robert W. Woodruff Library, Emory University, Atlanta).

107. Rovere, "The Klan Rides Again," 445–446; Theodore Irwin, "The Klan Kicks Up Again," *American Mercury* 50 (August 1940): 470–476; *New York Times,* March 12, 31, 1940.

108. Mrs. L. W. Alford to Ames, January 10, 1940; Ames to Mrs. Alford, August 6, 1940, reel 6, ASWPL Papers.

109. *New York Times,* May 10, 1940.

110. *New York Times,* May 17, 1940.

111. NAACP press release, July 3, 1940, series A, part 7, reel 28, NAACP Papers.

112. Oswald Garrison Villard to Patterson, July 8, 1940, reel 28, NAACP Papers.

113. Thurgood Marshall to Harry T. Moore, August 9, 1940, reel 28, NAACP Papers; *Norfolk Journal and Guide,* May 18, 1940, reel 231, Tuskegee Institute News Clippings File.

114. *Nashville Globe,* July 5, 1940, reel 232, Tuskegee Institute News Clippings File.

115. *Nashville Globe and Independent,* December 27, 1940, reel 231, Tuskegee Institute News Clippings File.

116. Harry T. Moore to White, August 5, 1940, reel 28, NAACP Papers.

117. White to Patterson, September 14, 1940, reel 28, NAACP Papers.

118. Ames to Lillian Smith, June 4, 1940, reel 2, ASWPL Papers.

119. *Wilmington Morning Star,* July 8, 1933, reel 227, Tuskegee News Clippings File.

120. *Richmond Times-Dispatch,* May 18, 1940, reel 28, NAACP Papers.

121. *Atlanta Daily World,* July 14, 1940.

122. *Jacksonville (Florida) Times-Union,* July 25, 1940, reel 232, Tuskegee Institute News Clippings Files.

123. Virginius Dabney, *Below the Potomac: A Book about the New South* (1942; reprint ed., Port Washington: Kennikat Press, 1969), 189.

124. NAACP press release, July 3, 1940, reel 28, NAACP Papers.

125. Patterson to White, July 13, 1940, reel 28, NAACP Papers.

126. White to Patterson, September 14, 1940, reel 28, NAACP Papers.

127. Patterson to Walter White, September 30, 1940, reel 28, NAACP Papers. Tuskegee officials and NAACP representatives met on October 23. At this meeting Tuskegee agreed to again send records of controversial cases to the NAACP. Ralph Davis to Walter White, December 5, 1940, reel 28, NAACP Papers.

128. Ralph Davis to Ames, December 5, 1940, reel 5, ASWPL Papers.

129. White to Thurgood Marshall and others, December 9, 1940, reel 28, NAACP Papers.

130. Marshall to White, December 11, 1940, reel 28, NAACP Papers.

131. "Summary of the Conference on Lynchings and Reports on Lynchings, Tuskegee Institute, Alabama, December 14, 1940," reel 8, ASWPL Papers.

132. *Raleigh News and Observer,* August 1, 24, November 14, 21, 1902.

133. "Summary of the Conference on Lynching and Reports on Lynchings, Tuskegee Institute, Alabama, December 14, 1940," reel 8, ASWPL Papers.

134. "Summary of the Conference on Lynchings and Reports on Lynchings, December 14, 1940," reel 8, ASWPL Papers.

135. "Summary of the Conference on Lynchings and Reports on Lynchings, Tuskegee Institute, Alabama, December 14, 1940," reel 8, ASWPL Papers.

136. *Nashville Globe and Independent,* December 20, 1940, reel 231, Tuskegee Institute News Clippings File.

137. Jessie Daniel Ames, *The Changing Character of Lynching* (Atlanta: Commission on Interracial Cooperation, 1942), 30.

138. Virginius Dabney to White, June 26, 1941, reel 28, NAACP Papers.

139. Marguerite Cartwright, "The Mob Still Rides—Tuskegee Notwithstanding," *Crisis* 60 (April 1953): 222–223.

140. See, for example, Stewart E. Tolnay and E. M. Beck, *Festival of Violence: An Analysis of Southern Lynchings, 1882–1930* (Urbana: University of Illinois Press, 1995), 260; Terence Finnegan, "'At the Hands of Parties Unknown': Lynching in Mississippi and South Carolina, 1881–1940" (Unpublished Ph.D. diss., University of Illinois, 1993), 111; Oliver Cox, *Caste, Class, and Race: A Study in Social Dynamics* (1948; reprint ed., New York, 1970), 549. Stephen Whitfield deals with this question with subtle precision in *A Death in the Delta: The Story of Emmett Till* (New York: Free Press, 1988), 24–31. Roberta Senechal de la Roche has made a sophisticated attempt to distinguish lynching from other forms of collective violence. See "The Sociogenesis of Lynching," in W. Fitzhugh Brundage, ed., *Under Sentence of Death: Essays on Lynching in the South* (Chapel Hill: University of North Carolina, 1997), 48–76. Brundage adopts the NAACP's "loose" definition in his *Lynching in the New South.* Lynching, he writes, took myriad forms and should not be limited to violent "dramatization[s] of the values and consensus of close-knit communities." Brundage, *Lynching in the New South,* 19. Brundage's formulation will overcome the popular image of lynching as crowd murder only with great difficulty. Brundage made little impact on Leon Litwack, for example, who still describes lynching as "a public ritual, a collective experience." Litwack, *Trouble in Mind: Black Southerners in the Age of Jim Crow* (New York: Knopf, 1998), 285.

141. *Chicago Tribune,* January 1, 1890.

142. George C. Wright, *Racial Violence in Kentucky. 1865–1940: Lynchings, Mob Rule, and "Legal Lynchings"* (Baton Rouge: Louisiana State University Press, 1990), 6n8.

CHAPTER EIGHT

1. Timothy M. Phelps and Helen Winternitz, *Capitol Games: Clarence Thomas, Anita Hill, and the Story of a Supreme Court Nomination* (New York: Hyperion, 1992), 331–377; Jane Mayer and Jill Abramson, *Strange Justice: The Selling of Clarence Thomas* (Boston: Houghton Mifflin, 1994), 280–300.

2. Kimberle Crenshaw, "Whose Story is it Anyway? Feminist and Antiracist Appropriations of Anita Hill," in Toni Morrison, ed., *Race-ing Justice, En-Gendering Power: Essays on Anita Hill, Clarence Thomas, and the Construction of Social Reality* (New York: Pantheon,

1992), 402–440; Sandra L. Ragan et al., eds., *The Lynching of Language: Gender, Politics, and Power in the Hill-Thomas Hearings* (Urbana: University of Illinois Press, 1996).

3. *Raleigh Gazette,* June 12, 1897.

4. Peter W. Bardaglio, *Reconstructing the Household: Families, Sex, and the Law in the Nineteenth-Century South* (Chapel Hill: University of North Carolina Press, 1995), 190–201.

5. *Washington Post,* June 28, 2000; *USA Today,* June 28, 2000; *Houston Chronicle,* June 28, 2000; *New York Daily News,* June 28, 2000; *Christian Science Monitor,* July 3, 2000; *Los Angeles Times,* July 12, 2000; *Arizona Republic,* July 12, 2000; *St. Louis Post-Dispatch,* July 13, 2000; *New York Times,* July 13, 2000; *Seattle Times,* July 16, 2000.

6. ABC News, "The Hanging Tree," *20/20* (July 7, 2000); CBS News, "FBI Looking into Rumors and Suspicions that a Black Teenager was Lynched In Mississippi," *CBS Evening News* (July 13, 2000); ABC News, "Tension in Small Town over Hanging Death of Raynard Johnson," *World News Tonight* (July 12, 2000); CNN, "Mississippi Hanging Investigation: Suicide or Lynching?" *Burden of Proof* (July 17, 2000); CNN, "Hanging Death Mystery in Mississippi: Suicide or Murder?" *Burden of Proof* (July 21, 2000).

7. *Vicksburg Post,* August 10, 2000.

8. *Leslie's Weekly* 97 (August 20, 1903): 182.

9. Leonard Dinnerstein, *The Leo Frank Case* (1966; reprint ed., Athens; University of Georgia Press, 1987), 1–61; Nancy Maclean, "The Leo Frank Case Reconsidered: Gender and Sexual Politics in the Making of Reactionary Populism," *Journal of American History* 77 (December 1991): 917–948. For local press coverage, see, for example, *Atlanta Journal,* April 28, 1913 and after.

10. *Frank v. Mangum,* 237 U.S. 326.

11. Dinnerstein, *The Leo Frank Case,* 114–147.

12. *New York Times,* March 8, 1982.

13. *Atlanta Journal,* April 28, 1913; *Chicago Tribune,* April 28, 1913; *New York World,* April 28, 1913.

14. "Statement of Facts," *State of Texas v. Jesse Washington,* District Court of McLennan County, March term, 1916. Transcript in the possession of William Carrigan and kindly loaned to the author.

15. James M. SoRelle, "The 'Waco Horror': The Lynching of Jesse Washington," *Southwestern Historical Quarterly* 86 (1983): 517–536; James Allen et al., *Without Sanctuary: Lynching Photography in America* (n.p.: Twin Palms, 2000), 174.

16. *New York Times,* May 16, 1916; *San Francisco Chronicle,* May 16, 1916; *Chicago Tribune,* May 16, 1916; *New Orlean Times-Picayune,* May 16, 1916; SoRelle, "The 'Waco Horror'," 517–536. The *New York Times* denounced the Washington lynching in an editorial, May 17, 1916.

17. A. A. Madden testimony, March 4, 1910, bill of exceptions, *Annie M. Rogers et al. v. V. S. & P. R. R. Co.,* case number 251, Circuit Court of the United States for the Western Division of the Southern District of Mississsppi (National Archives, Southeast Region, East Point, Georgia).

18. *Rogers, et al. v. Vicksburg, S. & P. R. Co.,* 194 F, 65 (1912).

19. G. O. Cundiff testimony, January 8, 1913, *Annie M. Rogers, et al. v. V. S. & P. R. R. Co.,* case number 251. Deposition of Thomas F. Wright, taken before Reginald H. Carter, esq., United States Commissioner, December 20, 1913, *Annie M. Rogers, et al. v. V. S. & P. R. R. Co.,* case number 295.

20. The Court's Instructions to the Jury, *Mrs. Annie May Rogers v. Vicksburg, Shreveport & Pacific Railroad Co and Alabama & Vicksburg Railroad Co.,* case number 251.

21. *Vicksburg Evening Post,* January 4, 1911.

22. Amended Declaration, filed June 28, 1910, *Annie May Rogers, et al. v. V. S. & P. Ry Co.,* case number 251.

23. Rebecca Stiles Taylor, chairman, and Mary E. Belcher, secretary, to the President, May 31, 1918, file 158260, straight numerical files, RG 60, Department of Justice (National Archives, College Park, MD)

24. John F. Monroe to Woodrow Wilson, received December 16, 1917, file 158260, straight numerical files, Department of Justice.

25. McChord to president, March 15, 1921, file 158260, straight numerical files, Department of Justice.

26. H. McK. Fedgham to Attorney General, June 19, 1919, file 158260, straight numerical files, Department of Justice.

27. Michael Hardt and Antonio Negri, *Empire* (Cambridge: Harvard University Press, 2000), 5.

28. Michael Emery, Edwin Emery, and Nancy L. Roberts, *The Press and America: An Interpretative History of the Mass Media,* Ninth ed. (Boston: Allyn and Bacon, 2000), 288–291, 244–245.

29. Maurine Beasley, "The Muckrakers and Lynching: A Case Study in Racism," *Journalism History* 9 (Autumn-Winter 1982): 86–91.

30. Ray Stannard Baker, "What is a Lynching? A Study of Mob Justice South and North: Lynching in the South," *McClure's Magazine* 24 (January 1905): 299–314; idem, "What is a Lynching? A Study of Mob Justice, South and North: Lynching in the North," *McClure's Magazine* 24 (February 1905): 422–430.

31. David Levering Lewis, *W. E. B. Du Bois: Biography of a Race, 1868–1919* (New York: Henry Holt, 1993), 409–427.

32. "The Waco Horror," supplement to the *Crisis* (July 1916): 1–8; SoRelle, "The 'Waco Horror'," 517–536.

33. Rogers Melton Smith, "The Waco Lynching of 1916: Perspective and Analysis," (M.A. thesis, Baylor University, 1971), 33–59.

34. *Chicago Defender,* January 29, 1910; Roi Ottley, *The Lonely Warrior: The Life and Times of Robert S. Abbott* (Chicago: Henry Regnery Co., 1955), 88–114; Theodore Kornweibel, Jr., "'The Most Dangerous of All Negro Journals': Federal Efforts to Suppress the *Chicago Defender* During World War I," *American Journalism* 11 (Spring 1994): 154–168; Alan D. DeSantis, "A Forgotten Leader: Robert S. Abbott and the Chicago *Defender* from 1910–1920," *Journalism History* 23 (Summer 1997): 63–71; Mary E. Stovall, "The *Chicago Defender* in the Progressive Era," *Illinois Historical Journal* 83 (1990): 159–172; Neil R. McMillen, "Black Journalism in Mississippi: The Jim Crow Years," *Journal of Mississippi History* 49 (1987): 129–138; James R. Grossman, "Blowing the Trumpet: The Chicago *Defender* and Black Migration during World War I," *Illinois Historical Journal* 78 (1985): 82–96.

35. Ottley, *Lonely Warrior,* 121–139.

36. Paula Marantz Cohen, *Silent Film and the Triumph of the American Myth* (New York: Oxford University Press, 2001), passim, but esp. 4–42.

37. J. Fred MacDonald, *Don't Touch That Dial: Radio Programming in American Life, 1920–1960* (Chicago: Nelson-Hall, 1979), 1–90, 327–370; Christopher H. Sterling and John M. Kittross, *Stay Tuned: A Concise History of American Broadcasting* (1978; 2nd ed., Belmont: Wadsworth, 1990), 50–93; Leonard C. Archer, *Black Images in the American Theatre: NAACP Protest Campaigns—Stage, Screen, Radio, and Television* (Brooklyn: Pageant-Poseidon, 1973), 225–262; Barbara Dianne Savage, *Broadcasting Freedom: Radio, War, and the Politics of Race, 1938 to 1948* (Chapel Hill: University of North Carolina Press, 1999).

38. *General Laws of the Legislature of Alabama Passed at the Session of 1919* (Montgomery: State Printers, 1919), 15–16, 808–809.

39. W. W. Callahan to Thomas E. Kilby, July 6, 1922, Governor Thomas E. Kilby Papers, SG22128 (Alabama Department of Archives and History, Montgomery); Kilby to E. W. Barrett, September 27, 1921, ibid.

40. *Moore v. Dempsey*, 261 U.S. 86 (1923).

41. *Moore v. Dempsey*, 261 U.S. 86 (1923).

42. James H. Madison, *A Lynching in the Heartland: Race and Memory in America* (New York: Palgrave, 2001), 70–92.

43. Dan T. Carter, *Scottsboro: A Tragedy of the American South* (1969; reprint ed., New York: Oxford University Press, 1975), 8–20. In 1976 NBC broadcast a docudrama about the Scottsboro case; Victoria Price, still living, sued the network for libel. "If Thomas Knight, the Scottsboro prosecutor, had had 'em executed," she told a reporter, "they done promised me I could push the button. And I'd do it. . . . I'd have pushed it and laughed." NBC chose to settle rather than pursue the case. *Washington Post,* January 4, 1982.

44. John Egerton, *Speak Now Against The Day: The Generation Before the Civil Rights Movement in the South* (New York: Knopf, 1994), 139–149; Ann Douglas, *Terrible Honesty: Mongrel Manhattan in the 1920s* (New York: Noonday, 1995), 31–72; M. K. Singleton, *H. L. Mencken and the American Mercury Adventure* (Durham: Duke University Press, 1962), 4–5, 102–103.

45. Interview with Martha Hunt Huie, June 14, 2001; Huie family scrapbook, Martha Hunt Huie collection; Egerton, *Speak Now Against The Day,* 59–61.

46. Carter, *Scottsboro,* 51–103; Egerton, *Speak Now Against The Day,* 144–146.

47. James Goodman, *Stories of Scottsboro* (New York: Vintage Books, 1994), 25.

48. *San Francisco Western Worker,* February 15, April 15, 1932, October 16, December 11, 1933.

49. *San Francisco Western Worker,* October 16, December 18, 1933, March 5, 1934.

50. *San Francisco Western Worker,* December 11, 1933.

51. Goodman, *Stories of Scottsboro,* 24–38, 85–89; Carter, *Scottsboro,* 137–173.

52. *Powell v. Alabama,* 287 U.S. 56.

53. *San Francisco Western Worker,* November 14, 1932.

54. Goodman, *Stories of Scottsboro,* 148; Carter, *Scottsboro,* 174–242.

55. Goodman, *Stories of Scottsboro,* 120–124; Carter, *Scottsboro,* 192–242.

56. The other defendants faced Judge William Washington Callahan, a more traditional Alabama judge. Callahan so openly sided with the prosecution that he first forgot to instruct the jury on how to acquit. Jurors sentenced Haywood Patterson and Charlie Weems to seventy-five years and Clarence Norris to death. When Alabama governor Bibb Graves refused to pardon the remaining five Scottsboro Boys, newspapers headlined the news, but thereafter the case drifted onto the back pages. For years, the five sat in the terrifying Alabama prison system. Authorities quietly released Weems in 1943. Norris and Ozie Powell left prison in 1946. Patterson escaped to Michigan two years later, where the governor refused to extradite. Alabama paroled Andrew Wright in 1950, the last of the Scottsboro Boys still in prison. Carter, *Scottsboro,* 330–413.

57. Richard C. Cortner, *A "Scottsboro" Case in Mississippi: The Supreme Court and Brown v. Mississippi* (Jackson: University Press of Mississippi, 1986), 28.

58. *Brown v. Mississippi,* 297 U.S. 278 (1936).

59. *NLRB v. Jones and Laughlin Steel Corp.,* 301 U.S. 1 (1937); *NLRB v. Friedman-Harry Marks Clothing Co.,* 301 U.S. 58 (1937); *Associated Press v. NLRB,* 301 U.S. 103 (1937); Barry Cushman, *Rethinking the New Deal Court: The Structure of a Constitutional Revolution* (New York: Oxford University Press, 1998), 139–225; Peter H. Irons, *The New Deal Lawyers* (Princeton: Princeton University Press, 1982), 203–289.

60. Howard Kester, "Lynching by Blow Torch," Howard A. Kester Papers, 1923–1972, reel 11 (microfilm, Manuscripts Department, Southern Historical Collection, University of North Carolina); *New York Times,* April 14, 1937; *Atlanta Constitution,* April 14, 1937.

61. *Jackson Daily News,* no date, in ASWPL Papers, reel 36.

62. D. B. Cooley to Theodore G. Bilbo, April 16, 1937, folder 17, box 303, Theodore G. Bilbo Papers (McCain Library and Archives, University of Southern Mississippi, Hattiesburg, Mississippi).

63. W. A. Sullivan to Bilbo, April 16, 1937, folder 17, box 303, Theodore G. Bilbo Papers; John Smith to Bilbo, ibid.

64. Mrs. Charles J. Sharp and Mrs. Mabel Jones West to Bilbo, January 25, 1939, folder 15, box 1057, Theodore G. Bilbo Papers.

65. Hamilton Basso to John Temple Graves, January 28, 1937, folder 3, John Temple Graves, Jr., Papers (Department of Archives and Manuscripts, Birmingham Public Library).

66. Brian Kelly, *Race, Class, and Power in the Alabama Coalfields, 1908–1921* (Urbana: University of Illinois Press, 2001).

67. "In the Matter of the Investigation of the Killing of Willie Beard [*sic*]," SG 12068, Governor Thomas Kilby Papers (Alabama Department of Archives and History, Montgomery); *New York Times,* January 17, February 3, 7, 21, 1921.

68. Roger K. Newman, *Hugo Black: A Biography* (New York: Pantheon, 1994), 201–203.

69. Bilbo to Alfred Stephens, January 13, 1940, folder 39, box 974, Theodore G. Bilbo Papers; Bilbo to Charles Petty, February 21, 1938, folder 13, box 1053, ibid.; Bilbo to Rev. Henry A. Boyd, February 17, 1938, folder 14, box 1053, ibid.

70. David Margolick, *Strange Fruit: Billie Holiday, Cafe Society, and an Early Cry for Civil Rights* (Philadelphia: Running Press, 2000), 21–25, 63–74, 88–94; Angela Y. Davis, *Blues Legacies and Black Feminism: Gertrude "Ma" Rainey, Bessie Smith, and Billie Holiday* (New York: Pantheon Books, 1998), 181–198.

71. Bruce Wilferth to Bilbo, January 9, 1939, folder 39, box 974, Theodore G. Bilbo Papers.

72. Art and Margaret Landes to Bilbo, May 2, 1940, folder 39, box 974, Theodore G. Bilbo Papers; Bilbo to Mr. and Mrs. Landes, May 6, 1940, ibid.

73. Dabney to Graves, June 20, 1941, folder 4, John Temple Graves, Jr., Papers.

74. William Bradford Huie, "The South Kills Another Negro," *American Mercury* 53 (November 1941): 535–545.

75. Henry A. Schweinhaut, "The Civil Liberties Section of the Department of Justice," *Bill of Rights Review* 1 (1941): 206–216; Sidney Fine, *Frank Murphy: The Washington Years* (Ann Arbor: University of Michigan Press, 1984), 76–98; Risa L. Goluboff, "The Thirteenth Amendment and the Lost Origins of Civil Rights," *Duke Law Journal* 50 (2001): 1615–1618.

76. *Chicago Tribune,* April 3, 1933; Goluboff, "The Thirteenth Amendment and the Lost Origins of Civil Rights," 1618–1627.

77. Thurgood Marshall to Wendell Berge, January 30, 1942, box A406, group II, NAACP Papers (Manuscript Division, Library of Congress, Washington, D. C.).

78. "Investigation into the Lynching of Cleo Wright at Sikeston, Missouri, January 23, 1942," box A407, NAACP Papers; Dominic J. Capeci, Jr., *The Lynching of Cleo Wright* (Lexington: University Press of Kentucky, 1998).

79. "Federal Jurisdiction in Lynching Cases," memorandum, March 24, 1943, box A407, group II. NAACP Papers.

80. *Chicago Defender,* November 13, 20, 1943.

81. *Vicksburg Post,* June 9, 1999, January 16, 2000.

82. Matthew William Dunne, "Next Steps: Charles S. Johnson and Southern Liberalism," *Journal of Negro History* 83 (Winter 1998): 1–34; Lee Todd, "Charles S. Johnson and the Sociology of Race Relations," *Southern Historian* 21 (2000): 56–65; *A Monthly Summary of Events and Trends in Race Relations* 1 (August 1943): 8–9.

83. *Chicago Defender,* September 19, 1942.

84. *Houston (Texas) Negro Labor News,* July 18, 1942.

85. Victor W. Rotnem, "The Federal Civil Right 'Not to be Lynched,'" *Washington University Law Quarterly* 28 (February 1943): 58.

86. Rotnem, "The Federal Civil Right 'Not to be Lynched,'" 57–73.

87. *Montgomery Advertiser,* April 22, 1943; *Chicago Tribune,* January 13, 1943; *Birmingham News,* April 25, 1943. All in reel 232, microfilm, Tuskegee news clippings file.

88. Patricia Sullivan, *Days of Hope: Race and Democracy in the New Deal Era* (Chapel Hill: University of North Carolina Press, 1996), 133–168.

89. Clark, *The Ox-Bow Incident;* Harry F. Tepker, Jr., "The Ox-Bow Incident," *Oklahoma City University Law Review* 22 (Fall 1997): 1209–1221; Max Westbrook, "The Archetypal Ethic of the Ox-Bow Incident," *Western American Literature* 1 (summer 1966): 105–118; Robert Cochran, "Nature and the Nature of Man in *The Ox-Bow Incident*," *Western American Literature* 5 (Winter 1971): 253–264.

90. Henry Fonda, as told to Howard Teichmann, *Fonda: My Life* (New York: New American Library, 1981), 178.

91. E. M. Ellis, Jr., testimony, transcript of record, *Screws v. United States,* box 3830, U. S. Supreme Court Appellate Case Files, RG 267 (National Archives, Washington, D.C.). Hereinafter cited as Screws transcript.

92. James P. Willingham testimony, Screws transcript.

93. *Baker County News,* February 12, 1943.

94. Prentice Thomas to E. Sprye, February 4, 1943, box A407, part II, NAACP Papers (Library of Congress, Washington, D.C.); Prentice Thomas to Victor Rotnem, February 15, 1943, ibid.; White to Marshall, February 18, 1943, ibid.; Wendell Berge to Roy Wilkins, February 25, 1943, ibid.

95. Thurgood Marshall to Tom C. Clark, December 27, 1946, box A410, group II, NAACP Papers; J. Edgar Hoover to Walter White, January 13, 1947, ibid.

96. Calhoun testimony, Screws transcript.

97. *Baker County News,* April 16, 1943.

98. Robert K. Carr, "*Screws v. United States:* The Georgia Police Brutality Case," *Cornell Law Quarterly* 31 (1945): 48–67; Woodford Howard and Cornelius Bushover, "The Screws Case Revisited," *Journal of Politics* 29 (1967): 617–620, 620 (quotation).

99. Petition for a writ of certiorari, *Screws v. United States,* box 3830, Supreme Court Appellate Case Files, RG 267 (National Archives, Washington, D.C.).

100. Frank Murphy, handwritten notes, Frank Murphy Papers, roll 129 (microfilm, Bentley Historical Library, Ann Arbor, Michigan); Liva Baker, *Felix Frankfurter* (New York: Coward-McCann, 1969), 256–268; C. Herman Pritchett, *The Roosevelt Court: A Study in Judicial Politics and Values, 1937–1947* (New York: MacMillan, 1948), 150–152.

101. Fine, *Frank Murphy,* 396–402.

102. *Screws et al. v. United States,* 325 U.S. 91 (1945); Carr, "*Screws v. United States:* The Georgia Police Brutality Case," 64–67; Taylor Branch, *Parting the Waters: America in the King Years, 1954–63* (New York: Simon and Schuster, 1988), 408–409; Pritchett, *Roosevelt Court,* 152.

   It is a comment on this decision that the biographers of Frank Murphy discuss it extensively. The biographers of Hugo Black and Felix Frankfurter, while extolling their subjects' commitment to civil liberites, entirely neglect the case of *Screws v. United States.* See J. Woodford Howard, Jr., *Mr. Justice Murphy: A Political Biography* (Princeton: Princeton University Press, 1968), 355–358; Fine, *Frank Murphy,* 396–402; Howard Ball, *Hugo L. Black: Cold Steel Warrior* (New York: Oxford University Press, 1996); Roger K. Newman, *Hugo Black: A Biography* (New York: Pantheon Books, 1994); Gerald T. Dunne, *Hugo Black and the Judicial Revolution* (New York: Simon and Schuster, 1977); James F. Simon, *The Antagonists: Hugo Black, Felix Frankfurter and Civil Liberties in Modern America* (New York: Simon and Schuster, 1989); Mark Silverstein, *Constitutional Faiths: Felix Frankfurter, Hugo Black, and the Process of Judicial Decision Making* (Ithaca: Cornell University Press, 1984); Baker, *Felix Frankfurter;* H. N. Hirsch, *The Enigma of Felix Frankfurter* (New York: Basic Books, 1981); Michael E. Parrish, *Felix Frankfurter and His Times: The Reform Years*

(New York: Free Press, 1982); Joseph P. Lash, *From the Diaries of Felix Frankfurter* (New York: W. W. Norton, 1975).

103. Clyde Miller to Arthur Hays Sulzberger, August 22, 1946, box A410, group II, NAACP Papers; John Egerton, *Speak Now Against the Day: The Generation Before the Civil Rights Movement in the South* (New York: Knopf, 1994), 369–371.

104. Jack E. Davis, "'Whitewash' in Florida: The Lynching of Jesse James Payne and Its Aftermath," *Florida Historical Quarterly* 68 (January 1990): 277–283.

105. Testimony of Millard F. Caldwell, *Crowell-Collier Publishing Company v. Millard F. Caldwell*, appeal from the District Court of the United States for the Northern District of Florida, civil action 152, box 43 (National Archives, East Point, Georgia.).

106. Millard F. Caldwell, complaint, *Crowell-Collier Publishing Company v. Millard F. Caldwell*.

107. Davis, "'Whitewash' in Florida," 277–298.

108. *Charleston News and Courier*, February 18, 19, 21, 1947; *Greenville News*, February 18, 19, 20, 21, 1947; David Redekop, "The Lynching of Willie Earle" (M.A. Thesis, Clemson University, 1987); Kari Frederickson, "'The Slowest State and 'Most Backward Community': Racial Violence in South Carolina and Federal Civil-Rights Legislation, 1946–1948," *South Carolina Historical Magazine* 98 (April 1997): 177–202.

109. *New York Times*, February 18, 1947.

110. *Greenville News*, February 21, 1947; *Charleston News and Courier*, February 21, 22, 1947.

111. "The Shape of Things," *Nation* 164 (May 24, 1947): 615.

112. "Trial by Jury," *Time* 49 (May 26, 1947): 27; "Story of a Lynching," *Newsweek* 29 (May 26, 1947): 29–30; "Twelve Good Men and True," *New Republic* 116 (June 2, 1947): 9; "Lynch Trial Makes Southern History," *Life* 22 (June 2, 1947): 27–31.

113. *New York Times*, May 21, 1947.

114. Victoria Glendinning, *Rebecca West: A Life* (London: Weidenfeld and Nicolson, 1987), 184.

115. Harold Ross, *Letters from the Editor: The New Yorker's Harold Ross*, ed. Thomas Kunkel, (New York: Modern Library, 2000), 233.

116. Ross, *Letters from the Editor*, ed. Kunkel, 332.

117. Glendinning, *Rebecca West*, 190.

118. Walter White memorandum to Wilkins and Harrington, June 13, 1947, box A406, part II, NAACP Papers.

119. *San Francisco People's World*, May 23, 1947.

120. William E. Leuchtenburg, "The Conversion of Harry Truman," *American Heritage* 42 (November 1991): 55–68.

121. Leuchtenburg, "The Conversion of Harry Truman," 55.

122. *McGee v. State*, 200 Mississippi 350 (1946).

123. *McGee v. State*, case 36411, Mississippi Supreme Court Records, (Mississippi Department of Archives and History); *McGee v. State*, 203 Mississippi 592 (1948).

124. McGee testimony, transcript of testimony, *McGee v. State*, case 36892, Mississippi Supreme Court Records; *McGee v. State*, 40 Southern Reporter, 2nd series 160 (1949).

125. *Time* 57 (May 14, 1951): 76; *Life* 30 (May 21, 1951): 44–45.

126. Carl T. Rowan, *South of Freedom* (New York: Knopf, 1952), 177.

127. Rowan, *South of Freedom*, 174–192.

128. Ben Green, *Before His Time: The Untold Story of Harry T. Moore, America's First Civil Rights Martyr* (New York: Free Press, 1999), 23–141.

129. Green, *Before His Time*, 168–254.

130. Stephen J. Whitfield, *A Death in the Delta: The Story of Emmett Till* (New York: Free Press, 1988), 25–27; David A. Shostak, "Crosby Smith: Forgotten Witness to a Mississippi Nightmare," *Negro History Bulletin* 38 (December 1974–January 1975): 320–325;

George E. Curry, "Killed for Whistling at a White Woman," *Emerge* 6 (July-August 1995): 24–32.

131. See above for the Scottsboro Boys, "Mother Mooney," and the Theodore Jordan case. See also the mother of Mrs. Rosa Lee Ingram, *San Francisco People's World,* March 19, 24, 1948.

132. Interview with Ernest C. Withers, June 14, 2001; *San Francisco People's World,* September 14, 21, 1955. Ruth Feldstein, "'I Wanted the Whole World To See': Race, Gender, and Constructions of Motherhood in the Death of Emmett Till," in Rima D. Apple and Janet Golden, ed., *Mothers and Motherhood: Readings in American History* (Columbus: Ohio State University Press, 1997), 131–170; Rick Halpern, *Down on the Killing Floor: Black and White Workers in Chicago's Packinghouses, 1904–54* (Urbana: University of Illinois Press, 1997), passim.

133. *San Francisco People's World,* September 20, 1955.

134. Whitfield, *A Death in the Delta,* 33–50; *Pictures Tell the Story: Ernest C. Withers Reflections in History* (Norfolk: Chrysler Museum of Art, 2000), 35–61; *New York Amsterdam News,* September 17, 24, 1955.

135. *Greenville Delta Democrat-Times,* September 18, 1955.

136. *New York Amsterdam News,* October 8, 1955; *Pictures Tell the Story,* 59.

137. William Bradford Huie, "The Shocking Story of Approved Killing in Mississippi," *Look* 20 (January 24, 1956): 46–50.

138. *Chicago Defender,* October 1, 8, 1955.

139. *Chicago Defender,* October 15, November 19, 1955.

140. Melba Pattillo Beals, *Warriors Don't Cry: A Searing Memoir of the Battle to Integrate Little Rock's Central High* (New York: Washington Square, 1994).

141. C. L. Wilson to J. P. Coleman, no date, folder 16, box 19, J. P. Coleman Papers, (Mississippi Department of Archives and History). For the Parker lynching generally, see Howard Smead, *Blood Justice: The Lynching of Mack Charles Parker* (New York: Oxford University Press, 1986).

142. J. Edgar Hoover to Attorney General, May 28, 1959, 144–41–304, Civil Rights Division files, Department of Justice, RG 60 (National Archives, College Park, Maryland). Hereinafter cited as Parker investigation.

143. J. Edgar Hoover to Attorney General, November 24, 1959, Parker investigation.

144. For Congressional protest, see, for example, Philip A. Hart to Thomas C. Hennings, January 15, 1960, Parker investigation. For the ABA, see Arthur Freund to William P. Rogers, May 26, 1959, ibid.

145. Lawrence Walsh to Thomas C. Hennings, February 8, 1960, Parker investigation.

146. John H. Wright to William P. Rogers, November 11, 1959, Parker investigation.

147. William Bradford Huie, "Lynching—Northern Style," *Cavalier* 10 (April 1960): 10–15.

148. William Bradford Huie, "Why the Army Hanged Emmett Till's Father," *Confidential* 4 (May 1956): 8–9, 50, 52.

149. Huie, "Lynching—Northern Style," 12.

150. Joel Williamson, "Wounds Not Scars: Lynching, the National Conscience, and the American Historian," *Journal of American History* 83 (March 1997): 1227.

151. William D. Carrigan, "Forgotten Lynchings: Mob Violence Against Mexican Americans, 1848–1928," (unpublished paper presented at the American Historical Association, January 2002, San Francisco, California).

EPILOGUE

1. William Bradford Huie, "The Shocking Story of Approved Killing in Mississippi," *Look* 20 (January 24, 1956): 46–50.

2. Huie, "Approved Killing," 47, 50.

3. Hugh Stephen Whitaker, "A Case Study in Southern Justice: the Emmett Till Case" (M.A. Thesis, Florida State University, 1963), 155, 171–177.

4. Whitaker, "Case Study," 107, 108, 127.

5. William Bradford Huie, "What's Happened to the Emmett Till Killers?" *Look* (January 22, 1957): 63–67.

6. Whitaker, "Case Study," 161–162.

7. Robert D. Putnam, *Bowling Alone: The Collapse and Revival of American Community* (New York: Simon and Schuster, 2000).

8. Reed Massengill, *Portrait of a Racist: The Man Who Killed Medgar Evers?* (New York: St. Martin's Press, 1994), 167.

9. Massengill, *Portrait of a Racist,* 167–171; Bobby DeLaughter, *Never Too Late: A Prosecutor's Story of Justice in the Medgar Evers Case* (New York: Scribner, 2001), 33–35.

10. Michal R. Belknap, *Federal Law and Southern Order: Racial Violence and Constitutional Conflict in the Post-Brown South* (Athens: University of Georgia Press, 1987), 229–251.

11. DeLaughter, *Never Too Late,* 28.

12. Maryanne Vollers, *Ghosts of Mississippi: The Murder of Medgar Evers, the Trials of Byron De La Beckwith, and the Haunting of the New South* (Boston: Little Brown, 1995), 341.

13. Vollers, *Ghosts of Mississippi,* 4–7; Adam Nossiter, *Of Long Memory: Mississippi and the Murder of Medgar Evers* (Reading: Addison Wesley, 1994), 11; Massengill, *Portrait of a Racist,* 14–16.

14. Vollers, *Ghosts of Mississippi,* 372.

15. Frank Sikora, *Until Justice Rolls Down: The Birmingham Church Bombing Case* (Tuscaloosa: University of Alabama Press, 1991); *New York Times,* May 3, 2001.

16. *Chicago Tribune,* January 5, 6, 1923; *New Orleans Times-Picayune,* January 8, 1923; *Palm Beach Post,* April 9, 1994; *Tampa Tribune,* May 29, 1995.

17. *New York Times,* February 21, 1999, February 5, 2000, March 1, 2001.

18. "An Act to Provide for the Acquisition and Publication of Data about Crimes that Manifest Prejudice Based on Certain Group Characteristics," 104 Stat. 140; James B. Jacobs and Kimberly A. Potter, "Hate Crimes: A Critical Perspective," *Crime and Justice* 22 (1997): 1–42; Marc Fleisher, "Down the Passage Which We Should Not Take: The Folly of Hate Crime Legislation." *Journal of Law and Policy* 2 (1994): 1–53.

19. 108 Stat. 2131.

20. 108 Stat. 2096.

21. *Charleston (Illinois) Times-Courier,* June 23, 1998.

22. *New York Times,* June 17, 1998.

23. *Washington Post,* June 13, 1998.

24. *Washington Post,* February 17, 1999.

25. *Boston Globe,* April 18, 1999.

26. *Washington Post,* June 14, 1998.

Bibliography

PERIODICALS

Alton (Illinois) Observer
American Citizen
Arizona Republic
Atchison (Kansas) Freedom's Champion
Atchison (Kansas) Squatter Sovereign
Atlanta Constitution
Atlanta Georgian
Atlanta Herald
Atlanta Journal
Baker County (Georgia) News
Birmingham Iron Age
Birmingham News
Boston Daily Advertiser and Patriot
Boston Liberator
Charleston (Illinois) Times-Courier
Charleston (South Carolina) Courier
Charleston (South Carolina) News and Courier
Chatham (Canada West) Provincial Freeman
Chicago American
Chicago Defender
Chicago Democrat
Chicago Tribune
Christian Science Monitor
Cincinnati Philanthropist
Clinton (Mississippi) Gazette
Colored Citizen
The Crisis
Daily Memphis Avalanche
Galena (Illinois) Galenian
Greensborough (North Carolina) Patriot
Greenville (Mississippi) Delta Democrat-Times
Greenville (South Carolina) News
Greenwood (Mississippi) Commonwealth
Harper's Weekly
Harrisburg (Pennsylvania) State Journal
Herald of Freedom
Houston Chronicle

Houston Negro Labor News
Indianapolis Freeman
Kansas City American Citizen
Kansas City Enterprise
Kansas Free State
Lexington (Kentucky) True American
Life
Los Angeles Star
Los Angeles Times
Louisianan
Louisville Advertiser
Memphis Appeal
Memphis Avalanche
Mobile (Alabama) Daily Register
Morning Courier and New-York Enquirer
Nashville Banner
Nashville Republican
Nation
National Baptist World
New Orleans Louisiana Advertiser
New Republic
New Richmond (Ohio) Philanthropist
New York Age
New York Amsterdam News
New York Colored American
New York Commercial Advertiser
New York Daily News
New York Emancipator
New York Evening Post
New York Freeman
New York Herald
New York Times
New York Sun
New York World
Newsweek
Niles' Register
Norfolk American Beacon
People's Friend
Portland (Maine) Daily Evening Advertiser
Pulaski (Tennessee) Citizen
Raleigh (North Carolina) Gazette
Raleigh (North Carolina) News and Observer
Richmond Planet
St. Louis Missouri Republican
St. Louis Observer
St. Louis Post-Dispatch
San Francisco Chronicle
San Francisco Elevator
San Francisco Evening Bulletin
San Francisco People's World
San Francisco Western Worker
Sangamo (Illinois) Journal

Savannah (Georgia) Daily Morning News
Savannah (Georgia) Tribune
Seattle Times
Tampa Tribune
Time
Topeka Colored Citizen
USA Today
Vicksburg (Mississippi) Daily Whig
Vicksburg (Mississippi) Evening Post
Vicksburg (Mississippi) Herald
Vicksburg (Mississippi) Register
Vicksburg (Mississippi) Weekly Whig
Virginia Gazette
Virginia Star
Washington (D.C.) Bee
Washington (D.C.) National Era
Washington (D.C.) People's Advocate
Washington (D.C.) Post
Washington (D.C.) Southern Press
Wichita National Baptist World

PRIMARY SOURCES

Alabama Department of Archives and History
    Governor Thomas Kilby Papers
Atlanta University
    Association of Southern Women for the Prevention of Lynching (microfilm, University Microfilms International)
Birmingham Public Library
    Birmingham Police Department, Surveillance Files
    John Temple Graves Papers
California Historical Society
    William T. Sherman letters (North Baker Research Library)
Emory University
    Ralph McGill Papers (Robert W. Woodruff Library)
Library of Congress
    William O. Douglas Papers
    NAACP Papers
Library of Virginia
    Bedford County Court Order books
    Pittsylvania County Court Order books
Louisiana State University Library
    James Burns Wallace diary
Mississippi Department of Archives and History
    J. P. Coleman Papers
    Mississippi Supreme Court Records
National Archives, College Park, Maryland
    Civil Rights Division Files, Department of Justice, RG 60
    Records of the Attorney General's Office, Department of Justice, RG 60
    Department of Justice Central Files, RG 60
    Department of Justice Numerical Files, RG 60

National Archives, East Point Georgia
    District Court of the United States for the Northern District of Florida
    Circuit Court of the United States for the Western Division of the Southern District
    of Mississippi
National Archives, Washington, D.C.
    U.S. Supreme Court Appellate Case Files, RG 267
Tuskegee Institute
    News clippings file (microfilm)
University of California, Berkeley (Bancroft Library)
    William T. Coleman Papers
    Joseph Bryant Crockett Papers
    John Neely Johnson Papers
University of Michigan
    Frank Murphy Papers (microfilm)
University of North Carolina (Southern Historical Collection)
    David Schenck diary
    Howard A. Kester Papers
University of Southern Mississippi
    Theodore G. Bilbo Papers

PUBLISHED PRIMARY SOURCES

ABC News. "The Hanging Tree." *20/20* (July 7, 2000).
———. "Tension in Small Town Over Hanging Death of Raynard Johnson." *World News Tonight* (July 12, 2000).
Ames, Jessie Daniel. "Editorial Treatment of Lynchings." *Public Opinion Quarterly* 2 (January 1938): 77–80.
———. *The Changing Character of Lynching*. Atlanta, 1942.
Annual Report of the Adjutant General to the Governor of the State of Ohio for the Fiscal Year Ending November 15, 1894. Columbus: Westbote Co., 1895.
Audubon, John James. *Delineations of American Scenery and Character*. New York: G. A. Baker, 1926.
Beals, Melba Pattillo. *Warriors Don't Cry: A Searing Memoir of The Battle to Integrate Little Rock's Central High*. New York: Washington Square, 1994.
Bell, Major Horace. *Reminiscences of a Ranger or Early Times in Southern California*. Santa Barbara: Wallace Hebberd, 1927.
Birkbeck, Morris. *Notes on a Journey from the Coast of Virginia to the Territory of Illinois*. 1817; rev. ed., London, 1818.
Birney, James G. *Letters of James Gillespie Birney, 1831–1857*. Dwight L. Dumond, ed. 1938; reprint ed. Gloucester: Peter Smith, 1966.
Blackstone, William. *Commentaries on the Laws of England*. 1765–1769; reprint ed., Chicago: University of Chicago Press, 1979.
[Blane, William Newnham.] *An Excursion through the United States and Canada during the Years, 1822–23*. 1824; reprint ed. New York: Negro Universities Press, 1969.
The Bloodstained Trail. Seattle: The Industrial Worker, 1927,
Brande, W. T., ed. *A Dictionary of Science, Literature and Art*. London: Longman's Green and Co., 1865.
Cartwright, Marguerite. "The Mob Still Rides—Tuskegee Notwithstanding." *Crisis* 60 (April 1953): 222–223.
CBS News. "FBI Looking into Rumors and Suspicions that a Black Teenager was Lynched in Mississippi." *CBS Evening News* (July 13, 2000).
CNN. *CNN Breaking News*. (September 11, 2001).

CNN. "Mississippi Hanging Investigation: Suicide or Lynching." *Burden or Proof* (July 17, 2000).

CNN. "Hanging Death Mystery in Mississippi: Suicide or Murder." *Burden of Proof* (July 21, 2000).

Cabell, Margaret Coach Anthony. *Sketches and Recollections of Lynchburg by the Oldest Inhabitant.* Richmond: Wynne, 1858.

Chamlee, George W. "Is Lynching Ever Defensible? The Motives of Judge Lynch." *Forum* 76 (December 1926): 811–817.

Clark, Walter Van Tilburg. *The Ox-Bow Incident.* New York: Random House, 1940.

Cobbs, Elizabeth/Petric J. Smith. *Long Time Coming: An Insider's Story of the Birmingham Church Bombing that Rocked the World.* Birmingham: Crane Hill, 1994.

Cohee. "Lynch Law." *Harper's New Monthly Magazine* 18 (May 1859): 794–798.

Congress, House. *Joint Select Committee to Inquire into the Condition of Affairs in the Late Insurrection States.* 42nd Cong., 2nd sess. 13 volumes.

Congress, House. *Papers in the Contested Case of Sheave vs. Tillman in the Fourth Congressional District of Tennessee.* House Misc. Document 53, 41st Cong., 2nd sess.

Congress, House. *Indemnity to Relatives of Luis Moreno: Message from the President of the United States, Transmitting a Report from the Secretary of State with Accompanying Papers, Touching the Lynching in 1895, at Yreka. Cal., of Luis Moreno, a Mexican Citizen, and the Demand of the Mexican Government for Indemnity.* House report 237. 55th Cong., 2nd sess.

Congress, House. *Heirs of Certain Citizens of Italy: Message from the President of the United States, Transmitting A Communication from the Secretary of State Relating to the Outrages Committed by Citizens of the United States upon Citizens of Italy, and Recommending an Appropriation by Congress for the Relief of the Heirs of the Sufferers.* House document 37, 55th Cong., 1st sess.

Congress, Senate. *Lynching of Florentino Suaste.* Senate report 1832, 56th Cong., 2nd sess.

Congress, Senate. *Correspondence Regarding the Lynching of Certain Italian Subjects, Message from the President of the United States, transmitting, in Response to Resolution of the Senate of May 6, 1897, Calling for the Correspondence Regarding the Lynching in Louisiana of Certain Italian Subjects, A Report from the Secretary of State, with Accompanying Papers.* Senate document 104, 55th Cong., 1st sess.

Congressional Globe.

Congressional Record.

Cornet, Florence Dell. "The Experiences of a Midwest Salesman in 1836." *Missouri Historical Society Bulletin* (July 1973): 227–235.

Corrothers, James D, *In Spite of the Handicap.* New York: George H. Doran, 1916.

Creecy, James R. *Scenes in the South and Miscellaneous Pieces.* Washington: Thomas McGill, 1860.

Crime in the United States: Uniform Crime Reports. Washington: U.S. Government Printing Office, 2000.

Crockett, David. *Narrative of the Life of David Crockett.* Baltimore: E. L. Carey and A. Hart, 1834.

Curtis, Michael Kent. "The 1837 Killing of Elijah Lovejoy by an Anti-Abolition Mob: Free Speech, Mobs, Republican Government, and the Privileges of American Citizens." *UCLA Law Review* 44 (April 1997): 1126–1128.

Daniels, Josephus. *Editor in Politics.* Chapel Hill: University of North Carolina Press, 1941.

Dawson, Marion L. "The South and the Negro." *North American Review* 172 (January 1901): 279–284.

Defensor. *The Enemies of the Constitution Discovered, or, an Inquiry into the Origin and Tendency of Popular Violence, Containing a Complete and Circumstantial Account of the Unlawful Proceedings at the City of Utica, October 21st, 1835; The Dispersion of the State Anti-Slavery Convention by the Agitators, the Destruction of a Democratic Press, and of the Causes which Led Thereto, Together with a Concise Treatise on the Practice of the Court of His Honour Judge Lynch.* New York: Leavitt, Lord & Co., 1835.

Dennehy, William Francis. "Irish 'Outrages' in the Olden Time." *Catholic World* 35 (June 1882): 417–428.

Dimsdale, Thomas J. *The Vigilantes of Montana or Popular Justice in the Rocky Mountains.* Virginia City: Tilton, 1866.

Douglass, Frederick. *The Frederick Douglass Papers.* Ed. John Blassingame. New Haven: Yale University Press, 1979–1992.

Du Bois, W. E. B. *The Philadelphia Negro: A Social Study.* 1899; reprint ed., New York: Schocken, 1967.

———. *The Souls of Black Folk: Essays and Sketches.* Chicago: A. C. McClurg, 1903.

———. "W. E. B. Du Bois' Confrontation with White Liberalism During the Progressive Era: a *Phylon* Document." *Phylon* 35 (September 1974): 246.

———. *The Autobiography of W. E. B. DuBois: A Soliloquy on Viewing My Life from the Last Decade of its First Century.* N.p.: International, 1968.

Edgerton, Mary. *A Governor's Wife on the Mining Frontier: The Letters of Mary Edgerton from Montana, 1863–1865.* Ed. James L. Thane, Jr. Salt Lake City: University of Utah Press, 1976.

"Editorial: Lynch's Law." *Southern Literary Messenger* 2 (May 1836): 389.

Faux, William. *Memorable Days in America: Being a Journal of a Tour to the United States, Principally Undertaken to Ascertain, by Positive Evidence, the Condition and Probable Prospects of British Emigrants. . . .* London: W. Simpkins and R. Marshall, 1823.

Featherstonhaugh, G. W. *Excursion through the Slave States.* London: J. Murray, 1844.

Felton, Rebecca Latimer. *Country Life in Georgia in the Days of My Youth.* Atlanta: Index Printing Co., 1919.

Flint, James. *Letters from America.* Ed. Reuben Gold Thwaites. Cleveland: Clark, 1904.

Florcken, Herbert G. "The Law and Order View of the San Francisco Vigilance Committee of 1856." *California Historical Society Quarterly* 14 (December 1935): 350–374; ibid., 15 (March 1936): 70–87; ibid., 15 (June 1936): 143–162; ibid., 15 (September 1936): 247–275.

Fonda, Henry, as told to Howard Teichmann. *Fonda: My Life.* New York: New American Library, 1981.

Gaudet, Frances Joseph. *"He Leadeth Me."* 1913; reprint ed., New York: G. K. Hall, 1996.

General Laws of the Legislature of Alabama Passed at the Session of 1919. Montgomery: State Printers, 1919.

Graham, H. "Harrow School." *The Ladies' Repository* 4 (September 1869): 182.

Grant, Ulysses S. *The Papers of Ulysses S. Grant.* Ed. John Y. Simon. Carbondale: Southern Illinois University, 1967-.

Grund, Francis J. *The Americans in their Moral, Social, and Political Relations.* 1837; reprint ed., New York: Johnson, 1968.

Hall, James. *Letters from the West.* 1828; reprint ed., Gainesville: Scholars' Facsimiles, 1967.

Hening, William Waller. *The Statutes at Large: Being a Collection of all the Laws of Virginia.* 13 vols. Richmond, 1809–1823.

Hildreth, Richard. *Despotism in America: An Inquiry in the Nature, Results, and Legal Basis of the Slave-Holding System in the United States.* Boston: John P. Jewet, 1854.

Historical Statistics of the United States, Colonial Times to 1957. Washington, D.C., 1960.

Hodgson, Adam. *Letters from North America Written During a Tour in the United States and Canada.* London, 1824.

Hone, Philip. *The Diary of Philip Hone, 1828–1851.* Ed. Allan Nevins. 1927; reprint ed. New York: Kraus, 1969.

Huie, William Bradford. "The South Kills Another Negro." *American Mercury* 53 (November 1941): 535–545.

———. "The Shocking Story of Approved Killing in Mississippi." *Look* 20 (January 24, 1956): 46–50.

———. "What's Happened to the Emmett Till Killers?" *Look* (January 22, 1957): 63–67.

Hutchinson, William T. and William M. E. Rachel, eds. *The Papers of James Madison.* Chicago: University of Chicago Press, 1962.

[Ingraham, Joseph Holt.] *The Southwest.* 2 vols. New York: Harper and Brothers, 1835.

Irving, Washington. *A Tour of the Prairies.* Ed. John Francis McDermott. 1835: reprint ed., Norman: University of Oklahoma Press, 1956.

Irwin, Theodore. "The Klan Kicks up Again." *American Mercury* 50 (August 1940): 470–476.

Jefferson, Thomas. *The Papers of Thomas Jefferson.* Ed. Julian Boyd. Princeton: Princeton University Press, 1954-.

Judges and Criminals: Shadows of the Past, History of the Vigilance Committee of San Francisco, Cal. San Francisco: privately printed, 1858.

Kellogg, Louis Phelps, ed. *Frontier Retreat on the Upper Ohio, 1779-1781.* Madison: Wisconsin Historical Society, 1917.

Kernan, Thomas J. "The Jurisprudence of Lawlessness." Paper read before the American Bar Association at St. Paul, August 30, 1906.

Kilgo, John Carlisle. "An Inquiry Concerning Lynchings." *South Atlantic Quarterly* 1 (January 1902): 4-13.

Langford, Nathaniel Pitt. *Vigilante Days and Ways.* Boston: Cupples, 1890.

Lieber, Francis, ed. *Encyclopedia Americana.* Philadelphia: Thomas, Coperthwait and Co., 1840.

The Life and Adventures of John A. Murrell, the Great Western Land Pirate. New York: H. Long, 1847.

Lincoln, Abraham. *The Collected Works of Abraham Lincoln.* ed. Roy P. Basler. New Brunswick: Rutgers University Press, 1953.

Lodge, Henry Cabot. "Lynch Law and Unrestricted Immigration." *North American Review* 152 (1890): 602-612.

"Lynch Law." *Harper's Monthly* 18 (May 1859): 794-798.

"Lynch's Law." *Southern Literary Messenger* 2 (May 1836): 389.

"Lynch Law and Treason." *Literary Digest* 55 (August 18, 1917): 12-13.

Lynch, John Roy. *Reminiscences of an Active Life: The Autobiography of John Roy Lynch.* Ed. John Hope Franklin. Chicago: University of Chicago Press, 1970.

McConnell, J. L. *Western Characters or Types of Border Life in the Western States.* New York: Redfield, 1853.

McGowan, Edward. *Narrative of Edward McGowan.* San Francisco: privately printed, 1857.

Madison, James. *The Papers of James Madison.* Ed. Robert A. Rutland. Charlottesville: University Press of Virginia, 1984-.

Marrs, Elijah P. *Life and History of the Rev. Elijah P. Marrs.* Louisville: Bradley and Gilbert, 1885.

Martineau, Harriet. *Retrospect of Western Travel.* London, New York: Harper and Bros., 1838.

Matthews, Albert. "The Term Lynch Law." *Modern Philology* 2 (October 1904): 172-195.

Matthews, Catherine Van Cortlandt. *Andrew Ellicott, His Life and Letters.* New York: Grafton, 1908.

May, Samuel J. *Some Recollections of Our Antislavery Conflict.* Boston: Fields, Osgood & Co., 1869.

"Music and the Drama." *Appleton's Journal* 12 (October 24, 1874): 541.

Narrative of the Late Riotous Proceedings against the Liberty of the Press in Cincinnati with Remarks and Historical Notices Relating to Emancipation. Cincinnati, 1836.

National Public Radio. *All Things Considered.* (September 11, 2001).

Nelson, Jill. *Police Brutality: An Anthology.* New York: Norton, 2000.

Newmark, Maurice and Marco R. Newmark, eds. *Sixty Years in Southern California, 1853-1913: Containing the Reminiscences of Harris Newmark.* 3rd ed. Boston: Houghton Mifflin, 1930.

Nichols, Thomas. "Preaching to the Conscience." *Presbyterian Quarterly and Princeton Review* (January 1875): 18.

Ohio Adjutant General. *Annual Report of the Adjutant General to the Governor of the State of Ohio for the Fiscal Year Ending November 15, 1984.* Columbui: Westbote, 1895.

Ovington, Mary White. *Black and White Sat Down Together: The Reminiscences of an NAACP Founder.* New York: Feminist Press, 1995.

Oxford English Dictionary. Oxford: Clarendon Press, 1882-.

Page, Thomas Nelson. "The Lynching of Negroes—Its Cause and Its Prevention." *North American Review* 178 (January 1904): 33-48.

Page, Thomas Walker. "The Real Judge Lynch." *Atlantic Monthly* 88 (December 1901): 731-743.

Palmer, William P., ed. *Calendar of Virginia State Papers and other Manuscripts* 1883; reprint ed., New York: Kraus, 1968.

Phillips, William. *The Conquest of Kansas by Missouri and Her Allies.* Boston: Phillips, Sampson and Co., 1856.

Pickins, William. *The Heir of Slaves.* Boston: Pilgrim, 1911.

Pictures Tell the Story: Ernest C. Withers Reflections in History. Norfolk: Chrysler Museum of Art, 2000.

Piercy, Frederick Hawkins. *Route from Liverpool to Great Salt Lake Valley.* Ed. Fawn M. Brodie. 1855; new ed., Cambridge: Harvard University Press, 1962.

Pillsbury, Albert E. "A Brief Inquiry into Federal Remedy for Lynching." *Harvard Law Review* 15 (March 1902): 707–713.

Power, Tyrone. *Impressions of America During the Years 1833, 1834, and 1835.* London: P. Bentley, 1836.

Proceedings in the Ku Klux Klan Trials at Columbia, S.C. in the United States Circuit Court, November Term, 1871. Columbia: Republic Printing Co., 1872.

Ross, Harold. *Letters from the Editor: The New Yorker's Harold Ross.* Ed. Thomas Kunkel. New York: Modern Library, 2000.

Rovere, Richard H. "The Klan Rides Again." *The Nation* 150 (April 6, 1940): 445–446.

Sherman, William Tecumseh. *Memoirs of General William T. Sherman.* 1875; reprint ed., New York: Library of America, 1990.

Simms, William Gilmore. *Guy Rivers: A Tale of Georgia.* 2 vols. New York: Harper and Bros., 1834.
———. *Mellichampe, a Legend of the Santee.* New York: Harper and Bros., 1836.
———. *Border Beagles: A Tale of Mississippi.* 2 vols. Philadelphia: Carey and Hart, 1840.
———. *The History of South Carolina.* New York: Redfield, 1860.

Singleton, Arthur. *Letters from the South and West.* Boston, 1824.

Soule, Frank, John H. Gihon, James Nisbet. *The Annals of San Francisco.* New York: Appleton, 1855.

Supplemental Report of Joint Committee of the General Assembly of Louisiana on the Conduct of the Late Elections and the Condition of Peace and Good Order in the State. New Orleans: A. L. Lee, 1869.

Stearns, Charles. *The Black Man of the South and the Rebels; or, the Characteristics of the Former, and the Recent Outrages of the Latter.* Boston: American News, 1872.

Stuart, James. *Three Years in North America.* 2 vols. Edinburgh, 1833.

Tappan, Lewis. *The Life of Arthur Tappan.* 1871; reprint ed. Westport: Negro Universities Press, 1970.

Thaw, Harry K. *The Traitor: Being the Untampered with, Unrevised Account of the Trial and All that Led to It.* Philadelphia: Dorrance and Co., 1926.

Tourgee, Albion W. *A Fool's Errand.* Ed. John Hope Franklin. Cambridge: Belknap Press, 1961.

Tuttle, William M., Jr., "W. E. B. DuBois' Confrontation with White Liberalism During the Progressive Era: A Phylon Document." *Phylon* 35 (September 1974): 241–258.

Twain, Mark. *Roughing It.* Hartford, Conn.: American Publishing Co., 1872.

Vigne, Geogrey T. *Six Months in America.* London, 1832.

Waddell, Alfred M. "The Story of the Wilmington, N. C. Race Riots." *Colliers Weekly* 22 (November 26, 1898): 4–16.

Walker, Francis A., comp. *A Compendium of the Ninth Census.* Washington: Government Printing Office, 1872.

Washington, Booker T. *The Booker T. Washington Papers.* Ed. Louis R. Harlan and Raymond W. Smock. Urbana: University of Illinois Press, 1981.

Watson, Thomas E. "The Official Record in the Case of Leo Frank, a Jew Pervert." *Watson's Magazine* 21 (September 1915): 256.

Webster, A. F. "American Summer Resorts—Long Branch." *Appleton's Journal* 12 (October 3, 1874): 431.

Wells, Ida B. *Crusade for Justice: The Autobiography of Ida B. Wells.* Chicago: University of Chicago Press, 1970.

———. *A Red Record: Tabulated Statistics and Alleged Causes of Lynchings in the United States, 1892–1893–1894.* Chicago, 1895.

———. *Southern Horrors: Lynch Law in all its Phases* in Jacqueline Jones Royster, ed. *Southern Horrors and Other Writings: the Anti-Lynching Campaign of Ida B. Wells, 1892–1900.* Boston: Bedford, 1997.

———. *Mob Rule in New Orleans: Robert Charles and his Fight to the Death.* Chicago, 1900 in Jacqueline Jones Royster, ed. *Southern Horrors and Other Writings: the Anti-Lynching Campaign of Ida B. Wells, 1892–1900.* Boston: Bedford, 1997.

———. *The Memphis Diary of Ida B. Wells.* Ed. Miriam Decosta-Willis. Boston: Beacon, 1995.

———. *Lynch Law in Georgia.* Chicago, 1899.

West, Goldsmith B. *The Hawes Horror and Bloody Riot at Birmingham: A Truthful Story of What Happened.* Birmingham: Caldwell Printing, 1888.

White, Walter. *Rope and Faggot: A Biography of Judge Lynch.* 1929; reprint ed., New York: Arno Press, 1969.

———. *A Man Called White: The Autobiography of Walter White.* 1948; reprint ed., Athens: University of Georgia Press, 1995.

———. "The Costigan-Wagner Bill." *Crisis* 42 (January 1935): 10–11.

Williams, Will. "Our London Letter." *Appleton's Journal* 13 (March 20, 1875): 330.

Worcester, James E. *A Universal and Critical Dictionary of the English Language.* Boston: Wilkins, Carter, and Co., 1846.

Zell's Popular Encyclopedia, a Universal Dictionary of English Language, Science, Literature, and Art. Philadelphia: Zell, 1871.

BOOKS

Acuna, Rodolfo. *Occupied America: A History of Chicanos.* 3rd ed. New York: Harper and Row, 1988.

Akers, Monte. *Flames After Midnight: Murder, Vengeance and the Desolation of a Texas Community.* Austin: University of Texas Press, 1999.

Allen, James, Hilton Als, John Lewis, and Leon F. Litwack. *Without Sanctuary: Lynching Photography in America.* N.p.: Twin Palms, 2000.

Apple, Rima D. and Janet Golden, eds. *Mothers and Motherhood: Readings in American History.* Columbus: Ohio State University Press, 1997.

Archer, Leonard C. *Black Images in the American Theatre: NAACP Protest Campaigns—Stage, Screen, Radio, and Television.* Brooklyn: Pageant-Poseidon, 1973.

Austin, J. L. *How to do things with Words.* 1962; reprint ed., Cambridge: Harvard University Press, 1975.

Ayers, Edward. *Vengenace and Justice: Crime and Punishment in the 19th-Century American South.* New York: Oxford University Press, 1984.

———. *The Promise of the New South: Life After Reconstruction.* New York: Oxford University Press, 1992.

Baker, Jean. *Affairs of Party: The Political Culture of Northern Democrats in the Mid-Nineteenth Century.* Ithaca: Cornell University Press, 1983.

Baker, Keith Michael. *Inventing the French Revolution.* Cambridge: Cambridge University Press, 1990.

Baker, Liva. *Felix Frankfurter.* New York: Coward-McCann, 1969.

Ball, Howard. *Hugo L. Black: Cold Steel Warrior.* New York: Oxford University Press, 1996.

Bancroft, Hubert Howe. *Popular Tribunals.* San Francisco: History Co., 1887.

Barak, Gregg. *Media, Process, and the Social Construction of Crime: Studies in Newsmaking Criminology.* New York: Garland, 1994.

Bardaglio, Peter W. *Reconstructing the Household: Families, Sex, and the Law in the Nineteenth-Century South.* Chapel Hill: University of North Carolina Press, 1995.

Barnes, Kenneth C. *Who Killed John Clayton? Political Violence and the Emergence of the New South, 1861–1893.* Durham: Duke University Press, 1998.

Bartley, Numan V., ed. *The Evolution of Southern Culture.* Athens: University of Georgia Press, 1988.

Bass, Jack. *Taming the Storm: The Life and Times of Judge Frank M. Johnson, Jr. and the South's Fight Over Civil Rights.* New York: Doubleday, 1993.

Bederman, Gail. *Manliness and Civilization: A Cultural History of Gender and Race in the United States, 1880–1917.* Chicago: University of Chicago Press, 1995.

Beik, William. *Urban Protest in Seventeenth-Century France: the Culture of Retribution.* Cambridge: Cambridge University Press, 1997.

Belknap, Michal R. *Federal Law and Southern Order: Racial Violence and Constitutional Conflict in the Post-Brown South.* Athens: University of Georgia Press, 1987.

Bellesiles, Michael A., ed., *Lethal Imagination: Violence and Brutality in American History.* New York: New York University Press, 1999.

Bensel, Richard Franklin. *The Origins of Central State Authority in America, 1859–1877.* Cambridge: Cambridge University Press, 1990.

Berwanger, Eugene H. *The Frontier Against Slavery: Western Anti-Negro Prejudice and the Slavery Extension Controversy.* Urbana: University of Illinois Press, 1967.

Birney, Hoffman. *Vigilantes.* Philadelphia: Penn Publishing, 1929.

Blee, Kathleen M. *Women of the Klan: Racism and Gender in the 1920s.* Berkeley: University of California Press, 1991.

Boder, David P. *I Did Not Interview the Dead.* Urbana: University of Illinois Press, 1949.

Braden, Waldo W., ed. *Oratory in the New South.* Baton Rouge: Louisiana State University Press, 1979.

Branch, E. Douglas. *The Sentimental Years, 1836–1860.* New York: Hill and Wang, 1962.

Branch, Taylor. *Parting the Waters: America in the King Years, 1954–63.* New York: Simon and Schuster, 1988.

Brooke, John L. *The Heart of the Commonwealth: Society and Political Culture in Worcester County, Massachusetts, 1713–1861.* Amherst: University of Massachusetts Press, 1989.

Brown, Herbert Ross. *The Sentimental Novel in America, 1789–1860.* New York: Pageant, 1959.

Brown, Mary Jane. *Eradicating this Evil: Women and the American Anti-Lynching Movement, 1892–1940.* New York: Garland, 2000.

Brown, Richard D. *Knowledge is Power: The Diffusion of Information in Early America, 1700–1865.* New York: Oxford University Press, 1989.

Brown, Richard Maxwell. *Strain of Violence: Historical Studies of American Violence and Vigilantism.* New York: Oxford University Press, 1975.

———. *No Duty to Retreat: Violence and Values in American History and Society.* New York: Oxford University Press, 1991.

Bruce, Dickson D., Jr. *Violence and Culture in the Antebellum South.* Austin: University of Texas Press, 1979.

Brundage, W. Fitzhugh. *Lynching in the New South: Georgia and Virginia, 1880–1930.* Urbana: University of Illinois Press, 1993.

———., ed. *Under Sentence of Death: Lynching in the South.* Chapel Hill: University of North Carolina Press, 1997.

Capeci, Domenic J., Jr. *The Lynching of Cleo Wright.* Lexington: University Press of Kentucky, 1998.

Carter, Dan. *Scottsboro: A Tragedy of the American South.* 1969; reprint ed., New York: Oxford University Press, 1975.

———. *When the War was Over: The Failure of Self-Reconstruction in the South, 1865–1867.* Baton Rouge: Louisiana State University Press, 1985.

Chadbourn, James Harmon. *Lynching and the Law.* Chapel Hill: University of North Carolina Press, 1933.

Clement, Maud Carter. *The History of Pittsylvania County, Virginia.* Lynchburg: J. P. Bell, 1929.

Cohen, Paula Marantz. *Silent Film and the Triumph of the American Myth.* New York: Oxford University Press, 2001.

Conway, Alan. *The Reconstruction of Georgia.* Minneapolis: University of Minnesota Press, 1966.

Cortner, Richard C. *A "Scottsboro" Case in Mississippi: The Supreme Court and Brown v. Mississippi.* Jackson: University Press of Mississippi, 1986.

Courtwright, David T. *Violent Land: Single Men and Social Disorder from the Frontier to the Inner City.* Cambridge: Harvard University Press, 1996.

Cox, Oliver. *Caste, Class, and Race: A Study in Social Dynamics.* 1948; reprint ed., New York, 1970.

Crouthamel, James L. *Bennett's New York Herald and the Rise of the Popular Press.* Syracuse: Syracuse University Press, 1989.

Cushman, Barry. *Rethinking the New Deal Court: The Structure of a Constitutional Revolution.* New York: Oxford University Press, 1998.

Cushman, Dan. *Montana—The Gold Frontier.* Great Falls: Stay Away Joe, 1973.

Cutler, James Elbert. *Lynch Law: An Investigation into the History of Lynching in the United States.* 1905; reprint ed., New York: Negro Universities Press, 1969.

Dabney, Virginius. *Below the Potomac: A Book about the New South.* 1942; reprint ed., Port Washington: Kennikat Press, 1969.

Dailey, Jane, Glenda Elizabeth Gilmore, and Bryant Simon, eds. *Jumpin' Jim Crow: Southern Politics from Civil War to Civil Rights.* Princeton: Princeton University Press, 2000.

Davis, Angela Y. *Blues Legacies and Black Feminism: Gertrude "Ma" Rainey, Bessie Smith, and Billie Holiday.* New York: Pantheon Books, 1998.

Davis, James E. *Frontier Illinois.* Bloomington: Indiana University Press, 1998.

Davis, Natalie Zemon. *Society and Culture in Early Modern France.* Stanford: Stanford University Press, 1975.

DeLaughter, Bobby. *Never too Late: A Prosecutor's Story of Justice in the Medgar Evers Case.* New York: Scribner, 2001.

Denham, James M. *"A Rogue's Paradise": Crime and Punishment in Antebellum Florida, 1821–1861.* Tuscaloosa: University of Alabama Press, 1997.

Dinnerstein, Leonard. *The Leo Frank Case.* 1966; reprint ed., Athens: University of Georgia Press, 1987.

Dittmer, John. *Local People: The Struggle for Civil Rights in Mississippi.* Urbana: University of Illinois Press, 1994.

Dollard, John. *Caste and Class in a Southern Town.* 1937; rev. ed. Garden City: Doubleday, 1957.

D'Orso, Michael. *Like Judgment Day: The Ruin and Redemption of a Town Called Rosewood.* New York: Putnam's Sons, 1996.

Douglas, Ann. *Terrible Honesty: Mongrel Manhattan in the 1920s.* New York: Noonday, 1995.

Downey, Dennis B., and Raymond M. Hyser. *No Crooked Death: Coatesville, Pennsylvania, and the Lynchings of Zachariah Walker.* Urbana: University of Illinois Press, 1991.

Dray, Philip. *At the Hands of Parties Unknown: The Lynching of Black America.* New York: Random House, 2002.

Dudziak, Mary L. *Cold War Civil Rights: Race and the Image of American Democracy.* Princeton: Princeton University Press, 2000.

Dunne, Gerald T. *Hugo Black and the Judicial Revolution.* New York: Simon and Schuster, 1977.

Dunning, William Archibald. *Reconstruction: Political and Economic, 1865–1877.* New York: Harper, 1907.

Eckenrode, H. J. *The Revolution in Virginia.* 1916; reprint ed., Hamden: Archon, 1964.

Egerton, John. *Speak Now Against the Day: The Generation Before the Civil Rights Movement in the South.* New York: Knopf, 1994.

Ellsworth, Scott. *Death in a Promised Land: The Tulsa Race Riot of 1921.* Baton Rouge: Louisiana State University Press, 1982.

Emery, Michael, Edwin Emery, and Nancy L. Roberts. *The Press and America: An Interpretative History of the Mass Media.* Ninth ed. Boston: Allyn and Bacon, 2000.

Evers, Mrs. Medgar, with William Peters. *For Us, the Living.* New York: Doubleday, 1967.

Fabian, Ann. *Card Sharps, Dream Books, and Bucket Shops: Gambling in 19th-Century America.* Ithaca: Cornell University Press, 1990.

Fairman, Charles. *Reconstruction and Reunion, 1864–88.* New York: Macmillan, 1987.

Farrell, Harry. *Swift Justice: Murder and Vengeance in a California Town.* New York: St. Martin's Press, 1992.

Fedo, Michael. *The Lynchings in Duluth.* 1979; reprint ed., St. Paul: Minnesota Historical Society, 2000.

Feldman, Glenn. *Politics, Society, and the Klan in Alabama, 1915–1949.* Tuscaloosa: University of Alabama Press, 1999.

Ferrell, Claudine L. *Nightmare and Dream: Antilynching in Congress, 1917–1922.* New York: Garland, 1986.

Findlay, John M. *People of Chance: Gambling in American Society from Jamestown to Las Vegas.* New York: Oxford University Press, 1986.

Fine, Sidney. *Frank Murphy: The Washington Years.* Ann Arbor: University of Michigan Press, 1984.

Fischer, David Hackett. *Albion's Seed: Four British Folkways in America.* New York: Oxford University Press, 1989.

Fleming, Walter L. *Civil War and Reconstruction in Alabama.* New York: Columbia University Press, 1905.

Foner, Eric. *Reconstruction: America's Unfinished Revolution, 1863–1877.* New York: Harper and Row, 1988.

Fossett, Judith Jackson and Jeffrey A. Tucker, eds. *Race Consciousness: African-American Studies for the New Century.* New York: New York University Press, 1997.

Frederickson, George M. *The Black Image in the White Mind: The Debate on Afro-American Character and Destiny, 1817–1914.* New York: Harper and Row, 1971.

Furet, François. *Interpreting the French Revolution.* Trans. Elborg Forster. Cambridge: Cambridge University Press, 1981.

Gaines, Kevin K. *Uplifting the Race: Black Leadership, Politics, and Culture in the Twentieth Century.* Chapel Hill: University of North Carolina Press, 1996.

Gale, Robert L., ed. *Nineteenth-Century American Western Writers.* Detroit: Gale, 1997.

Gambino, Richard. *Vendetta: A True Story of the Worst Lynching in America, the Mass Murder of Italian-Americans in New Orleans in 1891, the Vicious Motivations Behind It, and the Tragic Repercussions that Linger to this Day.* Garden City: Doubleday, 1977.

Garner, James W. *Reconstruction in Mississippi.* 1901; reprint ed., Baton Rouge: Louisiana State University Press, 1968.

Gilje, Paul A. *The Road to Mobocracy: Popular Disorder in New York City, 1763–1834.* Chapel Hill: University of North Carolina Press, 1987.

———. *Rioting in America.* Bloomington: Indiana University Press, 1996.

Gilmore, Glenda Elizabeth. *Gender and Jim Crow: Women and the Politics of White Supremacy in North Carolina, 1896–1920.* Chapel Hill: University of North Carolina Press, 1996.

Ginzburg, Ralph. *100 Years of Lynchings.* 1962; reprint ed., Baltimore: Black Classics Press, 1988.

Glendinning, Victoria. *Rebecca West: A Life.* London: Weidenfeld and Nicolson, 1987.

Goodman, James. *Stories of Scottsboro.* New York: Vintage, 1994.

Grant, Donald L. *The Way it was in the South: The Black Experience in Georgia.* New York: Carol, 1993.

Green, Ben. *Before His Time: The Untold Story of Harry T. Moore, America's First Civil Rights Martyr.* New York: Free Press, 1999.

Greenberg, Kenneth S. *Honor and Slavery: Lies, Duels, Noses, Masks, Dressing as a Woman, Gifts, Strangers, Humanitarianism, Death, Slave Rebellions, the Proslavery Argument, Baseball, Hunting, and Gambling in the Old South.* Princeton: Princeton University Press, 1996.

Greene, Melissa Fay. *The Temple Bombing*. Reading, Mass.: Addison Wesley, 1996.

Grimsted, David. *American Mobbing, 1828–1861: Toward Civil War*. New York: Oxford University Press, 1998.

Guilds, John Caldwell and Caroline Collins, eds. *William Gilmore Simms and the American Frontier* Athens: University of Georgia Press, 1997.

Hale, Grace Elizabeth. *Making Whiteness: The Culture of Segregation in the South, 1890–1940*. New York: Pantheon, 1998.

Hall, Jacquelyn Dowd. *Revolt Against Chivalry: Jessie Daniel Ames and the Women's Campaign Against Lynching*. Revised ed. New York: Columbia University Press, 1993.

Hall, Kermit, James W. Ely, eds. *An Uncertain Tradition: Constitutionalism and the History of the South*. Athens, London: University of Georgia Press, 1989.

Halpern, Rick. *Down on the Killing Floor: Black and White Workers in Chicago's Packinghouses, 1904–54*. Urbana: University of Illinois Press, 1997.

Halttunen, Karen. *Confidence Men and Painted Women: A Study of Middle-Class Culture in America, 1830–1870*. New Haven: Yale University Press, 1982.

Hardt, Michael and Antonio Negri. *Empire*. Cambridge: Harvard University Press, 2000.

Harlan, Louis R. *Booker T. Washington: The Making of a Black Leader, 1856–1901*. New York: Oxford University Press, 1972.

Harris, Trudier. *Exorcising Blackness: Historical and Literary Lynching and Burning Rituals*. Bloomington: Indiana University Press, 1984.

Harris, William C. *The Day of the Carpetbagger: Republican Reconstruction in Mississippi*. Baton Rouge: Louisiana State University Press, 1979.

Haskell, Thomas L. *The Emergence of Professional Social Science: The American Social Science Association and the Nineteenth-Century Crisis of Authority*. Urbana: University of Illinois Press, 1977.

Higginbotham, Evelyn Brooks. *Righteous Discontent: The Women's Movement in the Black Baptist Church, 1880–1920*. Cambridge: Harvard University Press, 1993.

Hirsch, H. N. *The Enigma of Felix Frankfurter*. New York: Basic Books, 1981.

Hodes, Martha. *White Women, Black Men: Illicit Sex in the 19th-Century South*. New Haven: Yale University Press, 1997.

Hoffman, Ronald, Thad W. Tate, and Peter J. Albert, eds. *An Uncivil War: The Southern Backcountry during the American Revolution*. Charlottesville: University Press of Virginia, 1985.

Holmes, William F. *The White Chief: James Kimble Vardaman*. Baton Rouge: Louisiana State University Press, 1970.

Horn, Stanley F. *Invisible Empire: The Story of the Ku Klux Klan*. 1939; reprint ed., New York: Haskell, 1973.

Horwitz, Tony. *Confederates in the Attic: Dispatches from the Unfinished Civil War*. New York: Pantheon, 1998.

Howard, Gene L. *Death at Cross Plains: An Alabama Reconstruction Tragedy*. University: University of Alabama Press, 1984.

Howard, J. Woodford, Jr. *Mr. Justice Murphy: A Political Biography*. Princeton: Princeton University Press, 1968.

Howe, Henry. *Historical Collections of Virginia; Containing a Collection of the Most Interesting Facts, Traditions, Biographical Sketches, Anecdotes, &c. Relating to its History and Antiquities*. Charleston: Babcock, 1852.

Huie, William Bradford. *Ruby McCollum: Woman in the Suwannee Jail*. New York: E. P. Dutton, 1956.

Hurt, Frances Hallam. *An Intimate History of the American Revolution in Pittsylvania County, Virginia*. Danville: Womack Press, 1976.

Ignatiev, Noel. *How the Irish Became White*. New York, London: Routledge, 1995.

Irons, Peter H. *The New Deal Lawyers*. Princeton: Princeton University Press, 1982.

Jackson, Jesse. *Legal Lynching: Racism, Injustice, and the Death Penalty*. New York: Marlowe, 1996.

Jordan, Winthrop D. *Tumult and Silence at Second Creek: An Inquiry into a Civil War Slave Conspiracy*. Baton Rouge: Louisiana State University Press, 1993.

Kaczorowski, Robert J. *The Politics of Judicial Interpretation: The Federal Courts, the Department of Justice, and Civil Rights, 1866–1876*. New York: Oceana, 1985.

Kantrowitz, Stephen. *Ben Tillman and the Reconstruction of White Supremacy*. Chapel Hill: University of North Carolina Press, 2000.

Kelly, Brian. *Race, Class, and Power in the Alabama Coalfields, 1908–21*. Urbana: University of Illinois Press, 2001.

Klein, Rachel N. *Unification of a Slave State: The Rise of the Planter Class in the South Carolina Backcountry, 1760–1808*. Chapel Hill: University of North Carolina Press, 1990.

Klinkner, Philip A., with Rogers M. Smith. *The Unsteady March: The Rise and Decline of Racial Equality in America*. Chicago: University of Chicago Press, 1999.

Lamar, Howard R., ed. *The New Encyclopedia of the American West*. New Haven: Yale University Press, 1998.

Lane, Ann J. *The Brownsville Affair: National Crisis and Black Reaction*. Port Washington, N.Y.: Kennikat, 1971.

Lash, Joseph P. *From the Diaries of Felix Frankfurter*. New York: W. W. Norton, 1975.

Lewis, David Levering. *W. E. B. Du Bois: Biography of a Race, 1868–1919*. New York: Henry Holt, 1993.

Litwack, Leon. *Been in the Storm So Long: The Aftermath of Slavery*. New York: Vintage, 1979.

———. *Trouble in Mind: Black Southerners in the Age of Jim Crow*. New York: Knopf, 1998.

Lockley, Fred. *Vigilante Days at Virginia City*. Portland: privately printed, n.d.

Logan, Shirley Wilson. *"We Are Coming": The Persuasive Discourse of Nineteenth-Century Black Women*. Carbondale: Southern Illinois University Press, 1999.

McCaslin, Richard B. *Tainted Breeze: The Great Hanging at Gainesville, Texas, 1862*. Baton Rouge: Louisiana State University Press, 1994.

MacDonald, Fred. *Don't Touch That Dial: Radio Programming in American Life, 1920–1960*. Chicago: Nelson-Hall, 1979.

McGovern, James R. *Anatomy of a Lynching: The Killing of Claude Neal*. Baton Rouge: Louisiana State University Press, 1982.

McIlhany. William H., II. *Klandestine: The Untold Story of Delmar Dennis and his Role in the FBI's War Against the Ku Klux Klan*. New Rochelle: Arlington House, 1975.

McMurry, Linda O. *To Keep the Waters Troubled: The Life of Ida B. Wells*. New York: Oxford University Press, 1998.

———. *Recorder of the Black Experience: A Biography of Monroe Nathan Work*. Baton Rouge: Louisiana State University Press, 1985.

McWhiney, Grady. *Cracker Culture: Celtic Ways in the Old South*. Tuscaloosa: University of Alabama Press, 1988.

Madison, James H. *A Lynching in the Heartland: Race and Memory in America*. New York: Palgrave, 2001.

Margolick, David. *Strange Fruit: Billie Holiday, Cafe Society, and an Early Cry for Civil Rights*. Philadelphia: Running Press, 2000.

Mars, Florence, with Lynn Eden. *Witness in Philadelphia*. Baton Rouge: Louisiana State University Press, 1977.

Massengill, Reed. *Portrait of a Racist: The Man Who Killed Medgar Evers?* New York: St. Martins Press, 1994.

Mather, R. E. and E. E. Boswell. *Hanging the Sheriff: A Biography of Henry Plummer*. Salt Lake City: University of Utah Press, 1987.

Mayer, Jane and Jill Abramson. *Strange Justice: The Selling of Clarence Thomas*. Boston: Houghton Mifflin, 1994.

Mercer, A. S. *The Banditti of the Plains or the Cattlemen's Invasion of Wyoming in 1892*. 1894; reprint ed. Norman: University of Oklahoma Press, 1954.

Miller, Ericka M. *The Other Reconstruction: Where Violence and Womanhood Meet in the Writings of Wells-Barnett, Grimke, and Larsen*. New York: Garland, 2000.

Mirande, Alfredo. *Gringo Justice.* Notre Dame: Notre Dame University Press, 1987.

Morris, Christopher. *Becoming Southern: The Evolution of a Way of Life, Warren County and Vicksburg, Mississippi, 1770–1860.* New York: Oxford University Press, 1995.

Morris, Willie, *The Ghosts of Medgar Evers: A Tale of Race, Murder, Mississippi, and Hollywood.* New York: Random House, 1998.

Morrison, Toni, ed. *Race-ing Justice, En-Gendering Power: Essays on Anita Hill, Clarence Thomas, and the Construction of Social Reality.* New York: Pantheon, 1992.

Mullen, Kevin J. *Let Justice Be Done: Crime and Politics in Early San Francisco.* Reno and Las Vegas: University of Nevada Press, 1989.

Murray, David, Joel Schwartz, and S. Robert Liechter. *It Ain't Necessarily So: How the Media Make and Unmake the Scientific Picture of Reality.* Lanham: Rowman and Littlefield, 2001.

Newman, Roger K. *Hugo Black: A Biography.* New York: Pantheon, 1994.

Niewyk, Donald L. *Fresh Wounds: Early Narratives of Holocaust Survival.* Chapel Hill: University of North Carolina Press, 1998.

Nossiter, Adam. *Of Long Memory: Mississippi and the Murder of Medgar Evers.* Reading, Mass.: Addison Wesley, 1994.

Novick, Peter. *That Noble Dream: The "Objectivity Question" and the American Historical Profession.* Cambridge: Cambridge University Press, 1988.

———. *The Holocaust in American Life.* Boston, New York: Houghton Mifflin, 1999.

O'Brien, Frank. *The Story of the New York Sun, 1833–1928.* New York, London: Appleton, 1928.

O'Brien, Gail Williams. *The Color of the Law: Race, Violence, and Justice in the Post–World War II South.* Chapel Hill: University of North Carolina Press, 1999.

Olsen, Otto. *Carpetbagger's Crusade: The Life of Albion Winegar Tourgee.* Baltimore: Johns Hopkins University Press, 1965.

Orr, Linda. *Headless History: Nineteenth-Century French Historiography of the Revolution.* Ithaca: Cornell University Press, 1990.

Ottley, Roi. *The Lonely Warrior: The Life and Times of Robert S. Abbott.* Chicago: Henry Regnery Co., 1955.

Paludan, Phillip Shaw. *"A People's Contest": The Union and Civil War, 1861–1865.* New York: Harper and Row, 1988.

Papashvily, Helen Waite. *All the Happy Endings: A Study of the Domestic Novel in America, the Women who Wrote it, the Women who Read it, in the Nineteenth Century.* New York: Harper, 1956.

Papke, David Ray. *Framing the Criminal: Crime, Cultural Work and the Loss of Critical Perspective, 1830–1900.* Hamden, Conn.: Archon Books, 1987.

Parrish, Randall. *Historic Illinois: The Romance of the Earlier Days.* Chicago: McClurg, 1906.

Pasley, Jeffrey L. *"The Tyranny of Printers": Newspaper Politics in the Early American Republic.* Charlottesville: University Press of Virginia, 2001.

Penn, I. Garland. *The Afro-American Press and Its Editors.* 1891; reprint ed., New York: Arno Press, 1969.

Percy, Alfred. *Origin of the Lynch Law, 1780.* Madison Heights, Va.: Percy Press, 1959.

Perkins, Kathy A., Judith L. Stephens, eds. *Strange Fruit: Plays on Lynching by American Women.* Bloomington: Indiana University Press, 1998.

Perman, Michael. *The Road to Redemption: Southern Politics, 1869–1879.* Chapel Hill: University of North Carolina Press, 1984.

———. *Struggle for Mastery: Disfranchisement in the South, 1888–1908.* Chapel Hill: University of North Carolina Press, 2001.

Phelps, Timothy M. and Helen Winternitz. *Capitol Games: Clarence Thomas, Anita Hill, and the Story of a Supreme Court Nomination.* New York: Hyperion, 1992.

Pitt, Leonard. *The Decline of Californios: A Social History of the Spanish-Speaking Californians: 1846–1890.* Berkeley: University of California Press, 1966.

Ponton, M. M. *Life and Times of Henry M. Turner.* 1917; New York: Negro Universities Press, 1970.

Pritchett, C. Herman. *The Roosevelt Court: A Study in Judicial Politics and Values, 1937–1947.* New York: MacMillan, 1948.

Putnam, Robert D. *Bowling Alone: The Collapse and Revival of American Community.* New York: Simon and Schuster, 2000.

Ragan, Sandra L., Dianne G. Bystrom, Lynda Lee Kaid, and Christina S. Beck. *The Lynching of Language: Gender, Politics, and Power in the Hill-Thomas Hearings.* Urbana, Chicago: University of Illinois Press, 1996.

Reid, John Phillip. *Policing the Elephant: Crime, Punishment, and Social Behavior on the Overland Trail.* San Marino: Huntington Library, 1997.

Richards, Leonard L. *"Gentlemen of Property and Standing": Anti-Abolition Mobs in Jacksonian America.* New York: Oxford, 1970.

Rohrbough, Malcolm J. *The Trans-Appalachian Frontier: People, Societies, and Institutions, 1775–1850.* New York: Oxford University Press. 1978.

———. *Days of Gold: The California Gold Rush and the American Nation.* Berkeley: University of California Press, 1997.

Rothert, Otto A. *The Outlaws of Cave-in-Rock.* Cleveland: Arthur H. Clark, 1924.

Royster, Jacqueline Jones. *Southern Horrors and Other Writings: The Anti-Lynching Campaign of Ida B. Wells, 1892–1900.* Boston: Bedford, 1997.

Savage, Barbara Dianne. *Broadcasting Freedom: Radio, War, and the Politics of Race, 1938 to 1948.* Chapel Hill: University of North Carolina Press, 1999.

Savage, W. Sherman. *The Controversy Over the Distribution of Abolition Literature, 1830–1860.* N.p.: Association for the Study of Negro Life and History, Inc., 1938.

Schechter, Patricia A. *Ida B. Wells Barnett and American Reform, 1880–1930.* Chapel Hill: University of North Carolina Press, 2001.

Schiller, Dan. *Objectivity and the News: The Public and the Rise of Commercial Journalism.* Philadelphia: University of Pennsylvania Press, 1981.

Schoolcraft, Henry Rowe. *Rude Pursuits and Rugged Peaks: Schoolcraft's Ozark Journal.* Fayetteville: University of Arkansas Press, 1996.

Secrest, William B. *Juanita.* Fresno: Saga-West, 1967.

Selby, John E. *The Revolution in Virginia, 1775–1783.* Williamsburg: Colonial Williamsburg Foundation, 1988.

Senkewicz, Robert M. *Vigilantes in Gold Rush San Francisco.* Stanford: Stanford University Press, 1985.

Sewell, William H., Jr. *A Rhetoric of Bourgeois Revolution: The Abbe Sieyes and What Is the Third Estate?* Durham: Duke University Press, 1994.

Shapiro, Herbert. *White Violence and Black Response from Reconstruction to Montgomery.* Amherst: University of Massachusetts Press, 1988.

Shinn, Charles Howard. *Mining Camps: A Study in American Frontier Government.* 1884; reprint ed., New York: Harper and Row, 1965.

Silverman, Kenneth. *Edgar A. Poe: Mournful and Never-Ending Remembrance.* New York: HarperCollins, 1991.

Silverstein, Mark. *Constitutional Faiths: Felix Frankfurter, Hugo Black, and the Process of Judicial Decision Making.* Ithaca: Cornell University Press, 1984.

Simon, Bryant. *A Fabric of Defeat: The Politics of South Carolina Millhands, 1910–1948.* Chapel Hill: University of North Carolina Press, 1998.

Simon, James F. *The Antagonists: Hugo Black, Felix Frankfurter, and Civil Liberties in Modern America.* New York: Simon and Schuster, 1989.

Singleton, M. K. *H. L. Mencken and the American Mercury Adventure.* Durham: Duke University Press, 1962.

Slotkin, Richard. *The Fatal Environment: The Myth of the Frontier in the Age of Industrialization, 1800–1890.* Middletown: Wesleyan University Press, 1985.

—————. *Gunfighter Nation: The Myth of the Frontier in Twentieth-Century America.* New York: Atheneum, 1992.

Smead, Howard. *Blood Justice: The Lynching of Mack Charles Parker.* New York: Oxford University Press, 1986.

Smith, Duane A. *Rocky Mountain Mining Camps: The Urban Frontier.* Bloomington: Indiana University Press, 1967.

Smith, Helena Huntington. *The War on Powder River.* Lincoln: University of Nebraska Press, 1966.

Smith, Kimberly. *The Dominion of Voice: Riot, Reason, and Romance in American Politics.* Lawrence: University Press of Kansas, 1999.

Snively, W. D., Jr., and Louanna Furbee. *Satan's Ferryman: A True Tale of the Old Frontier.* N.p.: Frederick Ungar, 1968.

Spencer, C. Tucker, ed. *Encyclopedia of the Vietnam War: A Political, Social, and Military History.* Santa Barbara: ABC-Clio, 1998.

Sterling, Christopher H. and John M. Kittross. *Stay Tuned: A Concise History of American Broadcasting.* 1978; 2d ed., Belmont: Wadsworth, 1990.

Stewart, James Brewer. *Holy Warriors: The Abolitionists and American Slavery.* New York: Hill and Wang, 1976.

Sunderland, Lane V. *Popular Government and the Supreme Court: Securing the Public Good and Private Rights.* Lawrence: University Press of Kansas, 1996.

Taylor, William. *Cavalier and Yankee: The Old South and American National Character.* Cambridge: Harvard University Press, 1979.

Thornbrough, Emma Lou. *T. Thomas Fortune: Militant Journalist.* Chicago: University of Chicago Press, 1972.

Thornton, J. Mills, III. *Politics and Power in a Slave Society: Alabama, 1800–1860.* Baton Rouge: Louisiana State University Press, 1978.

Tolnay, Stewart E. and E. M. Beck. *A Festival of Violence: An Analysis of Southern Lynchings, 1882–1930.* Urbana: University of Illinois Press, 1995.

Trelease, Allen W. *White Terror: The Ku Klux Klan Conspiracy and Southern Reconstruction.* Baton Rouge: Louisiana State University Press, 1971.

Tucher, Andie. *Froth and Scum: Truth, Beauty, Goodness, and the Ax Murder in America's First Mass Medium.* Chapel Hill: University of North Carolina Press, 1994.

Tucker, Spencer C., ed. *Encyclopedia of the Vietnam War: A Political, Social, and Military History.* Santa Barbara: ABC-Clio, 1998.

Vandal, Gilles. *Rethinking Southern Violence: Homicides in Post–Civil War Louisiana, 1866–1884.* Columbus: Ohio State University, 2000.

Vollers, Maryanne. *Ghosts of Mississippi: The Murder of Medgar Evers, the Trials of Byron de la Beckwith and the Haunting of the New South.* Boston: Little Brown and Co., 1995.

Waldrep, Christopher. *Roots of Disorder: Race and Criminal Justice in the American South, 1817–1880.* Urbana: University of Illinois Press, 1998.

Wang, Xi. *The Trial of Democracy: Black Suffrage and Northern Republicans, 1860–1910.* Athens: University of Georgia Press, 1997.

Watson, Charles S. *From Nationalism to Secessionism: The Changing Fiction of William Gilmore Simms.* Westport: Greenwood Press, 1993.

Wendt, Lloyd. *Chicago Tribune: The Rise of a Great American Newspaper.* Chicago: Rand McNally, 1979.

West, Cornel. *The American Evasion of Philosophy: A Genealogy of Pragmatism.* Madison: University of Wisconsin Press, 1989.

White, Walter. *A Man Called White: The Autobiography of Walter White.* 1948; reprint ed., Athens: University of Georgia Press, 1995.

—————. *Rope and Faggot: A Biography of Judge Lynch.* New York: Knopf, 1929.

Whitfield, Stephen J. *A Death in the Delta: The Story of Emmett Till.* New York: Free Press, 1988.

[Williams, Joseph S.] *Old Times in West Tennessee.* Memphis: W.G. Cheney, 1873.

Williams, Juan. *Thurgood Marshall: American Revolutionary.* New York: Random House, 1998.

Williams, Lou Falkner. *The Great South Carolina Ku Klux Klan Trials, 1871–1872.* Athens: University of Georgia Press, 1996.

Williamson, Joel. *The Crucible of Race: Black-White Relations in the American South since Emancipation.* New York: Oxford University Press, 1984.

Wirt, William. *Sketches of the Life and Character of Patrick Henry.* Philadelphia: Thomas, Cowperthwait, 1838.

Wright, George C. *Racial Violence in Kentucky, 1865–1940: Lynchings, Mob Rule, and "Legal Lynchings."* Baton Rouge: Louisiana State University Press, 1990.

Wyatt-Brown, Bertram. *Lewis Tappan and the Evangelical War against Slavery.* Cleveland: Case Western Reserve University Press, 1969.

———. *Southern Honor: Ethics and Behavior in the Old South.* New York: Oxford University Press, 1982.

Zangrando, Robert L. *The NAACP Crusade against Lynching, 1909–1950.* Philadelphia: Temple University Press, 1980.

Zboray, Ronald J. *A Fictive People: Antebellum Economic Development and the American Reading Public.* New York: Oxford University Press, 1993.

Zuczek, Richard. *State of Rebellion: Reconstruction in South Carolina.* Columbia: University of South Carolina Press, 1996.

ARTICLES

Alexander, Ann Field. "'Like an Evil Wind': The Roanoke Riot of 1893 and the Lynching of Thomas Smith." *Virginia Magazine of History and Biography* 100 (1992): 173–206.

Alviti, John V. and Mark H. Haller. "Loansharking in American Cities: Historical Analysis of a Marginal Enterprise." *American Journal of Legal History* 21 (1977): 125–156.

Amann, Peter H. "Vigilante Fascism: The Black Legion as an American Hybrid." *Comparative Studies in Society and History* 25 (July 1983): 490–524.

Baker, Ray Stannard. "What is a Lynching? A Study of Mob Justice South and North: Lynching in the South." *McClure's Magazine* 24 (January 1905): 299–314.

———. "What is a Lynching? A Study of Mob Justice, South and North: Lynching in the North." *McClure's Magazine* 24 (February 1905): 422–430.

Bardaglio, Peter. "Rape and the Law in the Old South: 'Calculated to Excite Indignation in Every Heart.'" *Journal of Southern History* 60 (1994): 749–772.

Beasley, Maurine. "The Muckrakers and Lynching: A Case Study in Racism." *Journalism History* 9 (Autumn-Winter 1982): 86–91.

Bedini, Silvio A. "The Survey of the Federal Territory: Andrew Ellicott and Benjamin Banneker," *Washington History* (Spring-Summer 1991): 77–95.

Belz, Herman. "New Left Reverberations in the Academy: The Antipluralist Critique of Constitutionalism," *Reviews of Politics* 36 (1974): 265–283.

Benson, Bruce L. "Reciprocal Exchange as the Basis for Recognition of Law: Examples from American History." *Journal of Libertarian Studies* 10 (Fall 1991): 53–82.

Betts, Vicki. "'Private and Amateur Hangings': The Lynching of W. W. Montgomery, March 15, 1863." *Southwestern Historical Quarterly* 88 (October 1984): 145–166.

Blee, Kathleen M. "Women in the 1920s' Ku Klux Klan Movement." *Feminist Studies* 17 (Spring 1991): 57–77.

Braden, Waldo W. "The Emergence of the Concept of Southern Oratory." *Southern Speech Journal* 26 (Spring 1961): 173–183.

Brown, Richard Maxwell. "Legal and Behavioral Perspectives on American Vigilantism." *Perspectives in American History* 5 (1971): 95–144.

Buckland, Roscoe L. "Contrasting Views of Lynching in Two Wister Stories." *Wyoming Annals* 65 (Winter 1993–94): 36–46.

Capozzola, Christopher. "The Only Badge Needed is Your Patriotic Fervor: Vigilance, Coercion, and the Law in World War I America." *Journal of American History* 88 (March 2002): 1354–1382.

Capeci, Dominic J., Jr., and Jack C. Knight. "Reckoning with Violence: W. E. B. Du Bois and the 1906 Atlanta Race Riot." *Journal of Southern History* 62 (November 1996): 727–766.

Carby, Hazel V. "'On the Threshold of Woman's Era': Lynching, Empire, and Sexuality in Black Feminist Theory." *Critical Inquiry* 12 (Autumn 1985): 262–275.

Childs, Ann Waybright. "A Hoosier Goes West: The Diaries and Letters of David Wallace Springer." *Wyoming Annals* 65 (Spring 1993): 7–20.

Clinansmith, Michael S. "The Black Legion: Hooded Americanism in Michigan." *Michigan History* 55 (Fall 1971): 243–262.

Cochran, Robert. "Nature and the Nature of Man in the *Ox-Brow Incident*." *Western American Literature* 5 (Winter 1971): 253–264.

Cornet, Florence Dally. "The Experiences of a Midwest Salesman in 1836." *Missouri Historical Society Bulletin* (July 1973): 227–235.

Curry, George E. "Killed for Whistling at a White Woman." *Emerge* 6 (July-August 1995): 24–32.

Curtis, Michael Kent. "The 1837 Killing of Elijah Lovejoy by an Anti-Abolition Mob: Free Speech, Mobs, Republican Government, and the Privileges of American Citizens," *UCLA Law Review* 44 (April 1997): 1109–1184.

Davis, Jack E. "'Whitewash' in Florida: The Lynching of Jesse James Payne and its Aftermath," *Florida Historical Quarterly* 68 (January 1990): 277–298.

DeSantis, Alan D. "A Forgotten Leader: Robert S. Abbott and the Chicago *Defender* from 1910–1920." *Journalism History* 23 (Summer 1997): 63–71.

Dunne, Matthew William. "Next Steps: Charles S. Johnson and Southern Liberalism." *Journal of Negro History* 83 (Winter 1998): 1–34.

Ellingson, Stephen. "Understanding the Dialectic of Discourse and Collective Action: Public Debate and Rioting in Antebellum Cincinnati." *American Journal of Sociology* 101 (July 1995): 100–144.

Fitzgerald, Michael. "The Ku Klux Klan: Property Crime and the Plantation System in Reconstruction Alabama." *Agricultural History* 71 (Spring 1997): 186–206.

Fleisher, Marc. "Down the Passage Which We Should Not Take: The Folly of Hate Crimes Legislation." *Journal of Law and Policy* 2 (1994): 1–53.

Frader, Laura L. "Dissent Over Discourse: Labor History, Gender, and the Linguistic Turn." *History and Theory* 34 (1995): 213–230.

Frederickson, Kari. "'The Slowest State' and 'Most Backward Community': Racial Violence in South Carolina and Federal Civil Rights Legislation, 1946–1948." *South Carolina Historical Magazine* 98 (April 1997), 177–202.

Fritz, Christian. "Popular Sovereignty, Vigilantism, and the Constitutional Right of Revolution." *Pacific Historical Review* 63 (February 1994): 39–66.

Gatell, Frank Otto, ed. "Postmaster Huger and the Incendiary Publications." *South Carolina Historical Magazine* 64 (October 1963): 193–201.

Goluboff, Risa L. "The Thirteenth Amendment and the Lost Origins of Civil Rights." *Duke Law Journal* 50 (2001): 1609–1680.

Grimsted, David. "Rioting in Its Jacksonian Setting." *American Historical Review* 77 (April 1972): 361–397.

Gross, Ariela. "Beyond Black and White: Cultural Approaches to Race and Slavery." *Columbia Law Review* 101 (April 2001): 640–689.

Grossman, James R. "Blowing the Trumpet: The *Chicago Defender* and Black Migration during World War I." *Illinois Historical Journal* 78 (1985): 82–96.

Hartog, Hendrik. "The Constitution of Aspiration and 'The Rights that Belong to us All,'" *Journal of American History* 74 (December 1987): 1013–1034.

Hicks, Jimmie. "The Frontier and American Law." *Great Plains Journal* 6 (Spring 1967): 60–61.

Higgenbotham, Evelyn Brooks. *Righteous Discontent: The Women's Movement in the Black Baptist Church, 1880–1920.* Cambridge: Harvard University Press, 1993.

Holden-Smith, Barbara. "Lynching, Federalism, and the Intersection of Race and Gender in the Progressive Era." *Yale Journal of Law and Feminism* 8 (1996): 31–78.

Holt, Thomas C. "The Lonely Warrior: Ida B. Wells-Barnett and the Struggle for Black Leadership." John Hope Franklin and August Meier, eds. *Black Leaders of the Twentieth Century.* Urbana: University of Illinois Press, 1982.

―――. "The Political Uses of Alienation: W. E. B. Du Bois on Politics, Race, and Culture, 1903–1940." *American Quarterly* 42 (June 1990): 301–323.

Hovland, Carl Iver and Robert R. Sears. "Minor Studies of Aggression: Correlation of Lynchings with Economic Indices." *Journal of Psychology* 9 (May 1940): 301–310.

Howard, Woodford and Cornelius Bushover. "The Screws Case Revisited." *Journal of Politics* 29 (1967): 617–636.

Hux, Roger K. "Lillian Clayton Jewett and the Rescue of the Baker Family, 1899–1900," *Historical Journal of Massachusetts* 19 (Winter 1991): 13–23.

Inverarity, James M. "Populism and Lynching in Louisiana, 1889–1896: A Test of Erikson's Theory of the Relationship between Boundary Crisis and Repressive Justice." *American Sociological Review* 41 (April 1976): 262–280.

Ireland, Robert M. "Frenzied and Fallen Females: Women and Sexual Dishonor in the Nineteenth-Century United States." *Journal of Women's History* 3 (Winter 1992): 95–117.

―――. "Insanity and the Unwritten Law." *American Journal of Legal History* 32 (1988): 157–172.

Istvan, Haller. "Lynching Is Not a Crime: Mob Violence against Roma in Post-Ceauscescu Romania." *European Roma Rights Center Newsletter* (Spring 1998):http://www.netsoft.ro/proeuro/HRO/Roma.htm

Jackson, David K. "A Poe Hoax Comes Before the U.S. Senate." *Poe Studies* 7 (1974): 47–48.

Jacobs, James B. and Kimberly A. Potter. "Hate Crimes: A Critical Perspective." *Crime and Justice* 22 (1997): 1–42.

Johnson, David A. "Vigilance and the Law: The Moral Authority of Popular Justice in the Far West." *American Quarterly* 33 (1981): 558–586.

Johnson, Manie White. "The Colfax Riot of April, 1873." *Louisiana Historical Quarterly* 13 (July 1930): 391–427.

Kelly, Joseph M. "Shifting Interpretations of the San Francisco Vigilantes." *Journal of the West* 24 (1985): 39–46.

Kornweibel, Theodore, Jr. "'The Most Dangerous of All Negro Journals': Federal Efforts to Suppress the *Chicago Defender* during World War I," *American Journalism* 11 (Spring 1994): 154–168.

Laska, Lewis L. and Severine Brocki. "The Life and Death of the Lottery in Tennessee, 1787–1836." *Tennessee Historical Quarterly* 45 (Summer 1986): 95–118.

Leach, Eugene E. "Chaining the Tiger: The Mob Stigma and the Working Class, 1863–1894." *Labor History* 35 (Spring 1994): 187–215.

Leuchtenburg, William E. "The Conversion of Harry Truman." *American Heritage* 42 (November 1991): 55–68.

Levy, Newman. "The Unwritten Law." *American Mercury* 35 (August 1935): 398–403.

Logan, Shirley W. "Rhetorical Strategies in Ida B. Wells's 'Southern Horrors': Lynch Law in All its Phases." *Sage* 8 (Summer 1991): 3–9.

Logue, Cal M. "Rhetorical Ridicule of Reconstruction Blacks." *Quarterly Journal of Speech* 62 (December 1976): 400–409.

―――. "The Rhetorical Appeals of Whites to Blacks During Reconstruction." *Communications Monographs* 44 (August 1977): 242–243.

Lowery, Charles D. "The Great Migration to the Mississippi Territory, 1798–1819." *Journal of Mississippi History* 30 (1968): 173–192.

Lupton, John A. "'In View of the Uncertainty of Life': A Coles County Lynching." *Illinois Historical Journal* 89 (Autumn 1996): 134–146.

"Lynch Law." *William and Mary College Quarterly Historical Magazine* 24 (October 1915): 73–74.

McDermott, John D, "Writers in Judgment: Historiography of the Johnson County War." *Wyoming Annals* (Winter 1993–94): 20–35.

McDowell, Winston. "Race and Ethnicity During the Harlem Jobs Campaign, 1932–1935." *Journal of Negro History* 69 (Summer-Fall 1984): 134–146.

MacLean, Nancy. "The Leo Frank Case Reconsidered: Gender and Sexual Politics in the Making of Reactionary Populism." *Journal of American History* 77 (December 1991): 917–48.

———. "White Women and Klan Violence in the 1920s: Agency, Complicity, and the Politics of Women's History." *Gender and History* 3 (Autumn 1993): 285–303.

McMillen, Neil R. "Black Journalism in Mississippi: The Jim Crow Years." *Journal of Mississippi History* 49 (1987): 129–138.

Miller, Kathleen Atkinson. "The Ladies and the Lynchers: A Look at the Association of Southern Women for the Prevention of Lynching." *Southern Studies* 2 (Fall and Winter 1991): 261–280.

Miller, Linda. "Poe on the Beat." *Journal of the Early Republic* 7 (Summer 1987): 147–165.

Mintz, Alexander. "A Re-Examination of Correlations Between Lynchings and Economic Indices." *Journal of Abnormal and Social Psychology* 41 (April 1946): 154–165.

Morrison, Howard Alexander. "Gentlemen of Proper Understanding: A Closer Look at Utica's Anti-Abolitionist Mob." *New York History* 62 (1981): 61–82.

Moseley, Clement Charlton. "The Case of Leo M. Frank, 1913–1915." *Georgia Historical Quarterly* 51 (March 1967): 42–62.

Naison, Mark D. "Communism and Black Nationalism in the Depression: The Case of Harlem." *Journal of Ethnic Studies* 2 (Summer 1974): 24–36.

Nord, David Paul. "The Paradox of Municipal Reform in the Late Nineteenth Century." *Wisconsin Magazine of History* 66 (Winter 1982–1983): 128–142.

———. "The Public Community: The Urbanization of Journalism in Chicago." *Journal of Urban History* 11 (August 1985): 411–441.

Northrup, Jeff. "The Hawes Riot: All the News Unfit to Print." *Journal of the Birmingham Historical Society* 5 (January 1977): 16–25.

———. "The Hawes Affair: Part II." *Journal of the Birmingham Historical Society* 6 (January 1979): 15–23.

Olsen, Otto H. "The Ku Klux Klan: A Study in Reconstruction Politics and Propaganda." *North Carolina Historical Review* 39 (Summer 1962): 340–362.

Petrie, Jon. "The Secular Word 'Holocaust': Scholarly Sacralization, Twentieth Century Meanings." http://www. berkeleyinternet.com/holocaust/.

Pfeifer, Michael J. "Lynching and Criminal Justice in South Louisiana." *Louisiana History* 40 (1999): 155–177.

Pilkington, Charles Kirk. "The Trials of Brotherhood: The Founding of the Commission on Interracial Cooperation." *Georgia Historical Quarterly* 69 (Spring 1985): 55–80.

Price, Eliphalet. "The Trial and Execution of Patrick O'Conner at the Dubuque Mines in the Summer of 1834." *Palimpsest* 1 (1920): 86–97.

Prince, Carl E. "The Great 'Riot Year': Jacksonian Democracy and Patterns of Violence in 1834." *Journal of the Early Republic* 5 (Spring 1985): 1–18.

"Recollections of a Retired Lawyer: Recollection II, Lynch's Law." *Southern Literary Messenger* 5 (March, 1839): 218–221.

Riss, Jean F. "The Lynching of Francisco Torres." *Journal of Mexican American History* 2 (Spring 1972): 90–121.

Rose, James A. "The Regulators and Flatheads in Southern Illinois." *Transactions of the Illinois State Historical Society for the Year 1906.* Springfield: Illinois State Journal, 1906.

Rotnem, Victor W. "Clarifications of the Civil Rights Statutes." *Bill of Rights Review* 2 (1942): 252–261.

———. "The Federal Civil Right 'Not to be Lynched'." *Washington University Law Quarterly* 28 (February 1943): 57–73.

Schmitz, Neil. "Murdered McIntosh, Murdered Lovejoy: Abraham Lincoln and the Problem of Jacksonian Address." *Arizona Quarterly* 44 (Autumn 1988): 15–39.

Schwartz, Thomas F. "The Springfield Lyceums and Lincoln's 1838 Speech." *Illinois Historical Journal* 83 (Spring 1990): 45–49.

Schweinhaut, Henry A. "The Civil Liberties Section of the Department of Justice." *Bill of Rights Review* 1 (1941): 206–216,

Sevitch, Benjamin. "The Well-Planned Riot of October 21, 1835: Utica's Answer to Abolitionism." *New York History* 50 (1969): 251–263.

Shostak, David A. "Crosby Smith: Forgotten Witness to a Mississippi Nightmare." *Negro History Bulletin* 38 (December 1974–January 1975): 320–325.

Smith, David A. "From the Mississippi to the Mediterranean: the 1891 New Orleans Lynching and Its Effect on United States Diplomacy and the American Navy." *Southern Historian* 19 (1998): 60–85.

Smurr, J. W. "Afterthoughts on the Vigilantes." *Montana* 8 (1958): 8–20.

Snorgrass, J. William. "The Black Press in the San Francisco Bay Area, 1856–1900." *California History* 60 (Winter 1981–1982): 306–317.

SoRelle, James M. "The 'Waco Horror': The Lynching of Jesse Washington." *Southwestern Historical Quarterly* 86 (1983): 517–536.

Stovall, Mary E. "The *Chicago Defender* in the Progressive Era." *Illinois Historical Journal* 83 (1990): 159–172.

Tepker, Harry F., Jr. "The Ox-Bow Incident." *Oklahoma City University Law Review* 22 (Fall 1997): 1209–1222.

Todd, Lee. "Charles S. Johnson and the Sociology of Race Relations." *Southern Historian* 21 (2000): 56–65.

Toews, John E. "Intellectual History after the Linguistic Turn: The Autonomy of Meaning and the Irreducibility of Experience." *American Historical Review* 92 (October 1987): 879–907.

Tucker, David M. "Miss Ida B. Wells and Memphis Lynching." *Phylon* 32 (Summer 1971): 112–122.

Tucker, Mark. "'You Can't Argue with Facts': Monroe Nathan Work as Information Officer, Editor, and Bibliographer." *Libraries and Culture* 26 (Winter 1991): 151–168.

Ulph, Owen. "The Virginian: Misbegotten Folk Hero." *Halcyon* (1983): 131–155.

"The Vigilantes: Nebraska's First Defenders." *Nebraska History Magazine* 14 (January-March 1933): 3–18.

Watson, Alan D. "The Lottery in Early North Carolina." *North Carolina Historical Quarterly* 69 (1992): 365–387.

Weigman, Robyn. "The Anatomy of a Lynching." *Journal of the History of Sexuality* 3 (1993): 445–467.

Westbrook, Max. "The Archetypal Ethic of the Ox-Bow Incident." *Western American Literature* 1 (Summer 1966): 105–118.

Whites, LeeAnn. "Rebecca Latimer Felton and the Problem of 'Protection' in the New South." In *Visible Women: New Essays on American Activism.* Urbana: University of Illinois Press, 1993: 41–61.

———. "Rebecca Latimer Felton and the Wife's Farm: The Class and Racial Politics of Gender Reform." *Georgia Historical Quarterly* 76 (Summer 1992): 354–372.

Williamson, Joel. "Wounds not Scars: Lynching, the National Conscience, and the American Historian." *Journal of American History* 83 (March 1997): 1221–1253.

Wolf, Charlotte. "Constructions of a Lynching." *Sociological Inquiry* 62 (February 1992): 83–97.

Young, Erle Fiske. "The Relation of Lynching to the Size of Political Areas." *Sociology and Social Research* 12 (March-April 1928): 348–353.

Zanjani, Sally Springmeyer. "The Curse of the Uber Lynching: Violence and Conscience on the Nevada Frontier." *American West* 19 (1982): 59–69.

UNPUBLISHED WORKS

Aydt, Gregory. "A Radical Cure: Thomas Dimsdale, Radical Republicanism, and the Montana Vigilantes during the Civil War." M.A. Thesis: Eastern Illinois University, 1999.

Balthrope, Robin Bernice. "Lawlessness and the New Deal: Congress and Antilynching Legislation, 1934–1938." Ph.D. diss.: Ohio State University, 1995.

Brumbaugh, Alice Louise. "The Regulator Movement in Illinois." M.A. Thesis: University of Illinois, 1927.

Carrigan, William D. "Between South and West: Race, Violence, and Power in Central Texas, 1836–1916." Ph.D. diss.: Emory University, 1999.

———. "Forgotten Lynchings: Mob Violence Against Mexican Americans, 1848–1928." Paper presented at the American Historical Association, January 5, 2002, San Francisco, California.

Crawford, Kristan J. "'Exciting the Rable to Riots and Mobbing': Community, Public Rituals, and Popular Disturbances in Eighteenth-Century Virginia." M.A. Thesis: Eastern Illinois University, 1995.

Ellis, Mary Louise. "'Rain Down Fire': The Lynching of Sam Hose." Ph.D. diss.: Florida State University, 1992.

Feimster, Crystal Nicole. "'Ladies and Lynching': The Gendered Discourse of Mob Violence in the New South, 1880–1930." Ph.D. diss.: Princeton University, 2000.

Finnegan, Terence. "'At the Hands of Parties Unknown': Lynching in Mississippi and South Carolina, 1881–1940." Ph.D. diss.: University of Illinois, 1993.

Fritz, Christian. "Legitimating Government: The Ambiguous Legacy of the People's Sovereignty, 1776–1860." (unpublished manuscript kindly loaned by the author).

Goluboff, Risa L. "A Road Not Taken: The Thirteenth Amendment and the Lost Origins of Civil Rights." Paper delivered at the American Society for Legal History Meeting, Princeton, N.J., 2000.

Gould, Lewis Ludlow. "Willis Van Devanter in Wyoming Politics, 1884–1897." Ph.D. diss.: Yale University, 1966.

Hines, Mary Elizabeth. "Death at the Hands of Persons Unknown: The Geography of Lynching in the Deep South, 1882–1910." Ph.D. diss.: Louisiana State University, 1992.

Howard, Walter T. "Vigilante Justice: Extra-Legal Executions in Florida, 1930–1940." Ph.D. diss.: Florida State University, 1987.

Kiracofe, David James. "Treason and the Development of National Identity in Revolutionary America, 1775–1815." Ph.D. diss., University of Connecticut. 1995.

Pfeifer, Michael J. "Lynching and Criminal Justice in Regional Context: Iowa, Wyoming, and Louisiana, 1878–1946." Ph.D. diss.: University of Iowa, 1998.

Phillips, Jeff. "A Riot's Events and Effects." Washington Senior High School history paper, not dated, Washington Court House, Ohio.

Redekop, David. "The Lynching of Willie Earle." M.A. Thesis: Clemson University, 1987.

Ross, John. "At the Bar of Judge Lynch: Lynching and Lynch Mobs in America." Ph.D. diss.: Texas Tech University, 1983.

Senechal de la Roche, Roberta. "Why is Collective Violence Collective?" Paper presented at the Annual Meeting of the American Society of Criminology, San Diego, November 1997.

Sipress, Joel M. "The Triumph of Reaction: Political Struggle in a New South Community, 1865–1898." Ph.D. diss.: University of North Carolina. 1993.

Smith, Rogers Melton. "The Waco Lynching of 1916: Perspective and Analysis." M.A. Thesis: Baylor University, 1971.

Stowell, Daniel W. "Why Redemption? Religion and the End of Reconstruction, 1869–1877." Paper presented at the Southern Historical Association, Birmingham, Ala., November 14, 1998.

Thompson, Mildred, "Ida B. Wells-Barnett: An Exploratory Study of an American Black Woman, 1893–1930." Ph.D. diss.: George Washington University, 1979.

Whitaker, Hugh Stephen. "A Case Study in Southern Justice: The Emmett Till Case." M.A. Thesis: Florida State University, 1963.

Index

Abbott, Robert S., 158–159
Abolitionism, 38–47
Alabama hill country resistance to KKK, 75–76
Alabama Constitutional Convention in 1901, 131
Aldridge, Georgia, 92
Alexander, Will, 132
Allen, Lewis. *See* Meeropol, Abel
Alta California, 51, 59
Alton riot (Illinois), 44–45
American Anti-Slavery Society, 38, 39
American Beacon, 45
American Citizen, 123
American Mercury, 145, 162–163, 167
Ames, Fisher, 20
Ames, Jessie Daniel, 127, 131, 132, 137; Methodism of, 132–133, 139; campaign for lynch-free year, 132–134, 142–150
Amos 'n' Andy, 160
Antilynching law, 164–166
Arp, Bill (columnist), 116
Asheville Citizen-Times, 140
Associated Negro Press, 136
Associated Press (AP), 143, 179
Association of Southern Women for the Prevention of Lynching (ASWPL), 132–133; disputes NAACP, 142–143
Atlanta, 153–154
Atlanta Constitution, 82, 128; Sam Hose lynching, 119–120
Atlanta Daily World, 146
Atlanta Herald, 93
Atwood, H. C. C., 123
Audubon, John James, 22

Baird, Willie (lynching victim), 166
Baker, Frazier B. (lynching victim), 118–119
Baker, Ray Stannard, 157–158

Baltimore Afro-American, 136
Baltimore Sun, 58
Bancroft, Hubert Howe (historian), 14, 93, 95
Barrett, W. T., 108
Baxley, William, 189–190
Beals, Melba Pattillo, 180
Beckwith, Byron De La, 187–189
Beckwith, James R. (U.S. Attorney), 77
Bedford County, Virginia, 15–17
Bennett, James Gordon, 33–34
Berge, Wendell, 170
Berry, Shawn Allen, 191
Biaggi, Mario, 189
Bilbo, Theodore, 166
Birmingham, Alabama, 94
Birmingham Age-Herald, 160
Birmingham Iron Age, 108–109
Birmingham Post, 162, 167
Birney, James, 43–44
Birth of a Nation, The, 159
Black, Hugo, 165–166, 171
Black Legion, 140–142
Black Legion, 169
Blackford, William T. (Alabama probate judge), 74
Blanding, William, 59
Blease, Cole, 121
Blountsville, Alabama, KKK in, 70
Boder, David P., 5
Bodley, Hugh S., 29, 31
Bolton County, Texas, 98
Boone County Recorder, 150
Booneville Observer (Missouri), 41
Boston Daily Advertiser and Patriot, 32, 33, 41
Boston Herald, 100
Boston Transcript, 126
Bradley, Mamie, 178–180
Brandeis, Louis, 161

Brevard County, Florida, 145
Brewer, David J., 153
Brewer, Lawrence Russell, 191
Brinkley, Alan, 5
Bristol, Tennessee, 109
Brooks, Preston, 40
Brown, Ed, 164
Brown, Miles W., 142
Brown, Richard Maxwell, 7
Brown v. Board of Education, 178, 183
Bryant, Carolyn, 178
Bryant, Roy, 1, 178–180, 185–187
Bulldozing, 77
Burdue, Thomas, 51–52
Burns, Andy (vigilante victim), 74
Butler, Pierce, 161
Butler, Santee, 74
Byrd, James, Jr. (murder victim), 190

Caldwell, Millard F. (Florida governor), 173
Calhoun, Marcus B. (FBI agent), 170–171
California, 49–61
Campbell, William, 15
Canton, Mississippi, 143
Carrollton massacre (Mississippi), 103–107
Cartwright, Marguerite, 149
Carruthers, J. S., 92
Casey, James P. (murdered James King of
    William), 52–53, 57
Cashman, John Gordon (lynching
    opponent), 128–129
Celina, Ohio, 95
Chambers, William (lynching victim), 111
Chambliss, Robert ("Dynamite Bob"),
    189–190
Chamlee, George W., 116–117
Charles, Robert (murdered in New
    Orleans), 122
Charleston (South Carolina) Courier, 32, 59
Charleston (South Carolina) News and Courier, 96,
    115
Charleston Post Office (South Carolina),
    38
Chicago American, 32
Chicago Defender, 158–159, 168, 180, 187
Chicago Inter-Ocean, 110, 123
Chicago Tribune, 77, 97, 106, 122, 126, 155;
    annual count of lynchings, 112–114,
    134, 150
Cincinnati Evening Post, 44
Cincinnati Republican, 44
Cincinnati Whig, 44

Clark, Walter Van Tilburg, 169
Clayton, Powell, (Arkansas governor), 75
Coit, A. B., 117
Colbert, Elias, 112–113
Coleman, William T., 51–52
Colfax Massacre, 77
Colliers, 158, 173–174
Collins, Levy ("Too Tight"), 180, 187
Columbia Statesman (Missouri), 41
Commission on Interracial Cooperation
    (CIC), 132
Communist party, 163, 177
Conway County, Arkansas (battleground
    between KKK and unionists), 75
Conyers, John, 189
Cooper, James Fenimore, 50
Cora, Charles (accused murderer), 52, 57
Cordele, Georgia, 134
Courtwright, David, 7
Cranford, Alfred, 119–120
Crawford, William H. (FBI agent),
    170–171
Creecy, James R., 28
Crisis, 158
Crockett County, Tennessee, 77
Crockett, David, 21
Crockett, Joseph B., 53
Cultural history, 6, 71, 138–139
Cummins, Eli (mob leader), 74
Cushman, Dan, 65
Cutler, James, 14, 131

Dabney, Virginius, 146, 147, 162, 167
Daniels, Josephus, 129–130, 149
Darrow, Clarence, 126
Davis, Mrs. H., 123–124
Day, Benjamin H., 33–34
Daytona Beach, Florida, disputed lynching
    in, 143
De Bar, George (lynching victim), 61
Defensor (pseudonym for abolitionist
    writer), 38–39
DeLaughter, Bobby, 188
Detroit News, 141
Devereaux, Nancy, 17
Diggs, John (lynching victim), 88
Dimsdale, Thomas J. (lynching apologist),
    65
Douglas Stephen (U.S. Senator), 45
Douglas, William O., 172
Dresser, Amos (abolitionist), 38–39
Du Bois, W. E. B., 137–138, 158

Dubuque, Iowa, 28
Duck Hill, Mississippi, 164–165
Dukes, John (lynching victim), 134
Dunning, William Archibald, 122
Dyer, Leonidas, 135

Earle, Willie (lynching victim), 174–175
East Point, Georgia, KKK in, 144, 146
Edgarton, Stanley (chief justice for Idaho Territory), 64
El Dorado, Arkansas, 142
Elaine, Arkansas, 134
Ellicott, Andrew, 20–21
Ellington, Arthur, 164
Enemies of the Constitution Discovered, 38
Espy, Mike, 188
Evers, Medgar, 187–189

False lynching reports, 112–114, 143, 152–153
Faux, William, 23
Fayette County, Ohio, 117
Felton, Rebecca Latimer, 133
Fifth Circuit Court of Appeals, 156
Fischer, David Hackett, 7
Flint, James, 22, 24
Floyd County, Georgia, 75
Fonda, Henry, 169
Foote, Henry S., 40
Forbes, Nat (lynching victim), 96
Force Bill of 1890 (Lodge Bill), 113
Ford, Benton (KKK victim), 144
Fortune, T. Thomas, 5, 98–101, 103, 110, 124; denounced Carrollton massacre, 106
Foster, Charles (unwillingly joined KKK), 76
Frank, Leo (lynching victim), 153–154, 161
Frankfurter, Felix, 171–172
Free Speech, 109
Freedom's Champion, 63
Freeman, Elizabeth (lynching investigator), 158
Freund, Arthur J., 181
Frontier, 21–25
Fury, 169

Gambling, 35
Garfield, James A., 81
Garrison, William Lloyd, 40, 41–42
Garrison, William Lloyd, II, 118
Gaston, Ike (KKK victim), 144–145, 146
Gibson, Orville (lynching victim), 181–182

Gihon, John H., 56
Globalism, 157
Good, Charley (KKK victim), 72
Good, Jim, 111
Grant, Ulysses S., 77, 81
Graves, Bibb, 162
Graves, John Temple, 128, 167
Greensborough Patriot (North Carolina), 58
Greenville, South Carolina, 174–175
Gringo Justice, 51
Grund, Francis J., 13–14
Gunn, Allen M. (opposed to KKK), 75
Gunthorpe, Osmond, (disenchanted with KKK), 76

Hale, John P., 40
Hale County, Alabama, 74
Hall, Grover, 162
Hall, Jacquelyn Dowd, 4
Hall, James, 23, 25
Hall, Rob F. (journalist), 179
Hall, Robert (murder victim), 170–173
Hamilton, Andrew, 20
Harding, Warren G., 130
Harpe, Micajah and Wiley, 24
Harper's Monthly, 27
Harris, Dan (lynching victim), 111
Harris, Trudier, 4
Hate crime, 10–11, 185–191
Heith, John (lynching victim), 115
Helms, Jesse, 190
Hicks, James, 179
Hill, Anita, 182
Hodgson, Adam, 22
Holliday, Billie, 166–167
Holmes, Oliver Wendell, 161
Holocaust, 5
Holt, Sam. *See* Sam Hose
Hone, Philip (Whig diarist), 37
Hoover, J. Edgar, 177–178
Hopkins, Jeff (lynching victim), 111
Hopkins, Sterling A., 54
Horn, Stanley (historian), 82
Hose, Sam (lynching victim), 119–120
Houston, Louis (lynching victim), 108
Huie, William Bradford, 162, 167; Emmett Till case, 180, 182, 185–186; Vermont lynching, 181–182
Hunter, William A., 125

Industrial Workers of the World (IWW), 125–126, 144

Ingraham, Joseph Holt, 24–25
International Labor Defense (ILD), 136,
　143, 163, 164
Irving, Washington, 23, 24, 25
Italian-Americans, 109

Jackson, Andrew, 35–38
Jackson, Jesse, 152
Jackson, Robert, 171
Jackson Daily News, (Mississippi), 165
Jacksonville Times-Union, (Florida), 146
Jameson, David, 19
Jansen, Charles J., 51
Jasper, Texas, 190–191
Jefferson, Thomas, 15–16
Jenkins, John (lynched by San Francisco
　vigilantes), 52
Jewett, Lillian Clayton, 118–119
Johnson County War, (Wyoming), 121–122
Johnson, Charles, 168
Johnson, David A., 50–51
Johnson, Elihu, (lynching victim), 134
Johnson, Gibson, (lynching victim), 134
Johnson, J. Neely (California governor), 54,
　59–60
Johnson, Leroy (lynching victim), 134
Johnson, Louis, (lynching victim), 134
Johnson, Raynard (disputed lynching),
　152–153
Johnson, Sam (lynching victim), 95
Johnson, William (governor's brother), 56
Jones County, Mississippi, 176–177
Jones, Frank, 170
Jones, H. C., 74
Jones, John C., 172

Kansas, 61–63
Kansas City Enterprise, 59, 62
Kansas Free State, 63
Kansas-Nebraska Act, 61
Kelly, Jim Bob, 170
Kelsen, Hans, 157
Kennelly, Barbara, 189
Kester, Howard (lynching investigator), 165
Key, Emmet (lynching victim), 96
Kibbe, William, 54
King, John William, 191
King of William, James (editor, murder
　victim), 52–53
Kokomo, Mississippi, 152
Ku Klux Klan, 9, 66, 68, 69–78, 97, 98, 122,
　163; in Ohio, 140; in East Point,

Georgia, 144; wrecking crews, 144–145;
　in Alabama, 166, 189–190
Labor violence, 136–137, 165–166
Lake City, South Carolina, 118–119
Latham, Robert, 140
Lathrop, Abial, 118
Lawless, Benjamin, 19
Lawless, Luke (judge), 44
League of Struggle for Negro Rights, 136,
　144
Legal lynchings, 151–152, 154; Scottsboro
　Boys, 161–164; Willie McGee, 176–177
Leibowitz, Samuel, 163–164
Leon County, Florida, KKK in, 70
Leslie's Weekly, 153
Lewis, John A. (KKK opponent), 75, 76
Lexington Intelligencer, 42
Liddell, James, 104
Life, 177, 182
*Life and Adventures of John A. Murrell, the Great
　Western Land Pirate,* 38
Limestone County, Alabama, 79; opposition
　to KKK, 75
Lincoln, Abraham, 32, 36–37, 43, 50
Little, Frank (lynching victim), 125
Little Rock Central High School (riot), 180
Loggins, Henry Lee, 180
London Times, 59
Look, 185–186
Loudon, Tennessee, 92
Louisville Advertiser, 28, 35
Louisiana Advertiser, 30–31, 32
Louisianian, 97
Lovejoy, Elijah (lynching victim), 44–45
Lowther, Henry (KKK victim), 74
Luce, Henry R., 173
Lynch, Charles (Mississippi governor), 45
Lynch, Charles (Virginia magistrate), 15–22,
　25
Lynch, John Roy (political leader), 80
Lynch, William, 19–22, 25
Lynchburg, Virginia, 45–46
Lynching: definition, 2–4, 183; origins of the
　term, 13–25; Vicksburg lynching,
　27–35; Andrew Jackson as Judge Lynch,
　35–38; abolitionists challenged, 38–47;
　western lynching, 49–66;
　Reconstruction violence, 67–84;
　journalists' metanarrative, 85–101; lack
　of ritual, 86–88; newspaper hyperbole,
　88–91; world, 13; racial, 103–126;
　justified by rape, 116–122; summit

conference on, 147–150; legal, 151–152, 161–164

Madison County, Mississippi, 29, 32, 38, 45
Madison, James H., 4
Maloney, James Reuben, 54, 58
Marion, Indiana, 161
Marshall, Thurgood, 2, 148, 170
Martinsburg, West Virginia, 96
Massengill, Reed, 188–189
McCain, John, 5
McCall, Willis, 177
McChord, John R., 156
McClure's, 157–158
McConnell, J. L., 50
McDowell, Calvin, 108
McGee, Willie, 176
McGowan, Edward, 58
McIntosh, Francis (lynching victim), 43, 44
McKinley, William, 117–118
McKenzie, Robert (lynched by San Francisco vigilantes), 52
Medill, Joseph, 112
Meeropol, Abel (Allen, Lewis), 166
Memphis Appeal, 95, 96–97, 104, 105
Memphis Avalanche, 96, 104, 105
Memphis Tri-State Defender, 179
Mencken, H. L., 162–163
Methodist Church, 124, 132–133, 143
Mexicans, lynching of, 51, 109, 183
Milam, J. W., 1, 178–180, 185–187
Millar, John S., 72
Mills, William, 29–30, 33
Milwaukee Sentinel, 40
Minden, Louisiana, 172
Mirande, Alfredo, 51
Mississippi Free Trader, 41
Mississippi Plan, 77
Mississippi Supreme Court, 176–177
Mississippian (pseudonym), 46
Missouri Republican, 58
Mitchell, Jerry, 188
Mobile Daily Register, 58
Monroe County, Mississippi, 74
Montana, 63–66
Montana Post, 65
Monterey County, California, 89
Montgomery County, Virginia (led mines), 16
Moore, Harry T., 145 (murdered), 177–178
Moore, Will (lynching victim), 156–157
Moores, Merrill, 135

Mooty, Rayfield, 1, 179
Morgan County, Alabama (resistant to KKK), 75
Morning Courier and New-York Enquirer, 42
Moss, Thomas (lynching victim), 108
Mount Vernon, Tennessee, 111
Movies, 159–160, 169
Muckraking, 157–158
Murphy, Frank, 167, 172
Murray, William W. (U.S. Attorney), 77
Nashville Banner, 87
Nashville Globe and Independent, 145, 149
Nashville Press and Times, 69

Natchez, Mississippi, 28
Nation, The, 145, 155
National Afro-American Council of the United States, 124
National Association for the Advancement of Colored People (NAACP), 10, 124, 127, 132, 143, 163, 164, 176, 177, 179; definition of lynching, 2; campaign against lynching, 134–150; muckraking, 158
National Baptist World, 123
National Police Gazette, 34
National Race Council, 124
Negro Labor News, 168
Neher, Ludwig, 92
New Departure, 82
New Orleans, Louisiana, 109, 122–123
New Orleans Times-Picayune, 122
New Orleans True American, 31, 32, 39
New Republic, 155
New York Age, 110
New York Amsterdam News, 179
New York Atlas, 32
New York Courier and Inquirer, 32
New York Gazette, 32
New York Globe, 98
New York Herald, 33–34, 42–43, 59
New York Sun, 27, 32–34
New York Times, 45, 57, 86–96, 99, 101, 113, 122, 131, 141, 142, 145, 155, 172, 174; and Ida B. Wells, 110–112; new emphasis, 114–116; Scottsboro Boys, 163
New York Tribune, 80
New Yorker, 175
Newberry, Vermont, 181
Niles, Henry C. (judge), 155–156
Niles, Hezekiah (journalist), 37
Niles' Register, 28, 33, 35, 36

Nisbet, James, 53, 56
Northern, William J. (opposed lynching), 128
Nossiter, Adam, 188–189
Novick, Peter, 5

O'Conner, Patrick, 28
O'Farrell, Charles T., 123
Ohio, Ku Klux Klan in, 140
Outrage (mob violence), 78–84
Ox-Bow Incident, 169

Page, Clarence, 190
Panama City, Florida, 142
Parker, Mack Charles (lynching victim), 181, 182
Patterson, Frederick Douglass, 146, 147
Patterson, Orlando, 191
Payne, Jesse James (lynching victim), 172
Pearce, John R. (lynching victim), 115
Pender County, North Carolina, 140
Pennsylvania Gazette, 34
Penny press, 33–34
Pensacola Gazette, 24
People's Advocate, 98
Phagan, Mary, 153–154
Philanthropist, 44
Phillips, William (lynching victim), 63
Pickens, William (author), 100
Pierce, Franklin, 55, 59–60
Piercy, Frederick Hawkins, 35
Pitney, Mahlon, 154
Pittsylvania County, Virginia, 19–20
Plummer, Henry, 64–66
Poe, Edgar Allen, 21
Police lynchings, 142, 170–173
Popular sovereignty, 20, 27, 39, 46, 55, 56,–57, 67–68, 93–94
Portland Daily Advertiser, 32
Power, Tyrone, 22, 23
Praeger, Robert, 125
Pratt, Daniel D., 71
Preston, William, 15, 16
Price, Victoria, 162
Prohibition, 160

Radio, 160
Raleigh News and Observer, 129–130
Randolph, A. Phillip, 169
Raper, Arthur, 148
Rawls, Sarah (KKK victim), 144
Reconstruction, 67–84

Reed, Willie, 179
Reeder, Andrew H, 62–63
Reid, Ira, 148
Reid, Richard C., 7
Reno, Janet, 152
Richmond Times-Dispatch, 146
Richmond Whig, 58
Rochester Union, 40
Rogers, Annie May (widow of Rogers, Robert T.), 155–156
Rogers, Doc (shot by police), 140
Rogers, Joe (disputed lynching), 143
Rogers, Robert T. (lynching victim), 125; law suit, 155–156
Rogers, William P., 181
Rolph, James, Jr. (endorsed lynching), 131
Roosevelt, Franklin D., 165, 168
Rosewood, Florida, 190
Ross, Harold, 175
Rotnem, Victor, 168–169, 170
Rowan, Carl, 177

San Francisco Chronicle, 89–90, 155
San Francisco Elevator, 71, 79
San Francisco Evening Bulletin, 52–54, 56, 59
San Francisco Herald, 55
San Francisco Vigilance Committee, 51–61
Sanders, Captain, 18
Sanders, Edward Clement, 82
Sanders, Wilbur, 64
Sanford, Edward, 161
Sangamo (Illinois) Journal, 32
Savannah (Georgia) Daily Morning News, 58
Schenck, David, 72
Schoolcraft, Henry Rowe, 22
Scottsboro Boys, 116–117, 136, 161–164, 178
Screven County, Georgia, 143
Screws, M. Claude, 170–172
Screws v. U.S., 170–172
Sentimental writing, 31, 41, 91–92
September 11, 5
Settle, Ara Lee, 130
Shannon, Marmaduke, 29
Shapard, William, 78
Sharpton, Al, 152
Shepard, William Jacob (KKK leader), 140–141
Sherman, William T., 55, 60, 61
Shields, Henry, 164
Shillady, John R., 138
Sikeston, Missouri, 168

Simms, William Gilmore (novelist), 23–24, 37–38
Singleton, Arthur, 22
Sixteenth Street Baptist church bombing, 189–190
Slaton, John M. (Georgia governor), 154
Smiley, J. Hockley, 158
Smith, Arthur A., 78
Smith, Henry (lynching victim), 110, 111
Smith, Joseph S. (Birmingham sheriff), 94
Snell, Lee (disputed lynching), 143
Soule, Frank, 56
Spingarn, Joel, 158
Squatter Sovereign (Kansas), 62
St. Louis Globe-Democrat, 105
St. Louis Republican, 28
Stewart, Henry, 108
"Strange Fruit," 166–167
Street, J. Gordon, 101
Stuart, James (lynched by San Francisco vigilantes), 51–52
Stuart, James (travel writer), 23, 25, 31–32
Sullivan, W. A., 165
Sumner, Charles, 40
Sumpter County, Alabama, 45
Sutherland, George, 161

Taft, William Howard, 161
Tallapoosa, Alabama, 70
Tallulah, Louisiana, 125
Tarpey, Matt ("woman murderer"), 89–90
Taylor, J. O. J. (lynching investigator), 143
"Taxicab Lynching," 174–175
Terkel, Studs, 167
Terry, David S. (California Supreme Court justice), 54–55
Thaw, Harry, 3, 7
Thomas, Clarence, 151–152, 182, 191
Thurmond, Strom, 174, 178
Till, Emmett, 1, 178–180, 182, 185–187
Tillman, Ben, 119, 120–121, 124
Time, 173–174, 177
Topeka (Kansas) Colored Citizen, 99
Tourgee, Albion, 78, 81, 83
Toussaint Louverture branch of the Savannah Chapter, (American Red Cross), 156
Treadaway, Francis Marion (KKK opponent), 75
Truman, Harry S, 175–176
Tulsa race riot, 190
Tunica County, Mississippi, 109

Turner, Henry M., 124
Tuskegee, Alabama, KKK in, 70
Tuskegee Institute, 10, 124, 136, 141–142, 144–150

University Commission on the Southern Race Question, 131
Unwritten law, 89
Urbana, Ohio, 117
U.S. Constitution, Fourteenth Amendment, 78, 99
U.S. Justice Department, 167, 168–173, 181, 189
U.S. Sentencing Commission, 189
U.S. Supreme Court, 77–78, 164–165, 171–172
U.S. v. Harris, 77–78
Utica, New York, 38, 39
Utica Standard and Democrat, 39

Van der Veer, McClellan (Birmingham journalist), 148
Vardaman, James K.(recounts Carrolton massacre), 105–106, 120
Vicksburg, Mississippi, 9, 27–47, 186
Vicksburg Register, 29–30, 33
Vicksburg Weekly Whig, 59
Vigne, Godfrey T., 22–23
Villard, Oswald Garrison, 145, 158
Virginian, the, 121
Vollers, Maryanne, 188

"Waco (Texas) Horror," 154–155
Walker, John Pershing, 181
Waller, William, 188
Walton County, Georgia, 176
Warren, Ed, 111
Washington, Booker T., 99–100, 124, 130
Washington County, Wisconsin, 61
Washington, George, 20
Washington, Jesse (lynching victim), 154–155, 157
Washington National Era, 60–61
Watson, Tom, 130
Watt, Sam R., 174–175
Weir, Leonard (lynched by KKK), 78
Wells, Ida B., 4, 5, 10, 85–86, 96, 99, 124, 138; Carrolton massacre, 103–107; lynching at the curve, 108–110; in England, 110, 117; and the *Chicago Tribune,* 114; Robert Charles, 122–123; gender, 123–124; definition of lynching, 131

Wells, P. M. (mob murder victim), 77

West, Rebecca, 162; Taxicab Lynching trial, 175

Western Characters or Types of Border Life in the Western States, 50

Western Worker, 125, 163

Wharton County, Texas, 98

Wheeling Gazette, 33

Whigs, 35–38

Whitaker, Samuel (lynched by San Francisco vigilantes), 52

White, Hugh (Mississippi governor), 178

White, Stanford, 3

White, Walter, 2, 138–139, 144, 145, 146, 147, 148, 170, 175

Wichita People's Friend, 123

Wilkins, Roy, 170, 179

Wilkinson County, Georgia, 74

Williams, Charlie (not lynched), 143

Williams, Elbert (lynching victim), 168

Willis, Hollie (lynching victim), 168

Wilmer, Cary Breckenridge, 130–131

Wilmington, North Carolina (race riot), 111

Wilmington (Delaware) Herald, 58

Wilmington (North Carolina) Morning Star, 146

Wilson, C. L., 181

Wilson, James, 20

Wilson, L. Alex (journalist), 179, 180, 187

Wilson, Woodrow, 156

Wister, Owen, 121–122

Withers, Ernest, 1, 179

Within Our Gates, 159–160

Women, as a justification for lynching, 53–54, 73, 75, 88–91, 116–122, 128, 130, 144–145, 165

Women's Christian Temperance Union, 133

Woods, Eliza (lynching victim), 107

Work, Monroe, of Tuskegee, 132, 134, 137; disputes NAACP, 134–135, 140, 142; Black Legion, 141–142

World War I, 125, 159

World War II, 167–169

Wright, Cleo (lynching victim), 3

Wright, Mose, 179

Yeager, Red, 65

York County, South Carolina (KKK stronghold), 70, 76

Zanuck, Darryl F., 169